SO-EIF-535

Programming in
Visual Basic.NET

.net series

Ted Coombs

ONWORD PRESS

THOMSON LEARNING

Australia • Canada • Mexico • Singapore • Spain • United Kingdom

ONWORD PRESS
TM
THOMSON LEARNING

Programming with Visual Basic .Net
Ted Coombs

Business Unit Director:
Alar Elken

Executive Marketing Manager:
Maura Theriault

Production Manager:
Andrew Crouth

Executive Editor:
Sandy Clark

Marketing Channel Manager:
Fair Huntoon

Art/Design Coordinator:
David Arsenault

Acquisitions Editor:
Gregory L. Clayton

Marketing Coordinator:
Karen Smith

Editorial Assistant:
Jennifer Luck

Executive Production Manager:
Mary Ellen Black

Library of Congress Cataloging-in-Publication Data.

ISBN: 0-7668-4868-X

NOTICE TO THE READER

This book is dedicated to Jason,
without whom I never would have learned all this stuff.

Contents

Acknowledgments

I would like to thank Roderico DeLeon for his tireless tech edits and suggestions, Josh Trupin at MSDN, and the whole .NET crew for their software support. Also, thanks to Greg Clayton for believing in this book, Jennifer Thompson and Jennifer Luck for helping me get this book published, and to the development team for their creativity and skill in designing this book.

Part I

Programming Essentials

Part I is made up of 10 chapters that cover programming basics in Visual Basic .NET. These chapters will be useful for people learning to program for the first time and for experienced Visual Basic programmers who need to adopt the new programming style and features adopted by Visual Basic.

The Common Language Runtime, the core of Microsoft's language architecture, has changed forever the way application development is accomplished. In Part I you will be introduced to .NET and learn about the new features in Visual Basic .NET and Visual Studio. Then, each chapter in this section tackles basic programming fundamentals and techniques. You will learn about variables, operators, conditional statements, procedures, arrays, building an application, and object orientation.

Object orientation was included in earlier versions of Visual Basic, but never to the extent that Visual Basic .NET has adopted it. It may take even skilled Visual Basic programmers a bit of time to learn to exploit the new power and freedom programming in this environment allows.

Introduction to Visual Basic .NET

Welcome to Visual Basic .NET, one of the most widely used application development tools that has just gotten better. It's difficult to call Visual Basic .NET the next version of Visual Basic, because both the development environment and the programming language have undergone a nearly complete redesign—one that will challenge millions of programmers to adopt a new programming paradigm.

Visual Basic .NET represents a significant advance in a relatively old programming language. The first BASIC program was run at 4:00 A.M., May 1, 1964, at Dartmouth University. BASIC was invented by John Kemeny and Thomas Kurtz, two university professors, as a learning tool for more complex programming languages. A short time later, in the 1970s, Paul Allen and Bill Gates wrote their own version of BASIC to run on an Altair computer, and later to run on computers such as the Commodore, Apple, and Atari. It is this programming language that has evolved over nearly 30 years to become one of the most utilized programming languages in the world.

Visual Basic .NET has upgraded some of the old features of Visual Basic while introducing some exciting new abilities into the language, including:

Greater access to system resources

Object inheritance

Garbage collection

Better memory management

Greater interoperability

Common Language Runtime (CLR)

This book is particularly important to existing Visual Basic programmers because Visual Basic .NET has gotten rid of many older forms of language syntax. This means that programs written in earlier versions (version 6.0 and earlier) may not compile without first being rewritten.

There are some new terms you should become familiar with. *Managed code* is program code written to run exclusively under CLR. *Unmanaged code* is program code that continues to rely on the Win32 API and COM. For example, code written in previous versions of Visual Basic is considered unmanaged code. The new Visual Basic .NET compiler creates managed code.

Whether you are new to programming or an experienced Visual Basic programmer, you will find that this latest incarnation of Visual Basic is exciting and challenging. While this version maintains a certain amount of the language constructs contained in previous versions, the entire foundation of the language has changed. Visual Basic, once considered "object-based," is now an "object-oriented" programming language. In Chapter 7, you will learn how to create the objects that are fundamental to the way the language operates. This book introduces the foundations of object-oriented programming, including inheritance, overloading, the **Overrides** keyword, interfaces, and constructors, all covered in Chapter 8.

In addition to object orientation, Visual Basic .NET has other new abilities, such as the ability to create multithreaded applications. The ability to create threads is a basic requirement of some advanced communications abilities, such as network communications. Chapter 15 will get you started in creating multithreaded programs.

Bringing Visual Basic closer to powerful development languages such as C++, features such as improved exception handling have been added in this new version. Chapter 10, on exception handling, dives into an improved way to handle errors in managed programs.

Introducing the Common Language Runtime

Visual Basic .NET, as well as other new Microsoft development languages such as C# and ASP.NET, all use a common programming framework known as the Common Language Runtime (CLR). As you develop applications in Visual Basic .NET, you will continually refer to the Common Language Specification (CLS), around which these various languages have been designed.

The need for a Visual Basic runtime layer has been completely eliminated. The CLR replaces the existing runtime layers of COM and COM+ (see Better Than COM, p. 10), as well as Microsoft Transaction Services (MTS). For backward compatibility, Microsoft has included a CLR to the COM integration layer. The plan, however, is to eventually migrate completely away from COM.

Because of this new foundation for Visual Basic, many new standards have been developed, such as data types and how objects are handled. This standardization allows you to use the components you build in Visual Basic .NET in other languages that use the Common Language Runtime. You can use components, objects, and classes from languages such as C# within your Visual Basic .NET.

One of the important standards that makes this level of integration possible is that the compilers of all managed languages must use the Microsoft Intermediate Language (MSIL) to compile dynamic linked libraries (DLLs) and executable files (EXEs). MSIL is similar to assembler code in how it executes low-level instructions that manage registers.

Programmers familiar with assembly-level programming will understand how information is pushed, popped, and moved in and out of registers. Where MSIL is different is that, like Java, it is no longer dependent on what operating system and hardware platform it is running on. When MSIL JIT compilers are created for applications other than the Windows–Intel platform, your applications should run on other platforms. Therefore, the write once–run anywhere feature of Java is also available for managed applications.

Applications compiled into the intermediate MSIL are not executable on their own. They must undergo an additional compilation step familiar to Java programmers, the JIT (Just In Time) compilation. The final JIT compilation converts the MSIL instructions into machine language specific to the operating system and hardware.

Programs created using the Common Language Runtime are much safer from system attacks because of the extra JIT compilation step. During this final compilation, the compiler verifies that the managed code is type safe, with no illegal type conversions, and that no nasty memory manipulation is being done. Because the JIT step is done on the user's computer, the user can feel safe that the code downloaded to their computer is somewhat safe.

Modules

Both MSIL and metadata are stored in managed binary files known as modules. These are DLL files and EXE files that describe the types contained in them. MSIL was covered previously, and descriptive metadata is like the information stored in a COM DLL type library, for example, public type information, interfaces, classes, structures, and enumerations. Because of this metadata, there is no longer a need for an intermediate language to describe types such as the Interface Definition Language (IDL) employed by COM.

Public, multi-use classes no longer require the developer to build an interface to be used by other managed languages. A default interface is built behind the scenes, making the developer's task easier.

Assemblies

Assemblies are the primary building block of Visual Basic .NET. There are two parts to an assembly: namespaces and the manifest. The *namespace* contains the set of resources and types that form the functionality of the assembly in MSIL form. The *manifest* contains the metadata that describes how the resources in the assembly relate to one another, type visibility, component versioning, and security.

This is a good place to introduce the concept of a namespace. Namespaces are organizational units that provide an organization to references when using large groups of objects, such as class libraries, preventing ambiguity. An assembly can contain one or more namespaces (metadata and MSIL). Each assembly can be considered to be a deployment unit.

In Visual Basic .NET, each project you create will typically represent a single assembly. When you want to use managed types from another assembly in your project, your Visual Studio project must include a reference to the other assembly.

Visual Basic .NET makes designing applications that have methods that will be used by other assemblies simple by allowing you to define the scope and accessiblity of a class, method, property, or interface using the keywords Public, Private, Protected, Friend, and Protected Friend.

Welcome to the World of Objects

Visual Basic .NET supports inheritance by allowing you to define classes that serve as the foundation for new classes. These new classes inherit and even extend properties and methods of the class from which they are inheriting. When you create a new class using inheritance you can also override the functionality of methods in the class you are inheriting, adding new functionality. The ability to create new classes by using inheritance is particularly useful when creating custom user interfaces. Controls, the visual objects used to create a user interface (Chapter 12), are classes, most of which can be inherited and extended. Even the Form itself, the foundational container for other controls, can be inherited.

Overloading

When you create procedures in Visual Basic .NET you can have more than one implementation of the procedure. Each implementation has the same name but accepts different arguments (parameters passed to the procedure). Each implementation performs similar functionality but with differing data types or numbers of parameters, or both. This ability is known as *overloading*.

Overriding

Another feature of inheritance, the ability to override the methods of the base class using the **Overrides** keyword, allows different implementations than the methods inherited from the base class. Rather than completely override the abilities programmed into the method of the base class, you can extend those abilities by calling the original implementation by specifying **MyBase** before the method name.

Constructors and Destructors

New to Visual Basic .NET is the ability to create your own constructor and destructor procedures. Constructors are special procedures that launch when a new object is instantiated from a class definition. This is where any initialization of the object is done. Destructors, on the other hand, are methods used when destroying an object. This is where you can free system resources, close files, and perform general housekeeping procedures.

Shared Members

There is a special type of property and procedure that is shared among all instances of a class. This special type of class member is known as a *shared member*. Shared members are considered static, and are only called from the base class type, never from an object instance. Shared members make implementing functionality for and storage between all implementations of a class very simple. This is the same functionality Java and C++ programmers have come to love.

Interfaces

Interfaces are similar to classes, but a type of class that has no implementation. They describe the members (properties and methods) of classes as a type of prototype. In Visual Basic .NET, use the keyword **Interface** to declare interfaces and the **Implements** keyword to create classes that follow the prototype set forth by the **Interface**.

Delegates

Delegates are intermediary objects. They call methods of objects on your behalf. One of the important uses of delegates is that they allow procedures to be specified as event handlers. Events are covered in detail in Chapter 7. Delegates are also widely used in writing multithreaded programs.

Catch Those Errors

In previous versions of Visual Basic, error handling was done using On Error and GoTo statements. Visual Basic .NET still supports the older-style error handling but has added the more versatile exception handling ability of the Try–Catch–Finally statements. These mananged exception handlers were once only found in languages such as C++ and Java.

The new structured exception handling now built into Visual Basic .NET allows you to run protected blocks of code and handle errors on a specific exception basis using filters. Structured exception handling using Try–Catch–Finally is a big improvement in the ability to create error-free applications.

Threads

The ability to perform multiple tasks simultaneously (sort of) has been a part of the Windows operating system, and most other operating systems, for quite a few years. Most languages allow you to write applications that can launch several branches that run simultaneously within the same application. Each program branch is known as a thread, and applications that run multiple, independent threads are known as multithreaded applications.

Each thread has the ability to block the process of other threads, wait on other threads to finish their tasks, communicate between threads, share data, and set flags. Multithreading an application is no simple task. Information being processed by different threads must be properly synchronized to avoid crashes and conflicts. When writing multithreaded applications, Visual Basic .NET has all the abilities of even the most powerful programming languages.

Windows Services

A Windows Service is an application that runs, normally without a user interface, as a background application. An example of a Windows Service is a Web server application, running unattended in the background, serving up Web pages.

In previous versions of Visual Basic it was not possible to write a Windows Service without resorting to programming trickery and kludges. Visual Basic .NET now includes a special project type for building Windows Services applications, simply and cleanly.

Tracing and Event Logging

The Diagnostics namespace contains a collection of classes that allow powerful tracing, debugging, and logging diagnostics in your application. In the past, this was a time-consuming bit of coding. The classes included in the CLR have made this task much simpler.

The **Trace** class exposes several shared methods such as the **Write** method, which writes messages to a log file, and the **Assert** method, which tests conditions and logs a message when a specified condition has tested false. The diagnostics functionality is covered in detail in Chapter 10.

Garbage Collection

Visual Basic .NET manages the lifetime of objects by placing references to them in a special memory location. Funny enough, this memory location is known as the garbage heap, or, more correctly, the garbage collection heap. When an application releases the last reference to an object, the garbage collector routine, built into Visual Basic .NET, schedules the object for removal from memory, ensuring that it will be removed. Garbage collection is an efficient and robust means of managing object lifetimes.

> **Note**
> There is some contention among advanced developers as to whether garbage collection is truly better than previous object management schemes.

Migrating to Visual Basic .NET

The most difficult thing about deciding to adopt a new technology is assessing the impact on your existing technology base. In other words, will the old code continue to run if you migrate to Visual Basic .NET? The answer: probably not without some work. If your application is large, and somewhat involved, it may take considerable effort to make the code compatible with this new version. There are some definite benefits to migration, some existing and some future.

The Common Language Runtime is based on an entirely new object-oriented class framework that is not completely compatible with previous versions. In fact, for many Visual Basic programmers, the newly introduced object-oriented features may require a significant learning curve. In previous versions of Visual Basic you could build a class, but now Visual Basic .NET supports shared class members, parameters for class constructors, method overloading, and inheritance.

Some parts of the previous language are included for compatibility, for example, error handling. Applications that use the On Error statement will continue to operate in the same manner as before. You might consider slowly migrating away from this older and more limited form of error handling. In fact, you can take advantage of the compiler directives now built into Visual Basic .NET, which will allow you to compile different parts of your application conditionally. In this manner, you can slowly update your application or create versioning within a single code base.

You will find that in Visual Basic .NET it will seem that there are two ways to do almost everything. This can be confusing at first. Many of the language features, such as type conversion, are still included in the language. You'll find that converting one type to another is easier using methods of the data type, rather than built-in functions. I recommend, whenever possible, a move away from the old language toward a completely object-oriented programming style.

Upgrading your Visual Basic 6.0 application to Visual Basic .NET will give your application access to the significant abilities built into the CLR classes, abilities such as Directory Services (replaces complicated ADSI programming), XML, improved database access (replaces ADO), and a full socket programming environment (not available in previous versions of Visual Basic) for building applications that communicate over a network.

One thing you might consider is mixing and matching. Visual Basic .NET has the ability to handle unmanaged code. Try replacing only the parts of an existing application that are no longer compliant with the CLR. This way, your application is not doomed to remain in the world of Visual Basic 6.0. You can take advantage of the significant advancements and abilities offered by the CLR and know that your application can continue to grow as new abilities are added in the future.

Visual Basic .NET no longer supports user-defined types or the Type keyword from previous versions of Visual Basic. These have been replaced with a more object-oriented approach. New types are simply new classes.

Better Than COM

A great deal of code and effort has been spent over the years developing the Common Object Model (COM). Many programmers must have some trepidation about replacing COM with the Common Language Runtime. New programmers as well as veterans will be happy to know that implementing the same functionality using the CLR is easier and more robust than writing a COM or COM+ application. All the best features of COM have been incorporated into the CLR.

The goal of COM was to allow distributed applications to interoperate. With a common foundation, distributed programs no longer have to be written in the same language as long as they are CLS-compliant. Programs written in different languages had a limited ability to interoperate using COM objects, but the task was far from simple. Thus, the goal of COM has not only been achieved, but improved upon.

Implementation of DLL files, once a programming nightmare, has a new ability known as side-by-side implementation. In the past, if you needed to install a new version of a DLL, you had to overwrite the old DLL, and then reboot the computer to get the old DLL out of memory. It's now possible to run two versions of the same DLL, side-by-side in memory, with different applications calling into the appropriate DLL version. That is because an application stores information about which DLL version it was compiled against. Applications can be further configured to load this DLL or to load the most recent build.

One of the advantages of using the CLR class framework is that different language implementations can map to built-in types within the CLR. This takes compatibility much further, but it isn't perfect yet. Visual Basic .NET supports many but not all of the built-in CLR types. For example, Visual Basic .NET does not support unsigned integers. When creating components that you hope will operate within applications written in other languages, the Common Language Specification should become your trusted reference. Writing applications and components that are CLS-compliant will ensure interoperability.

Hello to New Data Types, Goodbye to Others

Visual Basic .NET has new data types not included in previous versions. For instance, previous versions of Visual Basic did not include the **Short** data type. The **Char Data** type is used to store Unicode characters that greatly expand the character set available over the older ASCII character set. In Visual Basic .NET, the **Decimal** type is a 96-bit signed integer scaled by a power of 10.

Perhaps the most used data type in previous versions of Visual Basic is the **Variant** type. There was a certain elegance about having a catch-all data type. You never had to worry about the return value types of functions, just shove the result into a **Variant**. Alas, there was no place for the **Variant** in the Common Language Runtime. The **Variant** is gone.

Writing Visual Basic Programs

Visual Studio includes a powerful, integrated development environment (IDE). The visual interface allows you to quickly build a user interface by simply selecting controls from a Toolbox window and placing them on a form. Access to the Form and control's properties are only a mouse-click away. Double-clicking the Form or control will add code to handle the control's default event. All that's left for you to do is add the Visual Basic .NET code that provides functionality.

The code editor has many time-saving features, such as auto-formatting, auto-completion, and context-sensitive help. Automatic formatting and completion means you rarely have to worry about a missing **End If** statement or a **Loop** statement in the wrong place. You will rarely have to refer to the documentation to learn what parameters a method accepts, because they will appear in the editor as you type. When the method is overloaded, accepting different parameters, you can scroll to the argument set you desire.

Also integrated with the editor is the debugger. As you compile your application, warnings and errors are displayed in a Window adjoining the editor. Clicking the warning or error will take you directly to the offending line of code, and normally, a meaningful message will help you fix the problem.

The development environment, Visual Studio, has evolved over the years. The most recent version for the .NET development environment supports an expandable development interface. Visual Studio.NET offers several ways it can be customized. The built-in methods include programmable shortcut keys, tool window configurations, and command bars.

When you first start Visual Studio.NET, a splash screen will appear. Notice that the splash screen has some useful information. It displays which .NET development products you have installed. Make certain that Visual Basic .NET is one of them.

Note

As programmer-friendly as the Visual Studio development environment is, it's not required to write and compile Visual Basic .NET applications. You are free to use any text editor to write the programs, and use the Visual Basic .NET command-line utilities to compile the code. Many programmers have formed preferences for code editors, some containing time-saving macros or specific formatting preferences.

Getting Started

After loading Visual Studio.NET, the New Project dialog appears automatically (Figure 1.1). From this dialog you can first choose the type of project listed in the left window. As you click on each project type, you'll notice that templates for many types of applications appear in the window to the right of the New Project dialog. Table 1.1 lists the different

Table 1.1 Project Types

Project Type	Template
Visual Basic Projects	Windows Application
	Class Library
	Windows Control Library
	Web Application
	Web Service
	Web Control Library
	Console Application
	Windows Service
	Empty Project
	Empty Web Project
	New Project in Existing Folder
Setup and Deployment Projects	Cab Project
	Merge Module Project
	Remote Deploy Wizard
	Setup Project
	Setup Wizard
	Web Setup Project
Visual Basic Building Blocks	Business Facade
	Business Rules
	Data Access
	System
	Web Facade
	WebUI
	WinUI

types of projects applicable to Visual Basic, and the corresponding templates that come installed with Visual Studio.NET.

Once you've selected your project and template type, the applicable project template will be loaded, and appear ready for editing.

The Visual Studio.NET Integrated Development Environment (IDE)

There are two types of windows within the Visual Studio.NET IDE: tool windows and document windows. The different window types are listed below, while a description and explanation of how to use the tools found in each window follows in this chapter and throughout the rest of the book.

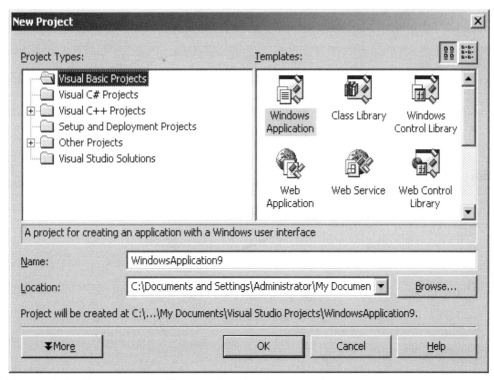

Figure 1.1   Create new applications by selecting a template.

The tool windows include:

Solution Explorer
Dynamic Help
Contents
Toolbox
Server Explorer
Output
Task List
Properties

The document windows include:

Form Design
Code Editor

Managing Files in Visual Studio.NET

Files in Visual Studio.NET are organized into containers called *solutions*. A solution consists of one or more *projects*, and each project consists of one or more files. Solutions can also contain files not contained within a project. This way, you are able to manage files not associated with a particular project. Manage and view this hierarchy of files and containers in the Visual Studio.NET Solution Explorer, as shown in Figure 1.2. When you first create a new solution, choosing a project template, the files required by the template are automatically added to the solution, and to the Solution Explorer.

Solution Explorer Commands

Depending on the type of file or container in the Solution Explorer, you can perform different tasks. If you right-click on the file or container, a pop-up menu appears. Clicking on a solution container allows you to perform the following tasks:

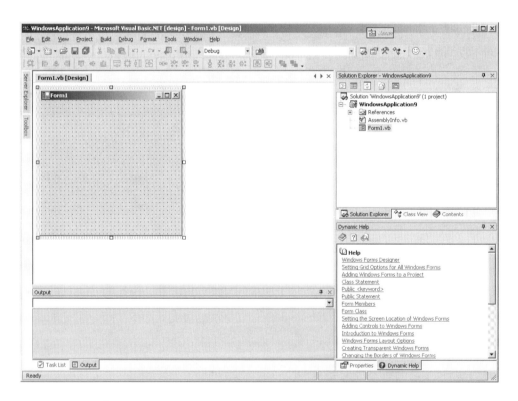

Figure 1.2   View solutions, projects, and files in the Solution Explorer.

Build, rebuild, batch build, and deploy

Launch the Configuration Manager

Add new projects and items

Set the startup project

Launch the debugger

Add the solution to source control

Solution file management such as save, rename, and properties

Selecting projects or individual files will dynamically update the pop-up menu to list tasks possible for the container or file type. Double-clicking on a file will open that file in the editor or design tool associated with that file type. If you wish to change the editor associated with a particular file type, instead of double-clicking, right-click and select **Open with...**, and select the application you'd like to associate with this file type.

You can select multiple files in the Solution Explorer by clicking either the Ctrl or Shift key while left-clicking with your mouse. The pop-up menus will only show selections that are applicable to all the file types you've selected. You can use multiple file selection to perform tasks on all files nearly simultaneously, such as Open, Exclude from Project, and standard file tasks such as Cut, Copy, and Delete.

The project displayed in bold is the startup project. The project designated as the startup project is the one that runs when you tell the debugger to start running the application. Change or add startup projects by selecting Startup Project from the pop-up menu when right-clicking on the solution name. If you select more than one startup project, the solution is displayed in bold.

Customizing Visual Studio .NET

One of the first things you might consider doing to customize Visual Studio.NET is to customize the behavior of the various windows that appear within the Visual Studio development environment. In the beginning of this chapter you learned that there are two types of windows in this environment: tool windows and document windows. Each type of window has a different ability to be customized.

Right-click on top of each window to bring up a window pop-up menu. The menu for tool windows includes the options found in Table 1.2.

Here are some quick tips for customizing the tool windows:

Set Windows to **AutoHide**, freeing desktop space for document window display.

Quickly set all tool windows to **AutoHide** by clicking the **Window** menu and then choosing **AutoHide all windows**.

If you don't like the configuration you've created and you'd like to return to the default Window settings, choose **Tools** from the main menu and then select **Options**. This

Table 1.2   Tool Window Options

Menu Option	Description
Dockable	This will "secure" a window to one side of the development environment. When you dock a tool window, the sizes of any open document windows are adjusted to allow the docked window to fit alongside.
Hide	This causes tool windows to minimize to an icon that appears on one side of the development environment.
Floating	This allows the tool window to float above document windows.
AutoHide	This setting causes windows to minimize to an icon along the side of the development environment whenever your mouse cursor is outside of the tool window. Windows can be restored by moving the mouse cursor over the window's label icon.

launches the Options dialog. Select **Environment** from the list on the left, revealing properties on the right side of the Options dialog. You should see a button labeled **Reset Layout**. Click this button and answer Yes to the warning dialog that asks if you're sure you want to do this. When you close the Options Dialog by clicking **OK**, your new, default settings should take effect.

Note
If your system supports multiple monitors, Visual Studio.NET supports this feature, allowing you to place tool windows on a different monitor from document windows.

Customizing the Environment

Select **Tools | Options** from the main menu. The Options dialog (Figure 1.3) will appear. Various configurable parts of Visual Studio.NET appear in a display window on the left of the dialog. Clicking each of these areas, marked by a folder, will display customizable features in the **Settings** area of the dialog.

The user-defined methods for customizing Visual Studio.NET include add-ins (Figure 1.4), wizards, macros, and the Visual Studio.NET integration program. Here is a short list of the areas within the development environment that can be modified by accessing the nearly 200 objects exposed by the Visual Studio.NET object model:

Code editor	Menus and commands
Project hierarchy	Build process
Code model	Tool windows
Debugger	Solution explorer

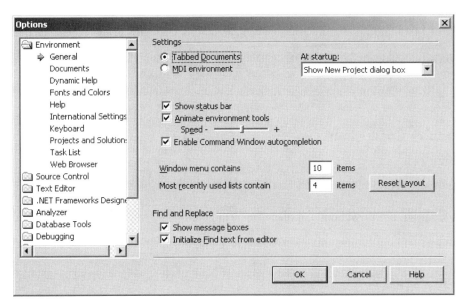

Figure 1.3   Configure Visual Studio.NET using settings in the Options dialog.

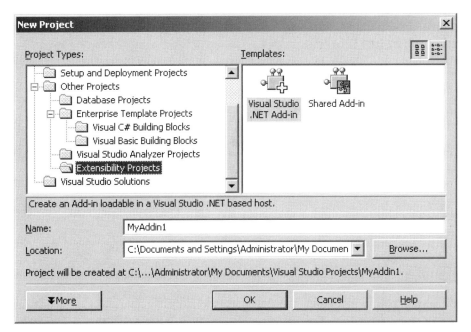

Figure 1.4   Find the Visual Studio.NET Add-in templates in the New Project Dialog.

Application Templates

Starting Visual Studio.NET allows you to choose which type of Visual Basic .NET application you'd like to build. There are many to choose from, and selecting the right project type is the first step.

Windows Application

The first choice of templates in the New Project dialog is the Windows application. This project type allows you to build a typical Windows application, complete with a user interface. The project loads a blank Form on which you can place controls such as buttons, text boxes, and list boxes. Windows applications compile into stand-alone executable files with an .EXE extension.

Class Library

Selecting the Class Library project type creates a framework that allows you to build classes, the foundation for objects, that you will use in other application types.

Windows Control Library

With the Windows Control Library project template you can build your own custom controls to be used in Windows Applications. When you load this project, Visual Basic .NET creates a new **UserControl** class. You can also create custom controls that are based on a **CustomControl** class.

Console Application

Not all applications require a graphic user interface. The Console Application runs from the command line without a user interface.

Windows Service

Similar to Console Applications, Windows Services do not require a user interface. This type of program can run in the background, providing Windows Services. This template sets up Visual Studio to make building a Windows Service easier.

Import Folder Wizard

The Import Folder Wizard is a wizard for creating a project in an existing folder.

Empty Project

Sometimes it's easier to start your application from scratch. The Empty Project loads a Visual Basic .NET project with no form or other added code.

ASP.NET Web Application

Active Server Pages (ASP.NET) use a language based on Visual Basic .NET to script Web applications. This type of project does not build a Visual Basic .NET application or component, but rather allows you to build Web page applications that are run using Web server software. This topic is not covered in this book.

ASP.NET Web Service

The ASP.NET Web Service project allows you to build Web services into your applications. Applications of this type have a user interface accessible through the World Wide Web. Building Web applications in not a topic covered in this book.

Web Control Library

With the Web Control Library template, you can build custom controls to include within Web pages. When the project is first loaded, Visual Basic . NET creates a new WebControl class. This topic is not covered in this book.

Empty Web Project

The Empty Web project template enables you to build a Web application from scratch. Web applications are not covered in this book.

Outlining and Hiding Code

The Visual Studio.NET editor gives you the option of creating a hierarchical, outlined view of your code. You can view your code files, no matter how large, in a table of contents–like fashion, with the ability to easily expand any section to view the code. This allows you quick access to your code, and allows you to have a big picture of the structure of your code.

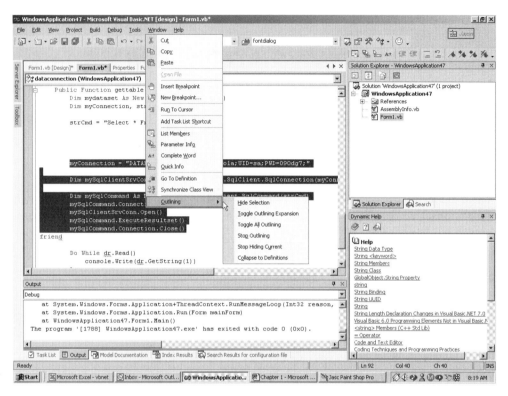

Figure 1.5 Highlight text you wish to outline.

Outlining Code

A simple way to manage and organize large amounts of code is by hiding the parts of the code you don't want to see. Outlining gives you the ability to collapse selected blocks of text, and expand the parts you want to view. Collapsing a block of text in no way affects the functionality of the program; it only hides text from your view, not the computer's.

Highlight the blocks of text you want to outline and select Outlining from the pop-up menu, as shown in Figure 1.5. Expand collapsed blocks of text by clicking the plus sign next to the outline definition.

You can undo outlining at any time by simply selecting the Stop Outlining menu selection. You can also globally expand all collapsed sections, or collapse all the sections simultaneously. One thing to keep in mind is that once you've defined a region, making changes to it could cause outlining in that region to be lost. Outlining is sensitive to the loss of blank lines and a change in indenting. Here are the outlining commands available from the pop-up menu:

Hide Selection   Hides the currently selected text. This menu command will not be active when no text is selected. You can use the keyboard shortcuts Ctrl+m then Ctrl+h. (Ctrl+z will undo this command.)

Toggle Outlining Expansion   A toggle is a two-position switch. Selecting this menu choice changes the state of the current collapsed or hidden section. The keyboard shortcut is Ctrl+m then Ctrl+m again.

Toggle All Outlining   Changes the state of all collapsed or expanded code. All code results in either collapsed or expanded code, not a combination. The keyboard shortcut is Ctrl+m then Ctrl+l (lowercase L).

Stop Outlining   Stops outlining and removes any outlining information in the whole document. All procedures are expanded and symbols removed. The keyboard shortcut is Ctrl+m then Ctrl+p.

Stop Hiding Current   This expands the current section and removes any outlining information. The keyboard shortcut is Ctrl+m then Ctrl+u again.

Collapse to Definitions   This selection creates regions from all your procedures, using the procedure name as the definition, then collapses them. The keyboard shortcut is Ctrl+m then Ctrl+o.

Summary

Whether you've decided to upgrade your current applications or are learning Visual Basic .NET for the first time, this book takes you through many of the basics. This chapter introduced many of the terms and concepts you will need to know to better use this book, and understand Visual Basic .NET. The first section of this book covers all the basics of programming with Visual Basic .NET. Even experienced programmers should review these sections because Visual Basic .NET programming has changed. Pay particular attention to the next chapter on variables.

Variables 2

The technical definition of a variable is the best one. Variables are named locations in your computer's memory. When a variable is *declared*, your program names a location in memory, and tries to reserve the amount of memory that will be needed to store a value there depending on the type of variable. This chapter will cover declaring variables, how to format them, and converting them into other variable types. We also cover some of the variable naming standards and best programming practices when working with variables.

Primitives

Data types supported directly by the compiler are known as *primitves*. These are types that map directly to types in the base class library. Here are some of the primitives supported by Visual Basic .NET:

Boolean

Byte

Collection

Date-Time

Double

Integer

Long

Object

Single

String

Most of the examples in this chapter will use the primitives in this list. You'll learn to create variables of these types, how to format them, and how to convert these primitives into other primitive types.

Declaring Variables

Declaring a variable means that you are preparing a place for information to live in the RAM memory of your computer. The variable name is simply a human-readable alias for a memory address. When declaring a variable, you do several things:

1. Name the variable, creating the alias for the memory location.
2. Specify the data type, which tells the computer how much space it needs in memory.
3. Specify the scope, which creates limits on which areas of the program can access to retrieve the value.

Dim

The **Dim** statement is the most common way to declare variables. It is short for the word "dimension." Oftentimes you will see the words "declare" and "dimension" used to mean the same thing. **Dim** is used to create a named space in memory.

```
Dim [With Events] VariableName [subscripts] [As .[New]
Type] [=Initial Expression]
```

WithEvents   This optional keyword is used to specify that this variable is used to handle events. We cover the use of this keyword and events in detail in Chapter 7.

VariableName   This is the name of the variable and is required. See the section on standards and conventions for more information on variable names.

Initial arraysize   When the variable is an array, you can specify the size of the array for all of its dimensions. Otherwise, this value is optional.

New   The New keyword is used when creating a new object while you are declaring it. Chapter 7 covers using the New keyword in greater detail.

Type   This specifies the data type of the variable. This chapter discusses each variable type in detail. Just a note here, in previous versions of Visual Basic, this keyword was optional, declaring the data type to be of type variant. Visual Basic .NET no longer supports the variant type, therefore, this is no longer optional. It is used with the keyword **As**.

Initial Expression   You may optionally initialize a variable with a default value. Initializing variables is covered later in this chapter.

Using Dim

Dim, one of the most commonly used Visual Basic .NET statements, is short for the word "dimension." There are several ways to declare a variable, and using Dim is only one of them.

The Dim statement must appear on a line by itself, and cannot be used within an expression. Below is an example of declaring a new integer variable.

```
Dim iCounter As Integer
```

You can also set an initial value to this Integer value like this:

```
Dim iCounter As Integer = 5
```

You can declare an array (covered in detail in Chapter 6) in a few different ways. The first way is to declare an empty array like this:

```
Dim iCountArray As Array
```

Next, you can declare an **Array** that includes empty members. Notice in this example, when creating empty members, we must declare the type of data they will hold like this:

```
Dim iCountArray(3) As String
```

You can also create an **Array** by initializing its values like this:

```
Dim aColors() As String = {"red", "blue", "green", "purple"}
```

The **Dim** statement can be used to declare variables of specific types, such as those discussed in this chapter, and user-defined types. When you create a new class in Visual Basic .NET, it becomes a type. Declaring a variable as a new class type is primarily a two-step process. First, declare the variable using **Dim** and then create a new object by using the **New** operator, setting the variable equal to a new instance of the class type. Until assigned an object (as shown below), the declared object variable has the value of **Nothing**, a Visual Basic .NET keyword that indicates that the variable does not refer to a particular instance of an object.

```
Dim myObject as myClass()

myObject = New myClass()
```

This can also be done in a single step using the **New** operator with the **Dim** statement.

```
Dim myObject as New myClass()
```

Classes and Objects are discussed in detail in Chapter 7.

Scope

The *scope* of a variable is the limitation on what parts of the program can access the value of a variable, or even see that the variable exists. Scope is determined by the placement of the variable within a Visual Basic .NET application, unless the scope is explicitly changed.

A way to picture this is with large and small boxes. The largest box contains smaller boxes. In the case of Visual Basic .NET, the largest box is the module. Classes and procedures are smaller boxes that are contained within a module.

Variables declared within the module itself are accessible by all of the other classes and procedures within the module. This type of variable is known as a *global variable*. The variable is globally accessible by all parts of the module. The degree to which other parts of the application can access a variable is often known as the *size* of the variable's scope.

When variables are declared using the **Dim** statement within a class or procedure, that variable is accessible only to that procedure, or to procedures and classes within it (small boxes containing other small boxes).

> **Note**
> Although it's not a requirement, best practices suggest that when using the **Dim** statement, it normally belongs at the beginning of the module, class, or procedure.

Public

The **Public** statement is similar to the **Dim** statement, except that the scope of the variable is forced. Variables that are declared using **Public** are accessible from all procedures, classes, and modules within the application.

The Syntax for the **Public** statement is nearly identical to that of the **Dim** statement:

```
Public [With Events] VariableName [subscripts] [As [New]
Type] [=Initial Expression]
```

Here is an example of using the **Public** keyword that declares a variable with the Public scope:

```
Public AppName As String = "Visual Basic .NET Programming"
```

Just as with the **Dim** statement, **Public** can also be used to declare a new object variable like this:

```
Public AppObject As New ApplicationClass
```

The **Public** statement cannot be used to declare local variables.

Great care must be taken when declaring variables public. The more places a variable is visible from within the application, the greater chance of inadvertently changing the variable. It is much better to pass arguments into procedures, as described in Chapter 5.

Private

With syntax similar to the **Dim** and **Public** statements, the **Private** statement can be used to declare variables that are only accessible to the module, class, or procedure in which it's declared, or procedures and classes within the module, class, or procedure where the variable is delared.

```
Public [With Events] VariableName [subscripts] [As [New]
Type] [=Initial Expression]
```

The scope might seem confusing. Below is a simple example.

```
Class testclass

    Private myPrivateVariable As String = "Test"

    Sub testme()

        console.Write(myPrivateVariable)

    End Sub

End Class

Class Main()

    Dim myTestObj = New testclass()

    myTestObj.Testme()

End Class
```

In this example, a class called **testclass** contains a private variable. The private variable, **myPrivateVariable**, is called from within a procedure within the class. Class **Main( )** simply creates an instance of testclass to prove that the word "Test" is actually written to the console window.

Note
Variables should always be defined with the smallest scope possible.

The Private statement cannot be used to declare local variables.
Table 2.1 lists the three levels of scope within a Visual Basic .NET application.

Constants

There is a special type of variable used to represent a literal value called a *constant*. As its name suggests, the value of a constant remains the same throughout the procedure in

Table 2.1   Levels of Variable Scope

Scope	Declaration	Accessible from
Global	Public when declared in the declaration section of a code module.	Accessible throughout the application.
Module level	Private when declared in the declarations section of a form or code module.	All procedures in the form or code module.
Procedure Level	Private when declared in a procedure or function.	The procedure or function where it is declared.

which it's declared. Constants are merely shortcuts to make the code more readable and accessible.

Declare a constant using the **Const** statement. Here is an example of a constant called **UserID**. It can now be used instead of the lengthy string that is assigned to it. The advantage of a constant over a regular variable in this case is that the value cannot be accidentally changed by your application. Once the value is set, it is set in stone and cannot be changed unless you manually change it in the **Const** statement.

```
Const UserID As String = "fdfhk83nf83r7389483"
```

The syntax for declaring a constant is similar to that of a normal variable:

```
[Public|Private|Protected|Friend|Protected Friend] Const
ConstantName[As Type] = Value or Expression
```

The value or expression cannot be constructed using functions, whether user-defined or Visual Basic .NET functions. You cannot use variables in building the expression. The As Type declaration is optional because the constant's type will be set automatically by the type of the value or expression to which it is set.

It's important to know that constants are private within the procedures or modules in which they are declared and their scope cannot be changed. Therefore, constants will follow the same rules of scope as any private variable.

Variable Naming Conventions

There are some definite do's and don'ts when creating variable names. This section covers some of the rules, and then recommends some conventions that will help make your application more readable.

Variable names in Visual Basic .NET cannot begin with a number. They can, however, begin with the underscore symbol (_). So the variable name 123Name is illegal and will throw an error. However, starting the same variable name with an underscore so that it reads **_123Name** is completely legal.

Variable names are case sensitive. This means that the following two examples declare completely different and valid variables:

string MyString;

string myString;

> **Warning!**
> It's easy to mistakenly create two variables thinking that you are working with a single variable. This is one reason why working with a strict naming convention can save you headaches later on.

Using upper- and lower-case in a variable is a matter of programming style and will not change the way your program operates. There are three styles of capitalization:

Pascal Casing   Capitalize the first letter of each word: MyName

Camel Casing   Capitalize the first letter of each word, except the first word: myName

Upper Case   Use only for identifiers of two characters or less: System.IO

It's suggested in the .NET Framework Design Guidelines that you use Pascal Casing for naming everything except protected instances and parameters. These two should use Camel Casing.

> **Note**
> There are many different standard styles. Microsoft recommends you follow the suggestions in the .NET Framework Design Guidelines.Descriptive

Variable and Procedure Names

When possible, the body of a variable or procedure name should use both upper and lower case. You can make your variable names as long as necessary to describe the value stored in the variable or the procedure's purpose. The Microsoft coding guidelines suggest that your procedure names answer the question "what" instead of "how." If you decide later that you want to change how a procedure is implemented, you will not have to change the procedure name.

Procedures such as Sub and Function (explained in detail in chapter 5) perform a task, and should contain a verb to denote that action. It's not necessary to use prefixes for scope or variable type. It is good, however, when naming functions that return a value, to describe the value to be returned. Here are some examples of procedure names:

```
ReverseValueOrder()

GetFileName()

SaveObjectReference
```

When naming variables and procedures it's best not to use abbreviations. You should be able to construct long and detailed names whenever necessary. If you find that you prefer using abbreviations, it is important that you use them consistently throughout the entire program. Switching back and forth between a full expression and its abbreviation (say, between *zipcode* and *zip*) within a project will cause errors.

Counters

One exception to the rule of descriptive variable names are those used as counters in loops. Still a matter or style, rather than using a variable name such as iCounter, many programmers prefer to use the letter "i." One advantage to using a single letter for loop counters is that you may often have several embedded loops, each with their own counter. In that case it is customary to begin with "i," and then continue the next embedded loop with "j" and so on through the alphabet. Normally the letters "o" and "l" are not used due to possible confusion with zero and one respectively.

Initializing Variables

You initialize a variable when you first store a value into it after declaring it. Visual Basic .NET allows you to initialize a variable at the same time you declare the variable like this:

```
Dim FirstName as String = "Mary"
```

This is simply a shortcut and is equivalent to:

```
Dim FirstName as String

FirstName = "Mary"
```

Variable Types

So far in this chapter we've discussed how to create variables and how to format their names. It's now important to understand what variable types are built into Visual Basic .NET. This section will also cover briefly how to use each type. Variable data types in Visual Basic .NET follow the standards set forth in the Common Language Specification. This way, there will be no problems interoperating with languages such as C#. Table 2.2 lists the built-in data types, the .NET framework object names, and the variables' data ranges.

Table 2.2   Visual Basic .NET Data Types

Data type	.NET Structure	Value range
Boolean	System.Boolean	True − False (1 − 0)
Byte	System.Byte	Unsigned 0 to 255
Char	System.Char	Unsigned 0 to 65,535
Date	System.DateTime	1/1/0001 − 12/31/9999
Decimal	System.Decimal	$+/-$ 0.0000000000000000000000000001 to 79,228,162,514,264,337,593,543,950,335
Double	System.Double	-1.79769313486231^{E308} to $-4.94065645841247^{E-324}$ for negative values; 4.94065645841247^{E-324} to 1.79769313486232^{E308} for positive values
Integer	System.Int32	−2,147,483,648 to 2,147,483,647
Long	System.Int64	−9,223,372,036,854,775,808 to 9,223,372,036,854,775,807
Object	System.Object	Range specific to object type. All types are objects.
Short	System.Int16	−32,768 to 32,767
Single	System.Single	-3.402823^{E38} to -1.401298^{E-45} for negative values; 1.401298^{E-45} to 3.402823^{E38} for positive values
String	System.String	Includes all Unicode characters (see Note, page 44)
User defined	System.ValueType	Range specific to type

Working with Boolean Variables

George Boole (1815–1864), self-taught mathematician, introduced the concept of boolean algebra in 1854 in his book, *An Investigation into the Laws of Thought, on Which Are Founded the Mathematical Theories of Logic and Probabilities*. This algebra incorporated logic and is based on the concept that expressions result in one of two states, True or False. Complex expressions can then be created using algebraic symbols, or in Visual Basic .NET programs, the boolean operators **AND**, **OR**, **XOR**, and **NOT**.

Use the **Dim** statement to declare a new boolean variable. When first declared, the boolean variable will be False, even before a value is stored in it. The following example shows the declaration of a boolean variable called myboolean. The result of this code snippet is that the word "false" will be written to the console.

```
Dim isTrueorFalse as Boolean

    If isTrueorFalse Then console.Write("true")

Else
```

```
        console.Write("false")

    End If
```

For more information about the **If** statement, refer to the chapter on conditional statements.

Notice in the preceding example that it was not necessary to use an expression, but simply the variable itself. This is because expressions used in conditional statements, such as **If**, will evaluate to either True or False, and the boolean variable is already True or False so there is no need for an expression.

Only values of True or False can be stored in a boolean variable. This includes the results of expressions that evaluate to True or False, such as in this example:

```
Dim isTrueOrFalse As Boolean

Dim myinteger As Integer = 3

isTrueOrFalse = (myinteger = 3)

If isTrueOrFalse Then

        console.Write("true")

Else

        console.Write("false")

End If
```

The result of this example is that, because myinteger in fact equals 3, isTrueOrFalse is True and therefore the word "true" is printed in the console.

As mentioned earlier, there are Visual Basic .NET operators specifically for working with boolean variables. These are **AND**, **OR**, **XOR**, and **NOT**.

AND

The best way to quickly understand the **AND** operator and boolean logic is by viewing a very simplified truth table (Table 2.3).

```
Dim bVal1, bVal2, bResult as Boolean

bVal1 = "True"
```

```
    bVal2 = "False"

    bResult = bVal1 AND bVal2

    console.write(iif(bResult,"True", "False"))
```

This is an example of the second row of Table 2.3. One value is True and the other is False, and the result is False, so the immediate If statement causes the console.write method to write the word "false" in the console window.

For more information on immediate if (**iif**), go to Chapter 4, on conditional statements.

OR

The **OR** operator is different from the **AND** operator. It's easiest to understand the **OR** operator by converting the expression into English. If value1 is true or value2 is true, then the result is going to be true. So, if either of the values is true, the result will be true. This is quite different from the **AND** operator, where the only way for an expression to be True is if both values are True. Of course, if neither value is True, the result will be False. This is the only way for an **OR** expression to end up False. Table 2.4 shows a boolean truth table for **OR**.

```
    Dim bVal1, bVal2, bResult as Boolean

    bVal1 = "True"

    bVal2 = "False"

    bResult = bVal1 OR bVal2

    console.write(iif(bResult,"True", "False"))
```

Table 2.3   Simple Boolean Truth Table for the AND Operator

Value 1	Operator	Value 2	Result
True	AND	True	True
True	AND	False	False
False	AND	True	False
False	AND	False	False

Table 2.4   Simple Boolean Truth Table for the OR Operator

Value 1	Operator	Value 2	Result
True	OR	True	True
True	OR	False	True
False	OR	True	True
False	OR	False	False

This example is very similar to the last code example, except the **AND** operator was exchanged for the **OR** operator, causing the word "true" to be printed in the console. This is an example of the second row of Table 2.4.

XOR

The **XOR** operator is known as the logical exclusion operator. This operator excludes all cases where both values of the expression are the same, whether they are both True or both False. Consequently, the first and last rows of Table 2.5 are False, while expressions where the values differ are True.

```
Dim bVal1, bVal2, bResult as Boolean

bVal1 = "True"

bVal2 = "True"

bResult = bVal1 XOR bVal2

console.write(iif(bResult,"True", "False"))
```

Because of the exclusion behavior of **XOR**, the result of this example will be False.

NOT

The **NOT** operator simply reverses the current state of a boolean variable. Therefore, **NOT** True is False and **NOT** False is True. You might be thinking, "That's silly. Why wouldn't you just write False or True instead of writing **NOT** True or Not False?" The

Table 2.5   Simple Boolean Truth Table for the XOR Operator

Value 1	Operator	Value 2	Result
True	XOR	True	False
True	XOR	False	True
False	XOR	True	True
False	XOR	False	False

NOT operator is commonly used in expressions where you need the expression to evaluate to True, while testing for falseness.

For example:

```
Dim bVal1 as Boolean = False

Do While NOT bVal1

    'statements

    bVal1 = True

Loop
```

Here, the loop is entered even though bVal1 is False because the **NOT** operator causes it to be read as True. So, when bVal1 is set to True within the loop, the loop will exit because NOT True is False. This example is quite simplified. When searching through the results of a database, there are times when you might only want to print the data. A stored value is then False. Here is an example where a recordset, **RS**, has a boolean type field name of **Employed**.

```
Do While NOT RS.EOF

    If NOT Employed Then

        'statements

    End If

Loop
```

The expression **NOT Employed** is **True** whenever the value stored in **Employed** is **False**.

Working with Byte Variables

Variables of the **Byte** data type store binary information of 1s and 0s only. A single byte can store 8 bits of information, a bit being a single 1 or 0. If you are converting binary arithmetic to base 10, the system we all know and love, a single byte can store a number from 0 to 255. In Visual Basic .NET the Byte data type is system.byte and is used to manipulate values in memory in their most raw format. Remember that data in memory is stored as binary values.

This example first converts decimal values to **Byte** using one of the conversion functions covered later in this chapter. You can manipulate a byte value as you would any number. The following example writes the number 6 into the console window.

```
Dim mybyte1 As Byte

Dim mybyte2 As Byte

mybyte1 = CByte(4)

mybyte2 = CByte(2)

console.Write(mybyte1 + mybyte2)
```

Visual Basic .NET has a set of operators for working with information at the Bit level known as *bitwise operators*: **BitAnd**, **BitOr**, **BitNot**, and **BitXOr**. The next several sections explain these in more detail.

BitAnd

Using the **BitAnd** operator is very similar to using the boolean **AND** operator. If you think about the 1s and 0s as being True and False, respectively you can view the information in Table 2.6 and see that 0 BitAnd 0 is the same as False **AND** False, and so on.

Let's take the number 25, which in binary form is 11001, and 24 (11000 binary) The **BitAnd** operator performs an analysis of each bit, with the results in Table 2.6. So, 11001 BitAnd 11000 = 11000 (see Figure 2.1).

Tip
An easy way to convert decimal to binary is using the Windows Calculator. From the View menu of the Calculator software select Scientific. Type in a decimal value, and then click the Binary radio button and the number will appear in binary format in the calculator. You can use this same method for converting to other useful computer bases, such as hexadecimal.

Table 2.6   BitAnd Result Table

Value 1	Operator	Value 2	Result
0	BitAnd	0	0
0	BitAnd	1	0
1	BitAnd	0	0
1	BitAnd	1	1

Figure 2.1 BitAnd Operation.

BitNot

The **BitNot** is similar to the boolean **NOT** where the value is reversed (*logical negation*). So, if a value is equal to 1, then adding **BitNot** in front of it would equate to 0.

BitOr

The simplest way to understand the use of the **BitOr** operator is to reference the results shown in Table 2.7. You'll find that the results are similar to the boolean **OR**.

BitXOr

The result table for the Bit Exclusive Or is shown below in Table 2.8

Table 2.7 BitOr Result Table

Value 1	Operator	Value 2	Result
0	BitOr	0	0
0	BitOr	1	1
1	BitOr	0	1
1	BitOr	1	1

Table 2.8 BitXOr Result Table

Value 1	Operator	Value 2	Result
0	BitXOr	0	0
0	BitXOr	1	1
1	BitXOr	0	1
1	BitXOr	1	0

Working with Char Variables

Char, or character type, variables hold a single Unicode character. (For more information on Unicode characters, visit www.unicode.org.) Each character is represented as a number between 0 and 65,535. You will most likely work with groups of characters, or *strings* of characters, but there are times you may want to store a single character value. There are utilities, *methods*, of the char type variable that make working with single characters quite powerful.

You can, for example, determine whether or not a char variable is a digit using the **IsControl** method like this:

```
Dim myChar As Char

Dim myResult As Boolean

myChar = CChar("T")

myResult = Char.IsDigit(myChar)

console.Write(myResult)
```

This sample writes False into the console window because T is not a digit. Determining if Char variables are digits is only one of the many methods available to this variable type. You can determine if the character is a letter, or a digit, upper- or lowercase, a symbol, punctuation, and much more. The Visual Studio.NET editor can help you choose the correct method. Typing char and a dot (.) will pop up a selection list of possible methods.

Working with DateTime Variables

DateTime variables are based on **System.DateTime**, which has many members for manipulating dates and times. There are too many to list in this book. You will have to refer to the full .NET Framework documentation for the complete list. In this section we've documented a few of the more commonly used methods. Before launching into working with dates you'll need to know about one additional type of object.

When working with **DateTime** type variables in Visual Basic .NET, it's important first to understand the idea of a *timespan*. A timespan is an object that represents the difference between one date and time and another measured in *ticks*. A property of a timespan object, ticks are units of measure, the smallest of which is 100 nanoseconds (one nanosecond is a billionth of a second).

Date

This property returns the date associated with an instance of a date object. The time is set to midnight. Here is a code snippet showing how this can be used:

```
Dim mydate As DateTime

mydate = CDate("08/01/2004")

console.Write(mydate.Date)
```

This example writes 8/1/2004 12:00:00 AM into the system console window.

Compare

This method of the **System.DateTime** class compares two dates to determine if they are exactly the same. If they are, the method returns 0, otherwise, the method returns a 1, as in the following example.

```
Dim mydate As DateTime

Dim todaysdate As DateTime

Dim isthesame As Integer

mydate = CDate("08/01/2004")

todaysdate = Today()

isthesame = System.DateTime.Compare(mydate, todaysdate)

console.Write(isthesame)
```

This example writes a 1 in the console window because today's date is not in the year 2004.

DaysInMonth

DaysInMonth(year, month) returns an Integer equal to the number of days in the specified month. The first parameter is the year, passed as an integer. This is important, because as in our example, the number of days in the month of February changes based on the year. Pass the month as the second integer parameter.

```
Dim howmanydays As Integer

howmanydays = System.DateTime.DaysInMonth(2001,2)

console.Write(howmanydays)
```

This example writes the number 28 to the system console window.

IsLeapYear

This method returns a boolean True or False depending on whether the year, passed as an integer argument, is a leap year.

```
console.Write(System.DateTime.IsLeapYear(2002))
```

This example writes the word False to the console window.

Now

This method returns the time and date from the system clock. This example declares a DateTime variable and then writes the current date and time to the console window.

```
console.Write(System.DateTime.Now)
```

You can also use this method without declaring a date variable like this:

```
console.Write(Now())
```

Today

This method returns today's date from the computer's system clock.

```
console.Write(System.DateTime.Today)
```

This example writes today's date into the console window along with the fixed time of 12:00:00 AM. Just like the Now method, you can also use the Today method without first declaring a date variable. This example passes Today( ) as an argument to the console.write method and is the equivalent to the code above.

```
console.Write(Today())
```

Working with Decimal Variables

The **Decimal** data type is used to store numbers with fractional portions, expressed as decimal values. The Decimal type is stored as a 96-bit value, enabling you to store numbers with as many as 28 decimal places. In Visual Basic .NET you can use the **Decimal** variable type to represent currency values.

> **Note**
> Visual Basic .NET no longer has the data type **Currency**, as in former versions.

Working with Double Variables

The **Double** variable type holds a 64-bit numeric value, capable of storing numbers with decimal fractions. It's very similar to the Decimal type except for the fact that the Double type is capable of storing its value.

The **Double** variable type consumes 8 bytes of memory when storing its value. This is true no matter the size of the number stored. If the value has been declared as type **Double**, it will use all 8 bytes to store the number. For this reason, you should use the **Double** type only when you're certain that a number with this degree of numeric precision is required. Otherwise, you will needlessly consume computer memory.

```
Dim myDouble As Double

myDouble = 12334555343.3423

myDouble = myDouble * 1435.334

console.Write(myDouble)
```

This example writes the number 17704206659180.9 to the console window.

Working with Integer Variables

Integer variables store negative and positive whole numbers from -2,147,483,648 to 2,147,483,647. **Integers** are one of the most commonly used types of numeric variables. They are used in counters and accept user information. Along with the **Decimal** variable type, you will find that for numbers under 2 billion, this will be your choice.

This example displays numbers by incrementing a counter variable in a loop. For more information on loops, see Chapter 4.

```
Dim myCounter As Integer

For myCounter = 1 To 100
```

```
        console.Write(myCounter)

        If myCounter <> 100 Then

            console.Write(", ")

        End If

    Next
```

You must be careful when using different numeric data types. The Visual Studio.NET editor will attempt to help you keep the numeric variable types straight. The following code seems simple enough, but will throw an error.

```
    Dim mynumber As Integer

    Dim myresult As Integer

    mynumber = 9

    myresult = mynumber / 4
```

This example throws an error because myresult will not equal an Integer, but a Double. Changing the code to read like this will solve this code's problem:

```
    Dim mynumber As Integer

    Dim myresult As Double

    mynumber = 9

    myresult = mynumber / 4
```

Working with Long Variables

A **Long** Variable is not a variable with a very long name; rather, a variable capable of storing a numeric value of 19 places whether positive or negative—in other words, very large numbers. The **Long** type uses 4 bytes of memory to store its numeric value.

```
    Dim mynumber As Long

    Dim myresult As Long

    mynumber.Write(myresult)
```

The code snippet above results in the following number being written to the console window: `64604646410464645`.   If you had tried to represent the number 12920929282092929 as an **Integer**, your code would have thrown an error, or the Visual Studio.NET editor would have complained that the number cannot be represented as an **Integer**.

Working with Short Variables

The term **Short** Variable has nothing to do with the length of the variable name. The **Short** variable type, also known as a **Short Integer**, is used to store negative and positive integers with less than 5 digits (-32,767 to 32,767), or to store real numbers with a total of four or fewer digits on both sides of the decimal point. The advantage of using a **Short** variable type is that it takes less memory in applications where the amount of memory used by variables is an issue. The **Short** type only requires 2 bytes of memory to store its value.

```
Dim mynumber As Short

Dim mymultiplier As Short

Dim myresult As Short

mynumber = 5

mymultiplier = 5

myresult = mynumber * mymultiplier

console.Write(myresult)
```

This example writes the number 25 into the console window. You must be careful when multiplying or adding short values. It's possible that the resulting number will no longer be handled by a **Short**. In cases where this might happen, make sure to have the variable that holds the result be declared as an Integer, rather than a Short.

Working with Strings

String variables were named because they were special variable types constructed of characters strung together like a string of pearls. Characters are what humans need to communicate easily with the computer. Of course, the computer has no need for characters to process information, and consequently converts all characters to numbers. As computers have continued to evolve, better communications with human beings of all nationalities became a priority.

The Unicode character set was created in an attempt to include every language character on Earth. Even though there are currently billions of characters, Visual Basic .NET supports only some of them. Of the supported 65,535 characters, the first 128 characters (0–127) correspond to the first 128 characters of the Unicode character set and the letters and symbols on a standard keyboard. The next 128 characters (128–255) are Latin-based alphabet letters, accents, currency symbols, fractions and other characters. The remaining characters consist of a variety of symbols, such as worldwide text characters, diacritics, math, and technical symbols.

For more information on Unicode symbols, visit www.unicode.org.

> **Note**
> In previous versions of Visual Basic it was possible to set the fixed length of a string when it was declared. Strings must now be declared without a length. Length is determined when a value is stored in the variable.

Strings are a little more complex to work with than other variable types because they are composed of many individual characters, thoughts, ideas, concepts, and, most of all, patterns. Of course, the computer doesn't understand thoughts, ideas, and concepts, but it certainly can recognize patterns of characters.

Strings, like other variable types, are defined as part of the .NET Framework of classes. Each class has methods (abilities). There are two kinds of methods of the string class: static methods and instance methods. Chapter 7 explains classes, objects, and methods in greater detail. For now, understand that these methods are abilities of the string.

Static methods are called like this: `system.string.methodname( )`

Static methods are called directly from the class, instead of from a string object. Instance methods require there to be a string object before they can be used like this:

```
StringObjectName.methodname()
```

Create a **String** object by simply declaring a variable of type **String**.

Table 2.9 lists the different member methods of the **String** class along with a short description of each method. This is followed by a brief explanation of some of the more useful methods. This section will also cover some of these methods in more detail. For complete instructions you will have to refer to the .NET Framework documentation.

Compare

This static method of the string class allows you to determine if one string exists within another. You can specify where to begin within the first string, the second string, the length of the string to compare, whether to ignore case, and finally, the culture.

Table 2.9   Static Methods of the String Class

Method	Description
Compare	Strings are compared to see if one string exists within another.
CompareOrdinal	Similar to the Compare method except that the comparison does not consider the local national language or culture settings.
Concat	Adds two strings together, or represents an object as a string.
Copy	Creates a new string variable by creating a copy of another, specified string.
Equals	Determines whether two strings are equal (have the same value).
Format	Replaces each format specification in a specified String with the textual equivalent of a corresponding object's value.
Intern	Retrieves a system reference to the specified String.
IsInterned	Retrieves a reference to a specified String.
Join	Concatenates a specified separator String between each element of a specified String array, yielding a single concatenated string.

```
Compare(String1, index1, String2, index2, Length,
IgnoreCase, Culture)
```

In this example, we will compare **mystring2** with part of **mystring1**, starting at index 4 (the fifth character in the string because the index is 0 based), and at the beginning of the second **string**, and comparing seven characters. This method returns an **Integer**: 0 if there is a match, and 1 if there is not.

```
Dim mystring1 As String = "justTesting"

Dim mystring2 As String = "Testing"

Dim myresult As Integer

myresult = String.Compare(mystring1, 4, mystring2, 0, 7)

console.Write(myresult)
```

Concat

The simplest thing to do with **Strings** is to add them together to form a larger **String**. This is a process known as *concatenation*. It's a big word for a simple thing. One way to concatenate (add together) **Strings** is using the special operator **&.**

```
Dim Greeting As String = "Dear "

Dim PersonName As String = "Bob "
```

```
Dim Salutation As String

Salutation = Greeting & PersonName

console.Write(Salutation)
```

This example writes Dear Bob into the console window, after concatenating two **String** variables, **Greeting** and **PersonName,** into the single variable, **Salutation**.

Concatenating **Strings** is pretty simple. It's often necessary to convert strings, either to uppercase or lowercase or another type of conversion. The **StrConv** function is particularly useful for this type of conversion.

Strings are objects and have methods that perform certain functions. One of those functions is concatenation. The **Concat** method of the string class is multipurpose. It's functionality changes with the number of arguments passed to the method. For example, when a single argument is passed to the **Concat** method, a string representation of the argument is returned.

```
Dim mystring As String

mystring = "I like it"

console.Write(mystring.Concat(23))
```

In this sample, the number 23 is written as a string to the console window. Another example of the **Concat** method's ability to offer up a string representation of an object (see Chapter 7 for more information on objects) is this example:

```
Dim mystring As String

console.Write(mystring.Concat(Me.button1))
```

The above example results in the following being written to the console window: System.Windows.Forms.Button, text: button1.

Copy

The **Copy** method of the **String** type will assign the value of one string into another. In this example, a value is stored into the variable **mystring1**. The **Copy** method then assigns the value into the variable **mystring2**.

```
Dim mystring1 As String

Dim mystring2 As String

mystring1 = "Visual Basic is fun."
```

```
mystring2 = System.String.Copy(mystring1)

console.Write(mystring2)
```

Using the **Copy** method probably seems like a lot of work. Visual Basic programmers have always simply created a new variable and stored the value of another string into it to make a copy. The code will still work. Here is an example:

```
Dim mystring1 As String

Dim mystring2 As String

mystring1 = "Visual Basic is fun."

mystring2 = mystring1

console.Write(mystring2)
```

Both samples write "Visual Basic is fun." into the console window. To better fit into the object-oriented programming paradigm, it's important for the **String** class to be able to make a copy of itself. This is an ability (explained more in Chapter 7) that belongs to **String** objects.

Equals

This method is quite simple in that it determines if the values in one string are exactly the same as in another string. Here are two equivalent examples, one that uses the **Equals** method and one that uses the equality operator (=).

```
Dim mystring1 As String

Dim mystring2 As String

mystring1 = "Visual Basic is fun."

mystring2 = "Visual Basic is fun."

console.Write(System.String.Equals(mystring1, mystring2))
```

The Equivalent of the previous code snippet is:

```
Dim mystring1 As String

Dim mystring2 As String
```

```
mystring1 = "Visual Basic is fun."

mystring2 = "Visual Basic is fun."

console.Write(mystring1 = mystring2)
```
Both examples write the word True into the console window.

Format

The **String.Format** method constructs new strings from other values and data types. Insert a formatting place holder (a whole number starting at 0) in braces, and then include the value you want displayed in its place as an argument to the format method. For example, {0} is replaced by **myInteger** in this code:

```
Dim myInteger As Integer = 150

Dim myString As String

myString = String.Format("Only {0} shopping days left.",
myInteger)

Console.WriteLine(myString)
```

This example displays the phrase:"Only 150 shopping days left." in the console window. This concept is very familiar to C and C++ programmers. The idea of replacing formatting characters in a string with values comes from the C programming language.

Continue adding formatting characters by incrementing each value to be replaced.

```
Dim myInteger As Integer = 47

Dim myDate As Date = Today()

Dim myString As String

myString = String.Format("I am {0} years old on {1}.",
myInteger, myDate)

Console.WriteLine(myString)
```

This example writes "I am 47 years old on 6/25/2001 12:00:00 AM" to the console window. The next section discusses formatting characters. You can include one of these formatting characters to further format your string by including it within the braces. In this next example you can see that the formatting character for currency is separated from the 0 in the braces by a colon.

```
Dim myInteger As Integer = 100

Dim myString As String = String.Format("I would like {0:C}
for my birthday.", myInteger)

Console.WriteLine(myString)
```

This example formats the integer as currency and writes, "I would like $100 for my birthday." to the console window. Another formatting feature is the ability to easily add white space to your string. This is simple enough to do without using a formatting character, although it makes adding a dynamic number of characters at runtime much simpler. Here is an example:

```
Dim myName As String = "Mary"

Dim myString As String = String.Format("Employee
Name:{0,3}", myName)

Console.WriteLine(myString)
```

This example writes "Employee Name: Mary" to the console window.

Join

Use the **Join** method to create new strings from arrays of strings. Join them together using a separator string, passed as an argument to the join method. The following example uses white space and a dash to join together a string array. This example has two members in the string array:

```
Dim MyString As String() = {"First Name:", "Rod"}

Console.WriteLine(String.Join(" - ", MyString))
```

This example writes "First Name: Rod" to the console window.

Instance Methods of the String Class

The previous sections covered methods that do not need a **String** object to use them. The methods are called directly from the string class. Don't worry if this seems a little confusing. It's covered in detail later in the book. What you need to know specifically about instance methods is that you have to have a string object to use them. Instead of the format stringclass.methodname, you use instance methods by using the variable name of the string, a dot, and the name of the method like this:

```
Dim myString As String = "Hello there."

Dim myString2 As String

myString2 = myString.Clone()
```

Table 2.10 lists the instance methods of the string class along with a brief description of each method.

Table 2.10   Instance Methods of the String Class

Method	Description
Clone	Returns a reference to this instance of String.
CompareTo	Overloaded; compares this instance with a specified object.
CopyTo	Copies a specified number of characters from a specified position in this instance to a specified position in an array of Unicode characters.
EndsWith	Determines whether the end of this instance matches the specified String.
Equals	Overloaded; overridden; determines whether two String objects have the same value.
GetEnumerator	Retrieves an object that can iterate through the individual characters in this instance.
GetHashCode	Overridden; returns the hash code for this instance.
GetType	Gets the Type of the current instance.
GetTypeCode	Returns the TypeCode for class String.
IndexOf	Overloaded; reports the index of the first occurrence of a String, or one or more characters, within this instance.
IndexOfAny	Overloaded; reports the index of the first occurrence in this instance of any character in a specified array of Unicode characters.
Insert	Inserts a specified instance of String at a specified index position in this instance.
LastIndexOf	Overloaded; reports the index position of the last occurrence of a specified Unicode character or String within this instance.
LastIndexOfAny	Overloaded; reports the index position of the last occurrence in this instance of one or more characters specified in a Unicode array.
PadLeft	Overloaded; right-aligns the characters in this instance, padding on the left with spaces or a specified Unicode character for a specified total length.
PadRight	Overloaded; left-aligns the characters in this string, padding on the right with spaces or a specified Unicode character, for a specified total length.

Table 2.10 Instance Methods of the String Class

Method	Description
Remove	Deletes a specified number of characters from this instance beginning at a specified position.
Replace	Overloaded; replaces all occurrences of a specified Unicode character or String in this instance, with another specified Unicode character or String.
Split	Overloaded; identifies the substrings in this instance that are delimited by one or more characters specified in an array, then places the substrings into a String array.
StartsWith	Determines whether the beginning of this instance matches the specified String.
SubString	Overloaded; retrieves a substring from this instance.
ToCharArray	Overloaded; copies the characters in this instance to a Unicode character array.

Clone

The clone method returns a reference to the **String** object. This means that a second variable points at the same string data. This is not the same as making a copy. If you change either the first or second variable, both will change because they point to the same place in memory. There is only a single copy of the data. Here's an example:

```
Dim mystring1 As String

Dim mystring2 As Object

mystring1 = "Visual Basic is fun."

mystring2 = mystring1.Clone()

console.Write(mystring2)

mystring2 = "vb is easy"

console.Write(mystring1)
```

String Properties

Strings, as complex as they are with all the many methods available, only have two properties. Properties, as you'll learn in Chapter 7, are stored information about an object. In the case of strings, the length of the **String** and individual characters can be retrieved. Table 2.11 lists these two properties.

Here is an example of using the properties of a string:

```
Dim myString As String = "Visual Basic is fun."

Dim myCharacter As Char

myCharacter = myString.Chars(2)

console.Write(myCharacter)
```

In this example, the letter "s" is written into the console window. Strings are arrays. You will learn about arrays in Chapter 6. Each character can be accessed by its position in the **String**, starting at 0. So, to access the first "V" in the string you would pass a 0 to the **Chars** property. The **Chars** property gets the character and returns it as a **Char** type variable, as in this example.

The **Length** property will get the length of the **String** as an integer like this:

```
Dim myString As String = "Visual Basic is fun."

Dim myLength As Integer

myLength = myString.Length

console.Write(myLength)
```

This code returns the number 20 and writes it to the console window.

Table 2.11 Properties of the String Class

Property	Description
Chars	Gets a character from a specific character position in the string.
Length	Gets the total number of characters in the string.

Table 2.12 StrConv Conversion Types

Visual Basic constant	Conversion type
UpperCase	All characters are converted to UPPERCASE.
LowerCase	All characters are converted to lowercase.
ProperCase	Returns a string where each word is returned with the first letter uppercase and the rest of each word lowercase. Note: In words such as UpperCase, where an internal letter is capitalized, it will be made lowercase by this conversion.
Wide	Converts single-byte charaters to double-byte characters for use only in Asian locales. This will throw an error if used in other locales.
Narrow	Converts double-byte charaters to single-byte characters for use only in Asian locales. This will throw an error if used in other locales.
Katakana	Converts Japanese Hiragana characters to Katakana.
Hiragana	Converts Japanese Katakana characters to Hiragana.
Simplified Chinese	Converts to simplifed Chinese, the official written language of mainland China.
Traditional Chinese	Converts to traditional Chinese, the older written language of China, the written language still used on Taiwan.
Unicode	Converts the string to Unicode.
FromUnicode	Converts a Unicode String to the default code page of the system.
None	No conversion takes place.

String Conversion

Occasionally, you may want to convert a string to a different case or language format. The **StrConv** function allows you to perform string-wide conversion.

```
StrConv(String, Conversion, LCID)
```

The syntax for the **StrConv** function is straightforward. The **String** argument is the variable name of the **String** to be converted. The Conversion parameter is the type of conversion, as listed in Table 2.12, and the LCID parameter is the localeID, if different from the system's localeID. The localeID is the information stored by your computer to keep track of your geographic locale, so as to properly format currency, dates, time, and character set.

Special String Formatting Characters

There are special formatting characters that can save you a great deal of effort when converting values to be displayed as a string. Using these characters will make displaying messages in message boxes, dialog windows, and other string display requirements simple. They work with most of the procedures that convert values to strings such as:

Format

ToString

Console.Write

This first section covers formatting numeric values, made much simpler using formatting characters.

Formatting Numeric Values

One of the most tedious things in programming can be the proper formatting of values, converted to the **String** type. Special formatting characters have made displaying these values as **Strings** quite simple. Mastering the use of these formatting characters will save you a great deal of time. Table 2.13 lists the various formatting characters that can be used to format numbers as **Strings**.

Note
Formatting characters are case sensitive, meaning either upper- or lowercase characters can be used, but in some conversions, changing the case of the character will provide a different result.

Table 2.13   Numeric Formatting Characters

Formatting Character	Format Description	Format Display
C	Currency	$XX,XX.XX
D	Decimal	[–]XXXXXXX
E	Scientific	[–]X.XXXXXXE+xxx
		[–]X.XXXXXXe+xxx
		[–]X.XXXXXXE-xxx
		[–]X.XXXXXXe-xxx
F	Fixed-point	[–]XXXXXXX.XX
G	General	This display varies and can be either general or scientific.
N	Number	[–]XX,XXX.XX
P	Percent	Displayed as a percentage.
R	Round-trip	Numbers converted into strings will have the same value when converted back to numbers.
X	Hexadecimal	Returns the minimum hexadecimal representation.

Currency

Depending on the culture specified on the computer on which the program is run, the currency is displayed in the local culture format. Using the formatting character shown in Table 2.10, methods that accept formatting characters will format the string as a currency. Include an integer after the letter C to specify how many decimal places you want included in the display. The default is two decimal places.

Here is an example:

```
Dim myInteger As Integer = 12005

Dim myString As String = myInteger.ToString( "c" )

console.Write(myString)
```

This example displays the number, formatted as currency: $12,005.00. Another example displays the same number with 4 decimal places:

```
Dim myInteger As Integer = 12005

Dim myString As String = myInteger.ToString( "c4" )

console.Write(myString)
```

Decimal

This formatting character, D, will take integer values and convert them into Base 10 decimal numbers. If the number happens to be negative in value, the number will appear with a negative sign (-). Here are examples of using the Decimal format:

```
Dim myString As String

Dim myInteger As Integer = 54321

myString = myInteger.ToString( "d6" )

console.Write(myString)
```

Assuming your computer's culture setting is set to U.S. English, myString will appear in the console window as 054321. Here is another example:

```
MyString = MyInteger.ToString( "d2" )

console.write(myString)
```

The value 54321 is written to the console window.

Exponential

Passing the letter E to methods that allow formatting will format strings in a scientific or exponent format. You can also pass a precision argument to set the number of digits to the right of the decimal point.

Note
In most cases, the case of the format character is insignificant. In the case of the exponential format, the case of the format specifier also determines the case of the exponent symbol.

```
Dim myInteger As Integer = 12345

Dim myString As String = MyInteger.ToString( "e" )

console.Write(myString)
```

This results in 1.234500e+004 being written to the console window. Adding the integer 3 as a precision specifier after the letter "e" has this effect:

```
Dim myInteger As Integer = 12345

Dim myString As String = MyInteger.ToString( "e3" )

console.Write(myString)
```

The value 1.235e+004 is written to the console window.

Fixed Point

Occasionally, you will need to display a whole number showing a certain number of decimal places; all zeros of course. The fixed-point format will insert a decimal to the right of the whole number and follow it with the number of zeros you've placed in the precision specifier.

Note
The default when no precision specifier is supplied is two zeros.

Here is an example of using fixed point formatting specifying three decimal places.

```
Dim myInteger As Integer = 12345

Dim myString As String = myInteger.ToString( "f3" )

console.Write(myString)
```

This results in 12345.000 being displayed in the console window.

```
Dim myInteger As Integer = 12345

Dim myString As String = myInteger.ToString( "f" )

console.Write(myString)
```

This results in 12345.00 being displayed in the console window.

General

Similar to the fixed-point and exponent formats, the general format displays a numeric value in either fixed point or exponential format. This format specifier returns the most compact string representation. Here is an example:

```
Dim myInteger As Integer = 12345

Dim myString As String = myInteger.ToString( "g" )

console.Write(myString)
```

This results in 12345 being written to the console window. After adding the integer 3 as the precision specifier in this next code snippet, you will see that it is displayed as the exponent 1.23e4 in the console window.

```
Dim myInteger As Integer = 12345

Dim myString As String = myInteger.ToString( "g3" )

console.Write(myString)
```

Another thing you should know about the general format is that it has a maximum precision of 17 digits when the variable type is **Double**. The default precision is 15 digits. If you want to use the maximum precision, make sure to specify 17 as the precision specifier.

Number

The number format displays a numeric value in the form "[-]d,ddd,ddd.dd." It's similar to the fixed-point format where a decimal is inserted followed by the number of zeros specified in the precision specifier. Just as in the fixed-point format, when no precision specifier is supplied, two zeros are inserted. Here is an example:

```
Dim myInteger As Integer = 12345

Dim myString As String = myInteger.ToString( "n" )

console.Write(myString)
```

With no specifier, the result in the console window is 12,345.00.

```
Dim myInteger As Integer = 12345

Dim myString As String = myInteger.ToString( "n4" )

console.Write(myString)
```

This code snippet results in 12,345.0000 being written to the console window.

Percent

The percent format will take a decimal value and display it as a percentage value. This is the same as multiplying the number by 100 before displaying it with the percent sign. Notice in this next example that specifying the percent format without a precision specifier causes the format to round to two decimal places, so that this code snippet displays 12.35% in the console window.

```
Dim myDouble As Double = .12345

Dim myString As String = myDouble.ToString( "P" )

console.Write(myString)
```

In this next example the precision specifier is set to 3 so that three-decimal-place accuracy is set and all the numbers are displayed:

```
Dim myDouble As Double = .12345

Dim myString As String = myDouble.ToString( "P3" )

console.Write(myString)
```

This results in 12.345% being displayed in the console window.

Round-trip

The round-trip format is special, in that it doesn't really do any formatting. Instead, it makes certain that a number, represented as a string, can be displayed with all of its precision and when parsed back into its original and complete numeric value. A perfect example of this is the **Double** data type, which has a maximum precision of 17 digits.

The following code snippet uses the round-trip format to preserve the value of the variable. In this example, the Double value is converted from a **Double** type to a **String** type and back again with no loss of precision.

```
Dim MyDouble As Double = 1.234567891234567

Dim myString As String = MyDouble.ToString( "R" )

console.Write(myString)

myDouble = Convert.ToDouble(myString)

console.Write(myDouble)
```

Note
Remember that console.write does an automatic conversion to string format before displaying in the console window.

Hexadecimal

The hexadecimal format converts a numeric value to a hexadecimal string representation of the number. Hexadecimal is base 16. Counting in hexadecimal goes like this: 0,1,2,3,4,5,6,7,8,9,A,B,C,D,E,F. So, the number 16 is represented as 10. Here is an example of using the hexadecimal formatting character:

```
Dim myInteger As Integer = 54321

Dim myString As String

myString = myInteger.ToString( "x" )

console.Write(myString)
```

This example writes the number d431 into the console window. If you replace the x with an uppercase X, the hexadecimal number will be written with uppercase letters: D431. Adding a precision specifier will set the number of significant digits, as in this example:

```
Dim myInteger As Integer = 54321

Dim myString As String
```

```
    myString = myInteger.ToString( "x6" )

    console.Write(myString)
```

This results in 00d431 being written to the console window. Notice that when six significant digits are specified, the number is stuffed with zeros to the left.

Picture Numeric Formatting

Visual Basic .NET has added an incredible amount of **String** formatting capability. In the last section you saw how numbers of almost any type can be formatted into **Strings**. If you're ever caught in a situation where the formatting provided by the list of characters so far in this chapter is not enough, take heart; there are many more ways to format numbers into **Strings** using picture-numeric formatting characters.

Using placeholder **Strings**, you can define how your number appears on both sides of the decimal point, both positive and negative. Table 2.14 lists the formatting characters you can use to build up a specific format.

> **Note**
> Numbers may appear formatted differently depending upon the culture setting of the computer displaying the number.

Here are some examples that demonstrate the use of the picture formatting characters:

```
    Dim myDouble As Double = 7.28934

    Dim myString As String = MyDouble.ToString( "000.##" )

    console.Write(myString)
```

This example displays the value 007.29 in the console window. Notice that the decimal point is also displayed as formatted. It will be included in the following examples without further explanation. For the sake of brevity, the following code snippets assume that variables have been declared and that a value is written to the console window.

```
    myString = myDouble.ToString( "0###.##" )
```

This example results in the following string: 0007.29.

```
    myString = myDouble.ToString( "%#.##" )
```

Similar to the percent formatting we've seen earlier in this chapter, the double type is converted to decimal by multiplying the number times 100. Therefore, this example results in the following string: %728.93.

Table 2.14   Picture Numeric Formatting Characters

Character	Description	Notes
0	Zero placeholder	This formatting character takes the place of a zero; when using this formatting character, a zero is printed whether the digit is significant or not.
#	Digit placeholder	Unlike the zero placeholder, the digit placeholder only replaces significant digits. If the value of the number is zero, nothing is displayed.
.	Decimal point	Simply displays the decimal point.
,	Group separator and multiplier	Acts as a number separator according to the culture defined on the computer. Standard English culture expects a comma before every fourth digit like this: 1,000.
%	Percent sign	Displays the percent sign.
E+0 E-0 e+0 e-0	Exponent notation	Formats the number according to scientific (exponent) notation.
\	Backslash	This is used to display special characters not interpreted as formatting characters. It is used with formatting sequences such as \t, which is the tab character.
{ }	Curly braces	Double curly braces are used for displaying single, literal, curly braces.
'text' "text"	Quote characters	Characters between single or double quotes are displayed literally.
;	Section separator (semi-colon)	Formats the output differently depending on whether the value is positive, negative, or zero.

Notice in this next example how a formatting character is inserted within a string and replaced in the output by the numeric value.

```
Dim myInteger as Integer = 27

myString = myInteger.ToString( "The magic number is #" )
```

This example results in the following string: "The magic number is 27."

Sections

There are three possible sections of a picture formatting string, each separated from the other by a semicolon (;). When only a single section is defined:

Section one: Formats the number

When a second section is defined:

Section one: Positive and zero values

Section two: Negative values

When three sections are defined:

Section one: Positive values

Section two: Negative values

Section three: Zero values

Here is an example of formatting with sections.

```
Dim iPI As Integer = 27

Dim iNI As Integer = -39

Dim iZero As Integer = 0

Dim myString As String

myString = iPI.ToString("Positive: #;Negative: -#;Zero:
#", Nothing)

console.Write(myString)
```

Because 27 is a positive value, only the positive portion of the formatting is paid attention. The result displayed in the console window is Positive: 27. In this example, if the numeric value were replaced with **iNI** instead of iPI, the second section of the formatting would have been used and the value Negative: -39 would have been displayed in the console window. Lastly, if the **iZero** value had been used, the result would have been Zero, with no following digit. Remember that the # format character does not display a zero when the value is zero.

DateTime Format Strings

It's possible to format dates and times in the same manner as the numeric values we've seen formatted so far in this chapter. Using the methods of the DateTime data type that convert values to string, such as the ToString method, you can provide formatted string data to appear anywhere string text is required.

Standard DateTime Format Strings   Table 2.15 lists the DateTime format strings. Note that the formatting characters are case sensitive, affecting the output that is listed

Table 2.15 Standard DateTime Formatting Characters

Character	Description	Output
d	Short date	6/26/2001
D	Long date	Tuesday, June 26, 2001
f	Partial full—This includes a long date and a short formatted version of the time	Tuesday, June 26, 2001 12:00 AM
F	Complete full—This includes a long date and a long time format	Tuesday, June 26, 2001 12:00:00 AM
g	General—This is a short date and a short time	6/26/2001 12:00 AM
G	General—This is a short date and a long time format	6/26/2001 12:00:00 AM
M, m	Character month and numeric day; both cases produce the same output	June 26
R, r	abbreviated day of the week, numeric day, abbreviated character month, full year, Greenwich Mean Time and GMT identifier; both cases produce the same output	Tue, 26 Jun 2001 00:00:00 GMT
s	Sortable DateTime string There is no uppercase S format character; using an uppercase S will throw an error	2001-06-26T00:00:00
t	Short time (hours and minutes)	12:00 AM
T	Long time (hours, minutes, seconds)	12:00:00 AM
u	Sortable DateTime string with Universal time	2001-06-26 00:00:00Z
U	Universal sortable DateTime string with Universal Time	Tuesday, June 26, 2001 7:00:00 AM
Y, y	Month, year	June, 2001

using June 26th, 2001, as the sample date. The number of characters determines if the output is short or long. Following the table of formatting characters, several examples are given of how dates and times are formatted as strings.

Note
The patterns produced by the format specifiers listed in Table 2.15 are influenced by the culture settings of your computer. Different areas of the world display dates and times differently.

The following example code produces the results listed below:

```
Dim myDate As DateTime = Today()

Dim myString As String

myString = myDate.ToString("formatting character")

console.Write(myString)
```

Custom DateTime Format Strings   You are not restricted to the format strings supplied in Table 2.15. You can build your own custom date-time formats. Use the characters listed below to build your custom format. Remember that the culture settings of the computer will affect the output.

Here is a custom time-date format created using the formatting characters in Table 2.16.

```
Dim myDate As DateTime = Now()

Dim myString As String

myString = myDate.ToString("zz ""from GMT"" dd/MM/yyyy
hh:mm:sss")

console.Write(myString)
```

This example results in: -07 from GMT 26/06/2001 11:56:18 being written to the console window. Notice that you can also include literal text in your format by embedding it in quotes. Because these quotes are embedded in a string, they must be formatted as double-double quotes as shown.

Table 2.16 Custom DateTime Formatting Characters

Characters	Description	Output
dd	Numeric day of the week Note: Single-digit days appear with a leading zero	26
ddd	3-letter abbreviation of the character day of the week	Tue
dddd	Full character day of the week	Tuesday
ff	2-digit seconds fraction	24
fff	3-digit seconds fraction	123
ffff	4-digit seconds fraction	1234
fffff	5-digit seconds fraction	12345
ffffff	6-digit seconds fraction	123456
fffffff	7-digit seconds fraction	1234567
g, gg. . .	Used alone, represents a general date; used with other formatting characters, represents the era	A.D.
hh, hhh. . .	Hour (12-hour clock) Note: Single-digit hours will appear with a leading zero	11
HH, HHH. . .	Hour (24-hour clock) Note: There is a leading zero in single-digit hours	13
mm, mmm. . .	The minutes in the time Note: Single-digit minutes have a leading zero	36
MM	The numeric month; single-digit months will have a leading zero	06
MMM	3 letter abbreviation of the month name	Jun
MMMM	The full name of the month	June
ss, sss. . .	The second; single-digit seconds will have a leading zero	14
tt, ttt. . .	AM or PM	AM or PM
yy	The year without the century. Note: When the year is less than 10, a leading zero is displayed.	02
yyy	The year including the century in 4 digits	2002
zz	Timezone offset from Greenwich, England (plus and minus signs are automatically included)	−07
zzz, zzzz. . .	Full timezone offset	−07:00
:	Time separator	:
/	Date separator	/

Table 2.17 Enumeration Formatting Characters

Format String	Result
G or g	String value
F or f	Treats this enum as if it had the Flags attribute set
D or d	Numeric value
X or x	Hexadecimal value

Enumeration Format Strings

Enumerators are English language shortcuts for numeric values. For example, the days of the week, normally represented by a number, can be represented as the character day of the week. Using the **ToString** method creates a new **String** that represents the numeric, hexadecimal, or **String** value of an Enum. Passing a formatting string, as listed in Table 2.17, will allow you to format the return value.

Note
Enumeration format characters are not case sensitive.

In this next example, the **TypeCode**, which is the enumerated value that identifies an object type, is set to the **Boolean** type. The code then accepts a formatting character with the results listed below.

```
Dim myType As TypeCode = TypeCode.Boolean

Dim myString As String = myType.ToString("format
character")

console.Write(myString)
```

The result of this code snippet is the following:

G returns Boolean

F returns Boolean

D returns 3

X returns 00000003

Variable Type Conversion

Unlike the formatting we've discussed so far in this chapter, it often becomes necessary to convert one data type to types other than **String**; for example, converting **Strings** into

Table 2.18 Visual Basic .NET Data Type Conversion Functions

Conversion Function	Description
Cbool	Converts numbers greater than 0 to True, all others to False; converts valid strings to True or False; valid Strings are "True," "False," "1," "0"
Cbyte	Accepts a Double between 0 and 255 and converts it to type Byte
CChar	Accepts a string value and converts a single string character to type Char
CDate	Accepts a string that represents a date and converts it to the DateTime type
CDbl	Accepts any valid number in the range of the Double data type and converts it to type Double
CDec	Accepts any valid number in the range of the Decimal data type and converts it to type Decimal
Cint	Accepts any valid number in the range of the Integer data type and converts it to type Integer; if the number is a fractional value, the fraction will be rounded to a whole number
Clng	Accepts any valid number in the range of the Long data type and converts it to type Long; if the number is a fractional value, the fraction will be rounded to a whole number
Cobj	Any valid expression is converted to type Object
Cshort	Accepts any valid number in the range of the Short data type and converts it to type Short; if the number is a fractional value, the fraction will be rounded to a whole number
Csng	Accepts any valid number in the range of the Single data type and converts it to type Single
CStr	Numeric values are converted to a string representation of the number; Boolean values are returned as string "True" or "False" and Dates are returned as a string in "mm/dd/yy" format

dates. There are a large number of conversion functions provided by Visual Basic .NET for converting one data type into another (see Table 2.18).

Caution!
Convert carefully, especially numeric values. You may end up with rounding issues you didn't expect. When the number passed to either the CLng or CInt functions has a fractional part exactly equal to .5, the number is rounded to the nearest *even* number, for example, 0.5 to 0, 1.5 to 2, 2.5 to 2.

When using the conversion functions, it's a good idea to refer to the values in Table 2.2, so you do not accidentally try to convert a value that is out of range.

Converting 239473489834 to a Single type using Csng( ) results in `2.394735E11`, as shown below:

```
Dim myLong As Long = 239473489834

Dim mySingle As Single

mySingle = CSng(myLong)

console.Write(mySingle)
```

Some value types cannot be converted to other types. For instance, the following conversion from string to single type will throw an error:

```
Dim myString As String = "Hi"

Dim mySingle As Single

mySingle = CSng(myString)
```

Value and Reference Types

There are two types of variables in Visual Basic .NET: value type and reference type. If you've used previous versions of Visual Basic, this will be a new and important concept for you.

When variables of the *value* type are created, a place in memory is reserved to store a value. Whenever the variable is used, either to retrieve or store a value, the value is located directly in the storage space assigned to it. This is the way primitive types are stored. Remember from the beginning of this chapter that primitive types include the String, Integer, Boolean, and other types.

As the name suggests, *reference* types store a reference. A reference is a memory address where the computer can expect to find a value, rather than the value itself. C programmers will recognize this as a pointer. The value points to a place in memory. To get to the actual value when programming in C, you had to "dereference" the pointer.

Here are examples of each, and how they behave differently:

```
Dim myString As String = "Test"        'This creates a
value type

Dim myForm As Form = New Form()  'This creates a reference
type
```

As an easy way to see how the **String** and **Form** are different, we'll make copies of each:

```
Dim myNewString As String

myNewString = myString

Dim myNewForm As Form

myNewForm = myForm
```

In the case where the **String** was copied, an entirely new String variable was created. Subsequently changing one string will not affect the other. However, where the form was copied, only a reference to myForm was copied. Now there are two references to the same form. No matter which variable we use to access the form, there is still only a single form.

In Chapter 5 you will learn about procedures. As a foundation to learning about procedures, you'll need to know that you can pass arguments (parameters) to a procedure. You have the choice of passing the arguments ByVal (by value) or ByRef (by reference). When you pass the argument by value, you have made an entirely new copy of the information. Changing the value within the procedure will not affect the original information. Passing the value by reference simply creates another reference to the same information. Any changes to the value within the procedure affects the original information. Remember that you are only passing a reference to a single value. Reference and value type variables are stored differently in memory. In this next section, you'll learn how they are stored.

Stacks and Heaps

There are two places where Visual Basic .NET allocates memory for storing values. The first is the *stack*, which is a structured area of memory managed such that memory is allocated on a first come, first served basis. This type of ordered management is done by the Common Language Runtime and is known as LIFO (Last-In, First-Out). Because it's possible to know the exact size requirements of primitive, value-type variables at compile time, they can be managed by, and have values stored on, the stack. Values are "pushed" onto the stack and are "popped off" when required.

The heap, on the other hand, is a pool of memory, normally set aside for data types, that is created at runtime. Before runtime it's impossible to know the exact storage requirements of some types of data. The Common Language Runtime allocates heap memory for things such as classes.

The CLR manages its allocated heap by requesting a *chunk* of the heap called a *heap block*. When the blocks are no longer needed they are returned to the heap. On a regular basis a special "garbage collection" routine makes blocks available that are no longer being used and reorganizes the available space in the heap in the same way you might defragment a hard drive. This is important because of the dynamic way in which heap blocks are allocated.

Because it's impossible to know at compile time the exact memory requirements of objects such as Forms, these types of objects are managed on the heap, rather than a stack, just as a local, primitive-type, variable might be stored.

Values that are stored in a heap require two values stored in memory, one is the actual heap memory, and the other is the hexadecimal memory address. It is that memory address that is the reference variable for objects stored in heap memory.

Summary

This chapter has covered almost everything you need to know about using variables in Visual Basic .NET. Covering any material as complex as this is difficult without referring to other parts of the book. You may want to refer to Chapter 6 on arrays when learning about strings and Chapter 7 on objects when learning about variable types. Each variable is an object.

A great deal of time was spent in this chapter on formatting strings. Most applications have user interfaces, and user interfaces require your application to communicate primarily in string values. Visual Basic .NET has very powerful formatting capabilities that you will be able to take advantage of when building your applications.

The next chapter introduces operators, the workhorses of any computer programming language. Most of the examples in this chapter used the (=) operator without a proper introduction. Chapter 3 will show you how to build complex expressions using the variables you learned about in this chapter and operators.

One of the most important skills a programmer can learn is to form valid programming expressions. Interestingly, the formation of expressions and use of operators is nearly identical among most programming languages. An expression is any legal combination of symbols, such as those in Table 3.1, that ultimately represents a value. That value may be a number, such as the math operation 1 + 1 = 2, or a **String** *concatenation*, the joining together of **Strings**, like this "This is" & "a string," or may result in a **Boolean** value such as 5 > 4 (5 is greater than 4), which would equal True.

The operators listed in Table 3.1 will form the foundation of complex expressions and even help develop shortcuts. For example, the += operator provides the following shortcut:

```
Dim iNumTotal As Integer = 5

'The long way

iNumTotal = iNumTotal + 6

'The short way

iNumTotal += 6
```

Rather than writing **iNumTotal** twice, using the += operator allows you to shortcut the process with the same result.

Table 3.1 includes a brief description and example of each operator's use.

Logical Operators

Boolean values, or **Boolean** expressions that result in values of True and False, form the majority of expressions in most applications. This is because **Boolean** expressions are used to form decisions about what code an application should execute. Chapter 4 explains conditional expressions in more detail.

Table 3.1 Operators

Operator	Example	Description
+	xVal1 = 1 xVal1 + 5 Results in the number 6	The addition operator is used to add two numeric values together.
−	xVal1 = 5 xVal1 − 3 Results in the number 2	The subtraction operator is used to subtract one numeric value from another.
*	xVal1 = 2 xVal1 * 5 Results in the number 10	The multiplication operator is used to multiply one number times another.
/	xVal1 = 10 xVal1 / 5 Results in the number 2	The division operator is used to divide one numeric value by another.
%	xVal1 = 10 xVal1 % 3 Results in the number 1	The modulus operator returns the remainder of a division expression.
=	x = 5 Result: x contains the integer 5	Used to assign a value to a variable or property.
&=	sString = "Good" sString &= "Morning" Result: sString contains the string "Good Morning"	Concatenates one string to another and assigns the result back to the same variable.
*=	xVal1 = 4 xVal1 *= 3 Result: xVal1 contains the integer 12	Multiplies the value of a variable or expression with another and assigns the result to the original variable.
+=	xVal1 = 4 Val1 += 1 Result: xVal1 contains the integer 5	Adds the value of a variable or expression to another and assigns the result to the original variable.
−=	xVal1 = 4 xVal1 −= 1 Result: xVal1 contains the integer 3	Subtracts the value of a variable or expression from another and assigns the result to the original variable.
/=	xVal1 = 4 xVal1 /= 2 Result: xVal1 contains the double 2	Divides the value of a variable by the value of another variable or expression and assigns the result to the original variable.
\=	xVal1 = 4 xVal1 /= 2 Result: xVal1 contains the long 2	Divides the value of a variable by the value of another and then assigns the integer result to the original variable.
^=	xVal1 = 5 xVal1 /= 2 Result: xVal1 contains the double 100	Raises the value of a variable to the power of an exponent and assigns the result back to the original variable.

True is a Visual Basic operator that equates to a value of 1 when used in an expression, and a 1 equates to a boolean true statement. Also, **False** equates to a boolean false, or 0. Here's a code snippet to prove this:

```
Dim a, b As Integer

a = 1

b = 0

If a Then

     MessageBox.Show("A is true")

End If

If b Then

     MessageBox.Show("B is true")

End If
```

There are special operators that allow you to manipulate boolean statements:

AND – Compares two boolean values according to a truth table. Shown in Table 2.5.
OR – Compares two boolean values according to a truth table. Shown in Table 2.6.
XOR – Compares two boolean values according to a truth table. Shown in Table 2.7.

Assignment Operators

Assignment operators assign a value to a variable. This action is the same as storing a value into a variable's memory location. The most common of all the assignment operators is the equals sign (=).

```
Integer1 = 10
```

This assigns the number 10 into the variable **Integer1**. As you learned in the last chapter, values you assign to variables must be of the type you declared the variables to be. **Strings** are assigned to **String** variables, integers to **Integer** variables, and so forth.

Note
Don't confuse the assignment operator with the equality operator. They look the same but perform completely different functions.

Here is an example of using an assignment operator as a shortcut. This example sets the **Text** property of a **TextBox** control on the **Form** when a button is clicked. This example uses some concepts you'll learn about in some of the chapters further in the book. In Chapter 5 you will learn about procedures such as the Sub in this example. In Chapter 9 you will learn more about **TextBox** controls and building a **Form**.

```
Private Sub button1_Click(ByVal sender As System.Object,
ByVal e As System.EventArgs) Handles button1.Click

    Dim ival As Long

    ival = 10

    ival \= 5

    textBox1().Text = CStr(ival)

End Sub
```

Here's an example that uses the division shortcut operator:

```
Dim myInteger1 As Integer = 9

Dim myInteger2 As Integer = 3

myInteger1 /= myInteger2

console.Write(myInteger1)
```

This writes the number 3 into the console window.

Note
You might have to turn off Option Strict for this example to work. To turn the option off, go to the top of the **Form** and write: `Option Strict Off`.

Comparison Operators

The operators in the preceding table were used to create numeric and string values. Another type of operator is called a comparison operator because values on either side of the operator are compared and the result is a boolean true or false. The most commonly used operator is the equals sign (=). You'll notice that it serves a dual purpose. It's both an assignment operator as well as a comparison operator. Here are examples of the two uses of the equals operator.

```
Dim MyInteger As Integer

'Assignment

MyInteger = 4

'Comparison

If MyInteger = 4 Then

'statements

End If
```

This example uses a conditional "if" statement, which is discussed in Chapter 4. You'll find that using comparison operators is done mostly in forming expressions that make logical decisions as part of a conditional statement. You can refer to Table 3.2 for a list of the comparison operators used in Visual Basic .NET.

Comparison operators are all used in the same way. They require two values to evaluate (compare) and return a boolean true or false. Here's an example of using the not equal (<>) operator.

```
Dim myString1 As String = "Strawberry"

Dim myString2 As String = "Peach"

If myString1 <> myString2 Then

' do something

End If
```

It doesn't matter that strawberries and peaches are both sweet and yummy, what matters is that the characters in the two strings do not match. The conditional statement is read in English: "If myString1 is not equal to myString2 then." In this example, it's true that they are not equal, so the expression returns True.

Table 3.2   Comparison Operators

Operator	Example	Description
=	A = B	Value A equal or equivalent to Value B
>	A > B	Value A greater than Value B
<	A < B	Value A less than Value B
>=	A >= B	Value A greater than or equal to Value B
<=	A <= B	Value A less than or equal to Value B
<>	A <> B	Value A not equal or equivalent to Value B

Bitwise Operators

Manipulating binary values (1s and 0s) in memory is an important ability, as ultimately every value in a computer program, including the program itself, ends up in binary form. Chapter 2 on variables covers the bitwise operators in more detail. We'll introduce each of the operators, BITAND, BITOR, BITXOR, and BITNOT. But, first you should be able to visualize exactly how binary arithmetic works. Binary has only two values, 0 and 1. Table 3.3 gives you an idea of how counting in binary appears.

Computers use binary arithmetic because of the electronic components involved. Tiny transistors, embedded in the integrated circuits of a computer, operate as a switch. They are either on or off. When the transistors are on, electricity flows through the transistor and the computer sees this flow of electricity as a 1 or "on" condition. When the transistor is turned off, the value is considered 0. Imagine the values in Table 3.3 as three transistors in a row. To represent the number 0, all transistors are turned off. To represent a value of 1, the far-right transistor is turned on, while the others are turned off. For the value 2, the two end transistors are off, the middle one is on, and so forth. It's easy to envision with only three transistors. In fact, only three transistors will allow you to count all the way to the number 8. Modern computers have millions and even billions of transistors. It's the job of computer programs to set the on and off conditions of those transistors. Each transistor represents one bit of information.

Visual Basic .NET has a set of operators for working with information at the Bit level known as *bitwise operators*, which are operators that act on individual bits rather than the value as a whole. The next several sections explain the bitwise operators in greater detail.

Table 3.3   Binary–Decimal Comparison

Decimal Value	0	1	2	3	4
Binary Value	0	1	10	11	100

BitAnd

Using the **BitAnd** operator is very similar to using the boolean **AND** operator discussed in Chapter 2. If you think about the 1s and 0s as being True and False, respectively, you can view the information in Table 3.4 and see that 0 BitAnd 0 is the same as False AND False, and so on.

Let's take the number 25, which in binary form is 11001, and 24 (11000 binary). The **BitAnd** operator performs an analysis of each bit, with the results in Table 3.4. So, 11001 **BitAnd** 11000 = 11000.

> **Tip**
> An easy way to convert decimal to binary is using the Windows Calculator. From the View menu of the Calculator software, select Scientific. Type in a decimal value, and then click the Binary radio button and the number will appear in binary format in the calculator. You can use this same method for converting to other useful computer bases, such as hexadecimal.

Here is a code example using the BitAnd operator:

```
Dim MyInteger1 As Integer = 5

Dim MyInteger2 As Integer = 6

Dim MyResult As Integer

MyResult = MyInteger1 BitAnd MyInteger2

console.Write(MyResult)
```

The result is a decimal 4 (100 binary). Here is how the result is reached:

5 is binary 00000101

6 is binary 00000110

Table 3.4   BitAnd Result Table

Value 1	Operator	Value 2	Result
0	BitAnd	0	0
0	BitAnd	1	0
1	BitAnd	0	0
1	BitAnd	1	1

Starting at the left, we see that 0 **BitAnd** 0 is 0, so we can skip through the first five numbers. The matching 1's will BitAnd to a 1 and the next two columns, where the bits do not match, will **BitAnd** to a 0, resulting in 100 (4 decimal).

BitNot

The **BitNot** operator performs logical negation on any numeric value. The value, of course, is represented as bits, and the negation is performed on individual bits instead of the entire numeric value. Here is an example followed by a more visual explanation of what you are actually accomplishing using BitNot:

```
Dim myInteger1 As Integer = 30

Dim myInteger2 As Long = 86859

Dim myDouble As Double = 45.86

Dim mySingle As Single = 2

console.Write(BitNot myInteger1)

console.Write(BitNot myInteger2)

console.Write(BitNot myDouble)

console.Write(BitNot mySingle)
```

Here are the results of the previous code example:

BitNot MyInteger1 = -31
BitNot MyInteger2 = -86860
BitNot MyDouble = -47
BitNot MySingle = -3

Taking one of these examples, the variable **mySingle** equals 2, which in binary is 10. The **BitNot** operator reverses each bit so that the **BitNot** result of 2 is 11111101. The easiest way to visualize this is to use the Microsoft Calculator included with Windows. Begin by entering the number 2 in decimal form, as shown in Figure 3.1.

Once you've entered the number 2, click the **Bin** radio button, converting the number 2 into its binary representation of 10, as shown in Figure 3.2.

The next step is to click the Byte radio button, selecting display of the binary information as a single Byte (8 bits). The display should not change. You will still see 10. On the far

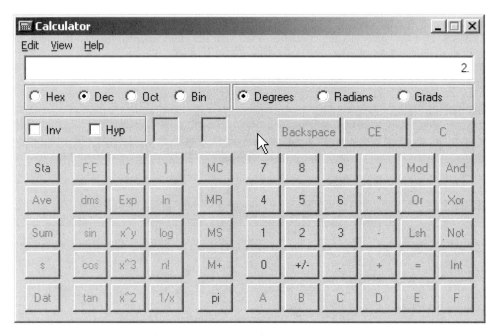

Figure 3.1   The Microsoft Calculator can help you visualize the BitNot operator's action.

right of the calculator you will see a red **Not** button. Clicking the **Not** button will per-form the **Not** operation on the binary number 10, resulting in 11111101 (Figure 3.3). Remember that the display was not displaying all of the zeros that the computer changed to 1's. In a signed number, the most significant bit is the sign, so the first thing that happens is that we change from positive to negative and the rest of the bits equals −3. If you want to assure yourself of that, follow these steps on the calculator.

1. Clear the calculator.
2. Switch to decimal mode and enter the number 2.
3. Click the **Not** button.

The result is −3.

BitOr

The **BitOr** operator compares individual bits in two numeric values and outputs a result based on the result values in Table 3.5. To give yourself an idea of what the result is going to be, you can first convert the numeric values into binary and compare the numbers by hand.

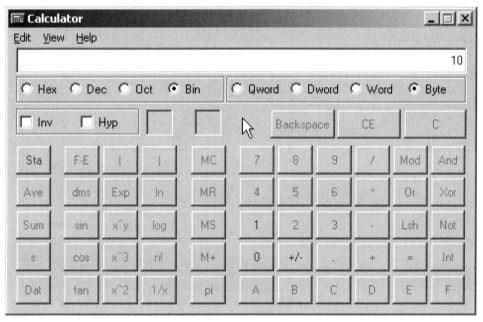

Figure 3.2   The binary representation of the number 2 is 10.

Here is an example that shows you how to use the **BitOr** operator followed by an explanation of how the result was reached:

```
Dim MyInteger1 As Integer = 5

Dim MyInteger2 As Integer = 6

Dim MyResult As Integer

MyResult = MyInteger1 BitOr MyInteger2

console.Write(MyResult)
```

Table 3.5   BitOr Result Table

Value 1	Operator	Value 2	Result
0	BitOr	0	0
0	BitOr	1	1
1	BitOr	0	1
1	BitOr	1	1

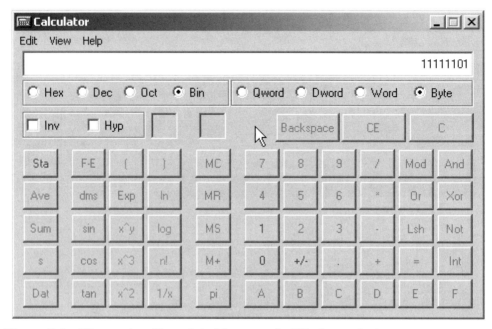

Figure 3.3   The number 10 result in binary on the Windows calculator.

MyResult is 7 and is written to the console window.
Here is how the **BitOr** operator arrives at 7:

5 is binary 00000101

6 is binary 00000110

Starting at the left, we see that 0 **BitOr** 0 is 0, so we can skip through the first five numbers.

The first 1's we come to are **BitOr** to 1. The next place has a 0 **BitOr** 1, which we see from Table 3.5 is equal to 1. So far we have 0000011. Once again, in the last place we have 1 **BitOr** 1, which is 1. The completed **BitOr** is now 00000111. Enter a binary 111 into your calculator. Then, click the **Dec** button, converting the binary value to decimal, and the result is 7.

BitXOr

Rather than a comparison of two numeric values, the **BitXOr** operator performs something called an *exclusion*. That's where the X in **BitXOr** comes from (Bit Exclusive Or).

Table 3.6   BitXOr Result Table

Value 1	Operator	Value 2	Result
0	BitXOr	0	0
0	BitXOr	1	1
1	BitXOr	0	1
1	BitXOr	1	0

Notice in Table 3.6 that the results of a **BitXOr** are quite different from a normal **BitOr**. Essentially, whenever the bits match you get a 0; when they don't, you get a 1.

Here is an example using the **BitXOr** operator:

```
Dim MyInteger1 As Integer = 5

Dim MyInteger2 As Integer = 6

Dim MyResult As Integer

MyResult = MyInteger1 BitXor MyInteger2

console.Write(MyResult)
```

The result of this code snippet is that the number 3 is written to the console window. Remember that 3 in binary is 11. When working with bitwise operators you rarely care about the decimal result, and most often care about the resulting individual bits.

Here is how the **BitXOr** operator arrives at the result of 3 (11 binary). Just as with the **BitOr** example:

5 is binary 00000101

6 is binary 00000110

Starting at the left, we see that 0 **BitXOr** 0 is 0, so we can skip through the first five numbers.

Now excluding the matching 1's, the result is 0, and neither of the next two places matches, resulting in 1's with a result of 11 (3 decimal).

Specialized Operators

You've seen so far in this chapter that there are essentially three types of operators: assignment; comparison; and operators, such as the bitwise operators, that perform a task. There are other operators that perform tasks that we haven't listed so far. The first operator is a holdover from previous versions of Visual Basic.

&

The **&** operator is used to join two strings. You learned in the last chapter that you can also join two **Strings** together using either the **Concat** method or the **Join** method of the **String** type. If you want your programs to be more object oriented, you should stick with those methods. But, for programs that are already written or for quick programs where adherence to object-oriented principles is not important, you can use the **&** operator. Placing the **&** operator between two **Strings** causes them to be joined into a single **String**. Here is an example of using the **&** operator.

```
Dim String1 As String = "Speak the speech I pray you "

Dim String2 As String = "as I pronounced it to you,
trippingly on the tongue."

Dim HamletLine As String

HamletLine = String1 & String2

Console.Write(HamletLine)
```

The example writes the string **HamletLine** to the console window as a single, joined string:

Speak the speech I pray you as I pronounced it to you, trippingly on the tongue.

MOD

The **MOD** operator is used to divide two numbers and returns only the remainder. For example, when dividing 9 by 4 the result is normally 2.25, but when using the **MOD** operator, only the remainder after the division into the 9 is performed. Therefore, a 1 is returned. Numbers that divide evenly, such as 9 divided by 3, where no remainder is returned, will return 0 when the **MOD** operator is used. Here is what these examples look like in code:

```
Dim myInteger1 As Integer = 9

Dim myInteger2 As Integer = 4

Dim myresult As Decimal

myresult = myInteger1 Mod myInteger2

console.Write(MyResult)
```

In this example, the number 1 is written to the console. In this next example, the numbers will divide evenly.

```
Dim myInteger1 As Integer = 9

Dim myInteger2 As Integer = 3

Dim myresult As Decimal

myresult = myInteger1 Mod myInteger2

console.Write(MyResult)
```

In this example, the number 0 is written to the console window.

Forming Complex Expressions

One purpose of using operators is to form expressions. So far in this chapter you've seen operators used to form simple expressions, such as Variable1 = 1 + 1. Expressions can be made quite complex by adding more variables and more operators. An important consideration, particularly with numeric expressions, is the order in which each part of the expression is analyzed.

Here is an example where confusion could possibly exist:

```
Dim myresult As Integer

myresult = 5 + 5 * 10

console.Write(myresult)
```

Is the answer 100 or 55? It depends on the order in which the expression is analyzed. Certain operators have precedence over others in the order in which they are executed. Here is a list of precedence:

1. multiplication and division
2. addition and subtraction

The result of the previous example is then 55, not 100. The multiplication is done first, then the addition. Making the example a little more complex:

```
Dim myresult As Integer

myresult = 5 + 5 * 10 / 2

console.Write(myresult)
```

This example results in the number 30 being written to the console window, because the multiplication and division are performed before the addition.

You can force a different precedence on the order by using parentheses. Here is how using parentheses will alter the example:

```
Dim myresult As Integer

myresult = (5 + 5) * 10 / 2

console.Write(myresult)
```

Expressions enclosed in parentheses are performed first. Therefore, the expression is now seen as 10 * 10 / 2, which equals 50 instead of 30. You can also use parentheses in non-numeric expressions to affect the order in which an expression is analyzed. This is common in boolean expressions, where the logic can get pretty confusing. In fact, oftentimes programmers will use parentheses in logical expressions, not to change the order, but to make it more apparent to the programmer. Here is an example of using parentheses in logical expressions:

```
Dim myresult, mybool1, mybool2, mybool3 As Boolean

mybool1 = True

mybool2 = False

mybool3 = True

myresult = mybool1 And (mybool2 Or mybool3)
```

In this example, the parentheses were not required. The result is True with or without them. But, it's much easier for the programmer to see the logic in the expression with the parentheses.

Summary

Operators are the workhorses of any computer programming language. Because of that, operators are almost the same no matter what language you are programming in. You can be pretty certain that using an operator in Visual Basic. NET will have the same effect in most any other language. You've seen how operators forming the foundation of all expressions store values in variables and perform important conversions. This information will also form the foundation for the next chapter on conditional statements. You'll learn how to direct the logical flow of your program using condition statements built from operators in this chapter.

Conditional Statements 4

Object orientation has changed the basic way application logic flows. Still, the underlying and basic flow, on a line-by-line basis, is one line of code after another until the application code is caused to start processing in a different object. Because application code is serial in nature (one life after another) it's necessary to be able to branch the code based on decisions made at runtime. This is known as *conditional* logic.

Conditional logic can cause certain blocks of code to either be processed, not processed, or processed more than once.

If

Decision, decisions! All program flow is based on a decision with ultimately a very simple answer, either yes or no, or in logic terms, true or false—or, more closely to the truth, 1 or 0. The simplest, and most common way to implement this type of conditional logic is by using an **IF** statement.

The conditional statement IF has three basic parts. We can get fancier in a moment. The first part involves the keyword IF, followed by some boolean (evaluating to true or false) expression followed on the same line with the keyword THEN. Here is an example:

```
If True Then
```

The second part of the IF statement is the code that will be executed whenever the expression in the first part resolves to True. Lastly, each IF ends with an END IF statement. The result looks like this:

```
Dim TestValue as String

Dim NewValue as String

TestValue = "ABC"

If TestValue="ABC" Then
```

```
        NewValue = "DEF"

    End If
```

In this case, if the value stored in the variable, **TestValue**, is equal to the **String** value "ABC," then the expression will evaluate to True and the line of code setting the variable **NewValue** is executed. Next, lets look at an additional statement that can be added into this condition. What happens if the expression in the **IF** statement evaluates to False? Well, in the example above the line, NewValue="DEF" would simply be skipped. The **ELSE** clause allows you to add an alternative set of code in the event the **IF** evaluates to False.

```
    Dim TestValue as String

    Dim NewValue as String

    TestValue = "ABC"

    If TestValue="ABC" Then

        NewValue = "DEF"

    Else

        NewValue="123"

    End If
```

In this example, the variable **NewValue** is set to the string value, "123," if **TestValue** is not equal to "ABC." What happens when there is more than one value to consider? The **ElseIf** clause can be added to create an additional evaluation. You can add as many **ElseIf** clauses as you need, and if all of them evaluate to False, then the **Else** clause, at the end, is executed. Here is an example:

```
    If mySon="Jason" Then

        hisSon = "Ocean"

    ElseIf mySon="Bob" Then

        hisSon="Bob Jr."

    ElseIf mySon="George" Then

        hisSon="Peter"
```

```
Else

    hisSon="someone else"

End If
```

Since, in the last example, we are only considering whether the **String** stored in **mySon** is equal to the corresponding **String** in the conditional expression, it's not possible for more than one of the **ElseIf** statements to be True. To evaluate conditions where more than one of these expressions can evaluate to True, you will need separate **If** statements.

You can embed an **If** statement within another **If** statement like this:

```
If MyCar="Ford" Then

    If MyModel="Bronco" Then

        Carsize="Medium"

    Elseif MyModel="Explorer" Then

        Carsize="Large"

    Else

        Carsize="unknown"

    End if

End if
```

There is no limit to the number of **If** statements you can embed within other **If** statements. When there are several **If** statements embedded within other **If** statements, care must be taken to ensure that each **If** is properly terminated with an **End If**.

Tip

When embedding many **If** statements within other **If** statements you should consider adding comments to your code. Otherwise, it's quite easy to lose track of **If** statements without **End If** statements, or logic errors due to incorrectly placed conditions.

Inline If

There is a simple and abbreviated way to write **If** statements called an *inline If*. You can write the **If**, expression, and **Then** on the same line followed by the statements that are executed when the expression evaluates to True. Each statement must be seperated by a colon.

```
If <expression> Then statement1 : statement2 :
statement3...
```

For simple **If** conditions, this is the cleanest syntax. It does come with some restrictions. First of all, you cannot include an **Else** condition. To include an **Else** condition see the next section, on **Immediate If**. Secondly, you cannot embed one inline If within another. Inline If statements must be the first statement on a line. That would not be true for a second inline If. Therefore, it's not a legal use of this type of statement and the compiler will throw an error.

Immediate If

Oftentimes, you will want to use an **If** statement simply to set a variable to one of two possible values. If one thing is true, set the value to value A, if it's not true, then set it to value B. Instead of writing a full **If**, **Then**, **End If** statement, you can use an *Immediate If* (IIF), a method of the Visual Basic .NET Interaction Class. The Immediate If accepts three parameters:

Expression

Value A—returned if the express is True

Value B—returned if the express is False

Here is an example:

```
Dim Adult as boolean

Adult = IIF(Age > 17, True, False)
```

Choose

You've seen how an **immediate IF** allows you to simply select one of two possible answers based on the value of an expression. The **Choose** function lets you select from an array of possible values. Each value is *indexed* (numbered). By passing in a number as a parameter to the **Choose** function, the array value whose index matches is returned.

The numeric value passed as a parameter must be of type **Double**. Unlike arrays in Visual Basic .NET, which are always 0-based, the Choose function that returns the first choice with a 1 is passed as the index parameter.

```
Dim anIndex = 4 as Integer

Dim rightChoice as String
```

```
rightChoice = Choose(anIndex, "Tom", "Dave", "Bob",
"Ted", "John")
```

The **rightChoice**, in this example and always, is Ted. One of the odd behaviors of this function is that, even though you pass as a parameter the index of the correct choice, the function looks at every other choice in the list. So, if your choices are objects that perform some type of processing, expect them to each be evaluated before the selected choice is returned.

Select Case

The example in the section on the **If** statement that included several **ElseIf** statements can be written in a different way, slightly more streamlined but with the same end result. The **Select Case** statement allows you to set up a list of possible results of an expression. Unlike **ElseIf**, where you can include many different expressions, the **Select Case** statement evaluates a single expression.

There are six parts to a Select Case statement:

The first part includes the keywords Select Case followed by the expression to be evaluated.

The second part is the word Case followed by the expected result of the expression in the Select Case statement.

Statements after each Case that are executed if the result is a match with the expression in the Select Case statement

Case Else statement

Statements executed when the Case Else is the default response

End Select statement ending the list of choices

Here is the previous **ElseIf** sample rewritten as a **Select Case** statement:

```
Dim mySon as String

mySon="Jason"

Select Case mySon

Case "Jason"

    hisSon = "Ocean"

Case "Bob"
```

```
        hisSon="Bob Jr."

    Case "George"

        hisSon="Peter"

    Case Else

        hisSon="someone else"

    End If
```

This example has only a single statement following each **Case**. You can have as many statements following each **Case** as needed.

Loops

When it becomes necessary to run the same program code many times, you can cause your program flow to loop continuously processing statements until a condition is met. The condition may be a counter, or it may be some expression evaluating to True.

There are two basic types of loops: Do loops and For loops. The Do loop is used to evaluate a condition while a For loop loops a specified number of times, or in the case of a For Each loop, through all the objects contained within a parent object, such as the values of an array.

Do Loops

Executing a block of code until a condition is met is the job of a Do loop. There are two basic ways of creating a Do loop. The first evaluates the condition before entering the loop, such that if the condition cannot ever be met, the code within the loop is never executed. The second form a Do loop evaluates is the condition at the end of the loop. This means that the code is run at least once before the condition is evaluated.

There is another wrinkle to consider. The Do loop can be caused to loop **While** a condition is True or **Until** a condition is met. One of these two keywords must be part of the conditional evaluation, whether at the beginning or end of the loop.

```
Do While <condition>

    <statements>

[Exit Do]
```

```
          <statements>

Loop

Do Until <condition>

          <statements>

  [Exit Do]

          <statements>

Loop

Do

<statements>

[Exit Do]

<statements>

Loop While <condition>


Do

          <statements>

     Exit Do

          <statements>

  Loop Until <condition>
```

The statements within a Do loop will continue executing until one of two things happens. Either the condition is met, or an **Exit Do** statement is encountered. The **Exit Do** statement causes program flow to continue after the Loop statement. In fact, the condition is optional. You can control when a loop is exited using only the **Exit Do** statement.

Here are a couple of brief examples of using a Do loop, showing the different results depending on whether the condition is at the beginning or end of the loop.

```
Dim bCondition as Boolean

bCondition = True

Dim iCounter = 1 as Integer


Do while bCondition

    If iCounter = 3 Then

        bCondition = False

    End if

    iCounter = iCounter + 1

Loop
```

In this example, the condition is met when the loop is first encountered, and then set to False after three times through the loop. When the condition is finally not met because **bCondition** is set to False, the program flow will continue after the Loop statement and **iCounter** will equal 4 because it was incremented one more time after **bCondition** was set to False.

In this next example, we set **bCondition** to **False**. In the previous example, the loop would never have been entered and **iCounter** would have equaled 1. Because the evaluation of the condition happens at the end of the loop, the statements within the loop will still be executed at least once.

```
Dim bCondition as Boolean

bCondition = False

Dim iCounter = 1 as Integer



Do

    If iCounter = 3 Then
```

```
              bCondition = False

      End if

      iCounter = iCounter + 1

   Loop while bCondition
```

Whether you evaluate at the beginning or end of the loop or perform no evaluation at all, you can exit the loop at any time using the **Exit Do** statement. Now, we'll change the behavior of the first loop example by putting in an **Exit Do** statement.

```
Dim bCondition as Boolean

bCondition = True

Dim iCounter = 1 as Integer

Do while bCondition

      If iCounter = 3 Then

            bCondition = False

            Exit Do

      End if

      iCounter = iCounter + 1

Loop
```

In this example, **iCounter** is left at 3 because processing jumps from the **End If** outside the loop, skipping the incrementing of **iCounter**.

Warning
If a loop has no condition or the condition never attains a value where the loop is exited, that's called an *endless loop*. An endless loop will continuously run until the program is forcibly halted. When there is a chance of an endless loop within your application, you can create error-handling code such as a counter that executes an **Exit Do** statement when a certain number of loops is achieved.

So far, only the **While** keyword has been used in our examples to evaluate a **Do** condition. The other keyword, **Until**, has a slightly different useage.

```
Dim finalAmount = 10 as Integer

Dim iCounter = 1 as Integer

Do Until iCounter = finalAmount

    iCounter += 1

Loop
```

Unlike a Do loop where the **While** keyword is used and the expression supplied must evaluate to True, the keyword **Until** expects an expression that when False allows the loop to continue processing. When it becomes True, the loop is exited. In the last example, **iCounter** was not equal to **finalAmount**, so the loop was entered and continued looping until the variable, **iCounter**, had incremented to where it was equal to **finalAmount**, at which point processing continued on the line after the **Loop** statement. In a nutshell:

Do While something is True

Do Until something becomes True

While Loop

The While Loop is very similar to the Do Loop. The While loop will continue looping while the condition remains True. When the condition, as shown in the following code snippet, turns False, the program continues processing the next statement after the End While.

```
While <condition>

<statements>

[Exit While]

<statements>

End While
```

Also similar to the Do loop, the While loop has an exit statement for exiting the loop before the condition is met. The While loop's exit statement is **Exit While**. One of the only differences between a While loop and a Do loop is that the condition in a While loop is not optional, whereas it is optional in a Do loop. This makes the While loop a little less flexible than the Do loop.

Here is an example of a While loop:

```
Dim xval As Integer = 10

While xval = 10

    xval -= 1

End While
```

The condition, xval = 10 is true, and it loops only once, because xval is decremented (lowered by a value of 1) in the first loop, causing the statement to be False in the next evaluation of the condition.

For Loop

The **For** loop is useful for looping through code statements a specific number of times. The **For** loop is sometimes known as the *For–Next* loop because it is terminated with the **Next** statement rather than the **Loop** statement.

```
For counter = begin To end Step step

[Exit For]

Next
```

When you know exactly how many times a loop needs to execute, the **For** loop is the simplest method. The *counter* is a variable, either Integer or Long, the *begin* value is the number at which the loop starts counting, and the *end* value is the last number.

```
Dim lval As Long

For lval = 1 To 6500

    console.write(lval)

Next
```

This example loops 6,500 times, incrementing the counter variable, **lval**, of each loop. This is simpler than a Do loop, where you would have to write code to increment a counter. The **For** loop has another feature, *step*, which makes the counter flexible. This is an optional value that tells the counter the value of each step. For example, when the *step* value is set to 5, the counter counts by 5's. When it is set to −2, the counter counts backward in increments of 2.

```
Dim lval As Long

For lval = 1 To 6500 Step 10

    console.write(lval)

Next
```

This example code snippet will loop only 650 times.

One common use of the For Next loop is to iterate through the elements within an array. Using the step variable, you can choose to access every array element or every other, or every fifth, depending on how the step value is set.

```
Dim indexval As Integer

Dim aColors() As String = {"red", "blue", "green",
"purple"}

For indexval = 1 To UBound(aColors)

    console.Write(aColors(indexval))

Next
```

This example will print the names of the colors in the array into your console window, as shown in Figure 4.1.

Note
When using a For Next loop to iterate through every array element, Visual Basic .NET arrays are 0 based, and therefore the *begin* value of the For loop must be set to 0.

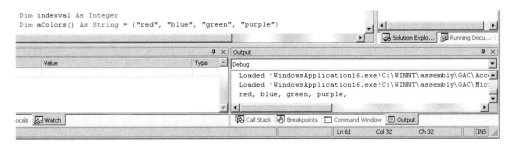

Figure 4.1   The output window displays the colors stored in the array.

Like other loops, there's a way out of the loop before the loop's condition becomes True. The **Exit For** statement causes the program to continue on the first statement after the **Next** statement.

For Each Loop

The For Each loop iterates through elements in an array or collection. This is a very handy way to move through an array without caring how many elements are in the object or the index number of the value within the array or collection.

```
For Each thingy in myarray

        'statements

[Exit For]

        'statements

Next
```

This next example is the equivalent of the sample used in the For Each section. Looking at both samples you can see that the same colors are printed, without having to keep track of the index number of the item being printed. Even though the processing is the same, the code in the For Each statement is much easier to read.

```
Dim aColors() As String = {J97 "red", "blue", "green",
"purple"}

Dim color As String

For Each color In aColors

      console.Write(color)

      console.Write(", ")

Next
```

Another reason the For Each loop is simpler for working with collections of objects, such as arrays, is that a For Next loop will fail if there are no elements in the array or collection. The example in the section on For Next would fail with no elements because the ubound( ) function requires that there be at least one element for there to be an upper bound. This kind of checking is not necessary with a For Each loop. If there are no elements in the object collection, the For Each loop is skipped and processing begins at the first statement to follow the Next statement.

As in other loops, the For Next loop uses the **Exit For** statement to exit the loop and continue program execution on the first statement after the **Next**. You can have as many **Exit For** statements in your loop as you require. They are normally found within an If–End If condition that tests some value, and if the condition is met, exits out of the loop.

For Each loops can be embedded within other loops of any type as deeply as you like. Care should be taken not to embed For loops too deeply, as performance may be affected when processing too many elements. One 10-item collection that loops through another embedded 10-item collection processes 100 items. This number can increase astronomically as loops are embedded.

Summary

Directing the flow of a program, allowing an application to make decisions based on input, is what makes computers more than simple adding machines. In Chapter 3, you learned how to build complex expressions using operators. In this chapter, you learned how to use those expressions to allow your program to make decisions, such as which path through the program will be taken or how many times the program will execute the same code in a loop. Chapter 5 continues by introducing the programming procedure. You will learn how to use the information in this chapter to direct the flow of processing to small subprograms, creating more compact and efficient programs through code reuse.

A *procedure* is a named block of code statements that allow you to reuse the same code within your program without rewriting it or copying it into your program over and over. All executable code in a Visual Basic .NET application must be within some type of procedure: either a subprocedure, a function, or a property procedure. Each procedure in Visual Basic .NET begins with a statement that defines it as either a subroutine, function, or property procedure. This chapter discusses each type of procedure and how it is used within a Visual Basic .NET program.

There are three required parts of a procedure: procedure header, code statements, and end procedure statement.

The syntax of the procedure header and end procedure statement are different depending on whether the procedure is a subroutine or a function.

Subroutines

Subroutines are the simplest type of procedure. They get their name from a time when computer programs were stored on punch cards. Routines, or programs as they are now called, were stored in decks of cards, and when a new routine was needed by the computer, a computer operator would load a new deck of punched cards into a computer card reader. Subroutines are small blocks of code that by themselves are not full programs but are reusable parts of the main routine, or program.

Subroutines accept parameters in the procedure header, enclose one or more lines of code (statements), and finish with an end procedure statement. A subroutine begins with the Sub statement and ends with an **End Sub**. But, unlike earlier versions of Visual Basic, Visual Basic .NET allows for a much more involved subroutine header. The following is the syntax for declaring a subroutine.

```
[Overloads | Overrides | Overridable| NotOverridable |
MustOverride| Shadows| Shared] [Private| Public |
Protected | Friend ] Sub Name[Parameter List]
```

```
    Statements

    [Exit Sub]

    Statements

    End Sub
```

Overloads

The **overloads** keyword tells the application that the subprocedure is overloaded. Remember that overloaded means that multiple versions of this procedure exist. Each version of the procedure must have a unique set of parameters. This keyword is optional.

Overrides

Overrides is an optional keyword that tells your application that this procedure has a name identical to a procedure in an inherited base class and that this procedure takes precedence over the inherited procedure. The data type of all parameters and the data type of the return value have to match exactly in both the inherited procedure and this procedure.

Overridable

Overridable is an optional keyword that lets the application know that it's possible for this procedure to be overridden in a derived class. The same rules apply regarding the parameters and return values being identical.

NotOverridable

There are times when you might not want an inheriting class to override your procedure. In this case you can use the optional **NotOverridable** keyword to disallow overriding of this procedure.

MustOverride

In some cases, you know that a procedure is necessary to perform some function, but the final implementation of that feature can't be known in a base class. For this reason, a procedure might exist that has no statements and the **MustOverride** keyword. This keyword is optional and indicates that inheriting classes must override this procedure.

Shadows

The **Shadows** keyword indicates that a derived class can shadow the name of inherited type members by redeclaring it. This keyword is optional.

Shared

The **Shared** keyword denotes a shared subprocedure, one that doesn't operate on a specific object instance. A shared subprocedure is called directly from a type rather than through an object instance. This keyword is optional.

Private

Procedures with the **Private** keyword are accessible only by other procedures within its declaration context. This includes any procedure calls embedded within the current procedure. This keyword is optional.

The scope value you enter determines what part of your application will have access to this subroutine. Scope is covered in detail in the chapter on variables (Chapter 2), but to touch on it quickly here, a procedure declared as **Public** will be accessible from any part of the application, and sometimes from other applications that are allowed to call procedures within your application. This is particularly true for applications that are compiled as dynamically linked libraries. A procedure declared as **Private** may only be called by other procedures within the same class, module, or structure in which it was declared.

Public

Procedures declared with the **Public** keyword are publicly accessible. This keyword is optional. It's important to know that all subprocedures are **Public** by default.

Protected

A **Protected** procedure contained in a class is accessible to variables and other procedures in that class and any derived classes. Access from a derived class requires that you precede the name of the procedure with the class name. This keyword is optional.

Friend

Procedures with the **Friend** keyword are accessible only within the program that contains the procedure declaration. This keyword is optional.

Note
Unlike with the **Private** and **Public** modifiers, a procedure can be declared with both the **Protected** and **Friend** modifiers, giving it both the accessibility of **Protected** and the **Friend** status.

Name

The name of the subprocedure is required. You should make the procedure name meaningful. Visual Basic .NET allows you to create very long procedure names.

Parameter List

The parameter list is a set of variables passed into the subprocedure. Each parameter or optional modifier (discussed below) is separated by a comma. Because subprocedures do not necessarily rely on information passed to them to process their statements, parameters are optional.

The parameter list has the following syntax:

```
[Optional] [ByVal|ByRef] [ParamArray] Variable[( )] [As
type] [=defaultvalue]
```

Optional Occasionally, you may want to specify a parameter to a procedure that is not required. The **Optional** modifier declares a parameter optional, meaning that no value need be passed when calling the procedure at runtime. In place of a passed parameter, all optional variables must be declared with a default value. The syntax above shows how to include a default value. Also, **Optional** cannot be used for a variable if the **ParamArray** modifier is used. One other very important thing: Any variable in the parameter list that is declared after an optional variable must also be declared as optional. So if only one of your variables is optional, make sure it's last in the list, like this:

```
Private Sub mysub(ByVal mytest As String, Optional ByVal
mytest2 As String = "test")
```

ByVal When a parameter is passed **ByVal**, or by value, a copy of the value passed into the procedure is made in memory. A value stored in memory that is declared outside the subprocedure is not changed by passing it into the procedure. Only the copy of that value is referred to or changed. Parameters in Visual Basic .NET are passed by value as a default, and so this modifier is completely optional.

ByRef A parameter passed by reference is quite different from one passed by value. Instead of a copy of the variable being passed to the subprocedure, a memory address pointing to a value already in memory is passed into the procedure. Values, passed by reference, can be changed within the procedure, changing the value in memory in a single location.

ParamArray   The **ParamArray** modifier indicates that the final variable in the parameter list is an optional array of Object elements. There is no limit to the size of the array. In this manner, at runtime you can pass as many or as few arguments to the procedure as you like. This statement is optional and is only used to modify the last argument in the list.

Variable   This is the name of the parameter variable. The **Variable** name is required when a parameter is passed.

Type   This modifier is the data type of the variable passed to the procedure, which may be of any data type, even user-defined types in procedures declared as **Private** or **Friend**. This statement is optional.

Defaultvalue   When a parameter has been declared to be **Optional**, it's required that you specify a default value. When the data type of the parameter is **Object**, the default value can only be set to **Nothing**. This statement is required only when the Optional modifier has been used.

Program Flow

Once a procedure has been entered, each statement is executed one after another. It is possible to branch from within a procedure to another procedure, but it is not possible to declare one procedure within another. Once processing in the called procedure has been completed, program flow continues on the next statement after the called procedure. It is not possible to completely exit a subprocedure by branching out of the procedure or by using the familiar GoTo statement.

One way to exit a subprocedure prior to the program encountering the **End Sub** statement is the **Exit Sub** statement. When program flow encounters an **Exit Sub** statement, it continues on to the first statement after the **End Sub** statement. You can have as many **Exit Sub** statements within a subprocedure as you find necessary. They are normally enclosed within some type of conditional statement, such as an If—End If, but this is not required.

Calling A Sub

Calling a **Sub** is not quite like calling a taxi. A Visual Basic .NET subprocedure is called using its name, any keywords or modifiers, and any parameters passed into the subprocedure. There is a **Call** statement within Visual Basic .NET, but it is not required.

Figure 5.1.   Variables of the A are available to B.

Variables and Scope within a Sub

The scope of variables can be a tricky thing if not managed carefully. Basically, there are two categories of variables you will use within a procedure. First, there are variables that you declare within the procedure itself. For further information on declaring variables, see Chapter 2. This includes any variables that are defined as part of the subprocedure header (the parameters). These variables are private (local) to the procedure by default, unless declared otherwise.

The other type of variables that can be used within a procedure are those that have been declared outside the procedure but within the scope of the subprocedure. In the case of a subprocedure that has declared variables and also calls a second subprocedure, the variables in the first subprocedure are available to the second. See Figure 5.1.

Functions

A *function* is a procedure type that accepts values passed as parameters, and returns a value to the code that called the function. The return values of functions in Visual Basic .NET are of a specified data type. A function is similar to a procedure with the exception of the return value.

Defining a Function

To define a function you need the following elements:

The keyword **Function**

Name of the function

Return type of the function

Return value

The **End Function** keywords

The syntax for declaring a function is nearly identical to the syntax for declaring a subprocedure. Therefore, we won't repeat the descriptions of each of the keyword modifiers. Refer to the previous section for a complete description of each modifier.

```
[Overloads| Overrides| Overridable| NotOverridable|
MustOverride| Shadows| Shared]

[Public| Private| Protected | Friend] Function Name[
Parameters ] [As Type]

     Statements

End Function
```

The main difference between the declaration of a function and of a subprocedure is that you must include the type of the return value using the **As *Type*** statement, where *Type* is the data type of the value the function will return to the calling procedure. Functions MUST return a value, and they must have a type.

If for some reason a value is not assigned by statements within a function, Visual Basic .NET assigns a default value:

Functions defined with numeric return values return 0.

Functions defined with a **Boolean** return value return False.

Functions defined with **String** return values return an empty string ("").

Functions defined as objects as return values return the value **Nothing**.

Working with Functions

The primary responsibility of a function is to return a value. Little or no processing has to actually go on within the function. It is valid to simply set the return value of the function and then return that value. There are two ways to set the return value of a function in

Visual Basic .NET: setting the name of the function equal to the return value and using the **Return** statement to specify the return value.

Here is an example of the first method of returning a value:

```
Private Function MyName(ByVal sFirst As String, ByVal
sLast As String) As String

    MyName = sFirst & " " & sLast

End Function
```

Note

When assigning a return value to the name of the function, it is not stored in a variable as it might appear. You cannot declare a variable with the same name as the function that it's in. The compiler will throw an error.

This style of returning a value from a function is fairly unique to Visual Basic, and was probably included for some backward compatibility. Most other languages require the use of the **Return** statement to specify the return value of the function like this:

```
Private Function MyName(ByVal sFirst As String, ByVal
sLast As String) As String

    Return sFirst & " " & sLast

End Function
```

So far, the examples have had a single statement, specifying the return value of the function. In many cases, this is all that is required. It is just as common that functions can contain a considerable amount of code and decision making before returning a value. Here is an example of a slightly more complex function:

```
Private Function Insure(ByVal bSmoker As Boolean, ByVal
iAge As Integer, ByVal bPreExisting as Boolean) As Boolean

    Dim RiskTotal As Integer = 0



    If Not bSmoker Then

        RiskTotal += 5
```

```
        End If

        If iAge > 50 Then

            RiskTotal += 10

        End If

        If bPreExisting Then

            RiskTotal += 25

        End If

        If RiskTotal >= 30 Then

            Return False

        Else

            Return True

        End If

    End Function
```

At times it may become necessary to have the program flow exit the function before all the statements are processed. This is done by using the **Exit Function** statement. Remember to set the return value of the function before exiting the function or the function will return a default value (listed above). Here is the same code snippet slightly changed so the test for **bPreExisting** conditions is performed first, and the insured is denied coverage.

```
    Private Function Insure(ByVal bSmoker As Boolean, ByVal
    iAge As Integer, ByVal bPreExisting as Boolean) As Boolean

        Dim RiskTotal As Integer = 0

        If bPreExisting Then

            Return False
```

```
            Exit Function

        End If

        If Not bSmoker Then

            RiskTotal += 5

        End If

        If iAge > 50 Then

            RiskTotal += 10

        End If

        If RiskTotal = 15 Then

            Return False

        Else

            Return True

        End If

    End Function
```

In this example, the **If** conditions are never evaluated when a preexisting condition exists. The program exits the function, with processing continuing on the first statement after the **End Function**. Without the **Exit Function** statement, the other conditions would have been evaluated and could have possibly changed the return value of the function. In complex functions it is important to manage program flow through the function so that the expected return value is set.

Using Functions

The fact that functions return a value makes their usage within a program quite different from a subprocedure. Subprocedures do not return a value; they are called on a line by themselves, and are never part of an expression. Functions, on the other hand, cannot appear on lines of code by themselves. Not only is it important that the functions return a value, it's equally important that the calling code provide a place to store or use that value.

Functions are always used as a part of an assignment statement or an expression. For example, when using the previous example function, you might assign the value like this:

```
Dim clientAge As Integer

Dim isASmoker, hasPreExistCondion, canInsure as Boolean

clientAge = 50

isASmoker = True

hasPreExistCondion = False

canInsure = Insure(bSmoker, iAge, bPreExisting)

If canInsure Then

    console.write("Insure this client.")

Else

    console.write("Sorry, this client is not insurable.")

End If
```

This example assigns the return value of the funtion to a variable. This same example, simplified, will demonstrate using a function as part of an expression.

```
Dim clientAge As Integer

Dim isASmoker, hasPreExistCondion as Boolean

clientAge = 50

isASmoker = True

hasPreExistCondion = False

console.write(iif(Insure(bSmoker, iAge, bPreExisting),
"Insure this client.", "Sorry, this client is not
insurable."))
```

Property Procedures

The last type of procedures discussed in this chapter is the *property procedures*, or *property accessors* as they are sometimes called. These are Visual Basic .NET procedures that enable you to read and write properties you define on modules, classes, and structures from within a property declaration.

There are two types of property procedures, and they are always found inside of a property declaration. For more information on property declarations, read Chapter 2.

The two types of property procedures:

Get—Gets the value of a property and returns it to the code requesting the property value.

Set—Sets property value to the value passed as an argument to the Set statement.

Both property procedure types are normally used together, one to **Get** the property value, and the other to **Set** it. In the case where a property is defined either as read-only or write-only, you may choose to use either **Get** or **Set** by itself.

This syntax shows the **Get** and **Set** syntax within a property declaration:

```
[Default] [Accessibility] Property name[parameters] As
Type

Get

     Return expression

End Get

Set [ByVal variable As type]

     lvalue = variable

End Set

End Property
```

In a **Set** procedure, the new property value is passed as an argument to the **Set** statement. When you declare an argument, you must declare it as the same data type as the property.

```
Private Sub button1_Click(ByVal sender As System.Object,
ByVal e As System.EventArgs) Handles button1.Click
```

```
        Dim newthing As testClass

        newthing = New testClass()


        newthing.thingcolor = "red"


        console.Write(newthing.thingcolor)


    End Sub

    Class testClass

    Dim p_color As String = "nothing"

    Public Property thingcolor() As String

        Get

            Dim colormod As String

            colormod = "Hot " & p_color

            Return colormod

        End Get

        Set(ByVal colorval As String)

            p_color = colorval

        End Set

    End Property

    End Class
```

Calling Property Procedures

Property procedures are fairly invisible to code that makes use of them. Properties are treated very much like you would set a value or get a value from a class or module. The one exception is that any necessary parameters must be included and the parameters must be enclosed within parentheses.

Note
When no parameters are supplied, you can skip the parentheses.

Here is an example of the code that makes use of the **Set** property procedure.

```
propertyname[(parameters)] = someValue
```

The following sample calls show allowable calling syntax for a **Get** property procedure:

```
someValue = propertyname[(parameters)]
```

Note:
Visual Basic .NET no longer uses the **Let** statement when assigning properties, but it is still considered a reserved word.

Summary

Computer programming made a great leap when it moved from programs that began on the first line and ended on the last. With no ability to reuse code, applications became cumbersome and prone to error. Procedures, such as the Visual Basic .NET Sub and Function, allow you to write compact and efficient applications with the ability to reuse code that you've written and debugged in many places within your application. Procedures also form the foundation of class members, giving objects abilities. This use of procedures is covered in more detail in Chapter 7.

In the next chapter, you will learn about a variable type, arrays, that allows you to maintain many values in a list. You will find arrays particularly useful when passing arguments to and from procedures, as they enable you to pass an indeterminate number of values.

Arrays 6

In Chapter 2, we covered information about data types. This chapter discusses a data type that is very different from other types. An *array* is a named place in memory, capable of storing a collection of values of the same data type. You might think of this collection as a chest of drawers; one storage place with many drawers. Standard variable types allow you to store a single value, such as a single number in an integer type variable, or a single string, however long. In an **Array**, you can store many values, each tagged with a number called an *index*.

The index value in Visual Basic .NET **Arrays** always begins at 0. In previous versions of Visual Basic you could start the index at 1 or 0 (see the tip about OPTION BASE). This has now changed. Figure 6.1 gives you a visual example of an **Array** with a place to store four individually wrapped bits of information. Each storage place in an **Array** is known as an *element*. Each element is numbered with an index. Notice in Figure 6.1 that the numbering begins with 0, so that the fourth element is number 3.

Tip
The OPTION BASE statement is no longer supported by Visual Basic. The .NET Framework allows **Arrays** with an index value lower than zero, although they are not considered CLS-compliant. You can't declare them directly in most CLS-based languages and should refrain from using them.

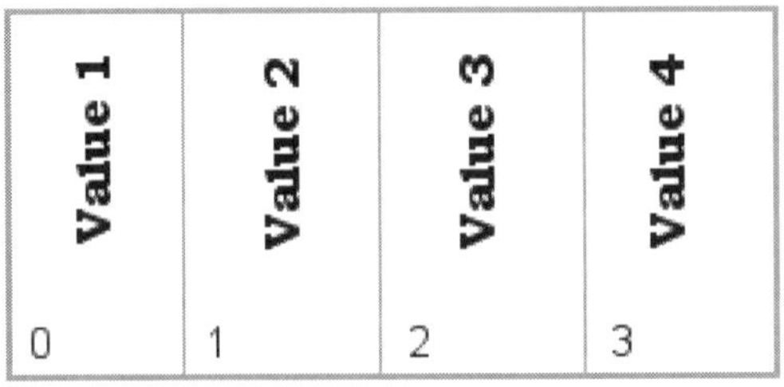

Value 1	Value 2	Value 3	Value 4
0	1	2	3

Figure 6.1 Four-element **Array**.

Declaring an Array

There are several ways to declare an **Array**. You can declare an **Array** that specifies an initial number of elements in the **Array**, declare the **Array** while also initializing the values in the **Array**, or declare an empty **Array**.

To declare an **Array** specifying the size of the **Array**, include the size as an argument:
`arrayname(`*`size`*`)`

The *size* of the **Array** is the total number of elements. This is also known as the **Array**'s *upper bound*.

Here are two equivalent examples of delaring an **Array**:

```
Dim aColors(3) As String

Dim aColors() As String = New string(3) {}
```

In these examples, the **Array** size is 3, even though each of the elements is currently empty and able to accept a string value. Just as in other variable types, it's possible to initialize the value of the elements at the same time the **Array** is declared. The following is an example of declaring an **Array** while also setting the values in the **Array**:

```
Dim aColors() As String = {"red", "blue", "green",
"purple"}
```

After setting the members of the **Array** equal to a string value, you can refer to the value in each member by including the index number in parentheses like this:

```
Dim aColors() As String = {"red", "blue", "green",
"purple"}

console.Write(aColors(2))
```

This example will print the color green in the console.

Note
Arrays in Visual Basic .NET are declared differently than in previous versions of Visual Basic. Visual Basic .NET does not allow you to declare an **Array** with a fixed size. All **Arrays** in Visual Basic .NET can be changed using the ReDim statement.

ReDim

The **ReDim** statement is used to reallocate storage space for an **Array**. It's one of the only ways to change the size of an **Array** dynamically. When you use **ReDim**, you must specify the size of the **Array**. This first code snippet creates an **Array** with four elements. If we needed to add yellow to the list, we would need a new **Array** element.

```
Dim aColors() As String = {"red", "blue", "green",
"purple"}
```

We can reallocate space for the **Array aColors** using **ReDim** like this:

```
ReDim aColors(5)
```

Now, the **Array aColors** has five elements. There is only one problem: reallocating the space overwrote all the values in the **Array**, so that aColors is an empty **Array**, five elements long. To save the existing values, you must include the **Preserve** keyword like this:

```
ReDim Preserve aColors(5)
```

After this statement you have an **Array** with the original element values still intact and the last (in this case the fifth) element empty. In other words, adding elements will always be done at the end of the **Array**. Once you've added the new element, you can store a value into that element like this:

```
aColors(5) = "Pink"
```

You can also use **ReDim** to reallocate space for a multidimensional **Array**. Multidimensional **Arrays** are described in more detail later in this chapter.

Note
The ReDim allows you to optionally specify the data type of the **Array**. You cannot use this feature to change an **Array** type from one data type to another.

The Array Class

Each data type in Visual Basic .NET is defined by a *class*. Classes and objects are covered in more detail in Chapter 7. The class contains the very definition of an object type, and in this case, the Class **Array** defines a variable type capable of holding a list of elements of the same type. The class also defines methods, abilities in the form of procedures, that can be used to manipulate information stored in an **Array**. The **Array** type in Visual Basic .NET is the **System.Array**, inherited from **System.Object**. This next section covers the methods of **System.Array** and their ability to handle data stored within an **Array**. This first section covers methods that can be called directly from the **System.Array** class.

Static Methods

Static methods are called directly from the Array type, and not from an actual **Array** object. Of course, you'll need actual **Arrays** for these methods to perform their tasks. Arrays, able to contain many values stored in elements, are designed to have many powerful methods to deal with this group of values stored in an **Array**. There are methods for copying, searching, changing the order of the values, and completely clearing the **Array**

Table 6.1 Static Methods

Method	Description
Binary Search	Finds an object within an array.
Clear	Clears the values of an array. Numeric are set to zero, all others set to Null.
Copy	Copies one single dimension array to another, starting at the lower bound to the index specified by the length parameter.
CreateInstance	Creates a new instance of an array.
IndexOf	Finds a value within an array and returns the index number. If there is more than one matching value within the array, only the index of the first match is returned.
LastIndexOf	Finds a value within an array, starting from the last element, and returns the index of the last matching value.
Reverse	Reverses the order of the array by index number.
Sort	Sorts the elements of an array by value.

altogether. When calling static methods, you precede the name of the method with the class name like this:

```
array.methodname()
```

Table 6.1 lists the static methods of the **Array** class and offers a brief description of their use. Each method is then covered in more detail throughout this chapter.

BinarySearch   The **BinarySearch** method allows you to perform a search through an **Array**'s elements matching the binary information (1's and 0's). The **BinarySearch** method accepts two parameters; the **Array** to search followed by the value to search for. Here's the exact syntax:

```
array.Binary Search(array as system.array, value as
object)
```

Here's an example that searches through an **Array** of strings looking for a binary match:

```
Dim aColors() As String = {"red", "blue", "green",
"purple"}

Dim bColors(5) As String

Dim Result As Integer

array.Copy(aColors, bColors, 4)
```

```
Result = array.BinarySearch(bColors, "green")

console.Write(Result)
```

This example writes the number 2 into the console window.

Copy   You can use the **Copy** method of the Array class to copy a one-dimensional **Array** to another. The fact that it will only copy a single dimension makes it fine for most **Arrays**, but when **Arrays** have more than one dimension, as covered later in this chapter, this method will not work for copying the **Array**.

```
array.copy(sourceArray as system.array, destinationArray
as system.array, length as Integer)
```

Here's an example of using the **Copy** method:

```
Dim aColors() As String = {"red", "blue", "green",
"purple"}

Dim bColors(4) As String

Dim Color As String

array.Copy(aColors, bColors, 4)

For Each color In bColors

        console.Write(Color)

        console.Write(vbCrLf)

Next
```

In this example you see that the source **Array** is of type **String** and has a size of 4. The destination **Array** must also be of the same type, in this case **String**, and have enough elements declared to hold the **Array** being copied into it. So, a size in the destination **Array** will also work. A destination **Array** with a different type of element or size will throw an error.

The **Copy** method has a third argument, the number of elements to be copied. This number must not be greater than the number of elements in the source **Array**. If it is smaller than the number of elements in the source **Array**, only part of the source **Array** will be copied, starting at the first element, element 0.

CreateInstance   **CreateInstance** is a static method of the Array class that creates an object instance of the class. (Classes and objects are covered in detail in Chapter 7.) This is an alternative way of creating an **Array** object.

Here's the syntax for the **CreateInstance** method:

```
array.CreateInstance(element.type as system.type, length
as Integer) As System.Array
```

In this next example, you will see how we've made specifying the type using the **Get-Type** method. The **GetType** method has the correct return value expected by the **CreateInstance** method. This example first declares myArray as an **Array** type and then uses the static method of the **Array** class, **CreateInstance**, to create an object of type **Array**, with elements of type **String** and only two elements long:

```
Dim myarray As Array

myarray = Array.CreateInstance(GetType(String), 2)
```

IndexOf   Each element in an **Array** has an index number beginning at 0. Therefore, the first element is element 0, the second element is element 1, and so on. It may become necessary to find the occurrence of an item within an **Array** and return the index number. This is when you can use the **IndexOf** method. Here is the syntax for the **IndexOf** method:

```
array.IndexOf(array as system.array, value as object) As
Integer
```

This example looks for a match between the string "green" and returns its position within the **Array** as an index number.

```
Dim result As Integer

Dim aColors() As String = {"red", "blue", "green",
"purple"}

result = array.IndexOf(aColors, "green")

console.Write(result)
```

Because the **IndexOf** method is looking for a match to the string "green," this example returns the number 2 and prints it in the console window.

LastIndexOf   Occassionally an **Array** will have more than one occurrence of the same value stored within it. The **IndexOf** method allows us to find the first occurrence of a value stored within the **Array**. The **LastIndexOf** method, as its name suggests, allows us to find the index of the very last occurrence of a value in the **Array**. The syntax for the **LastIndexOf** method is quite similar to the **IndexOf** method, and is shown below:

```
array.LastIndexOf(array as system.array, value as object)
As Integer
```

In this example, we have added a second occurrence of the color "red" within the **Array**. The **LastIndexOf** method will ignore the first occurrence and return the index of the last occurrence.

```
Dim result As Integer

Dim aColors() As String = {"red", "blue", "green",
"purple", "red"}

result = array.LastIndexOf(aColors, "red")

console.Write(result)
```

This example writes the number 4 into the console window. Remember that even though the second occurrence of the string "red" is the 5th member, the index returned is 4.

Reverse   Once in a while it becomes necessary to reorder the elements of an **Array**. For example, if an **Array** is being used to print values to the screen, and the end-user is given the opportunity to see the list in reverse order, the **Reverse** method can reorder the elements in reverse order. Here is the syntax:

```
array.reverse(array as system.array)
```

This method reorders the elements of the **Array** by index number in reverse order. The first element becomes the last and the last becomes the first, regardless of the values stored in the **Array**.

```
Dim aColors() As String = {"red", "blue", "green",
"purple"}

array.Reverse(aColors)

Dim i As Integer

For i = 0 To 3

    console.Write(aColors(i) & " ")

Next
```

This example writes the string "purple green blue red" to the console.

Sort   Similar to the **Reverse** method, the **Sort** method also reorders the elements of the **Array**. The sorting is performed based on the type of object being sorted. The example we show is a **String** type **Array**, and therefore, the values are sorted in alpha order. If the elements were numeric, they would be sorted in numeric order. This is the syntax for the **Sort** method:

```
array.sort(array as system.array)
```

Here's an example that sorts the values in the **Array**'s four elements alphabetically.

```
Dim aColors() As String = {"red", "blue", "green",
"purple"}

array.Sort(aColors)

Dim i As Integer

For i = 0 To 3

    console.Write(aColors(i) & " ")

Next
```

This code snippet causes the string "blue green purple red" to be written to the console window.

Instance Methods

There are methods of the Array class known as *instance methods*. Instance methods can be called from an **Array** object to operate on the data, specific to that "instance" of the **Array** class. An instance of a class is an object of that particular class type. Table 6.2 lists the instance methods of the Array class along with a short description of each method. We then cover each method in greater detail.

Clone   When an **Array** is cloned, a new **Array** object is created that contains a reference to the elements of the original **Array**. Because the copy is a shallow copy, no objects will be copied by the **Clone** method. The clone **Array** is the same type as the original **Array**. Here is the syntax:

```
arrayObject.clone()
```

A further description of cloning **Arrays**, along with an example of using the **Clone** method, appears at the end of this chapter.

CopyTo   The **CopyTo** method copies one single-dimension **Array** into another. You must declared a new variable of type **Array** into which the existing **Array** will be copied. Use the **CopyTo** method of the **Array** class to copy values into the new **Array**.

Table 6.2   Instance Methods

Method	Description
Clone	Creates a shallow copy of the **Array**.
CopyTo	Copies one single-dimension **Array** to another.
Equals	Returns True or False, depending on whether one array is the same instance as another **Array**.
GetEnumerator	Returns an Ienumerator for the **Array**.
GetHashCode	Serves as a hash function for a particular type, suitable for use in hashing algorithms and data structures like a hash table.
GetLength	Returns the number of elements in the **Array** or **Array** dimension.
GetLowerBound	Returns the lower bound of the **Array** or **Array** dimension.
GetType	Returns the type of the object.
GetUpperBound	Returns the upper bound (max number of elements) of the **Array** or **Array** dimension.
SetValue	Sets an **Array** element to a specified value.
GetValue	Returns the value stored in a specified array element. You specify which element by passing in the index.
ToString	Returns a string that represents the current object.
Initialize	Initializes every element in the **Array** with the default initialization value based on the type of the **Array** elements.

The **CopyTo** method accepts two parameters. The first parameter is the empty **Array**, and the second is the index at which to start copying. Here is the syntax:

```
ArrayObject.CopyTo(array, index)
```

For example:

```
Dim bColors(4) As String

Dim aColors() As String = {"red", "blue", "green",
"purple"}

aColors.CopyTo(bColors, 0)

Dim i As Integer

For i = 0 To 3

    console.Write(bColors(i) & " ")

Next
```

In this example, **bColors** is declared as a four-element, empty **Array**. The **CopyTo** method copies the string values from the **aColors Array** to the **bColors Array**. If the second argument to the **CopyTo** method were changed to 1, **bColors** would contain only the colors blue, green, and purple.

Equals   The **Equals** method returns True or False, depending on whether one **Array** is the same instance as another **Array**. This can be a little confusing. It does not return True if two **Arrays** contain elements that exactly match. It only returns True if the **Array** is actually pointing at the same members. This example shows two **Arrays** that are not equal:

```
Dim bEqualityResult As Boolean

Dim bColors(4) As String

Dim i As Integer

Dim aColors() As String = {"red", "blue", "green",
"purple"}

aColors.CopyTo(bColors, 0)

bEqualityResult = aColors.Equals(bColors)

console.Write(bEqualityResult)
```

This sample prints the word **False** into the console. Even these two **Arrays** are a copy of one another, and have exactly the same values in each element. They are not equal because they do not point to the same instance. Here is an example of where the **Equals** method would return True:

```
Option Strict Off

Dim bEqualityResult As Boolean

Dim bColors As Array

Dim i As Integer

Dim aColors() As String = {"red", "blue", "green",
"purple"}

bColors = aColors
```

```
bEqualityResult = aColors.Equals(bColors)

For i = 0 To UBound(aColors)

    console.Write(" acolors(" & CStr(i) & ")=" &.
aColors(i))

    console.Write(" bcolors(" & CStr(i) & ")=" &
bColors(i))

Next

console.Write(bEqualityResult)
```

In the previous example, **bColors** is declared as type Array. The **Array** is empty and its element type is undefined. When **bColors** is set to **aColors**, you can consider **bColors** to be an alias for **aColors**. Both **Arrays** point at the same place in memory. Changing a value in either **Array** changes it in both. You can verify this by printing the values in both **Arrays**, as this sample has done. The **Equals** method returns **True** because the two are pointing at the same instance.

GetEnumerator   The **GetEnumerator** method returns an **Ienumerator** object for the **Array**. Enumerators are used for reading data in a collection, such as an **Array**. They are not meant to be used for modifying the data.

> **Note**
> The enumerator object does not have exclusive access to the **Arraylist**. Therefore, changes made to the **Arraylist** while enumerating through it, such as add, change, or delete, can throw an error when using the the **current** or **movenext** methods of the **iEnumerator** object.

Here's an example:

```
Dim aColors() As String = {"red", "blue", "green",
"purple"}

Dim colorEnum As CharEnumerator

colorEnum = aColors.GetEnumerator()
```

GetHashCode   The **GetHashCode** method returns an integer used in hashing algorithms and data structures such as a hash table. Here's an example:

```
Dim aColors() As String = {"red", "blue", "green",
"purple"}

console.Write(aColors.GetHashCode)
```

This example writes a number representing the hash code to the console window.

GetLength   The **GetLength** method returns the number of elements in the **Array** or **Array** dimension. If the **Array** is a single-dimension **Array**, pass 0 as the dimension, just as in this example.

```
Dim myarray As Array

myarray = Array.CreateInstance(GetType(String), 2)

myarray.SetValue("Red", 0)

myarray.SetValue("Blue", 1)

console.Write(myarray.GetLength(0))
```

This example returns the value 2 into the console window because there are two elements in the **Array**. Remember that the **Array** can have elements that are counted but do not contain initialized values.

GetLowerBound   The **GetLowerBound** method returns the lower bound of the **Array** or **Array** dimension. With the base of all **Arrays** in Visual Basic .NET set to 0 (best practices dictates that you do not change this), then **GetLowerBound** should always return 0.

GetType   The **GetType** method returns the type of the object. The following is an example of using the **GetType** method:

```
Dim myarray As Array

myarray = Array.CreateInstance(GetType(String), 2)

console.Write(myarray.GetType())
```

This code snippet will write `System.String[ ]` into the console window.

GetUpperBound   The **GetUpperBound** method returns the upper bound (maximum number of elements) of the **Array** or **Array** dimension (multidimensional **Arrays** are covered later in this chapter).

The **GetUpperBound** method accepts one required argument, the numeric value of the dimension for which you are returning the upper bound.

Here's an example:

```
Dim myArray As Array

myArray = Array.CreateInstance(GetType(String), 2)

myArray.Initialize()

console.Write(myArray.GetUpperBound(0))
```

This example writes the number 1 into the console window.

SetValue Along with **GetValue**, the **SetValue** method is one of the most important **Array** methods. As its name suggests, this method sets the value of an element within an **Array**. This example demonstrates how to set the values of an **Array** created using the **CreateInstance** method.

```
Dim myarray As Array

myarray = Array.CreateInstance(GetType(String), 2)

myarray.SetValue("Red", 0)

myarray.SetValue("Blue", 1)
```

GetValue The **GetValue** method returns the value stored in a specified **Array** element. You specify which element by passing in the index of the element. In this example, when 0 is passed, the value "Red" is returned into the console window.

```
Dim myArray As Array

myArray = Array.CreateInstance(GetType(String), 2)

myArray.SetValue("Red", 0)

myArray.SetValue("Blue", 1)

console.Write(myArray.GetValue(0))
```

ToString The **ToString** method is mainly used for debugging. It returns an unformatted string version of whatever object happens to be stored in an element. It's not good to use this to display values of **Array** elements. Here is an example that returns the word "blue" in the console when run:

Table 6.3   Array Properties

Property	Description
IsFixedSize	Returns a boolean True or False, depending on whether the array is designated.
IsReadOnly	Returns True or False, depending on whether the array was designated as ReadOnly (elements within a ReadOnly array cannot be modified).
IsSynchronized	This value has to do with threads and whether the array is synchronized between threads (threads are covered in Chapter 15).
Length	This returns the total number of elements within the array. Elements can be empty.
Rank	This returns the total number of dimensions in the array.
Syncroot	This gets an object used when synchronizing access to the array between threads.

```
Dim aColors() As String = {"red", "blue", "green",
"purple"}

console.Write(aColors(1).ToString())
```

Initialize   The **Initialize** method stores a default initialization value based on the type of the **Array** elements into each element of the **Array**. In this next example, empty **Strings** are stored into the **Array**'s two elements.

```
Dim myArray As Array

myArray = Array.CreateInstance(GetType(String), 2)

myArray.Initialize()
```

Array Properties

The **Array** class has six properties, listed in Table 6.3. The two most interesting properties are **Length** and **Rank**. These two properties will let you know the size of the **Array** and how many dimensions it has.

Multiple Dimensions

So far we've discussed **Arrays** as lists of variables or objects. It's possible to create an **Array** that extends its storage capacity so that each **Array** element can also contain an **Array**.

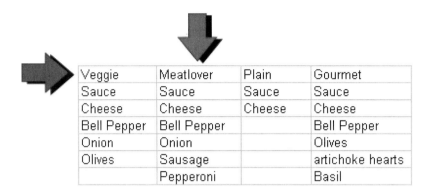

Figure 6.2   Multidimensional pizza **Arrays**.

This type of **Array** is known as a *multidimensional array* and the number of dimensions within the **Array** is known as the **Array**'s *rank*. Figure 6.2 gives you a visual look at how a multidimensional **Array** might appear.

Table 6.4 shows how the multidimensional **Array** shown in Figure 6.2 is indexed. The first **Array** is in the top row and is numbered from 0 to 3. This **Array** contains **Arrays**,

Table 6.4   Multidimensional Arrays

Veggie 0,0	Meatlover 1,0	Plain 2,0	Gourmet 3,0
Sauce 0,1	Sauce	Sauce	Sauce
Cheese 0,2	Cheese	Cheese	Cheese
Bell pepper 0,3	Bell pepper		Bell pepper
Onion 0,4	Onion		Olives
Olives 0,5	Sausage		Artichoke hearts
	Pepperoni		Basil

running down in columns. Each subsequent **Array** begins its index at 0. Notice the first column has six elements numbered from 0 to 5. Accessing the value "Artichoke hearts" is done using the index (3,5).

Arrays are not limited to two dimensions. Each dimension can include another, with a limit of 60 dimensions. Be assured that **Arrays** with ranks beyond three are extremely rare. As mentioned earlier, the resulting number of dimensions is known as the **Array**'s rank.

Declaring a Multidimensional Array   Declare a multidimensional **Array** in the same fashion as you would a single-dimension **Array** and pass the size of the additional dimensions in a comma-separated list. In this two-dimensional **Array** of **Integers**, the first argument, 10, represents an **Array** of 10 rows, and the second argument, 15 columns.

```
Dim myArray (10,15) As Integer
```

As the number of dimensions increases, it's impossible to continue referring to the dimensions as rows and columns. To declare an **Array** with three dimensions, simply add the size of the third dimension like this:

```
Dim myArray (10,15,20) As Integer
```

Using Multidimensional Arrays   You can directly access any element in any dimension by referring to it by index number. For instance, if you have a multidimensional **Array** with a rank of 3 (three dimensions) called **MyArray**, you can refer to a specific **Array** element like this: MyArray(4,2,6). You can set this value or retrieve this value.

It gets more fun when you need to access every element of an **Array** in each dimension. In Chapter 4, you learned how to construct For loops, both For-Next and For-Each. This is the easiest way to iterate through an **Array**. Here are some examples:

```
Dim myMultiDimArray(5, 6, 7) As Integer

Dim element As Integer

Dim counter, counter2, counter3 As Integer

For counter = 0 To 4

    'The first dimension is set here

    myMultiDimArray(counter, 0, 0) = counter

    For counter2 = 0 To 5

        'The second dimension is set here
```

```
            myMultiDimArray(counter, counter2, 0) = counter *
10 + counter2

        For counter3 = 0 To 6

            'The third dimension is set here

            myMultiDimArray(counter, counter2, counter3) =
counter * 100 + counter3

        Next

    Next

Next

'This part of the code reads the array values

For Each element In myMultiDimArray

    console.Write(element)

    console.Write(vbCrLf)

Next
```

In the previous example, there are three embedded For-Next loops that loop through each of the **Array**'s three dimensions. As the loops traverse the dimension, each element is set with an **Integer** value. Of course, if the **Array** were set to contain a different type of information, such as a **String**, then the elements would be set to **String** values.

In the second part of the example, the **Array** values are read back in a single For-Each loop and written to the console window. You could choose to iterate through individual dimensions using For-Next loops similar to the ones used when setting the values.

Changing Dimensions   You can change the size of each dimension within a multidimensional **Array** using **ReDim**, discussed earlier in this chapter, but you cannot change the number of dimensions once they have been declared.

```
ReDim MyArray(10,20,30) 'change the number of elements
```

If changing the number of dimensions becomes necessary, you will have to declare a new **Array**, and copy the values from the old **Array** into the new **Array**. This is not quite as simple as it sounds. Both the **Copy** and **CopyTo** methods, talked about earlier in this chapter, copy one-dimensional **Arrays** only. The following code first loads a multidimensional **Array**, then creates a new **Array** with an additional dimension. Using similar For-Next loops, the **Array** elements are copied one at a time as the **Arrays** iterate through each dimension. This example is in the click event of a button, so you can try it yourself.

```
    Private Sub button1_Click(ByVal sender As
System.Object, ByVal e As System.EventArgs) Handles
button1.Click

        Dim myMultiDimArray(5, 6, 7) As Integer

        Dim element As Integer

        Dim counter, counter2, counter3 As Integer

        For counter = 0 To 4

            myMultiDimArray(counter, 0, 0) = counter

            For counter2 = 0 To 5

                myMultiDimArray(counter, counter2, 0) =
counter * 10 + counter2

                For counter3 = 0 To 6

                    myMultiDimArray(counter, counter2,
counter3) = counter * 100 + counter3

                Next

            Next

        Next

        Dim myNewArray(5, 6, 7, 8) As Integer

        For counter = 0 To 4

            myNewArray(counter, 0, 0, 0) =
myMultiDimArray(counter, 0, 0)
```

```
                For counter2 = 0 To 5

                        myNewArray(counter, counter2, 0, 0) =
    myMultiDimArray(counter, counter2, 0)

                    For counter3 = 0 To 6

                            myNewArray(counter, counter2,
    counter3, 0) = myMultiDimArray(counter, counter2,
    counter3)

                    Next

                Next

            Next


        For Each element In myNewArray

            console.Write(element)

            console.Write(vbCrLf)

        Next


    End Sub
```

This example takes some time to run because the new **Array** is quite large, with four dimensions, and so takes a while to write the results to the console window. You may notice a large number of zeros printing along with the numbers. The values in the fourth dimension of the **Array** have not been set to a new value yet. Therefore, the fourth dimension values will print as zeros.

You'll notice in this example that the exact size of each **Array** is specified. Most of the time, the exact size of the **Array** is not known while programming, and is only known at runtime. You will need to dynamically figure out the size of each **Array** dimension using the **GetLength** method.

Note
When changing the size of a multidimensional **Array**, you can only modify the last dimension if you use the **Preserve** keyword.

Cloning Arrays

In the last section you saw that copying **Array** elements can become quite tedious and, although not impossible, it can be tricky if the number of dimensions is dynamic. A much easier way to deal with **Arrays** is cloning. Yes, just like Dolly the sheep, you end up with an identical **Array** without all the effort involved in making your own copy the hard way.

The downside to cloning is that it gives you an exact copy, which means that you're still stuck with manually copying if you need to change the number of dimensions. However, for creating exact copies of multidimensional **Arrays**, cloning is the way. Here's an example:

```
Dim myMultiDimArray(5, 6, 7) As Integer

Dim member As Integer

Dim counter, counter2, counter3 As Integer

For counter = 0 To 4

    myMultiDimArray(counter, 0, 0) = counter

    For counter2 = 0 To 5

        myMultiDimArray(counter, counter2, 0) = counter
        * 10 + counter2

        For counter3 = 0 To 6

            myMultiDimArray(counter, counter2, counter3)
            = counter * 100 + counter3

        Next

    Next

  Next

Dim myNewArray As Array

'Here is where we create a new clone.

myNewArray = myMultiDimArray.Clone()
```

```
For Each member In myNewArray

        console.Write(member)

        console.Write(vbCrLf)

Next
```

This example will print exactly the same values that would have been printed if you had written the results of **myMultiDimArray** instead of **myNewArray**.

Array Assignment

Arrays are objects. The next chapter will cover objects in greater detail. Because **Arrays** are objects, you can use them in assignment statements. There are a few things you will need to know. The first is the difference between a value type element and a reference type element.

Value type elements are straightforward data types such as **String** and **Integer**. Remember from Chapter 2 that these are primitive types. The elements directly contain values like "ABC" or "123." Reference type elements contain memory addresses as values and are normally used to point to values that are more complex, and can contain values themselves. Examples of reference types are classes, interfaces, and delegates.

If you are going to assign one **Array** object to another, there are some basic rules that apply.

Both **Arrays** must have the same type of elements: reference or value type.

For value-type elements, the **Array** data types must be the same.

When both **Arrays** have reference-type elements, you must employ a widening conversion from the source element type to the destination element type.

The number of dimensions of both **Arrays** must be the same.

Returning an Array from a Function

In Chapter 5, we covered procedures. You learned that functions can return a single value. When that value is an **Array**, you can actually return as many values as you like, as long as they are of the same type.

> **Note**
> Chapter 7 will discuss returning objects from procedures where you can return several values of different types.

A function can return an **Array** of values. In this example, a function, **GetStuffBack**, creates an **Array** of strings and returns the **Array** as the return value of the function. The click event of **Button1** calls the function and returns the **Array** into the **myColors Array**. To prove that it works, the contents of the **Array** are written to the console window.

```
Private Sub button1_Click(ByVal sender As System.Object,
ByVal e As System.EventArgs) Handles button1.Click

    Dim myColors() As String

    Dim color As String

    myColors = GetStuffBack()

    For Each color In myColors

        console.Write(color)

        console.Write(vbCrLf)

    Next

End Sub

Private Function GetStuffBack() As String()

    Dim aColors() As String = {"red", "blue", "green",
    "purple"}

    Return aColors

End Function
```

Using an **Array** to return values from functions can save you a great deal of trouble if you have more than one value to return.

Array Limits in a Nutshell

Each dimension is limited in size (number of elements) to the maximum value of a **Long** data type.

The maximum number of dimensions is 60. The total size of the **Array** in bytes is limited to your computer's available memory.

Note
When you create **Arrays** that are larger than your RAM memory, your computer will swap memory to the hard drive. This is the computer's way of dealing with out-of-memory conditions. Reading and writing the data to and from the hard drive is time-consuming, causing your application to run very slowly.

The total size limit of an **Array** varies, based on your operating system and how much memory is available. Using an **Array** that exceeds the amount of RAM available on your system is slower because the data must be read from and written to disk.

Summary

Arrays are a special kind of data type capable of containing multiple values of a single type, in a single or multidimensional pattern, all indexed by one or multiple zero-based long integer values. Programmers who used the standard Visual Basic array will find that this standard type varies significantly from an instance of the **Array** class.

Some of the differences between standard **Arrays** and a instances of the Array class include:

The **Type.IsArray** method will only return a True value for a standard **Array**. Instances of the Array class are objects.

The **Type.GetElementType** method will not return a value for instances of the Array class.

The Array class provides a **CreateInstance** method, which allows for late bound access.

Arrays are very useful when you need to group together many values of the same type. One of those uses include returning multiple values from functions. The members of the Array class provide a considerable number of tools for managing the elements within the **Array**. The next chapter will go into greater detail concerning classes and objects.

Classes and Objects 7

Object orientation allows programmers to better model the real world in their programs. In the world around us, there are things, or entities, and these entities all have two things in common. First, entities can be described, and second, entities are capable of doing something. For example, describe a rock as an entity. It has color, mineral composition, weight, size, and many other descriptive *properties*. You may be thinking that rocks don't do much, but in fact (ask any geologist) they do quite a lot. First and foremost, a rock, having weight, applies that weight to whatever is below it.

You often hear that object orientation is a new concept. You might be surprised to hear that object orientation was first conceived by the Norwegian Kristen Nygaard in the early 1950s and realized in a computer language developed by Ole-Johan Dahl and Kristen Nygaard in the early 1960s, called SIMULA. It's said that one of the first applications of object orientation was to programmatically describe the actions of tugboats in a fjord.

For a more complete history of the SIMULA programming language you can visit:

> http://java.sun.com/people/jag/SimulaHistory.html

Because programming languages in the United States were very entrenched in a serial (one command after another) concept, it was almost 25 years after the invention of object orientation that it was first implemented in a commercially used language called C++. Previous versions of Visual Basic were considered *object based*, but not truly object oriented. Even though Visual Basic .NET is not fully object oriented, Microsoft has added many additional features that bring it much closer.

The goal of object orientation is to describe an entity programmatically. We begin with a programming concept known as a *class*. A class is a programmatic description of a "class" of entities, also known as objects. If we were creating a class to describe rocks, we might give that class properties such as color, composition, weight, and size. We might also give that class an ability that we might humorously call **SitThere**.

A class is little more than a recipe for an entity. It forms the descriptive foundation that contain *properties* and abilities, known as *methods*. Together, properties and methods are known as *Instance Members* of a class, or simply *members*. A class can be used to create another type of programmatic construct called an *object*. An object, created from a class, is the actual entity, and can contain actual properties and abilities.

In our rock example, the method, **SitThere**, may accept a unit of gravity as a parameter. The method may then set the **weight** property based on the level of gravity. The properties of the object may be set directly without the use of a method, in the same manner as you might set any variable.

There are volumes written on the topic of object orientation, and it is beyond the scope of this book to cover these concepts in great depth. This chapter will help you through the practical implementation of classes and objects in Visual Basic .NET.

Classes

A class can be considered the documented design, or blueprint, from which objects are created. Said a different way, objects are tangible implementations of a class. A single class can be used to create many objects of the same type, design, and structure. When designing a class you must ask yourself two questions: what data does the future object need to collect about itself and what programmable abilities should that object have?

Creating a Class

The most important part of creating a class is designing the class before you start coding. Object-oriented design is largely common sense. Classes and objects mirror objects in the real world. When you think about anything in nature you can describe it in terms of properties and abilities. Think about your program as though you could bring each procedure to life as a real thing or person. Later in this chapter, we give the example of a zookeeper and zoo animals as objects. The properties and abilities of a well-designed object should only reflect the description and abilities associated with that type of object. For example, if you create an object for database searching, you would probably not give it the ability to change screen resolution.

```
Public Class MyClass

'class member declarations

End Class
```

Classes inherit from **System.Object**, meaning that they derive all their abilities from that object. Inheritance is covered in the next chapter. Therefore, the previous example is the same as:

```
Public Class MyClass

Inherits System.Object
```

```
'class member declarations

End Class
```

Members

As mentioned at the beginning of this chapter, classes are constructed of members. Members include properties, events, and methods. Properties store information while events and methods do the real work of an object. Remember that properties describe while methods create the ability of a class and/or object to perform tasks. If you were designing a robot instead of a class, you might first describe it in terms of its properties, height, weight, and maybe even name. Then you might describe its abilities, such as travel from room to room, speak, and possibly deliver drinks. This section covers creating properties and methods in more detail.

Properties

Properties are used for storage of information. Properties are also sometimes known as *fields*, and are simply variables in which data is stored. This means that an object's properties can be of any valid data type, or even custom data types created by you. Properties can be both public and private. Public properties are those that can be accessed by parts of the program that are not part of the object. Private properties are those that can only be accessed by the object itself, and are not visible outside the object. Placing data and functionality together in a single unit, and hiding that functionality to other parts of the program, is a principle called *encapsulation*.

While it's possible to access public variables directly, properties in Visual Basic .NET are more powerful than, and different from, public variables in the following ways:

Rather than a single declaration statement, you implement a property of a class with executable code called *property procedures*.

Property procedures are executed when the property value is set or retrieved. This allows a class to perform custom actions when client code accesses the property.

A property does not have a storage location associated with its declaration. Although property procedures often define local variables and constants, these are usually not available to the code accessing the property. Therefore, while you can include a variable or a field as a member of a structure or array, you cannot do this with a property.

You can define a property as read-only, write-only, or read/write. The default is read/write.

Property Declaration   A property itself is defined by a block of code enclosed within the **Property** and **End Property** statements. Inside this block, each property procedure appears as an internal block enclosed within a declaration statement (**Get** or **Set**) and an **End** statement. The syntax for declaring a property and its procedures is as follows:

```
[Default|ReadOnly|WriteOnly] Property PropertyName
([parameters]) [As Type]

    Get

        [Code Block]

    End Get

    Set

        [Code Block]

    End Set

  End Property
```

Here is an example that defines a property called **environment** in the class called **animal**. Taking a look at this class, we find a private instance variable called **HomeEnvironment**. This variable is not publicly accessible from outside the class. The property, **environment**, is used to set that private value and retrieve it using **Set** and **Get** statements as in the following example:

```
Class Animal
    Dim HomeEnvironment As String
    Property environment() As String
        Get
            Return HomeEnvironment
        End Get
        Set(ByVal Value As String)
            HomeEnvironment = Value
        End Set
    End Property

    Public Function HomeType() As String
        Return environment
    End Function

End Class
```

You can define properties in classes, structures, and modules. Properties are public by default, which means you can call them from anywhere in your application. You can also pass arguments into your property **Get** and **Set** declarations.

Argument Declaration   One of the powerful features of a property is that it accepts arguments (parameters). You declare each argument of Get and Set statements in the same manner as you would for a **Function** or **Sub** procedure, except that the value must be passed **ByVal**.

The syntax for each argument in the argument list is as follows:

```
[Optional] ByVal [ParamArray] argumentname As datatype
```

Arguments can be declared as optional, meaning that when a property is accessed within a program, the programmer can decide to include or not include the argument. But, when an argument is declared as **optional**, you must also supply a default value in its declaration, as follows:

```
Optional ByVal argumentname As datatype = defaultvalue

[Default] [Accessibility] Property name[argument list]
As Type

Get

   Return expression

End Get

Set [ByVal variable As type]

   lvalue = variable

End Set

End Property
```

Methods

Methods are procedures and functions that perform some functionality related to the class of objects. They are the workhorses of the class. Just like properties (fields), methods can also be public or private. Visual Basic .NET procedures start with **Sub** and end with **End Sub**. Because procedures are members of a class, there are many new ways to customize procedure development. This chapter will cover the new concepts you'll need to understand to make use of these new features. Here is the syntax of the **Sub** statement:

```
[Overloads | Overrides | Overridable | NotOverridable |
MustOverride | Shadows | Shared | Private | Public |
Protected | Friend | Protected Friend ] Sub name [argument
list]
```

You can see that there are many keywords that can precede the **Sub** statement. Once you understand the concepts behind each of them you'll have an amazing set of tools at your disposal. The rest of this chapter will cover each of these in considerable detail.

In addition to the arguments supplied with the Sub statement, the argument list also has a set of optional keywords:

```
[optional] [ByVal] [ByRef] [ParamArray] Varname[( )] [As
Type] [= defaultvalue]
```

Optional   This keyword indicates that an argument is not required. When used, all arguments following the one marked optional must also be optional.

ByVal   This keyword indicates that the argument is passed to the method by value.

ByRef   This means that the argument is passed by reference.

ParamArray   An optional array of objects. Cannot be used with Optional, ByVal, or ByRef.

Varname   This is the required name of the variable you are passing as an argument.

Type   Designates the data type passed as an argument.

DefaultValue   Optional parameters can specify a value.

Overloading

In traditional programming, it was never possible to include more than one function or procedure with the same name. You would throw an error. Object-oriented design actually allows this practice. Classes can contain methods with exactly the same name. The idea that you can have methods with the same name is called *overloading*. Methods that have the same name usually have the same purpose, but must always accept different parameters. A good example of this would be a method called **MyFormat( )**. See in the following example how the same method name is called with different parameters. The functionality, to format the input, is the same, but the processing is completely different.

```
Overloads MyFormat(ByVal TheString as String)

Overloads MyFormat(ByVal TheNumber as Integer)
```

Overloading isn't necessary in this case. You could always have created methods with different names, such as **MyFormatString** and **MyFormatNumber**. Overloading is a convenience, especially in complex programs, where limiting the number of unique method names simplifies the complexity of the program for the programmer. It's also an important ability to support backward compatibility in a program. If a program had always accepted **Integer** type values, and new versions must be designed to accept **Long** values while still supporting the ability to accept **Integers**, overloading would solve this problem. Visual Basic .NET will automatically detect the type of the argument being passed to a method and determine which method should be called, depending on the type of the argument. So, one method handles the **Integer** value while the other handles the **Long** value.

Creating Overloaded Methods To create methods that are overloaded, simply create two methods in the same class, with the same name. Each of the overloaded methods must accept different parameters from the other methods of the same name. They must also be marked with the **Overloads** keyword, as in the preceding example.

Shared

Procedures can be declared as *shared*. When you are creating a class, you are basically designing a new variable type. The types you learned about in the chapter on variables are built into Visual Basic .NET. You aren't limited to using these types. Classes allow you to design new types. Just as you can create a new value of a certain type by dimensioning it as a type, you can do the same with classes. When you call a shared procedure, it does not operate on a specific object instance, but rather on the class type itself. In other words, a shared procedure may be called directly from a type rather than through a specific instance of a type. So, *Shared Members* differ from standard members because they can be called without creating an instance of the class. A class can contain both shared methods and shared fields.

A shared method or shared field can be accessed simply by using the dot notation along with the name of the class, like this:

```
Classname.methodName

Classname.fieldName
```

Scope

Methods and properties are accessible within a defined *scope*. Scope refers to the parts of an application that "see" class members and can perform operations with or on them. The scope of a method or property can be either *private* or *public*.

Private Class members that are designated private are only visible to other members of the same class. They are used primarily to form the inner workings of a class. For example, a class that performs financial calculations may have a method that calculates interest rate. This method may only be used by other methods, and not publicly available to other objects. Private members are declared using the keyword **Private**.

Public   Members declared with the keyword **Public** are accessible by any other entity without restriction. So, these members can be called from within an object instance of the class, or by other objects.

Protected

The **Protected** keyword is optional. Members declared with the **Protected** keyword have protected access. A protected property or method is only visible within its own class or its subclasses.

Protected access is not the same as **Friend** access.

Friendship

Because object orientation is based on the real world, it makes sense that there be a concept called *friend*. Members designated with the different friend keywords are granted a special level of access, similar to the idea that your friends have different access to your personal life than do strangers.

Friend   Members declared as friends can only be accessed within the program that contains them.

Protected Friend   Members with **Protected Friend** status carry both the rights of a friend entity, as well as the protection afforded by the Protected status.

Events

An event is a message sent by the system signaling an application that something of note has occurred. Applications react to events with special procedures, called *event handlers*, designed to handle the occurrence of such a signal. In this way, event handlers are triggered, rather than called. For example, on a form, button objects have events defined. When a user clicks on the button with a mouse cursor, a *buttonname_Click* event is triggered, and any code within that event is run. Events are slightly different from procedures. For example, events cannot accept optional parameters nor have paramarray arguments. Events, when declared as part of a class, are always declared **Public**.

Adding Event-Handling Routines   Most programmers use very few of the events available to them. Visual Basic .NET controls and Forms have an encyclopedic array of events that can turn your application from a lifeless program to one that reacts to the end-user's every move.

For instance, the click event of a button is just about the only event most programmers ever write to. Instead of writing to the click event, what if you wanted to write to the **mouseenter** event, the one that's fired (*raised*) whenever the mouse passes over the control? Here is an example that changes the background color of the button when the mouse enters and changes it back to its original color when it leaves. The button simply writes "click" to the console when clicked.

```
Private Sub button1_Click(ByVal sender As System.Object,
ByVal e As System.EventArgs) Handles button1.Click

    console.Write("click")

End Sub

Private Sub button1_mouseenter(ByVal sender As
System.Object, ByVal e As System.EventArgs) Handles
button1.mouseenter

    Me.button1.BackColor =
System.Drawing.SystemColors.Desktop

End Sub

Private Sub button1_mouseleave(ByVal sender As
System.Object, ByVal e As System.EventArgs) Handles
button1.mouseleave

    Me.button1.BackColor =
System.Drawing.SystemColors.ControlDark

End Sub
```

For this example, event handling was set up when the button was added to the Form. This is the line of code that dimensions the variable that will later be instantiated into a button object. Notice the keyword **WithEvents**.

```
Private WithEvents button1 As System.Windows.Forms.Button
```

If you look through your Form's code you will see the line where the button object is actually instantiated:

```
Me.button1 = New System.Windows.Forms.Button()
```

Looking at the event handler code for the button's click event, you see that the subprocedure accepts two parameters and uses the keyword **Handles** followed by the object and the event name.

```
Private Sub button1_Click(ByVal sender As System.Object,
ByVal e As System.EventArgs) Handles button1.Click

    console.Write("click")

End Sub
```

The two arguments passed to the procedure include an object that represents the object sending the event (*event sender*), and the second is a system.EventArgs object that contains any arguments passed to the event handler. Objects capable of being event senders include forms, controls, and user-defined objects.

Creating an Event Handler   In the previous section you learned what it takes to create event-handling code for objects that already exist. New classes and objects you create may also contain events for which you want to create event handlers.

This example begins by creating a new class called **pinballmachine**.

```
Class pinballmachine

    Public Event tilt()

End Class
```

The only thing in the class is the declaration of an event called **tilt**. We could declare the event to also accept parameters, but at this stage it's best to keep it simple. The example continues by adding a declaration of the variable that will be the new pinballmachine object. Because variables declared to handle events are module-level variables, the variable **Superdude** is declared in the Declarations section of the form.

```
Private WithEvents Superdude As pinballmachine
```

Once again, just as in the previous section, when declaring the variable you must include the WithEvents keyword to let Visual Basic .NET know that this object is going to handle events. Then, instantiate the **Superdude** object.

```
Me.Superdude = New pinballmachine()
```

The Visual Basic .NET code editor makes it simple to create an event handler. Click the left drop down over the code editor and select Base Class Events. Select an event from the drop down on the right and an event handler will be created for you. (See Figure 7.1)

Writing Code to Handle an Event   Once a variable has been declared using WithEvents, the variable name appears in the left-hand drop down of the code editor.

Next, you need to create the event handler. Now, because the **tilt** event was not designed to accept any parameters, this is fairly simple:

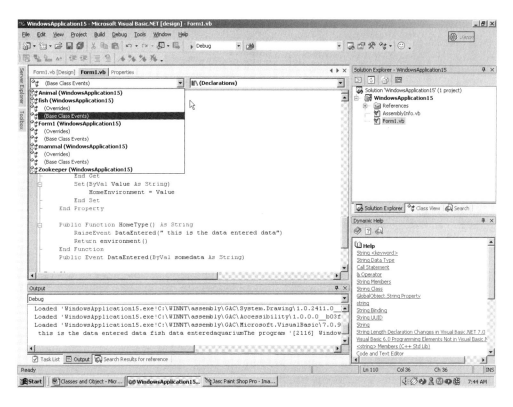

Figure 7.1 First select from the left-hand drop down, then the right, to create or edit an event procedure.

```
Private Sub superdude_tilt() Handles Superdude.tilt

    console.Write("tilt")

End Sub
```

Normally, you will want to specify parameters for your event handlers. The typical event handler declaration accepts these two parameters:

```
ByVal sender As System.Object, ByVal e As System.EventArgs
```

Manually Triggering an Event   To trigger an event, use the **RaiseEvent** statement.

```
Public Event DataEntered (ByVal SomeData as String)
```

```
Sub

    RaiseEvent DataEntered("some data")

End Sub
```

To associate this event with an event handler, use the With Events or AddHandler statement.

To Terminate Event Handling for a WithEvents Variable   To terminate event handling, you can set the variable associated with the event to **Nothing**.

```
Set variablename = Nothing
```

When a WithEvents variable is set to Nothing, Visual Basic .NET disconnects the object's events from the event procedures associated with the variable.

> **Note**
> A WithEvents variable contains an object reference, just like any other object variable. This object reference counts toward keeping the object alive. When you are setting all references to an object to **Nothing** in order to destroy it, don't forget the variables you declared using **WithEvents.**

Adding and Removing Event Handlers   The method you use to construct an event handler depends on how you want to associate the handler with the event. Best practices suggests that you create an event handler using the **Handles** keyword with the **WithEvents** keyword. Visual Basic .NET provides a second way to handle events, using the **AddHandler** keyword. **AddHandler** and **RemoveHandler** allow you to dynamically start and stop event handling for a specific event. You can use either method, but it's not recommended that you use both **WithEvents** and **AddHandler** with the same event.

If you want to add an event handler, and you are not using the WithEvents keyword method of creating event handlers, then you use the **AddHandler** statement, as shown below.

```
AddHandler MyObject.Event1, AddressOf Me.MyEventHandler
```

The **RemoveHandler** statement disconnects an event from an event handler and uses the same syntax as **AddHandler**. For example:

```
RemoveHandler MyObject.Event1, AddressOf Me.MyEventHandler
```

Handling Events Using AddHandler   As stated in the previous section, you use the AddHandler statement to dynamically connect events with event handler procedures.

Declare an object variable. Declare it to be of the class type for which you want to handle events. One advantage of the **AddHandler** over the **WithEvents** statement is that the object variable does not have to be a module-level variable but can be declared as a local variable.

```
Dim MyObject As New ClassWithEvents()
```

Use the **AddHandler** statement to specify the name of the event sender, and the **AddressOf** statement to provide the name of your event handler; for example:

```
AddHandler MyObject.EventName, AddressOf TheHandler
```

> **Note**
> You do not have to create a special procedure just for event handling. Any procedure can act as an event handler. The one restriction is that it supports the correct arguments specified for the event being handled.

Finally, add the code to the event handler that will be processed when an event message has been received. Here is an example:

```
Public Sub EventHandler(ByVal sender As System.Object,
ByVal e As System.EventArgs)

    console.Write("Event has been triggered.")

End Sub
```

This example employs a concept known as inheritance, covered in detail in the next chapter.

Events Inherited from a Base Class   New classes can be created from existing classes. This concept is known as inheritance and is covered in detail in the next chapter. The underlying class is known as the base class, and your application can handle events raised by this class. The newly created class is known as the *derived class*. Use the **Handles MyBase** statement to handle events in a derived class.

To handle events from a base class, declare an event handler in the derived class by adding a **Handles MyBase.<***event name***>** statement to the declaration line of your event handler procedure. Here is an example of creating a class with an event and another class that uses the **Handles MyBase** statement:

```
Class pinballmachine

    Public Event tilt(ByVal bumper As Integer)

End Class
```

```
Public Class PinBallWizard

    Inherits pinballmachine

    Sub EventHandler(ByVal bumper As Integer) Handles
    MyBase.Tilt

      console.write("Tilt")

    End Sub

End Class
```

Objects

Objects are implementations of classes. It's a little tricky to simply say that a class is a template and an object is the realization of that template because some classes have abilities without ever having an object implementation. However, it's not quite the chicken-and-egg problem because all objects must be derived from a class. In this case, you can think of a class definition as creating a variable type, and an object is a value of that newly defined type. For that reason, you can create as many objects of a specific class type as you need.

Chapter 6, on arrays, explained that you can create very complex arrays by storing one array within another. The same is true of objects. You can create very complex objects by storing objects as properties within another object. You can use the physical example of a pet dog. Dogs are objects that can contain other objects, such as intestinal parasite objects or flea objects.

When an object is realized by creating an *instance* of the object, it has two basic traits. It has abilities, depending on the methods and events it contains, and it has properties, values stored within the object that somehow describe the object.

> **Note**
> Giving an object abilities or storing values within an object that are not directly related to an object type is simply bad design.

Creating Objects

Using the **New** Operator, objects are created in a manner similar to variables. Just as with creating variables, where you first declare the variable and then store a value into it, creating an object is a two-step process. You must first create a place in memory for the objects using the **Dim** statement like this:

```
Dim newemployee As mynewclass()
```

The **newemployee** variable example will be of type **mynewclass**, a class type you have already created, or of an existing Visual Basic .NET class type. The next step is to use the **New** operator to actually create an instance of the object like this:

```
Dim newemployee As mynewclass()

newemployee = New mynewclass()
```

As you may remember, you can create most variable types while storing a value in a single statement. This is also true of objects. Include the **New** operator in the **Dim** statement like this:

```
Dim newemployee As New mynewclass()
```

This example is the equivalent of first using **Dim** and then using the **New** operator in a separate statement. The result is an object called **newemployee** of type **mynewclass**. All of the properties and methods of the object are then accessible.

Accessing Object Properties and Methods

Objects use *dot notation* to give access to properties and methods. Dot notation requires the name of the object, followed by a dot (period) and then the name of the property or method:

```
Dim newemployee As New mynewclass()

Dim Hiredate as Date = cdate("01/01/2004")

newemployee.name = "Bob"

newemployee.hire(Hiredate)
```

A shortcut for accessing the properties of an object uses the **With** keyword. Following the With keyword is the objectname, and then each line following With has a property name preceded by a dot. Here is an example:

```
With MyObjectName

    .Name = "Bob"

    .Age = 66

    .Gender = "Male"

End With
```

End With designates the end of the **With** statement for that object.

Create a new class called **MyClass1** and create a new member function called **writestuff( )**. The return value of this function is a string, so remember when creating the member function to specify the type of the return value using the **AS** statement.

Once you have created the new class, **MyClass1**, you can create a new object of type **MyClass1** in the **Click** event of the button you've placed on the form. You can see in the example that you can declare the new object and create the instance all on the same line. Once you have an object, which this example calls **MyTask**, you can call its member function, **writestuff( )**. Since **writestuff( )** returns a **String**, you can set the value of the **TextBox's Text** property with that **String**. So, clicking the button sets the value of the **TextBox**.

```
Private Sub button1_Click(ByVal sender As System.Object,
ByVal e As System.EventArgs) Handles button1.Click

        Dim MyTask As New MyClass1()

        textBox1().Text = MyTask.writestuff()

End Sub

Public Class MyClass1

    Public Function writestuff() As String

        Return "This is a test"

    End Function

End Class
```

Binding

An understanding of binding will help you write better code. *Binding* chooses a method or methods to be executed in response to a request. Different object languages support different criteria and times for binding an operation to a method for execution. Examples are *early binding,* at compile time, and *late binding,* at runtime.

Early binding occurs when an object variable is declared as a class type. When a variable is declared as a class type, at compile time it's already known what the object type is, and what methods and properties need to be supported. This increases efficiency in your program.

It's not always possible to know at compile time what objects your program will need to support. This creates the need for late binding, which occurs in Visual Basic .NET when you declare an object variable to be *As Object*. Variables of type object can hold any type of object. Therefore, an object variable of this sort can expect to reference any object and any number of methods and properties without knowing until runtime what those objects, methods, and properties are. It would not be possible to have a variable as an object type without late binding. All objects are early bound by default.

There are advantages and disadvantages to both types of binding. We already mentioned that the advantage of early binding is program efficiency. Also, with early binding we can take advantage of the compiler's ability to know if we have correctly specified correct parameters, or accessed methods that actually exist. It's not necessary for your application to discover the object type and the methods and properties supported by the object. The disadvantages of early binding are the advantages of late binding, which primarily is flexibility. The Visual Basic .NET runtime must dynamically determine, when making late-bound method calls, if the target object actually has a matching method. If the method is found, it then invokes that method on our behalf.

When programming it may become necessary to have a variable accept more than one type of object. Let's take for example an application that manages a zoo. Your zoo management application may have a zookeeper object that processes new arrivals of many different animal object types. The zookeeper object has a method that accepts different types of animal objects and assigns cages.

```
Option Strict Off


Private Sub button1_Click(ByVal sender As System.Object,
ByVal e As System.EventArgs) Handles button1.Click

        Dim bass As New fish()

        bass.environment = "water"

        Dim moose As New mammal()

        moose.environment = "land"

        Dim Joe As New Zookeeper()

        console.Write(Joe.Cageme(bass))

    End Sub

End Class
```

```
Class Zookeeper

    Public Function Cageme(ByVal ZooAnimal As Object) As
String

        Dim cagetype As String

        Dim EnvironmentNeed As String

        Try

            EnvironmentNeed = ZooAnimal.HomeType()

        Catch

            'Some error handling code

        End Try

        If EnvironmentNeed = "water" Then

            cagetype = "aquarium"

        ElseIf EnvironmentNeed = "land" Then

            cagetype = "savannah"

        Else

            cagetype = "box"

        End If

        Return cagetype

    End Function

End Class
```

```
Class Animal

    Dim HomeEnvironment As String

    Property environment() As String

        Get

            Return HomeEnvironment

        End Get

        Set(ByVal Value As String)

            HomeEnvironment = Value

        End Set

    End Property


    Public Function HomeType() As String

        Return environment

    End Function


End Class


Class mammal

    Inherits Animal

End Class

Class fish

    Inherits Animal

End Class
```

This example writes "aquarium" to the console window when the button is clicked. The zookeeper, Joe in this case, does not know at compile time what type of object will be received. When, at runtime, the fish object is passed to the zookeeper, the correct method is called and the right cage is returned. Fish belong in an aquarium.

Another advantage to late binding is that there are cases where an object must dynamically change the properties and methods it exposes. Not knowing which properties and methods should be exposed and when, at compile time, late binding once again comes to the rescue.

To support late binding you must set **Option Strict Off** at the beginning of the source file. This is because the Visual Basic .NET development environment enforces the default early binding of objects.

```
Option Strict Off

Module MyLateBindingTest.

   Public Sub MySubroutine(MyObj As Object)

      Try

         MyObj.SomeMethod()

      Catch

         'error handling code goes here.
      End Try

      End Sub
End Module
```

Summary

This chapter just scratched the surface of object-oriented programming in Visual Basic .NET. Understanding classes and objects is key to developing skills as a programmer of any language. Other languages, such as C++, C#, and Java, and scripting languages, such as Visual Basic, all use object-oriented principles. The next chapter introduces one of the more advanced topics of object orientation: inheritance.

Inheritance 8

One of the most powerful concepts of object orientation is *inheritance*. Inheritance is the concept that foundational classes can be constructed. From these foundational classes, new classes are built that inherit the members of the foundational class, also called a *base class*. For instance, if a new class called **Person** is created with the properties called **Name** and **Address**, a new class called **Employee** could be created that inherits the **Person** class, and the new **Employee** class would then already have a **Name** and an **Address** property. The new class is derived from the base class, and is therefore known as a *derived class*.

Inheriting classes is quite simple using the **Inherits** statement. When you want to create a new class that inherits the methods and properties of an existing base class, simply add the **Inherits** statement along with the name of the base class like this:

```
Class Employee

Inherits Person

    ' Employee methods and properties go here

End Class
```

In this example, the new class, **Employee**, comes equipped with any of the members already designed into the **Person** class. You can then include additional members or choose to override and change the members on the base class. This chapter goes into detail explaining all the things you can do with inheritance.

Base Classes

Base classes form the foundation of new classes. There are two types of base classes: the type from which objects can be derived and the type from which no object instance can be created, which only allows new classes to inherit them.

Tip

If you want to create a class that cannot be used as a base class, include the keyword **NotInheritable** in your class. This will keep other classes from inheriting from this class.

There is nothing special that has to be done to create a class that is considered a base class. Most of the work in creating a good base class is in program design, rather than coding. A good base class should include methods and properties that are generic and inclusive without becoming too specific. For example, an example **Employee** class may include the new property **EmployeeID** but should not include **HourlySalary**. It is likely that all employees will have an ID number of sorts, but not all employees will be paid hourly. Instead, new classes **HourlyEmployee** and **SalariedEmployee** can be created, inheriting from the **Employee** class.

Override

It's possible to *override* methods and properties of base classes in the derived class. Overriding methods and properties allows you to have the same method and property names with different abilities and values than the base class. For example, if your **Person** class has a method called **CreateSchedule( )** whose functionality creates a job search schedule, and then you derive a new class called **Employee**, the **CreateSchedule( )** method will have very different functionality (unless they aren't very good employees!).

```
Class Person

Overridable Function CreateSchedule()

'Code to create a job search schedule.

End Function

End Class


Class Employee

    Inherits Person

    Overrides Function CreateSchedule()

    'Code to create work schedule.
```

```
        End Function

  End Class
```

There is one thing you'll have to do to make it possible to override the methods and properties of a base class. Each public method and property is considered **NotOverridable** (not capable of being overriden) by default. Adding the **Overridable** statement allows derived classes to override the members of this base class.

There are times when a base class may create methods and properties as a type of template, but with no functionality. This is the second type of class, one where no object instance is ever created. When classes of this type include the keyword **MustInherit**, only new classes can be created by inheriting these base classes.

Using the **MustOverride** statement forces the inheriting class to override any method or property containing this statement. When using the **MustOverride** statement with procedures or functions, they may not contain any code after the **Sub** or **Function** statement. So, make sure you don't end any procedure or function with **End Sub** or **End Function** when using **MustOverride**. Whenever **MustOverride** is used, it must be within a class containing the **MustInherit** statement.

Here's an example:

```
  MustInherit Class Person

      MustOverride Function PlanSchedule(ByVal DayOfTheWeek)
      As String

      MustOverride Sub SortFriends()

      Function MakeFriends() As String

          Dim CoolFriend As String

          'Here is the code to make friends

          Return CoolFriend

      End Function

  End Class
```

Here are the things to look for in this example:

The class definition includes the **MustInherit** keyword. No objects of this type can be created. Only classes can be derived from this example class.

The **PlanSchedule** function and the **SortFriends** procedure are both labeled as **MustOverride**. Remember that this is only allowed in classes that are labeled as MustInherit. Also notice that these procedures do not include **End Function** or **End Sub**.

The function **MakeFriends** is a normal method, and does not require the person implementing a derived class to override this function. The functionality designed into the base class will be included in the derived class. Of course, you can still choose to include the overridable keyword in this function so that you can override this function in the derived class. The **MakeFriends** function is not overridable by default.

> ### Interesting Tidbit
>
> *The ability to override members of a base class in a derived class is an object-oriented concept called polymorphism. Polymorphism is a term borrowed from biology that refers to the ability of members within a species to have different characteristics, such as hair and eye colors, while having a common ancestor. Later in this chapter we discuss interfaces that can be used to implement polymorphism in Visual Basic .NET.*

MyBase

There is a very handy tool for referring to public members of a base class when overriding members in a derived class. The **MyBase** keyword refers to either the immediate base class or to a base class somewhere in the inheritance hierarchy. It is used in the following contexts: invocation expression and instance constructors.

An *invocation expression* is the technical term used to describe calling or invoking a method. So, you can use **MyBase** when calling methods, like this:

```
MyBase.methodname(argument)
```

An instance constructor is the member of a class that initializes (constructs) an instance of the class. In Visual Basic .NET, the constructor is given the member name **New**. Because a constructor will not return a value, it is a **Sub** rather than a **Function**. When building a class constructor, it is required that you have a call to the constructor of the base class, where all the code is implemented to actually create the class instance (object). The way to make this call to the base class constructor is using **MyBase** like this:

```
Public Sub New()

    MyBase.New
```

```
         ' Other things you want to initialize during
    construction of the object

End Sub
```

Here is an example of using MyBase when overriding the dispose( ) method:

```
Overrides Public Sub Dispose()

     MyBase.Dispose

     'This line disposes of the components on a form.

     components.Dispose

End Sub
```

MyClass

MyClass gives you the ability to call an overridable method in the current class or a base class. Call a method using **MyClass** in the current class, making certain that you are truly calling the method from the current or base class and not implementation in some derived class. **MyClass** is used strictly for invocation expressions, as explained in the section on **MyBase**.

```
MyClass.MethodinCurrentClass()
```

Interfaces

An *interface* is similar to a class that defines, or, more correctly, *prototypes* members. Prototyping a member means that you define the member's name, what parameters and parameter types the member accepts, and any return values. All of the interface's members, such as methods and properties, are simply declarations, empty of any processing code.

Interfaces are very misunderstood, and few people realize their importance. There are many benefits to using interfaces in your program design and implementation. Here are a few of them:

With interfaces you have the ability to maintain and extend your application code once it's been put into production. When you release program code into the marketplace, there is no way for you to retrieve it all and change it. So changing the underlying code without breaking everything is the job of the interface.

Another one of the benefits of an interface is that you can group together types of members, which a class later implements. This is similar to class inheritance, but with the ability to group members on a finer level of detail than in a class. A class can implement several interfaces.

Unlike inheriting from base classes, you can create new classes by implementing many interfaces.

Interfaces are useful in cases where you cannot use class inheritance. For example, structures cannot inherit from classes, but they can implement interfaces.

The idea behind an interface is that it sets forth a structure that can evolve without breaking the code that depends on it. When using inheritance, it's not only possible, but likely, that in time the need to change a class member will occur. This can be disastrous if the class acts as a base class for other classes. All other classes derived from the base class may operate on certain assumptions, such as the fact that a method returns a particular data type, such as string. If you change this to something such as Boolean later on, all the code that relies on this assumption will break. Using an interface takes care of this situation by letting you publish an updated interface that accepts the new data type.

Because the compiler will not allow you to compile a program that does not completely implement an interface, you are guaranteed that classes that implement interfaces will adhere to a basic, underlying structure. In this way, you can enforce design restrictions in your applications.

> **Note**
> Previous versions of Visual Basic were able to implement interfaces, but only in Visual Basic .NET are you allowed to create new interfaces.

Creating Interfaces

To create an interface, begin with the keyword **Interface** and end with **End Interface**. Within the interface definition, you can define properties, events, and methods.

```
Interface Employee

    Function NewHire(ByVal eName As String) As String

    Function Terminate(ByVal eName As String) As String

    Property Age As Integer

    Public Event ChangeStatus(ByVal xValue As Integer)

End Interface
```

You can see from this example that no processing code, not even an **End Function**, is included in the interface definition. You might notice that this is similar to an abstract class definition. This forms a template that classes must follow when implementing this interface. The actual processing code, or implementation, of each method or event is completely arbitrary.

One interface can inherit from another. So, when defining new interfaces, you can use the **Inherits** keyword like this:

```
Interface HourlyEmployee

    Inherits Employee

    Sub AddHours(ByVal iHours As Integer)

End Interface
```

The **HourlyEmployee** interface now includes all the methods, events, and properties of the **Employee** interface and adds the additional procedure **AddHours**.

Implementing Interfaces

When using an interface as a template for a new class, use the keyword **Implements** followed by the name of the interface you want to use as a template. The **Implements** keyword should appear on the next line after the class declaration like this:

```
Class SalariedEmployee

    Implements Employee

End Class
```

Of course, adding the **Implements** statement is not enough. When you create a class that implements an interface, you need to implement all the public members of the interface. This example gives you an idea of what that might look like:

```
Class SalariedEmployee

    Implements Employee

    Function NewHire(ByVal eName As String) As String
    Implements Employee.NewHire

    Function Terminate(ByVal eName As String) As String
    Implements Employee.Terminate
```

```
              Property Age As Integer Implements Employee.Age

              Public Event ChangeStatus(ByVal xValue As_
              Integer) Implements Employee.ChangeStatus

      Get

              'code to return the value of the property

          End Get

          Set

              'code to set the property

          End Set

      End Property

  End Class
```

Here is an implementation of an interface, **employee**, in the class called **mynewclass**. This example writes the number 52 in the console.

```
  Interface employee

          Function addhours(ByVal iHours As Integer) As
          Integer

      End Interface



      Class mynewclass

      Implements employee

      Function addhours(ByVal iHours As Integer) As
      Integer Implements employee.addhours

          iHours = iHours + 40
```

```
        Return iHours

    End Function

End Class


Private Sub button1_Click(ByVal sender As
System.Object, ByVal e As System.EventArgs) Handles
button1.Click

    Dim newemployee As New mynewclass()

    Dim theresult As Integer


    theresult = newemployee.addhours(12)

    console.Write(theresult)

End Sub
```

We have talked about inheritance a great deal in this chapter, and interfaces are not really a way to implement inheritance. But the concept is so close that this seemed like a logical place to cover the information. In the next section, we mention that classes inherit from a single base class. This is only true for Visual Basic .NET and is not an object-oriented rule. There is a concept known as multiple inheritance, whereby new classes can inherit from two or more classes, inheriting the members of each class.

Interfaces are similar to multiple inheritance because you can implement multiple interfaces in a single class. Rather than shortcutting your programming tasks, as inheritance might do, it forces a structure by which your new class must represent and implement possibly many interfaces.

Inheritance Rules to Live By

Here are some rules to live by when using inheritance in Visual Basic .NET:

New classes may inherit from a single base class. This may seem obvious, but some languages allow you to inherit from more than a single class. Multiple inheritance is not currently supported in Visual Basic .NET.

Classes may implement any number of interfaces.

Public classes cannot inherit friend classes.

Public classes cannot inherit private classes.

Friend classes cannot inherit private classes.

Even though Visual Basic .NET does not support the concept of multiple inheritance, there is no limit to the number of levels of inheritance an application might have. Each level of inheritance can add a new and deeper range of object abilities.

Remember also that one object can contain other objects. So, instead of a single class defining all of an object's capabilities, you might consider designing a class that is a container for many different types of objects. This is one way to design a class that mimics the capability of multiple inheritance. Changing one of the objects contained in your class will change the ability of new objects of that class type.

Summary

The advantages to object-oriented programming are code reuse and a natural, heuristic design. Programs reflect life. This probably sounds esoteric, and like something one of the great philosophers might say. In fact, it's a paradigm that is quite difficult for the procedural programmer to grasp. It's not a difficult concept, it's just difficult to think in terms of objects rather than pathways through the code. Instead of a tree-structured design, your application becomes full of living entities with personalities and abilities that can form the foundation of new entities with even more abilities.

It would be completely possible to have an object-oriented program without using inheritance. You could construct new and unique classes for each type of object you might find necessary. But why work that hard? In the next chapter, we have the perfect example of how object design has made programming easier. Visual components rely heavily on inheritance. In the next chapter, we begin the adventure of the user interface, keeping in mind the power of what we've learned in the last two chapters.

Form Development 9

So far this book has covered the foundations of the Visual Basic language, and some of the basics of programming. The next step is to learn how to create a user interface. Computer programs can run without interacting with a human user. We will be covering that type of application later in the book. Most applications require input from an end-user. For that purpose, computer applications are capable of carrying on a two-way conversation with a person. The computer prints information to the screen, and it has the ability to wait for input from the keyboard, or some other input device such as a mouse, touch screen, or industry-specific devices such as bar code readers, cash drawers, or optical scanners.

In the past, computer programs interacted using only text. With the invention of graphic operating systems came the ability to communicate with the end-user with a wider variety of tools, such as windows, clickable buttons, drop down lists, scroll bars, and many more graphic objects.

Forms are objects that form the foundation of most client-based Windows applications. They represent any window you will display in your application. In Visual Basic, the word *form* and *window* are synonymous. Visual Basic .NET can create several types of forms:

standard window

tool window

borderless

floating

modal dialog box window

Application Types

There are two basic types of Windows applications that interact with an end-user: *single* and *multiple* document interfaces. An application that employs single, main, window, and dialog windows is known as a Single Document Interface (SDI).

A single main window contains the user interface in an SDI application. The information represented within this window can change dynamically. You can also pop up supplemental windows such as dialog windows to supplement the information displayed or requested in the main window.

There are several methods of presenting information in a single window application. An excellent example of an SDI application is Windows Explorer. It's used so often that you can easily forget that it is a stand-alone, powerful application. Information is presented in two window "panes" that interact to present differing views of the files and folders stored on a hard drive. Menu selections allow you to alter the view within each window. Other ways to present different views include the tab view, sometimes known as the folder view. Clicking the graphic tab or folder presents a new set of information within the main window.

You can also create applications that employ a special user interface known as the *Multiple Document Interface* (MDI). This type of application specifies one window to be the application's parent window, in which you can open many document windows. Examples of applications that employ the Multiple Document Interface are Visual Studio or most of the Microsoft Office applications, such as Word and Excel. For example, in Word you can have many documents open simultaneously within the main application window. The main window of the application normally contains the main menu and toolbars.

Visual Studio.NET includes a visual Forms Designer that allows you to quickly and easily design and build user interfaces for your applications. The Forms Designer includes the ability to do the following tasks:

Place controls on a form using many different alignment tools

Edit event code for the form or for controls on the form

Edit the properties of the form and controls

In this visual development environment, you can quickly build forms that are used as main application windows and multiple document interface (MDI) windows, like those used in applications such as Visual Studio.NET, where a main application allows you to have multiple document windows open. Forms are also used as dialog boxes and display surfaces for graphics routines. Chapter 12 will introduce many of the powerful features included in the .NET class framework.

Forming an Application

Launching Visual Studio and selecting a Windows Application template will present you with a blank form. This form contains all the code necessary to act as the foundation of a complete Windows application. You could (not that you'd really want to) save an empty form and run it.

If you'd like to edit a form in an existing application, select the form in the Solution Explorer by double-clicking it. The form should appear in the Form Designer document window. Remember that if the Solution Explorer is not visible, you can launch it by pressing Ctrl-Alt-L or by selecting it from the **View** menu.

To add a new **Form** to your application using the Visual development environment:

1. Right-click the name of the project in the Solution Explorer.
2. From the pop-up menu, select Add. Then either select Add Windows Form or Add Inherited Form.
3. In the Add New Item window, make certain the Form template is selected.
4. Enter a name for the **Form**, keeping the .vb file extension.

You will see an icon representing the new form appear in the Solution Explorer and the new, blank **Form** will appear in the edit window.

Sizing the Form

The **Form** should be just large enough to hold each of the visual components layed out in a design that is not too crowded and confusing for the user of the application. Notice that the **Form** is surrounded by a frame with drag points (small rectangles) on each corner and side. Placing your mouse cursor over any of these drag points will change the cursor to a double arrow pointing in the directions the window side can be dragged (shortened or lengthened). Notice that dragging the corners will adjust the height and width of the **Form** simultaneously.

One thing to keep in mind when sizing a **Form** is the size of the form when the application is running on computers with different screen resolutions. It's very easy to develop applications on a computer running in 1024 **x** 768 pixel resolution, only to find that when someone runs the application in 640 **x** 480 resolution, the **Form** does not fit within the active desktop.

Notice in Figure 9.1 that at 1024 **x** 768, the default **Form** size is quite small. The running application appears next to the design mode version.

Now see, in Figure 9.2, how the same exact **Form**, running at 640 **x** 480 resolution takes up considerably more screen real estate.

Form Properties

Because **Forms** are objects, they have properties. For more information about properties of an object, you can refer to Chapter 7. There are two ways to edit a **Form's** properties. The first is by setting the initial properties of the form in the Form Properties window (see Figure 9.3) of Visual Studio.NET. The second is to change them within your application at runtime.

So far in this book we haven't really stressed the advantages of Visual development. Being able to set the properties of objects such as forms by using a properties window is one of the rapid application development features of a visual development environment.

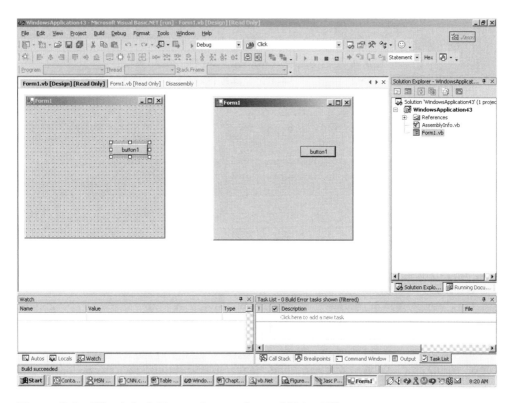

Figure 9.1   The default **Form** size running at 1024 x 768.

Changing the Form's Appearance   The default **Form** appearance is pretty plain. There are many ways to enhance the way a **Form** appears to the end-user. We've already talked about resizing the **Form**. This section discusses the properties available to change the **Form**'s appearance. The properties are:

BackColor
BackgroundImage
BorderStyle
Cursor
Font
ForeColor
RightToLeft
Text

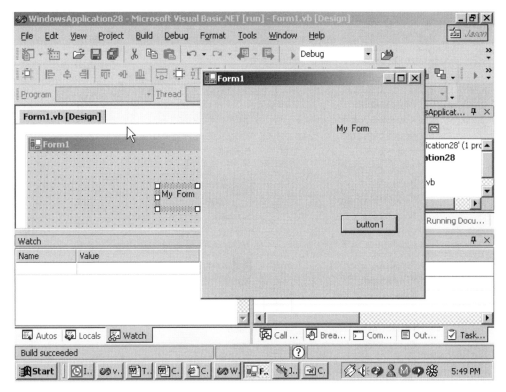

Figure 9.2   The default **Form** size running at 640 × 480.

These properties can be set within the form's property window, as shown in Figure 9.3, or set within the code.

The **BackColor** property sets the background color of the form. By default the background color is gray, also simply called **control**. Using the Form Properties Window, you can easily give your **Form** a new background color by clicking the drop down within the property value setting. A Color Picker window will appear, allowing you to select a color. The Color Picker window has three tab settings; Custom, Web, and System. The Custom color tab presents 64 custom colors for you to choose from. The Web tab presents a list of standard Web development colors, and the System tab lists the colors set by your computer's system color settings. When selecting one of these colors, the **Form** background will change colors whenever the system color settings change, or when the application is run on a computer with a different system color setting.

Note
Set the system color settings in the Display applet of the computer's Control Panel.

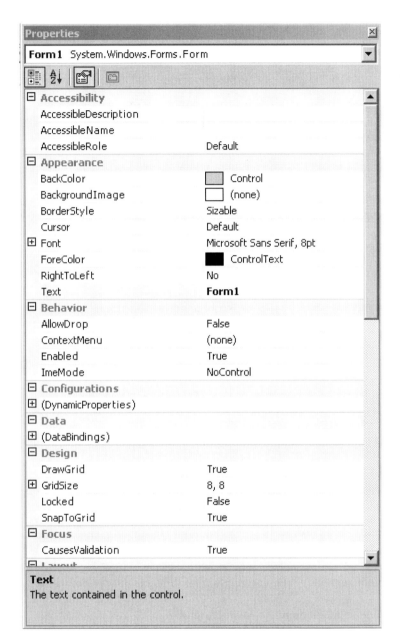

Figure 9.3 Configure the **Form's** properties in the Form Properties Window.

Rather than simply changing the background color of your **Form**, you might consider using a background image. A well-chosen image can create a powerful and professional appearance for your application. To add a background image, follow these steps:

1. From the properties window, select BackgroundImage.
2. Click the icon with the three dots.
3. Browse your computer for the image.
4. Select the image and click Open.

Figure 9.4 gives you a simple example of a small application with a single button on the form. Be aware that when you add a background image, if it's too small to fit on the form, it will repeat itself in a tile fashion across the face of the form. If the image is too large to fit on the face of the form, the image will be truncated.

The next section covers the BorderStyle property in detail. The Cursor property sets the mouse cursor that will appear when the mouse is over the active window. Be careful when changing the mouse cursor. Each cursor type is associated heuristically with an

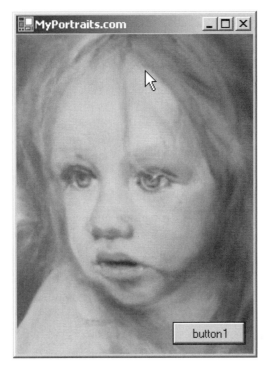

Figure 9.4   Adding a background image adds power to your application.

action. The end-user, seeing a particular mouse cursor, will assume a certain program state. For example, changing the mouse cursor to an hourglass-shaped WaitCursor will make it appear that an action is taking place and the user will assume that none of the form's controls will be active until the action has completed.

You can change the cursor dynamically at runtime to communicate information such as wait states to the end-user. Here's an example:

```
Private Sub button1_Click(ByVal sender As System.Object,
ByVal e As System.EventArgs) Handles button1.Click

        Me.Cursor = System.Windows.Forms.Cursors.WaitCursor

        Dim i As Long

        'loop for a while to kill some time

        For i = 1 To 100000000

        'do nothing here

        Next

        Me.Cursor = System.Windows.Forms.Cursors.Default

End Sub
```

You can change the font and foreground color used on the Form object. All objects placed on the form will be affected by the change in font and foreground color. Text, such as that displayed on buttons or in text labels, will appear in the font and color specified by the Font and ForeColor properties of the form.

> **Note**
> When designing a **Form** that contains an image you might consider selecting a Transparent background so that controls such as buttons and text labels do not obscure the image. Make sure to select a foreground color light or dark enough to be visible within the image.

The **RightToLeft** property affects how text is aligned on the form and within controls. By default text is left-aligned. Changing this property to read "Yes" will cause text to be right-aligned.

Creating Different Window Types   The form properties window gives you edit access to all the forms properties. Modifying the properties of the form affects the appear-

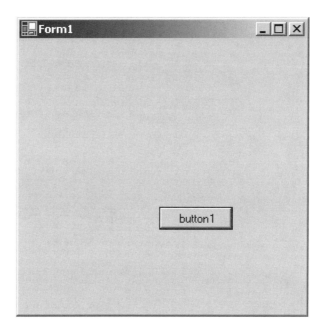

Figure 9.5   The Fixed Single window style has a single edged border and can't be resized.

ance and behavior of the form. Remember that forms can appear as many different types of windows. Properties such as **BorderStyle** determine the type of window that will appear to the end-user. Using the **BorderStyle** property, you can set an enumerated value that determines if the window is resizable, appearing as a dialog or standard window, among other styles. The complete list of Form properties can be found in the Visual Basic .NET documentation or by accessing the Properties window of the form. They are too numerous to list here.

The FixedDialog appearance (Figure 9.6) is very similar to the FixedSingle (Figure 9.5) selection. Resizable window style is also similar in appearance to the FixedDialog and FixedSingle, but notice in Figure 9.7 that placing the mouse cursor over the windows edge or corner changes the cursor to a double-arrow, allowing you to drag the sides and corners to resize the window while the application is running.

The tool windows can also be set as fixed or resizable. The most noticeable difference is that they do not include the minimize and maximize buttons in the frame.

Once you've decided on a frame type you may want to customize the font and color scheme of the form, as discussed in the previous section. About half of the form class properties are inherited from the Control Class. Many of the properties that deter-

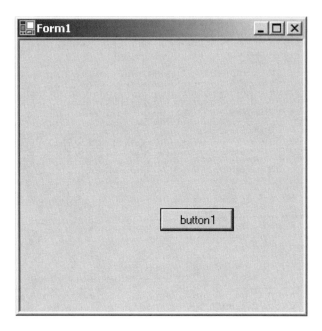

Figure 9.6 The Fixed 3D window style includes a 3D border.

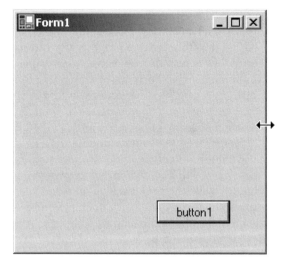

Figure 9.7 Resizable window style.

mine how the form appears are these inherited properties, such as **Font**, **ForeColor,** and **BackColor**.

> **Note**
> To create a form that will act as the main window of a Multiple Document Interface application, set the **IsMDIContainer** property to True.

Remember to set the **Text** property, the string value that displays in the Windows title bar. Now that we've touched on the topic of the title bar, be sure to control whether your form can be minimized and maximized by setting the **MinimizeBox** and **Maximize-Box** properties. As mentioned with regard to the tool window, these window options are not available for every window border style.

Accessibility Properties   There are several properties included to support Active Accessibility, which the ability to support accessibility aids such as screen enlargers and screen readers for the visually impaired and voice input for persons unable to use a keyboard and mouse. For more information on Microsoft's assistive technology, visit:

http://www.microsoft.com/enable/microsoft/technology.htm

The accessiblity properties of the form are inherited from the **Control Class**. Accessible Objects support the **iAccessible** interface.

AutoScroll Properties   An important set of properties that affect the behavior of the form as it appears as a window in your application are the **Autoscroll** properties. These affect when and where scroll bars automatically appear. If **AutoScroll** is enabled, the **AutoScrollMargin** property and the **AutoScrollMinSize** and **AutoScrollPosition** properties determine when to turn on the scroll bars, depending on how the controls fit into the window's client area. If a window is not large enough to include all of the controls, including their margin, a scroll bar will appear. You can see that setting a larger margin around controls will cause the scroll bars to appear sooner.

Form Methods

Using the methods of the **Form** object, you can control the behavior of your form. Visual Studio creates a standard template for form-based applications that contain all the correct methods to initialize and launch the primary form of a Windows application. When you create forms programmatically you will need to understand which methods of the form class control actions, such as making the form visible to the user. For example, the **Show( )** method launches a form. **The ShowDialog( )** method is used to launch a form as a modal dialog box. Here are the various form methods:

Activate   Activates a visible form, brings it to the front and gives it focus.

Show   Makes a form visible.

ShowDialog   Displays the form as a modal dialog box.

Close   Closes a form but does not destroy it.

LayoutMDI   Arranges the forms in an MDI application.

This example uses two forms. To create this example, follow these steps:

1. Create a new Windows application.
2. On the form, add a Button control.
3. In the Visual Studio.NET Solution Explorer, right-click on the name of the project.
4. Add a new form to the solution. It will be called **Form2** by default.
5. Add a new button control to **Form2**.
6. Right-click the button on **Form2** and select View Code.
7. Add the following code to the button's click event.

```
Private Sub button2_Click(ByVal sender As System.Object,
ByVal e As System.EventArgs) Handles button2.Click

        Me.Close()

End Sub
```

8. On Form1, add the following code to the button.

```
Private Sub button1_Click(ByVal sender As System.Object,
ByVal e As System.EventArgs) Handles button1.Click

        Dim MySubWindow As New Form2()

        MySubWindow.Show()

End Sub
```

Note
Your Button might have a different default name.

This example involves two forms. The second form, **Form2**, is created from the class that was created by the visual development environment. **Form2** uses the Close() method on the Button to close the form when the Button is clicked.

The Button on **Form1** creates an instance of **Form2** called **MySubWindow**, and launches the window using the **Show( )** method. This example demonstrates two principles. The first one is how to create new form classes and include them in your application. The second is the use of the form methods to launch and close forms.

Dynamic Forms

As you saw in the last section, using the visual development environment is the fastest way to create new forms. There may be times when you need to create forms and launch them dynamically in your application. Remember that a form is simply an object, which is created from the **Form** class. Therefore, to create a dynamic form, you only need to create a new object of class **Form( )**. Set any of the property values on the form. To launch the form, call the **show( )** method, as shown in the following code snippet. When this click event fires, a new form object is created and launched.

```
Private Sub button1_Click(ByVal sender As System.Object,
ByVal e As System.EventArgs) Handles button1.Click

        Dim MySubWindow As New Form()

        MySubWindow.Show()

End Sub
```

So far in this chapter, the examples have only shown forms being launched in the click event of a **Button**. Actually, they can be launched anywhere within your code. For example, you may launch a modal dialog window to handle an error condition. Chapter 10 covers programming to handle error conditions, also known as exception handling.

Form Events

Forms are actually controls that can respond to Windows events, such as mouse clicks, opening and closing, and keyboard presses. Some user interface elements, such as Buttons, are useless without responding to events such as the Buttons click event. Form events (listed in Table 9.1) are sometimes overlooked, because they appear to be simple, flat containers for other controls. The truth is quite the contrary. Forms are incredibly dynamic objects, inheriting events from the **Control** and **RichControl** classes (discussed later in the chapter) while adding a number of additional events.

Table 9.1   Form Events

Event	When event occurs
Activated	When a Form is activated in code or by the user
ChangeUICues	When focus, keyboard, or both cues have changed
Click	When the control is clicked
Closed	When the Form is closed
Closing	When a Form is closing
ControlAdded	When a new control is added
ControlRemoved	When a control is removed
Deactivate	When the Form loses focus and is not the active form
DoubleClick	When the control is double-clicked
DragDrop	When a mouse drags an object
DragEnter	When an object being dragged enters another object
DragLeave	When an object being dragged leaves another object
DragOver	When an object being dragged is over another object
Enter	When a control is entered
GiveFeedback	When Feedback is given
GetFocus	When a control receives focus
HandleCreated	When a handle is created for a control
HandleDestroyed	When a control's handle is destroyed
HelpRequested	When help is requested, context-sensitive help arguments are passed to this event
InputLangChange	Occurs after the input language of the form has changed
InputLangChangeRequest	When the user attempts to change the input language for the form
Invalidated	When an area of a window is invalidated
KeyDown	When a keyboard key is pressed down while a control has focus
KeyPress	When a keyboard key is pressed while a control has focus
KeyUp	When a keyboard key is released while a control has focus
Layout	When a control's layout properties have been modified
Leavez	When the control is left by giving focus to another object
LostFocus	When the control loses focus
MDIChildActive	When an MDI child form is activated or closed
MenuComplete	When a menu in a form loses focus
MenuStart	When a menu in a form receives focus
MouseDown	When the mouse pointer is over the control and a mouse button is pressed
MouseEnter	When the mouse pointer enters a control
MouseHOver	When the mouse pointer hovers over a control

Table 9.1 Form Events

Event	When event occurs
MouseLeave	When the mouse pointer leaves a control
MouseMove	When the mouse pointer is moved over a control
MouseUp	When the mouse pointer is over the control and a mouse button is released
MouseWheel	When the user moves the optional mouse wheel while a control has focus
Move	When the control is moved
Paint	When a repaint of a control occurs
PropertyChanged	When a property of a control has changed
QueryAccessibilityHelp	When the user requests accessibility Help, this event handler receives Query Accessibility Event arguments
QueryContinueDrag	As a drag-drop is occuring, this event returns the status of the drag operation
Resize	When a control has been resized
Validated	When a control has finished validating
Validating	While a control is validating

Here is an example of handling a **Form** event. Complete instructions for creating event handlers are in Chapter 7. First, click in the left drop down and select (Base Class Events). Second, click the right drop down and select the event you'd like to handle. This example will handle the click event. The editor will automatically create a new subprocedure to handle the selected event and take you right to it. This event handler simply writes "event handled" to the console window when the user clicks on the form.

```
Private Sub Form1_Click(ByVal sender As Object, ByVal e
As_ System.EventArgs) Handles MyBase.Click

    console.Write("event handled")

End Sub
```

This is a simple example. Some events will remain simple, while others will involve very complex program logic.

Controls

Forms aren't very interesting without *controls*. Controls are the graphic objects that appear on a form that interact with an end user. Placing these controls on the form is simple.

Adding code that does something when a user interacts with a control will form one of the most important parts of your application.

Tip
Proper placement and behavior of a control determines the user interface design of your program. A poor user interface design can make even the most powerful application difficult to use causing users to abandon the application.

Here are most of the standard Windows controls that come installed with Visual Basic .NET and a description of their functionality (Table 9.2).

Table 9.2   User Interface Controls

Control	Description
Button	Buttons perform a single task, they fire events depending on the mouse interaction with the button. Associate code with events such as a button's on_click event to start or stop a process.
CheckBox	This rectangular control allows an X or check to be placed as a selection, returning a value of Checked when an X is placed in the box.
CheckedListBox	This is a list of items with a checkbox next to each item in the list. This is a replacement for the terrible way you had to select multiple items in a list in past versions.
ColorDialog	The ColorDialog has its own color picker dialog window. Adding this control to a form allows you to launch this dialog by calling its showDialog method.
ComboBox	ComboBox Controls are similar to listboxes, except they also have an edit field where the user may enter data manually. The user can choose to enter data or select from the drop-down list.
ContextMenu	This control allows you to pop up a menu when the user clicks the right mouse button on an object.
DataGrid	This control allows you to view and edit data from a database.
DateTimePicker	This control pops up the standard Windows data-time dialog window.
DomainUpDown	This control allows you to select text in a spin control.
FontDialog	This control pops up a dialog that allows you to select a font from the fonts installed in the Windows system.
GroupBox	This control visually groups controls together on a form. Controls in a group can be moved as a unit. Similar to the Panel Control.
ImageList	An object used to store collections of images used in other controls. This object accepts bitmaps or icon images.
Label	The label is a text display control. Text in a label cannot be edited by the end-user of an application.

Table 9.2   User Interface Controls

Control	Description
LinkLabel	Similar to the label control, except that it can contain a URL used as a hyperlink, similar to a link on a Web page.
ListBox	A selection control that allows the end-user to select from a list of string values.
ListView	The ListView class operates similar to Windows Explorer, where you can choose to view items in a list as icons, a list, or in report format.
MainMenu	This control displays a Window main menu at runtime. This control can be visually configured.
NumericUpDown	This is the Windows up-down control that displays numeric values.
OpenFileDialog	This control is the standard Windows File Open dialog box.
Panel	The Panel Control groups controls together on a form, and unlike the GroupBox control, panel controls can include scroll bars.
PictureBox	This control serves as a canvas on which images can be displayed.
PrintDialog	This control is the standard Windows Print dialog box.
RadioButton	A selection control allows you to choose one item from several selection choices. When one choice is selected, any other choice is deselected.
RichTextBox	This edit control acts similar to a Word processor.
SaveFileDialog	This control is the standard Windows Save File dialog.
StatusBar	A control that can display the status of another control's progress.
TabControl	A control that displays pages selectable by a stylized tab appearance.
TextBox	Text input control used for accepting small amounts of text.
Toolbar	Use this control when you need a toolbar in your application.
TrackBar	Similar to a Window scrollbar, but more configurable.
TrayIcon	This control creates an icon in the Windows System Tray.
TreeView	This control displays hierarchical data in a collapsible tree configuration.

Nonvisual Controls

There is a class of controls that do not require a user interface, known as *nonvisual controls*. This type of control is also known as a *component*, and like any control, is designed to be reusable.

To add a nonvisual control to a form, select it from the Toolbox, and drag it to the **Form**. Once you've added a component to the form, an icon representing the control will be displayed in the resizable tray along the bottom of the form. Clicking this icon will allow you to set the properties of the component.

Nonvisual controls can be added to your application while it is running (at runtime). Simply create a new instance of the control as an object as you would any object. An example of a nonvisual object is the **messageQueue** object:

```
Dim myMessageQ as New System.Messaging.MessageQueue
```

ActiveX and COM Components

Visual Basic .NET supports adding legacy ActiveX controls to a form. The form in this version of Visual Basic is not optimized for ActiveX controls. In fact, Microsoft cautions that there may be performance degradation of your application when using legacy ActiveX controls.

*Begin by adding ActiveX controls to the Toolbox. ActiveX controls must appear in the Toolbox before they can be added to the form in the visual development environment. Add ActiveX controls to the Toolbox by choosing the **Customize Toolbox…** from the **Tools** menu selection and then clicking the COM Control tab. The available COM components are displayed with a checkbox next to it. Check the COM component you'd like to add to the Toolbox and click **OK** (see Figure 9.8).*

Once the component appears in the Toolbox, add it to your form by double-clicking on it in the Toolbox. It will then be added to your form. You should consider upgrading ActiveX controls to Windows Form Controls to overcome possible performance problems.

Adding Controls to a Form

There are two ways to add controls to a form: visually and programmatically. One of the great time-saving advantages to visual development is the ability to drag and drop controls onto a form. Visual Studio.NET makes dropping controls onto a form and arranging them very easy.

Begin by creating a Visual Basic application and Visual Studio will present you with a blank form. Locate the Toolbox window, as shown in Figure 9.8. The window may be hidden, requiring you to click on the Toolbox icon along the edge of the Visual Studio interface window. Notice that the Toolbox has three categories of controls, accessible by clicking the appropriate tab. For now, make certain that the Windows Forms tab is selected, displaying the list of visual controls. These correspond to the controls listed in Table 9.2.

Click on the desired control in the Toolbox, selecting it. Then click near the desired location on the form. Some controls require that when they are dropped on the form, you drag your mouse to size the object as it is being placed.

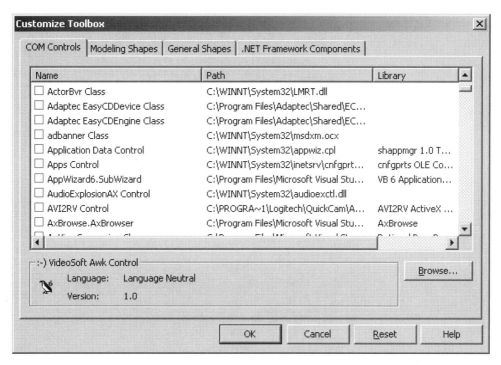

Figure 9.8   Select ActiveX components to add to your Toolbox.

Note:
It isn't important to get your sizing perfect as you drop the control on the form.
You can resize the form manually, or by using one of several control-sizing and
-placement utilities.

Control Properties

To set the properties of a control in the Visual development enviroment, right-click on the
control and select Properties from the pop-up menu. A Properties tab page will load, displaying all of the control's properties.

In Figure 9.10 you can see the properties of a button. You will most likely want to
change the **Text** property of the **Button** from its default value of **button1** to something
a bit more meaningful. Changing the **Text** property does not change the object's name.
You can change the name of the object by changing the **Name** property. Notice that the
properties are divided into expandable sections. You can expand or collapse a group of

Figure 9.9   Select the Windows Forms tab from the Toolbox window

properties by clicking once on the + icon to the left of the section name. For example, the **name** property is in the **Design** section.

Setting the properties of some controls is more involved. For example, the **DataGrid** control requires that you set the values in the **Data** properties. This will bind the **Data-Grid** control to a data source.

Visual Control Placement   You can move controls around the form by clicking on them, and moving them around the form. Your mouse pointer will change when moved over a selected control. The four-arrowed pointer means your control can be moved by left-clicking the mouse and dragging the control to its new location on the form.

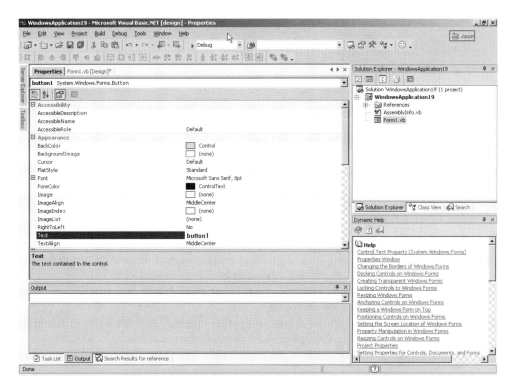

Figure 9.10   Use the Properties tab to set the properties of a control in the Visual development environment.

Visual Studio.NET incorporates a set of tools that will assist you in aligning your controls with respect to each other. Moving controls around with the mouse is fairly simple, but can become very tedious on a large form with many controls. The tools identified in Table 9.3 allow you to align controls with respect to one another, change the spacing evenly between controls, and align them with respect to the form.

The tools in this table can be accessed by using the Visual Studio toolbar, or by selecting the tool from the Visual Studio main menu. Once you've placed a control on the form using the Visual development environment, the **Format** menu choice will appear. Choose a tool from these menu selections.

Adding Controls Programmatically   Adding controls programmatically is an important ability. While it's easy and fun to add them visually, quite often forms are constructed

Table 9.3   Control Placement and Sizing Tools

Placement and Sizing Tool	Behavior of Tool
Align to grid	Moves controls to nearest alignment grid intersection.
Align Lefts	Aligns the left sides of all selected controls to the first selected control.
Align Centers	Moves controls so that all selected controls are vertically centered on the vertical center of the first selected control.
Align Rights	Aligns the right sides of all selected controls to the first selected control.
Align Tops	Aligns all selected controls along their tops using the first selected control as the guide.
Align Middles	Aligns controls so that the selected controls are horizontally centered using the horizontal center of the first selected control as a guide.
Align Bottoms	Aligns selected controls along the bottoms of the controls using the first selected control as a guide.
Make Same Width	Adjusts the width of all selected controls so that they are the same width as the first selected control.
Size to Grid	Adjusts the size of either individual or all selected controls so that the edges of the control are moved to the nearest grid line.
Make Same Height	Adjusts the height of all selected controls so that they are the same height as the first selected control.
Make Same Size	Adjusts both the height and width of all selected controls so that they match the height and width of the first selected control.
Make Horizontal Spacing Equal	Adjusts the horizontal spacing between controls so that they match the horizontal spacing between the first two selected controls. The left and rightmost controls do not move. Only the controls that are between them horizontally are adjusted.
Increase Horizontal Spacing	Adjusts selected controls so that the horizontal spacing between them increases by one horizontal grid space.
Decrease Horizontal Spacing	Adjusts selected controls so that the horizontal spacing between them decreases by one horizontal grid space.
Remove Horizontal Spacing	Adjusts the position of selected controls so that all horizontal space between them is removed. The control on the right is always moved toward the left no matter which control is selected first.
Make Vertical Spacing Equal	Adjusts the position of selected controls so that the veritical spacing between them is equal. The top and bottom selected controls do not move. Only the controls between them are adjusted.

Table 9.3   Control Placement and Sizing Tools

Placement and Sizing Tool	Behavior of Tool
Increase Vertical Spacing	Adjusts the position of selected controls so that the vertical spacing between them increases by one vertical grid space.
Decrease Vertical Spacing	Adjusts the position of selected controls so that the vertical spacing between them decreases by one vertical grid space.
Remove Vertical Spacing	Adjusts the position of selected controls so that there is no vertical space between them. All controls are adjusted up toward the top selected control no matter which order the controls were selected.
Center Horizontally	Center all selected controls on the form to the horizontal center of the form.
Center Vertically	Center all selected controls on the form to the vertical center of the form.
Bring to Front	Adjusts the order of controls or selected objects so that the selected control moves to the front when objects or controls are overlapped by other controls.
Send to Back	Adjusts the order of controls or selected objects so that the selected control moves to the back when objects or controls are overlapped by other controls.
Lock Controls	Locks the position of controls on the form. All controls are locked in place regardless of whether they are selected or not. Controls added after locking controls will not be locked until Lock Controls is once again selected.

dynamically depending on the logic of the application. After a demonstration of adding controls to the form, we give an example of adding controls to the form dynamically.

Create a new object of the control type you wish to create.

Set the control's properties (covered in the next section).

Using the Add method of the Form's Controls container, add the new control object to the form.

This example creates a new form object and places a label control in the upper left-hand corner. (See Figure 9.11)

```
Private Sub button1_Click(ByVal sender As System.Object,
    ByVal e As System.EventArgs) Handles button1.Click

        Dim MySubWindow As New Form()
```

```
        Dim myLabel As New Label()

        myLabel.Text = "Test"

        myLabel.Location = New Point(1, 1)

        MySubWindow.Controls.Add(myLabel)

        MySubWindow.Show()

End Sub
```

Changing a Control's Properties Programmatically   All controls share many of the same properties, because all control objects are inherited from the same **control** class. When creating new **Control** objects within your program, rather than using the visual

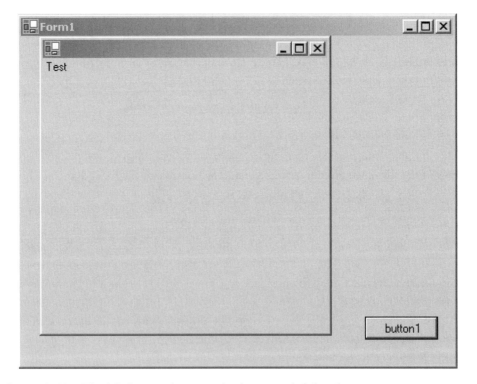

Figure 9.11   The label control appears in the upper left-hand corner.

development environment, you will need to set some of the basic properties normally set automatically for you when placing a control visually, such as the size and location of the control.

This example includes all the code for a form with a button and a label control. Clicking the button both moves the label control and resets the **Text** property. Notice the use of the keyword **Me**. The **Me** keyword is a Visual Basic .NET shortcut to refer to the currently active instance of the object, in this case, **Form1**.

```
Public Class Form1

    Inherits System.Windows.Forms.Form

#Region " Windows Form Designer generated code "

    Public Sub New()

        MyBase.New()

        'This call is required by the Windows Form
        Designer.

        InitializeComponent()

        'Add any initialization after the
        InitializeComponent() call

    End Sub


    'Form overrides dispose to clean up the component
    list.

    Public Overrides Sub Dispose()

        MyBase.Dispose()

        If Not (components Is Nothing) Then

            components.Dispose()

        End If
```

```
End Sub

Private WithEvents button1 As
System.Windows.Forms.Button

Private WithEvents button2 As
System.Windows.Forms.Button

Private WithEvents label1 As
System.Windows.Forms.Label

'Required by the Windows Form Designer

Private components As System.ComponentModel.Container

'NOTE: The following procedure is required by the
Windows Form Designer

'It can be modified using the Windows Form Designer.

'Do not modify it using the code editor.

<System.Diagnostics.DebuggerStepThrough()> Private Sub
InitializeComponent()

    Me.button1 = New System.Windows.Forms.Button()

    Me.label1 = New System.Windows.Forms.Label()

    Me.button1.Location = New
System.Drawing.Point(160, 104)

    Me.button1.TabIndex = 0

    Me.button1.Text = "button1"

    Me.label1.Location = New System.Drawing.Point(24,
32)

    Me.label1.TabIndex = 1
```

```
      Me.label1.Text = "label1"

      Me.AutoScaleBaseSize = New System.Drawing.Size(5,
      13)

      Me.ClientSize = New System.Drawing.Size(292, 273)

      Me.Controls.AddRange(New
      System.Windows.Forms.Control() {Me.label1,
      Me.button1})

      Me.Text = "Form1"

   End Sub

   Private Sub button1_Click(ByVal sender As
   System.Object, ByVal e As System.EventArgs) Handles
   button1.Click

      Me.label1.Location = New System.Drawing.Point(5,
      5)

      Me.label1.Text = "I've moved"

   End Sub

 #End Region

 End Class
```

Notice in this example the values of **Label1** are initially set on the form. You can change any of the properties at runtime. This particular example causes the text label to move, and to display the text "I've moved." Rearranging the user interface is only one example of why you might want to change a control's properties at runtime. You may want to change a control based on changes in a database or based on user input.

Visual Inheritance

Visual Basic .NET supports visual inheritance. This means that you can create a form, and then inherit from that form to create other forms that have the same layout, controls, and behaviors.

The simplest way to see how this works is by example. The example begins by creating a new form, Form1, and placing a label and a button on the form, dragging them from the Toolbox onto the form. Next, we can programmatically create a new class we'll call **sono-faform**. This new form will inherit the controls and layout of the initial form, **Form1,** by using the keyword **Inherits**, as shown in the code example that follows. In this example, the controls and properties of **Form1** are inherited by the new class, **sonofaform**. You can extend the new form by adding additional controls, or by modifying its properties. For example, in addition to the inherited button, **sonofaform** adds an additional Button like this:

```
Class sonofaform

    Inherits Form1

    Private WithEvents mybutton As
    System.Windows.Forms.Button



    <System.Diagnostics.DebuggerStepThrough()> Private Sub
    InitializeComponent()

      Dim resources As System.Resources.ResourceManager =
      New System.Resources.ResourceManager(GetType(Form1))

      mybutton() = New System.Windows.Forms.Button()

      mybutton().Location = New System.Drawing.Point(200,
      200)

      mybutton().TabIndex = 0

      mybutton().Text = "Our New Button"

    End Sub

  End Class
```

The example now has a new **sonofaform** class. The next step is to create a new object of type **sonofaform** called **MySubWindow**. The example continues by adding a **label** control and launches the new **Form** object using the **Show( )** method.

```
      Private Sub button1_Click(ByVal sender As
```

```
System.Object, ByVal e As System.EventArgs) Handles
button1.Click

        Me.label1.Location = New System.Drawing.Point(5,
        5)

        Me.label1.Text = "I've moved"

        Dim MySubWindow As New sonofaform()

        Dim myLabel As New Label()

        myLabel.Text = "Test"

        myLabel.Location = New Point(1, 1)

        MySubWindow.Controls.Add(myLabel)

        MySubWindow.Show()

    End Sub
```

There are several reasons why you might want to create a base **Form** from which other forms are inherited. For instance, if your application has a standard response dialog, and you'd like to provide some basic formatting such as the layout of the **OK Cancel Buttons**, border type, color, graphics, and font properties, you can create that once and create new forms that inherit each of these properties, saving you the trouble of creating the same form over and over again.

Just as you can inherit a form, you can also inherit any control. Not only can you benefit by creating controls that inherit "default" properties, you can also modify the behavior of the controls by modifying the event behavior of the control. For instance, all **Buttons** may play a click sound when the click event is triggered.

Summary

Forms are the foundation of most visual applications created using Visual Basic .NET. They are special, contained controls that represent various types of Windows on which you can place other controls. Forms can be designed and built using the visual design tools of Visual Studio, or created dynamically in your application. Because controls are objects, you can modify them and inherit from them as you can other types of objects. You may want to refer back to this chapter when reading Chapter 12, where the information here forms the foundation of more complex graphic user interface design.

Exception Handling 10

Error handling, or *exception handling*, is one of the most important tasks to writing bug-free, user-friendly programs. In past versions of Visual Basic, exception handling was accomplished through the OnError statement, branching the program using GoTo statements. This is known as *unstructured* exception handling and is described in detail later in this chapter. Visual Basic .NET now supports both *structured* and *unstructured* exception handling. If you're experienced in programming with other languages, you may remember structured exception handling from such languages as Visual C++ and Java.

Before launching into exception handling at the code level, it's important to know what tools are available for helping you debug your application using Visual Studio. Selecting Exceptions from the Debug menu launches the Exceptions window. Using this tool you can customize how Visual Studio reacts to exceptions as they occur in your application.

Customize Visual Studio by selecting individual exception types and specifying whether you want Visual Studio to continue the application, ignoring the exception, or break into the debugger. You can specify these settings for exceptions that are both handled and unhandled in your code. Figure 10.1 shows how you can select exceptions from the Common Language Runtime, Win32 exceptions, Native Run-Time checks, and C++.

Structured Exception Handling

Structured exception handling is more efficient and has simplified the development of good error handling. When using structured exception handling, blocks of code are marked as *protected*. Each marked block of code has its own error-handling routine. When an error occurs within the marked block of code, the error-handling routine is called.

Structured exception handling begins with the **Try** statement and ends with the **End Try** statement. Code that runs within the **Try** and **End Try** statements is considered protected. By themselves, the **Try** and **End Try** statements will not handle errors. You include a **Catch** statement for each exception you'd like to catch and handle. The code to handle each error condition is included after each **Catch** statement. There is no limit to the number of Catch statements you can include within a **Try** and **End Try** statement.

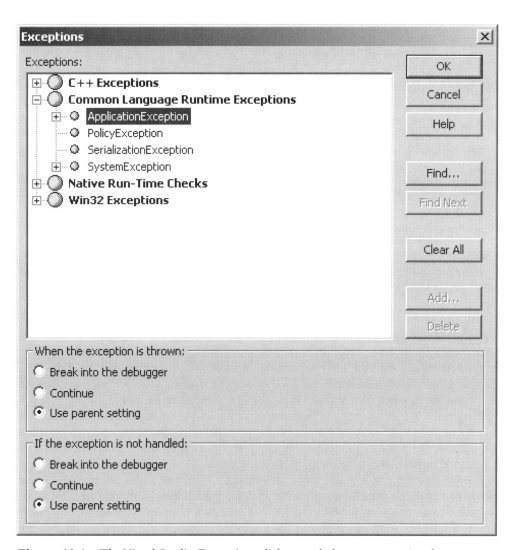

Figure 10.1   The Visual Studio Exceptions dialog can help you customize the debugger.

```
Try

Catch <exception> As <type> When <expression>

[Exit Try]

Finally

End Try
```

Try statements are required. This is the program code where an error condition can occur.

Catch (optional) Try – End Try blocks do not require a Catch statement.

Finally (optional) Try – End Try blocks do not require a Finally statement.

Even though both **Catch** and **Finally** are optional, a **Try** block requires that either a **Catch** or a **Finally** statement is included. There is no other reason to mark your code as protected if you have not included one of these statements. Visual Basic .NET will throw a compile error if you have not included one of these two statements within a Try—End **Try** block.

You can embed Try—End Try statements within each other. This is a way to create error-handling code that will handle errors that are more generic to many blocks of code, with more specific Try—End Try blocks within them. For example, you might have error handlers that run when a **File Open** condition produces an error. Within that Try—End Try block, you may have many other file processes, such as reads and writes. You may have more specific handling instructions for each read and write access to a file.

In each procedure where an exception occurs, the exception-handling code is called. If you do not have an exception handler in that procedure, the calling procedure is searched for an exception handler and the search continues up the line, until an exception handler is found. If none is found, the program is stopped, and an error message is displayed. Here is an example of a simple math error that is caught when run within the protected **Try** block. The error is the well-known divide-by-zero error. When we try this code by clicking the button, as shown in this example, a messagebox is launched, printing the "Math Error" message. The Finally block contains a Beep( ) statement just to indicate that the finally statement was run.

```
Private Sub button1_Click(ByVal sender As System.Object,
ByVal e As System.EventArgs) Handles button1.Click

        Dim MyInt1, MyInt2, MyInt3 As Integer

        MyInt1 = 5
```

```
        MyInt2 = 0

        Try

            MyInt3 = MyInt1 \ MyInt2

        Catch ' Exception

            MessageBox.Show("Math Error")

        Finally

            Beep()

        End Try

    End Sub
```

You can instantly see the advantage of error handling. There are no ugly runtime errors, programs stopping, hair pulling, name calling, or angry support calls. Instead, a friendly message appears. Of course, this example has forced this error. If the error had happened due to user input, you could direct the end-user to reenter the correct information and try again.

There are times when you want more information, rather than the simple, friendly message to the user. This next section covers a means to give you more information using **Catch** filters.

Catch Filters

The **Catch** statement has the ability to catch the exception type thrown by the error. You can then provide more information, or handle a specific error more efficiently. Taking another look at the syntax for the **Catch** statement, you can see that it's possible to further filter the **Catch** statement.

```
Catch <exception> As <type> When <expression>
```

In the last section, we simply used the **Catch** statement to catch any exceptions that have occurred. You can include a parameter that passes information from the exception to a variable you can use within your **Catch** statement to further handle the error gracefully. In the syntax above, you see that you can accept an exception as type. The exception can be any variable name. Do not declare this variable ahead of time. Specify **exception** as the type to catch all exceptions, like this:

```
Catch cexcept as Exception

'Exception handling code goes here
```

You don't have to catch all exceptions. You can filter which exceptions your code handles. The Catch statement can filter errors in two ways: the first is by class of exception and the second is based on any conditional exception such as by error number. Here is an example of filtering by class of exception:

```
Catch cexcept as ClassLoadException

'Exception handling code goes here
```

Here is an example of the same error condition as shown in the last section, the divide-by-zero error. This time, instead of just catching the error and printing a generic message, this example prints all the information passed to it by the Visual Basic .NET exception handler.

```
Private Sub button1_Click(ByVal sender As System.Object,
ByVal e As System.EventArgs) Handles button1.Click

        Dim MyInt1, MyInt2, MyInt3 As Integer

        MyInt1 = 5

        MyInt2 = 0

        Try

            MyInt3 = MyInt1 \ MyInt2

        Catch cexcept As Exception

            MessageBox.Show(cexcept.ToString)

        Finally

            Beep()

        End Try

End Sub
```

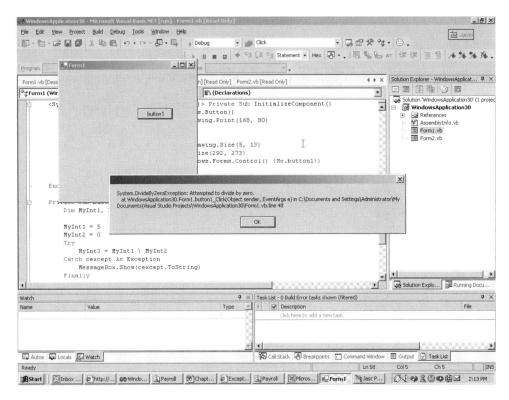

Figure 10.2 The messagebox contains the string version of the exception.

This example prints information about the exception to the MessageBox that appears when the error is caught. See Figure 10.1 to see the MessageBox. The variable, **cexcept**, is set with the value of the exception when it occurs.

The **Exception** class has methods and properties that can help you provide more information about the exception. The **Message** property is useful for printing the actual error message for the exception.

This example, instead of printing all the information shown in Figure 10.2, prints only the error message, "Attempted to divide by zero."

```
Private Sub button1_Click(ByVal sender As System.Object,
  ByVal e As System.EventArgs) Handles button1.Click

  Dim MyInt1, MyInt2, MyInt3 As Integer

  MyInt1 = 5
```

```
    MyInt2 = 0

    Try

        MyInt3 = MyInt1 \ MyInt2

        Catch cexcept As Exception

            MessageBox.Show(cexcept.Message)

        Finally

            Beep()

    End Try

End Sub
```

You can use the **Source** property to get the name of the application or object throwing the error. Even more useful when debugging an application is the **StackTrace** property. Use this to return the name of the application, name of the procedure, name and location of the source file, and line number on which the error occurred. For instance, replacing the **MessageBox** in the previous example with one that prints out the **StackTrace** property would result in this:

at WindowsApplication30.Form1.button1_Click(Object sender, EventArgs e) in C:\Documents and Settings\Administrator\My Documents\Visual Studio Projects\WindowsApplication30\Form1.Visual Basic.NET:line 48

The **TargetSite** property returns a **MethodBase** object referring to the procedure where the exception was thrown. Notice in this example that we use the **ToString** method of the object returned to print the result into the **MessageBox**.

```
    Private Sub button1_Click(ByVal sender As System.Object,
    ByVal e As System.EventArgs) Handles button1.Click

        Dim MyInt1, MyInt2, MyInt3 As Integer

        MyInt1 = 5

        MyInt2 = 0

        Try
```

```
        MyInt3 = MyInt1 \ MyInt2

    Catch cexcept As Exception

        MessageBox.Show(cexcept.TargetSite.ToString)

    Finally

        Beep()

    End Try

End Sub
```

This example launches a **MessageBox** with the message:

void button1_Click(System.Object, System.EventArgs)

Another property of the **Exception** class, the **InnerException** property, allows you to catch an exception in your code that will cause another exception to be thrown, saving the first exception to the **InnerException** property and thus allowing you to handle this type of exception more appropriately by analyzing the exception first thrown.

When filtering on conditions other than by class of exception, include the **When** conditional statement with the **Catch** statement like this:

```
Catch When <condition>

'Exception handling code goes here
```

Oftentimes, the **When** clause is used with the **Err** object, which contains additional information about an error such as the error number that has occurred. In the next example, rather than using an exception object, we use the number property of the **Err** object to determine which error has occurred.

```
Private Sub button1_Click(ByVal sender As System.Object,
ByVal e As System.EventArgs) Handles button1.Click

    Dim MyInt1, MyInt2, MyInt3 As Integer

    MyInt1 = 5

    MyInt2 = 0

    Try
```

```
        MyInt3 = MyInt1 \ MyInt2

    Catch When Err().Number = 11

        MessageBox.Show(Err().Description)

    Finally

        Beep()

    End Try

End Sub
```

This example launches a **MessageBox** that displays the **Description** property of the **Err** object, in this case, "Attempted to divide by zero." You can use the **Raise** method of the **Err** object to raise an error. In this example, we raise a user-defined error, giving it our own number, specifying the source and description. You can also specify **HelpFile** context as well. Notice that this example has changed the code so that a divide-by-zero exception is not thrown. We raised an error for no reason at all other than to demonstrate how to raise an error. Figure 10.3 shows the system error when this error is not handled.

```
Dim MyInt1, MyInt2, MyInt3 As Integer

    MyInt1 = 4

    MyInt2 = 2

    Try

        MyInt3 = MyInt1 \ MyInt2

        Err().Raise(Number:=1051, Source:=
        "ButtonClick", Description:="not a cool thing
        to do.")

    Catch When Err().Number = 11

        MessageBox.Show(Err().Description)

    End Try
```

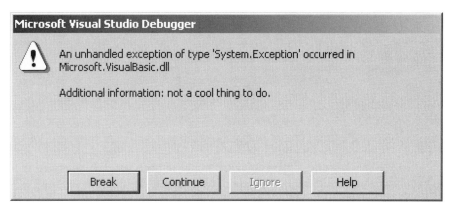

Figure 10.3   When the raised exception is not handled, you get a system error dialog.

Changing the code around just a little more to handle the user-defined exception allows the application to continue after handling the exception.

```
Catch When Err().Number = 1051

        MessageBox.Show(Err().Description)
```

With this modification to the previous example, a **MessageBox** is launched that displays the user-defined error description. You can also catch user-defined errors without knowing which error is going to occur by catching them with the exception object like this:

```
Private Sub button1_Click(ByVal sender As System.Object,
ByVal e As System.EventArgs) Handles button1.Click

        Dim MyInt1, MyInt2, MyInt3 As Integer

        MyInt1 = 4

        MyInt2 = 2

        Try

            MyInt3 = MyInt1 \ MyInt2

            Err().Raise(Number:=1051, Source:=
            "ButtonClick", Description:="not a cool thing
            to do.")
```

```
        Catch cexcept As Exception



            MessageBox.Show(cexcept.Message)

        End Try

    End Sub
```

This example also launches a **MessageBox** displaying the same user-defined message, in this case, "not a cool thing to do." The cool thing about creating user-defined errors in this way is that they can be used for data validation and allow you to catch user-entered or database data errors and handle them at runtime without worrying that your program will crash.

Throw

In the last section, you saw how you can use the **Raise** method of the **Err** object to cause error conditions to occur, whether user-defined or system-defined errors. There is another way to cause an error condition on purpose in your application that is more in keeping with the **Try** and **Catch** method of error handling. The **Throw** statement generates an error condition that is handled by a **Catch** statement.

You can place a Throw statement within your code, causing an error condition where an error condition may not normally be thrown. Based on the type of error you throw, the code you've placed in the **Catch** statement will handle the condition. You can also put a **Throw** statement within a **Catch** statement to rethrow the error to the next error handler.

In this example, the variable **MyException** is cast as an **ArgumentException**. The **Throw** statement throws that error, once again for no good reason other than example. This code would normally work fine and not throw an exception.

```
Private Sub button1_Click(ByVal sender As System.Object,
ByVal e As System.EventArgs) Handles button1.Click

    Dim MyInt1, MyInt2, MyInt3 As Integer

    MyInt1 = 4

    MyInt2 = 2

    Dim MyException As ArgumentException
```

```
    Try

        MyInt3 = MyInt1 \ MyInt2

        Throw MyException

    Catch cexcept As Exception

        MessageBox.Show(cexcept.Message)

    End Try

End Sub
```

This example launches a **MessageBox** and displays the error message:

An exception of type SystemNullReferenceException was thrown.

Custom Exceptions

Earlier in the chapter you learned how it was possible to create custom errors using the **Raise** method of the **Err** object. It's possible to create your own custom exception object that can be thrown using the **Throw** statement. So far in this chapter we have focused on the **Exception** object, which involves exceptions thrown by the Common Language Runtime exclusively. There is a class type called **ApplicationException** that is derived from **Exception** but does not extend any of its behaviors. The **ApplicationException** is used to create custom exceptions. If you try to modify an **Exception** object you'll find that its properties are read-only.

In this next example of creating your own custom exception, the constructor of the **ApplicationException** object accepts two parameters: the first is the error message as a string and the second, optional, parameter is a **System.Exception** that is the inner exception, if any.

```
Private Sub button1_Click(ByVal sender As System.Object,
ByVal e As System.EventArgs) Handles button1.Click

  Dim MyInt1, MyInt2, MyInt3 As Integer

   MyInt1 = 4

   MyInt2 = 2

   Dim MyException As New ApplicationException("This thing
   is broken.")
```

```
   Try

       MyInt3 = MyInt1 \ MyInt2

       Throw MyException

    Catch cexcept As Exception

        MessageBox.Show(cexcept.Message)

    End Try

 End Sub
```

If you replace the cexcept.Message in the previous example with cexcept.ToString, you will see the entire ApplicationException object printed to string format, as shown in Figure 10.4.

Finally

The **Finally** block of the Try-Catch–protected block is run every time code in the **Try** block is run. Unlike the code in the **Try** block, errors in the **Finally** block are not captured by the **Catch** block. Therefore, this is the perfect place to put housekeeping functionality, such as destroying objects and closing files. It's not a good idea to put code in this block that could fail or cause a runtime error.

In the examples throughout this chapter, the **Beep( )** function was included in the **Finally** block. This function causes the computer's system speaker to sound a short tone. It was in the examples just to show you that each time the code in the **Try** block was run, the **Finally** block also ran.

Figure 10.4   The full ApplicationException is sent to the messagebox.

Here is a more complete example that puts the information covered in this chapter so far to use:

```
Public Class UserInfo

    Sub GetUserInfo()

        Dim userinputwindow As New Form2()

        Try

            userinputwindow.Show()

        Catch cexcept As Exception

            Dim errorstring As String

            errorstring = "Error opening Form2 " & _
            cexcept.Message

            messagebox.Show(errorstring)

        Finally

            userinputwindow = Nothing

        End Try

    End Sub

End Class
```

This is the code for the button on **Form1**:

```
Private Sub button1_Click(ByVal sender As System.Object, _
ByVal e As System.EventArgs) Handles button1.Click

    Dim MyUserInfo As New UserInfo()

    Try

        MyUserInfo.GetUserInfo()
```

```
      Catch cexcept As Exception

          MessageBox.Show(cexcept.ToString)

      End Try

   End Sub
```

This example should catch any errors that occur in this portion of your application. (Chapter 9 explains Forms in more detail.)

Unstructured Error Handling

Previous versions of Visual Basic relied completely on unstructured error handling using the **On Error** statement. This method of error handling came from the very old and, happily, nearly defunct, method of controlling the flow of a program using the **GoTo** statement. Program flow was improved when programming languages became more procedural and, later, object-oriented.

On Error

The **On Error** statement controls error handling by redirecting program flow to a line marked with a label, or to a specific line number. It can also be used to cause your application to ignore all errors, continuing to run while ignoring errors as they occur.

In the absence of error handling of any type, all errors that occur in your application are considered fatal and will completely stop program execution and display the fatal error message. It's preferred that you use structured error handling when writing new Visual Basic .NET applications. However, there are millions of Visual Basic applications that still rely on unstructured error handling, which, for the purposes of backward compatibility, have remained a part of Visual Basic .NET.

The ways to control program flow using unstructured error handling are listed in Table 10.1.

> **Note**
> Similar to the **On Error GoTo Label** statement, the Visual Basic .NET documentation also includes **On Error GoTo Line**, where the program flow jumps to a specified line number within the same procedure. But this command is rarely used because line numbers change so frequently that it is nearly impossible to make it work. And in creating an example for this statement I learned that this functionality, even though it appears in the documentation, does not appear to be supported in Visual Basic .NET. For both these reasons it has been excluded from this chapter.

Table 10.1   On Error Statements

On Error Statement	Description
On Error GoTo Label★	When an error occurs, the program flow continues at the label specified in the On Error statement.
On Error Resume Next	Program flow continues on the line following the one where the error occurred.
On Error GoTo 0	Enables system-level error handling. If an error occurs, the program halts and displays an error message.
On Error GoTo -1	Disables any enabled exceptions within the procedure, resetting them to nothing.

★See the following Note.

Because the **On Error** statement affects errors of all types, when using the **On Error** statement to handle exceptions, the **Err** object can be used to determine which error has occurred. You can refer to the **Err.Number** property to determine the specific error, or use the **Err.Description** property for a detailed description, as do the examples in this section.

Error handlers must reside in the same procedure where an error might occur. Because of this, when using the **On Error** statement to branch control to a line number or label, it's important to use one of the **Exit** statements before the line or label to keep the error handling code from executing each time. Use **Exit Sub**, **Exit Function**, or **Exit Property** statements to jump out of the procedure just before the error handler.

> **Note**
> Errors that occur within DLLs (Dynamic Linked Libraries) do not throw exceptions. The only way to know if an error has occurred within a DLL is to check the return value of each procedure called from the DLL or check the **LastDLLError** property of the **Err** object.

The **On Error Goto Label** sends the program flow to the line containing a label that matches the one specified in the **On Error** statement. Labels must start with a letter of the alphabet (not a number) and end with a colon (:). Labels must also start in the first column, meaning you can't indent them with white space or tabs.

```
Private Sub button1_Click(ByVal sender As System.Object,
ByVal e As System.EventArgs) Handles button1.Click

    On Error Goto Errorhandler

    Dim MyInt1, MyInt2, MyInt3 As Integer

    MyInt1 = 5
```

```
      MyInt2 = 0

      MyInt3 = MyInt1 \ MyInt2

      Exit Sub

   Errorhandler: Messagebox.Show(Err().Description)

End Sub
```

Occasionally you might want a behavior similar to the **Try** and **Catch** statements discussed earlier in this chapter. In other words, try to execute the code (for example, open a file) and don't do anything if an error is thrown (for example, if the file does not exist). Instead, continue on the line after the line that may or may not throw the error. In this case it would be prudent to test for the existence of the file handle before proceeding with any reads or writes, which would continue to throw errors if the file did not successfully open. The **On Error Resume Next** statement forces all error handling, by the system or within your code, to be ignored. The **On Error Resume Next** statement is like a switch. Once it has been run, error handling is ignored until a different **On Error** condition, such as **On Error Goto 0**, is reached.

On Error Goto 0 forces the system to catch all the errors. This is a little severe because every error after an **On Error Goto 0** statement is fatal, and will stop your application without the ability to resume execution. The application must be restarted, and hopefully, whatever caused the error in the first place is corrected. When using unstructured error handling, it's best to keep the application in the **On Error Goto 0** state when possible so that errors you have not specifically handled in your code are caught by the system, even though they will be fatal. Then, institute specific **On Error Goto Label** statements within each procedure.

Here's an example of using both **On Error Goto Label** and **On Error Goto 0**:

```
Private Sub button1_Click(ByVal sender As System.Object,
ByVal e As System.EventArgs) Handles button1.Click

    On Error Goto Errorhandler

    Dim MyInt1, MyInt2, MyInt3 As Integer

    MyInt1 = 5

    MyInt2 = 0

    MyInt3 = MyInt1 \ MyInt2
```

```
        On Error Goto 0

        console.Write("Error handling has been reset to 0.")

        Exit Sub

    Errorhandler:

        Messagebox.Show(Err().Description)

    End Sub
```

Notice in this example that any errors, such as our purposeful divide-by-zero error, that occur after the **On Error Goto Errorhandler** statement will jump to that label further in the code. This is true until the **On Error Goto 0** statement. If for some reason the system cannot write to the console window, the error handler will not be called, but rather the system will catch this error and stop the application, displaying an error message. Of course, you can have as many error-handling routines as needed, each with their own label, and you can redirect the error handling to different handlers as often as needed within your code.

The **On Error Resume Next** statement causes the error condition to be completely ignored, and also causes processing to continue on the next line of code. It's highly recommended that unless it makes no difference in your code if an error occurs that you do additional error checking when setting the **On Error** condition to **Resume Next**. Remember that setting the **On Error** condition is like flipping a switch. All errors will continue to be skipped until a new **On Error** condition is set.

On Error Goto −1 is not an attempt to redirect program flow to line negative one. In fact, if it were possible to have a line numbered negative one, this would still not redirect program flow there. This statement specifically takes an exception within a procedure and sets it to nothing. Here is an example:

```
Private Sub button1_Click(ByVal sender As System.Object,
  ByVal e As System.EventArgs) Handles button1.Click

    On Error Goto Errorhandler

    Dim MyInt1, MyInt2, MyInt3 As Integer

    MyInt1 = 5

    MyInt2 = 0
```

```
        MyInt3 = MyInt1 \ MyInt2

        On Error Goto -1

        console.Write("The exception has been set to nothing .")

        Exit Sub

    Errorhandler:

        If MyInt1 = 0 Then

            MyInt1 = 1

        End If

        If MyInt2 = 0 Then

            MyInt2 = 1

        End If

        MyInt3 = MyInt1 \ MyInt2

        Resume Next

    End Sub
```

Resume Statement

Error handlers occur at the end of a procedure, usually after some sort of **Exit** statement, separating them from the normal processing code of the procedure. To continue processing code after the error-handling code has done its thing, you will need a way to redirect the processing flow back to where the error occurred or to another point in the application. The **Resume** statement is used in error handlers to redirect program flow. In fact, trying to use **Resume** outside of an error handler will cause a related error.

Note
The **Resume** statement is only used in unstructured error handling. It's not possible to use **Resume** within a Try—Catch block.

Resume   Using **Resume** without any arguments will cause program flow to resume with the program statement that caused the error.

> **Warning**
> If you do nothing in the error-handling code to correct the error, the error will continue to occur, and your program will be caught in an endless loop between the offending line and error-handling code.

Here's an example:

```
Private Sub button1_Click(ByVal sender As System.Object,
ByVal e As System.EventArgs) Handles button1.Click

    On Error Goto Errorhandler

    Dim MyInt1, MyInt2, MyInt3 As Integer

    MyInt1 = 5

    MyInt2 = 0

    MyInt3 = MyInt1 \ MyInt2

    On Error Goto 0

    console.Write("Error handling has been reset to 0.")

    Exit Sub

Errorhandler:

    If MyInt1 = 0 Then

        MyInt1 = 1

    End If

    If MyInt2 = 0 Then

        MyInt2 = 1

    End If
```

```
        Messagebox.Show(Err().Description & vbCrLf & "Error
corrected. Zero value set to 1.")

        Resume

End Sub
```

In this example, the divide-by-zero error causes the program to branch to the error handler where the zero value is set to one. The resume statement forms another branch back to the line where the error first occurred, and this time the program runs successfully. The **On Error** condition is then set to 0, and a message is written to the console window.

Resume Next   **Resume Next** is similar to the **Resume** statement with no arguments except that it includes the keyword **Next**. Processing continues on the line following the line where an error occurred. What is significant about that is the fact that if you attempt a procedure, such as opening a file, it will not be reattempted unless you reattempt to open the file in the error-handling routine.

```
Private Sub button1_Click(ByVal sender As System.Object,
ByVal e As System.EventArgs) Handles button1.Click

    On Error Goto Errorhandler

    Dim MyInt1, MyInt2, MyInt3 As Integer

    MyInt1 = 5

    MyInt2 = 0

    MyInt3 = MyInt1 \ MyInt2

    On Error Goto 0

    console.Write("Error handling has been reset to 0.")

    Exit Sub

Errorhandler:

    If MyInt1 = 0 Then

        MyInt1 = 1
```

```
      End If

      If MyInt2 = 0 Then

          MyInt2 = 1

      End If

      MyInt3 = MyInt1 \ MyInt2

      'notice that the offending line was reattempted

      Resume Next

End Sub
```

Note
Visual Basic .NET does not support **Resume *line***, even though the documentation may say otherwise. It's never a good idea to specify a specific line number when programming anyway because of the dynamic nature of programming.

Debugging

It's a far better thing to debug than to error-handle. A well-behaved application should have to use its error-handling code a minimal amount. Of course, there are always errors beyond the control of the programmer, and these are the errors you want to catch. It's impossible to know when programming if a user will erase a file the application will try to open, or if an expected network connection is lost or nonexistent. Unfortunately, far too many bugs are not the result of the unforseen, but rather just faulty programming logic. For this reason, Visual Basic .NET has included some very powerful debugging tools.

Debug and Trace

The **Debug** and **Trace** classes allow you to print debug messages to a number of different output types as well as check logic using special statements known as *assertion statements*, or simply an **assert**. Even though the **Debug** and **Trace** classes are quite similar, there is an inherent difference between the two. **Debug** is used during development, and **Trace** can be used in your release versions to monitor the ongoing health of your application. The following sections explain these classes and the other helper classes used with them to provide information about your application's state as it is running.

Debug   Using methods of the **Debug** class will not increase the size of your release application. **Debug** statements are only included in the debug builds of your application, and completely ignored in release builds. If you use methods in the **Debug** class to print debugging information and check your logic with assertions, you can make your code more robust without impacting the performance and code size of your shipping product.

> **Note**
>
> Chapter 11 has information about creating debug and release builds of your application.

The **Debug** class provides methods to display an **Assert** message in either a dialog box or the output window of Visual Studio. The **Debug** class also provides the following **Write** methods:

Write – Writes debug output

WriteLine – Writes debug output and includes a carriage return line feed at the end of each debug message.

WriteIf – Writes a message based on a boolean condition.

WriteLineIf - Writes a message based on a boolean condition and ends the message with a carriage return line feed.

To turn on debugging in your application, add this flag to the compiler command line:

```
/d:DEBUG=True
```

Trace   Within the CLR **System.Diagnostics** namespace you will find the **Trace** class. This class not only allows you to debug programs using its shared methods, it monitors the health of the release builds of an application.

Similar to the **Debug** class, the **Write** methods of the **Trace** class write messages to a number of different output types, including the console window, a log file, or informational dialog windows.

The **Assert** method, covered in more detail later in this chapter, outputs a message when a specific condition is false.

Both the **Debug** and **Trace** classes output messages to objects in its **Listeners** collection. Each object in this collection is of a class that inherits from **System.Diagnostics.TraceListener** and are further described in the next section.

To turn on tracing in your application, add this flag to the compiler command line:

```
/d:Trace=True
```

Listeners   Listeners produce formatted output from the debug output. There are three types of **TraceListeners** built into Visual Basic .NET:

DefaultTraceListener – Writes to the OutputDebug string.

TextWriterTraceListener – Writes data to the TextWriter class, which has the ability to output character data.

EventLogTraceListener - The class provides the **EventLog** property to get or set the event log that receives the tracing or debugging output, and the **Name** property for the name of the **EventLogTraceListener.**

By default, the collection contains an instance of the **DefaultTraceListener** class.

The **TraceListenerCollection** is used to specify the output listeners for both the **Debug** and **Trace** classes. You can retrieve this collection using the **Listeners** property of both classes.

Here is code that will indicate what **TraceListeners** are active in your application using the **Listeners** property of the **Debug** class:

```
Private Sub button1 Click(ByVal sender As System.Object,
ByVal e As Syst,e.EventArgs) Handles button1.Click

    Dim mylisteners As TraceListenerCollection

    Dim listener As TraceListener

    mylisteners = debug.Listeners

    For Each listener In mylisteners

        console.Write("-" & listener.ToString)

    Next

End Sub
```

In this example, only a single listener was part of the collection and

```
--System.Diagnostics.DefaultTraceListener
```

was printed to the console window.

This next example moves away from using the default listener. We first use the **Clear** method of the **Trace.Listeners** class to clear all listeners. This keeps an application from doing the extra work of writing to more than one listener. Create a stream that is set to write to a text file that will act as a log file. Then, using the Add method, add a new **TextWriterTraceListener** to the collection. Using the **WriteLine** method of the **Trace** class, we send a string that is then handled by the **TextWriterTraceListener**. Be sure to use either the **Close** or **Flush** methods of the **Trace** class, perhaps in a **Finalize** block of a Try-Catch-Finalize block. This will ensure that any data in the trace buffer is written to the log file. In fact, in this next example, you won't see anything appear in the log file until the Trace is closed.

```
Private Sub button1_Click(ByVal sender As System.Object,
ByVal e As System.EventArgs) Handles button1.Click

    Trace.Listeners.Clear()

    Dim mystream As New IO.FileStream("c:\log.txt",
    IO.FileMode.Create, IO.FileAccess.Write)

    Trace.Listeners.Add(New
    TextWriterTraceListener(mystream))

    Trace.WriteLine("This is a test")

    Trace.Assert(False)

    Trace.Close()

End Sub
```

In this example, we could have used the **Remove** method rather than the **Clear** method. When removing many or an unknown number of listeners, it's easier to use **Clear**. When removing only the default listener, it may be easier to simply use the **Remove** method.

The **Debug** and **Trace** classes provide properties to get or set the **IndentLevel**, the **IndentSize** (default four spaces), and whether to **AutoFlush** after each write. You've already seen how important it is to flush the buffers to make certain that data is written to the output stream and not held in cache. This is even more important if you want to make every attempt possible to retrieve data if an application is about to crash. If it crashes before you've called the **Flush** method, you could be out of luck. So, the **AutoFlush** property makes certain that the data is written to the output stream after every write.

Further customize the output of your debug messages by setting the **AutoFlush** and **IndentSize** properties. You can set the **AutoFlush** and **IndentSize** by editing the configuration file that matches the name of your application. The configuration file should be formatted like this:

```
<configuration>
<system.diagnostics>
<debug AutoFlush="True" IndentSize="5" />
</system.diagnostics>
</configuration>
```

Assert   An assertion, in the English language, is a positive statement about something you believe to be true; something that is arguably true. In the Visual Basic .NET programming language it is the same. It's an expression you believe to be true. When the expression is not true, a failure message is generated.

Therefore, when using the **Assert** method of the **Debug** and **Trace** classes, a message will print only when the assertion fails. In this next example, you can see how the value of a variable is tested by the expression passed to the Assert method. Since **MyInt1** will never equal 4, the **Assert** will fail.

```
Private Sub button1_Click(ByVal sender As System.Object,
ByVal e As System.EventArgs) Handles button1.Click

    Dim MyInt1, MyInt2, MyInt3 As Integer

    MyInt1 = 5

    MyInt2 = 2

    MyInt3 = MyInt1 \ MyInt2

    Trace.Assert(MyInt1 = 4)

End Sub
```

Here is the message that prints when the assertion in the previous code fails.

```
---- ASSERTION FAILED ----
---- Short Message


---- Long Message
```

```
        at Form1.button1_Click(Object sender, EventArgs e)
C:\Documents and Settings\Administrator\My Documents\Visual
Studio Projects\WindowsApplication30\Form1.vb(48)
    at Control.OnClick(EventArgs e)
    at Button.OnClick(EventArgs e)
    at Button.OnMouseUp(MouseEventArgs mevent)
    at Control.WmMouseUp(Message& m, MouseButtons button)
    at Control.WndProc(Message& m)
    at ButtonBase.WndProc(Message& m)
    at Button.WndProc(Message& m)
    at     System.Windows.Forms.Control+ControlNativeWindow.
    OnMessage(Message& m)
        at System.Windows.Forms.Control+ControlNativeWindow.
WndProc(Message& m)
        at NativeWindow.DebuggableCallback(IntPtr hWnd, Int32
msg, IntPtr wparam, IntPtr lparam)
        at UnsafeNativeMethods.DispatchMessageW(System.Windows.
Forms.NativeMethods+MSG& msg)
        at System.Windows.Forms.Application+ComponentManager.
System.Windows.Forms.UnsafeNativeMethods+IMso ComponentManag-
er.FPushMessageLoop(Int32 dwComponentID, Int32 reason, Int32
pvLoopData)
        at System.Windows.Forms.Application+ThreadContext. Run-
MessageLoop(Int32 reason, ApplicationContext context)
    at Application.Run(Form mainForm)
    at Form1.Main()
```

BooleanSwitch and TraceSwitch   The **BooleanSwitch** and **TraceSwitch** classes provide means to dynamically control the trace and debug output. The **BooleanSwitch** is an on/off switch depending on whether the switch is enabled or not, and the **TraceSwitch** is multilevel and responds based on the trace levels that are set. One of the benefits of using **TraceSwitch** is that you can change the values of the multilevel switch at runtime without recompiling your application.

You can set the switch level by using:

- A registry setting
- An environment variable
- A setting within your application code

Table 10.2   Trace Level Enumeration

Enumeration	Description of Trace and Debug level
Error	Error messages only
Info	Informational messages, warnings, and error messages
Off	Does not output messages
Verbose	Any debug and trace message
Warning	Warnings and error messages only

You can set the value of the switch within a configuration file by adding these lines:

```
<Switches>

<add name="myNewSwitch" value="20" />

</Switches>
```

Table 10.2 lists the different trace and debug levels. When no initial value is set, the default trace and debug level is set to Off, turning off all debug and trace messages.

Here is an example that shows how **TraceSwitch** can be used to selectively display certain error messages. This example will not work unless you have set the trace levels using a configuration file or environment variable.

```
Private Sub button1_Click(ByVal sender As System.Object,
ByVal e As System.EventArgs) Handles button1.Click

    Dim resultstring As String

    resultstring = myTestMethod()

    console.Write(resultstring)

End Sub


Function myTestMethod() As String

    Dim MySwitch As New TraceSwitch("MyDisplayName",
"Description of Switch")
```

```
    Dim MyException As ArgumentException

    Try

        Throw MyException

    Catch cexcept As Exception

        MessageBox.Show(cexcept.Message)

    End Try

    If MySwitch.TraceError Then

        Return "Error message."

    End If

    If MySwitch.TraceVerbose Then

        Return "Verbose message."

    End If

End Function
```

Logging

So far in this chapter you've seen how to create custom log files using **Trace** and **Debug**. It's not necessary to reinvent the wheel. Windows already maintains a number of log files with which your application can interact. The **EventLog** class allows your application to interact with the Windows event logs.

The **EventLog** class gives you quite a bit of functionality over log files, including:

- Reading from existing log files
- Writing to log files
- Creating or deleting event sources
- Deleting logs
- The ability to respond to specific log entries
- Create new log files when creating an event source

To create an array that contains a list of all the event logs, use the **EventLog. GetEventLogs** method. You can loop through this array, or to determine if a source exists, you can use the **Exists** method, which returns True if the log already exists. By default, there are three log files on most computers running as servers:

Application – Used by applications and services. Your application will most likely use this log.

System – Device drives use the system log file.

Security – This is where logon and security access audit events are stored.

Don't be surprised if your computer has more log files installed. For example, if your server is running as a DNS server, it will likely also have a DNS server log. Here is a sample application that will allow you to view which logs have been installed by viewing them in the console window.

```
Private Sub button1_Click(ByVal sender As System.Object,
ByVal e As System.EventArgs) Handles button1.Click

    Dim myLog As New EventLog()

    Dim loglist As Array

    Dim logname As EventLog

    loglist = myLog.GetEventLogs

    For Each logname In loglist

        console.Write(logname.Log.ToString & vbCrLf)

    Next

End Sub
```

Writing to Logs

Your application can write to existing logs by setting the value of the **Log** property to the name of the log. In the last section, you learned to find out the names of all existing logs by iterating through the list returned by the **GetEventLogs** method. Once you know the name of the log you would like to write to, set the **Log** property as shown in the following example. Then, use the **WriteEntry** method to write to the log. There is no need to flush a buffer as you may have done when tracing or debugging. The **LogEntry** class does not have a **Flush** method. All entries are immediately written to the log file.

Before you can write to the log you will need to specify the source by adding it to the Source property. This is required and is usually the name of the application or individual procedure. The actual entry can be any string. This might be the text of an exception, or simply an entry of some importance you want noted in the log.

Warning
To keep the size of the log file to a minimum, try to keep the number of messages to a minimum. You might consider setting a level of logging in your application, such as a debug level or release level, and write detailed information to the log while in debug mode and minimal log entries in release mode.

```
Private Sub button1_Click(ByVal sender As System.Object,
ByVal e As System.EventArgs) Handles button1.Click

    Dim myLog As New EventLog()

    myLog.Log = "Application"

    myLog.Source = "This application"

    myLog.WriteEntry("Visual Basic .NET is cool.")

End Sub
```

Reading from Logs

You can read a log and access the messages written to the log and either print or act on the entries based on the event's **Message**, **Category**, **TimeWritten**, and **EntryType**. Here is an example that simply writes all the messages in the Application log to the console window. Notice in this example that you need an **EventLogEntryCollection** object to hold the collection of messages stored in the log. Store all the log entries into the new collection object by assigning the value of the **Entries** property into it. Now you can do what you would normally do with any collection. You can further filter the collection, search it, or iterate through it as this example does using a For Each loop:

```
Private Sub button1_Click(ByVal sender As System.Object,
ByVal e As System.EventArgs) Handles button1.Click

    Dim myLog As New EventLog()
```

```
    Dim myLogEntryCollection As EventLogEntryCollection

    Dim myLogEntry As EventLogEntry

    myLog.Log = "Application"

    myLogEntryCollection = myLog.Entries()

    For Each myLogEntry In myLogEntryCollection

        console.Write(myLogEntry.Message)

        console.Write(vbCrLf)

    Next

End Sub
```

In this example you might notice that it is not necessary to specify a source when only reading from a log file. The source is only important when writing to a log file. If you are reading logs from a remote computer you will have to specify the MachineName of the remote computer, otherwise your local computer is accessed by default.

Custom Logs

In addition to using the logs already set up on your computer, you can create custom log files on both local and remote computers. Of course, remote computers must be accessible over a network. Creating a custom log can help you maintain information specific to your application. You can also reset the log without resetting the contents of a system or application log.

> **Note**
> When creating new logs, the file names are limited to only eight characters.

When you create a custom log, the method is similar to writing to an existing log file, such as the Application log. You must enter values in both the Log property as well as the Source property. A source can only be registered to one log at a time. When the **Source** property is set for an instance of EventLog, you can't modify the **Log** property for that **EventLog** without changing the value of **Source**. You can also call DeleteEventSource. If you try to modify the **Log** property once the **Source** property has been set, your application will throw an exception.

Creating a New Source   You may need to create a new source for your log. If you are changing sources for an existing log, remember to remove the existing source by first using the **DeleteEventSource** method. Then create a new event source using the **CreateEventSource** method.

This example first checks for the existence of the event source "MySource," and when it doesn't exist uses the **CreateEventSource** method of **EventLog** to create a new event source. Then, a new **EventLog** object is created and its source is set to the new Source.

```
Private Sub button1_Click(ByVal sender As System.Object,
ByVal e As System.EventArgs) Handles button1.Click

    'Create a new event source

    If Not EventLog.SourceExists("MySource",
"MyMachineName") Then

        EventLog.CreateEventSource("MySource", "MyNewLog")

        Console.WriteLine("CreatingEventSource")

    End If

    'Create a new eventlog and set the source to the new
source

    Dim myLog As New EventLog()

    myLog.Source = "MySource"

    myLog.WriteEntry("EventLog Message.")

End Sub
```

Summary

Error and exception handling are often the most overlooked and least understood parts of programming, and yet remain equally as important all other types of application logic, such as the user interface, decision logic, and database access.

Visual Basic .NET now has the ability to include structured exception handling using Try Catch Finally blocks. This structured method of exception handling is far superior to the older, unstructured method using the Visual Basic On Error mechanism, which is still included for backward compatibility. If at all possible try to replace unstructured exception handling, and in new development attempt to use only structured exception handling.

Because no one is perfect, and not every error throws an exception, good debugging is important. The **Debug** class adds powerful debugging abilities to your application without adding overhead in release versions. Similar to **Debug** is the **Trace** class, which is active in release builds and can monitor the continued operations of your application. Both classes have powerful abilities to handle debug and trace messages, including the ability to write custom handlers. It's even possible to have remote applications send you real-time trace messages over the Internet.

Logging is included in this chapter because it is often the last-resort tool for debugging an application. The logging abilities include both the ability to manipulate the logs already active on your computer as well as create new logs.

Some of the compile options important to debugging, logging, and tracing will be covered in the next chapter, where compiling a Visual Basic program is covered in detail. In Chapter 11 you will learn how to create debug and release builds of your well-structured application. One final recommendation: Even though it's beyond the scope of this book to go into more detail about all the tools included with Visual Studio, for even more information about your runtime applications, consider using Visual Studio Analyzer. This application creates a profile of your running application on one or many computers, and analyzes the overall performance of your application. Unlike debuggers or low-level analyzers, this application will provide you with a high-level set of reports about the performance of your application.

Part II

The .NET Framework

The first half of this book dealt with programming basics and the principles of object orientation. This next section allows you to use that knowledge while building applications using the .NET Framework of classes.

We begin this second part with a detailed explanation of building user interfaces with the myriad of built-in controls. The controls are located in the System.Windows.Forms namespace, and because of the object-oriented abilities now built into Visual Basic .NET, you can customize these controls or create your own custom controls.

Because most applications use data, Chapter 13 gives you a good primer on accessing data within a database using the .NET Framework classes. A foundational technology, XML is used in objects that manage data. You can also use the classes in the System.XML namespace to manage XML sent to you, create new XML files and schemas, and use data in XML format as the input for data-bound controls.

A new ability in Visual Basic .NET is creating Windows Services applications (Chapter 16). Included in the .NET Framework are classes that allow you to simply build a Windows Service, or manage the services that already exist. Building network applications (Chapter 18) is another new ability of Visual Basic .NET. Classes allow you to build low-level protocol-handling applications, right down to the socket level.

Building components has long been a popular feature of Visual Basic. You can now build and deploy components built upon managed code. Also included are classes that help you manage licensing of your commercial components.

Today's applications rely heavily on the ability to manage graphics. The System.Drawing namespace contains classes that allow you to create and manipulate bitmap files, icons, and other types of graphic information.

This part concludes with a chapter on directory services and the ability to manage data and perform system administration in active directories, as well as use LDAP and NDS as data repositories. When you're finished with this section you will have a good foundation in the fundamentals of the .NET Framework, and how to build applications using this framework of classes. The Framework is not guaranteed not to change. In fact, it may have changed by the time you have purchased this book. You will still be able to apply the fundamentals in this book to any changes within the framework, however.

Have fun!

Building and Deploying Applications 11

The Visual Basic programming language has come a long way since the days when it was an interpreted language, not unlike many of today's scripting languages. Visual Basic applications can be compiled and released as standalone executable applications. This chapter covers compiling an application into executable code and then deploying an application.

Compiler Directives

The Visual Basic .NET compiler pays attention to special directives (instructions) when compiling an application. These instructions are only paid attention to by the compiler and affect the completely compiled application. Once compiled, an application no longer sees these directives. Their job is done.

#Const

Chapter 2 explains the use of constants and how they are replaced with literals at compile time. The **#Const** is similar to using standard Visual Basic .NET constants, with one exception. **#Const** statement is used to create constants as part of conditional compilation. In other words, rather than replacing a value that is used in the application at runtime, it's a value that is replaced and used only at compile time.

To create a conditional constant, use the compiler directive **#** symbol followed by the word **Const** with no spaces. You must include the name of the constant followed by the value as a literal value or expression, compiler constants previously defined, math expressions, or logical operators, except for the **Is** operator.

```
#Const constant_name = expression
```

There are normally restrictions when creating a **Const**, but creating a **#Const** is even more restrictive. Here are some of the restrictions:

Constants are private to the module you are building. There is no such thing as a global constant.

233

Only conditional compiler constants and literals can be used in creating the *expression*. You cannot use standard Visual Basic .NET constants in creating the *expression*.

Constants defined using the compiler directive # symbol can only be used during conditional compilation. They are ignored during runtime. A good example of how and why you might use **#Const** is when keeping several versions of the same code to do the same thing, each slightly different. For example, you can do versioning in your application by maintaining several versions in the same source code and defining an **Application Version** constant, as shown below:

```
#Const ApplicationVersion = 2
```

Define constants at the beginning of the module or procedure. With this constant defined you can use conditional compiler directives, covered later in this chapter, to selectively compile different blocks of code in your application. Here is an example we'll discuss in more detail in the next section:

```
Private Sub button1_Click(ByVal sender As System.Object,
ByVal e As System.EventArgs) Handles button1.Click

#If ApplicationVersion = 2 Then

    messagebox.Show("Welcome to Version 2")

#ElseIf ApplicationVersion = 1 Then

    Messagebox.Show("Welcome to Version 1")

#End If

End Sub
```

You can define compiler constants for any number of things. Another common reason for using a compiler constant is to compile certain blocks of code, depending on the platform for which you are compiling the application.

#If

In the last section you saw how to use compiler constants together with conditional compiler directives. Similar to the standard **If** statement, you can tell the compiler which blocks of code to include or exclude when compiling. Precede the **If**, **ElseIf**, **Else**, and **End If** statements with a # sign, like this:

```
#If expression Then
```

```
#ElseIf expression Then

#Else

#End If
```

The expression in a compiler directive cannot contain variables. Remember that variables only contain values at runtime. Therefore, variables are useless at compile time. Instead, the expression can contain literal values such as numbers:

```
#Const ApplicationVersion = 5

Private Sub button1_Click(ByVal sender As System.Object,
ByVal e As System.EventArgs) Handles button1.Click

#If ApplicationVersion = < 5 Then

    messagebox.Show("Welcome to the old version.")

#ElseIf ApplicationVersion = 5 Then

    Messagebox.Show("Welcome to the current version.")

#End If

End Sub
```

Or, you can evaluate based on other variable types. Here is an example that compiles certain blocks of code based on the platform, and uses the String variable type:

```
#Const PlatformType = "DOTNET"

Private Sub button1_Click(ByVal sender As System.Object,
ByVal e As System.EventArgs) Handles button1.Click

#If PlatformType = "DOTNET" Then

    messagebox.Show("Common Language Runtime
compilation.")

#ElseIf PlatformType = "Win32" Then

    Messagebox.Show("Win32 PC compilation")
```

```
#End If

End Sub
```

#Region

The **#Region** directive is used to make programming in the Visual Studio environment simpler by allowing you to define regions of code.

Using the Visual Studio.NET Outline mode, you can expand and collapse certain blocks or regions of code. Chapter 1 contains more information on Outlining code. Creating regions is particularly useful when including blocks of code that are being reused, have been debugged, or should not be modified. Here is the syntax of the **#Region** directive.

```
#Region [nodebug] "Identifier"
```

The **nodebug** keyword is optional, but can be used to have the debugger skip certain blocks of code when running the application in debug mode. This will speed up the performance of an application running in debug mode. Once again, when including code that has already been debugged, there is no reason to make the debugger do extra work by debugging it again.

The identifier is any string that identifies the block of code. For example, you'll notice that Visual Studio, when creating a new Windows application, creates a region for the Form.

One restriction in using the **#Region—#End Region** directive is that it must start and end in a single block of code defined using the **#If—#End If** directives.

Building an Application

Building an application launches the Visual Basic .NET compiler and, based on the build configuration, compiles the application into an executable file. The executable file, once created, is stored in the **bin** folder of your project's folder, on your hard drive.

You can manage the build process of your application by modifying the properties found in the Configuration Manager. There are three ways to access the Configuration Manager dialog window.

- The Build menu
- The Solution Property Pages dialog window
- The Configuration Manager drop down in the main toolbar.

Select Configuration Manager from the Build menu selection. This launches the Configuration Manager window, as shown in Figure 11.1. On the Configuration Manager

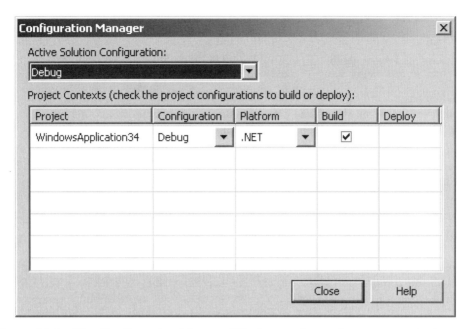

Figure 11.1   The Configuration Manager Window can be used to manage solution build configurations.

window you'll see a drop down, labeled **Active Solution Configuration**, which lists the available build types, such as Debug and Release.

Selecting the **Debug** build will cause your application to send debug messages according to the debug configuration you have created for your application. Chapter 10 covers configuring your **Debug** configuration within your code.

Selecting the **Release** build will exclude any **Debug** information, although **Trace** will still be active so you can monitor your application's continued performance. You can select either of these two standard build types or create new build types, such as a QA (Quality Assurance) build.

Create a new solution configuration by selecting <New…> from the Active Solution Configuration drop down. In the New Solution Configuration dialog, enter a new Solution Configuration Name. Also specify what build type you want to use as the template of your new configuration, and then specify whether you want Visual Studio to create a new project configuration by selecting or deselecting the checkbox.

Creating a new solution configuration causes Visual Studio to determine default project configurations for the project it will build from the project type you specify. New projects built using this configuration will be named to match the configuration, and any platform specified like this:

```
<custom configuration name> <platform name>
```

When you create a project configuration and select Also create new project configuration(s), Visual Studio matches a solution build configuration for each platform.

Visual Studio assigns solution build configurations by determining:

When project configurations omit a platform or specify a single platform, the solution build configuration whose name matches that of the new project configuration will be found or added. The new configuration will not include a platform name.

When a project supports more than one platform, a build configuration is found or added for each project configuration on each platform. The name of each solution build configuration will include both the project configuration name and the platform name, as shown above.

Configuring Builds

Configuring a build requires that you select the components that will be built or deployed from all the components in the project, and select how they will be built. You can also configure builds to run on specific platforms. There are two types of build configurations in Visual Studio: Solution Level Build and Project Level Build.

In the Solution Explorer you can right-click on each resource and choose to exclude it from the project, or choose to edit Properties. The properties in the Solution Explorer include:

- Build Action
- Custom Tool
- Custom Tool Namespace
- File Name
- Full Path

Of concern to us here is the Build Action property. Click the drop down next to this property and you'll see that the build actions include None, Compile, Content, and Embedded Source. By default, project files will be set to Compile. To exclude a file from compilation, you can set its build action to None.

Solution Configuration

There is a special naming convention for Solution Builds maintained by the IDE. The naming convention includes the Project Configuration Name, and is optionally followed by the Platform Name. The Platform Name is omitted when all builds are for the same platform.

```
<Project Configuration Name><Platform Name>
```

Selecting a build configuration also affects the IDE. The toolbars will update, depending on what type of application is being built.

Project Configuration

To configure your application's project, launch the Project Property Pages dialog window. This window will allow you to view and edit both the Common and Configuration properties for your project. To launch the Project Property Pages dialog, right-click on the name of the project in the Solution Explorer window and select **Properties** from the pop-up menu. In this dialog you can set both Common properties and Configuration properties. The properties in the Common categories include:

- General
- Build
- Imports
- Reference Path
- Sharing
- Designer Defaults

The Configuration properties include:

- Debugging
- Optimizations
- Build

The following sections cover these properties in more detail.

Common Properties   In the Project Property Pages dialog window (Figure 11.2) you can set many types of properties. Beginning with the General properties, you can set the:

Assembly Name – This is the name of the final executable file. Notice that changing this value changes the information printed beneath the entry boxes on this dialog.

Output Type – Choose between Windows Application, Console Application, and Class Library.

Startup object – This identifies the object first called when the application starts. For most Windows applications this will be the startup Form.

Root Namespace – This identifies the root namespace for this application.

In the Build properties you can change your application's icon. Notice that the default icon is the same as that for Visual Studio. Also, on the Build properties page, you can specify the three compiler options: **Explicit**, **Strict**, and **Compare**. These are the same settings you can place at the beginning of a module in your source code.

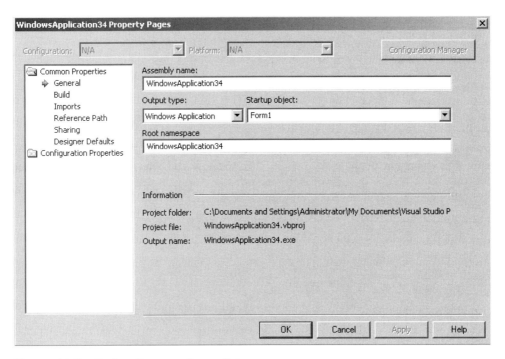

Figure 11.2 Project Property Pages dialog.

In the Imports properties page you can specify which files are imported into your application. Specify new import files or remove those listed in the Project Imports section.

Note
Don't be afraid to remove portions of the Common Language Runtime that you are not using. If you don't need to import these classes, then don't. They don't shave off a great deal of size, but every little bit helps when creating efficient release applications.

Set the Reference path to any folder containing parts of your application on the Reference Path properties page. These folders will be searched at compile time.

In the Sharing properties page you can choose to generate a shared name. This security measure makes certain that the code cannot be modified or accessed by hackers. Shared assemblies use public key cryptography to sign the compiled project. The originator field contains the public key, while the assembly is encrypted with the corresponding private key.

Note
Generate a key pair using the external program SN.EXE. This program can be run from the command line of your operating system's Command window.

Also on the Sharing properties page is the Key container field. This field provides access to the crypto key container, which is a database installed by the Common Language Runtime.

The Designer Defaults are properties for setting up Web projects. They configure the page layout, target schema, client-side scripting language, session state setting, and server-side scripting language.

Configuration Properties   The Configuration Properties of the project allow you to modify how your application is built. The Property types include:

Debugging Properties – Sets values that affect how your application interacts with the debugger.

Optimizations Properties – Sets properties that affect the performance of your application.

Build Properties – Sets values that create specific types of builds.

Modifying each of these properties will change the way your application outputs debugging information and the overall performance of your application.

Setting the Debugging Properties   Chapter 10 explained the output from an application in debug mode in some detail. Before your application can output that information, it must be set to create a *Debug Build*, a build that outputs debug information, and is usually not intended for final release. Remember that outputting debug information will impact the performance of your application.

When you configure a Debug Build, you specify additional actions that are taken when the application is run. Begin setting these actions with the Start action. This property identifies what you want to start when you run your application in Debug mode. You can start:

- The project – Your application. This is the default setting.
- Custom Program – You may want to run an external debugger or some other application when in Debug mode.
- URL – This selection will launch a URL in your Web browser when this debug project starts.
- None – Nothing is started when the application is in debug mode.

You can set command-line arguments that feed information into your application on startup. This is useful when setting default values to test your application. For example, some applications may read system information. This system information could be correct for some computers, but not all, and passing the system information as a command-line argument allows you to test your application for more than one environment.

Set the Working directory your application will use when it first starts up. The default is the working directory of your Visual Studio project. You may choose to create a special directory for your Debug projects, and this allows you to specify which directory to use when running the application.

When you've specified a URL as the startup type, the Web browser you've declared to your system will launch. It's common for many developers to have more than one Web browser type installed to debug Web applications using more than one browser because of display and scripting incompatibilities. You can ask the debugger to always launch Internet Explorer when launching your application.

When your application involves Active Server Pages scripting, you may want the debugger to allow script debugging. You can specify whether your Web project is debugged as an ASP.NET application or standard ASP application.

If your application makes use of unmanaged code, such as calls to COM and ActiveX objects, you can choose to have this code debugged along with the managed code in your Visual Basic .NET application.

Setting the Optimization Properties   Optimization properties affect the performance of your application as it runs. Visual Basic .NET has two application optimization properties. The first allows you to set whether or not your applicatoin checks for integer overflows (when the value of an integer exceeds the limit for integers). Setting **Remove integer overflow checks** will increase the performance of your application.

One of the checkboxes on this property page enables or disables optimization in your application. When creating DLL applications you can also set the default memory address the DLL will load into. To set this, enter a Base Address in hexadecimal form.

Build Properties   The Build properties allow you to configure the output path of your application and several other features related to debugging and tracing of your application.

- Output path – The folder where all output from a project is directed. This is set to the /Bin folder beneath your root project folder. You can modify this property to point to any valid folder on your computer or use file names and UNC-paths for client-based projects.

- Generate debugging information – Checking this box lets your application know whether it should output debug information. In debug builds this must be checked.

- Warnings – You can specify whether the build warnings are enabled by checking the checkbox in this section.

- Treat warnings as errors – When build warnings are enabled you can also tell Visual Studio to treat warnings as errors. When warnings are treated as errors, compilation will not result in a build.

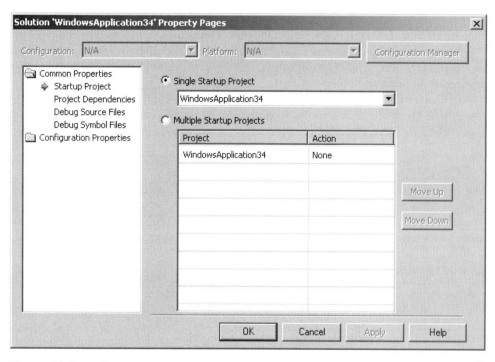

Figure 11.3   Solution Property Pages dialog.

- Conditional compilation constants – This section allows you to set the debug and trace constants that affect whether debugging and tracing are part of your build.
- Define DEBUG constant – Checking this check box sets the DEBUG constant equal to 1. This will enable debugging in the application.
- Define TRACE constant – Checking this check box sets the Trace value to 1, enabling tracing in your application.
- Custom constants – In this text box you can define new, custom constants to be used during compilation. Chapter 10 discusses these constants in more detail. Rather than defining them directly in your code, you can define them here, in this text box.

The Common Properties include:

- Startup Project
- Project Dependencies
- Debug Source Files
- Debug Symbol Files

The configuration properties, available by expanding the folder of the same name, are identical to those found in the Solution Property Pages dialog window (see Figure 11.3).

In the Startup Project properties you can specify whether there is a single or multiple startup projects, and what they are. You can also specify a build action. The build actions include None, Start, and Start without Debugging.

The Project Dependencies list any dependencies. This configuration item cannot be edited here. The Debug Source Files property allows you to specify the paths to search for source files. The Debug Symbol Files property lets you specify paths to any symbol files.

Configuration Files

Configuration files are used in Web applications and allow you to store dynamic values (*dynamic properties*) that your application may need to load at runtime. It's not always possible to know every single value while you're designing an application, and you may want the behavior of your application to change based on values stored in a configuration file. Some of the uses for configuration files are:

- Set business rules, such as tax percentages, which change on a regular basis.
- Set user information: nonprivate information such as user name and preferences, can be stored in a configuration file.
- Set administrative policies and computer configuration values.

The format of a configuration file is based on the XML standard (eXtended Markup Language). For more information on XML, you can refer to Chapter 14. In a nutshell, XML labels values with markup tags, similar to tags used in a Web page to format the page.

Tags are enclosed within parentheses and are followed by values or more embedded XML tags. Here is an example of setting the level of tracing in your application:

```
<configuration>

<system.diagnostics>

<switches>

<add name="myTraceSwitch" value="10" />

<add name="AnotherSwitch" value="20" />

</switches>

</system.diagnostics>

</configuration>
```

Notice that XML tags have begin and end tags, the end tag starting with a backslash (/) denoting an end to the information begun by a matching named tag. All configuration files begin with a <configuration> tag and end with a </configuration>, as shown in the previous example. This is known as the root tag. Notice also in this last example that you can set values specific to certain classes, such as the system.diagnostics class.

There are certain requirements when creating a configuration file. First, the configuration file must reside in the same folder as the application. Second, the filename of the application must match the name of the executable file and carry the **.config** file extension. Also, configuration files may only be used for applications that compile into an executable file. You cannot use configuration files for DLL projects. The exception to this is Web applications, which use a Web.config file.

To create custom values to be stored within your application, place them in an application root setting such as this:

```
<appsettings>

</appsettings>
```

To add keys (name–value pairs), use the add key tag like this:

```
<appsettings>

    <add key="myobject.configurablevalue" value="my
    value"/>

</appsettings>
```

This dynamic value is set in a special section reserved for application settings. You can create your own custom settings areas like this:

```
<configuration>

<buttonsettings>

    <add key="buttontext" value="my test button"/>

</buttonsettings>

</configuration>
```

Notice that all values in a configuration file are stored as strings. To use a value of a different data type you will have to convert the value from a string after you've retrieved it from the configuration file.

Summary

Preparing your application for compilation into executable form is an important part of developing applications. This chapter has covered the concepts of compiler directives, allowing you to compile only parts of an application, as well as creating Debug and Release applications. You can also build configuration files that allow your application to load dynamic properties at runtime.

Chapter 12 picks up where Chapter 9 left off, demonstrating how to use the power of the controls built into Visual Basic .NET as well as create your own custom controls.

Building the Windows User Interface

12

The application user interface is an audio–visual environment, often a multimedia environment, for interacting with human beings. I understand there is now software for pets, but for the most part, you're designing software for humans. User interfaces, once simply text on a monochrome screen, are now composed of powerful, visual, graphic controls.

In Chapter 9 we began introducing the user interface with the form control. You can think of the form as the canvas upon which you can create masterpieces. Creating a good user interface is an art or a science, depending on whom you are talking with. This chapter will introduce some of the many controls available to you, and how you can use them to interact with the end user.

Your creativity does not have to be stunted by a limited number of controls. Thanks to object orientation, you can inherit from any control to create new, custom controls. But, before launching into creating new forms, let's begin by taking a look at the classes within the WinForms namespace.

Controls

The **System.WinForms** namespace contains many classes you can use to create rich user interfaces for your Windows-based application. Each class defines a control designed for a different type of user interaction. Some interactions are as simple as clicking a button, while others have more complex listing, selection, and editing capabilities. This section will cover the abilities, properties, and uses of many of the classes in the WinForms namespace. Some classes, such as those used in database interactions, are covered in other chapters of this book. Those covered in this chapter will allow you to build most complete user interfaces.

Before launching into all the controls, it's a good idea to familiarize yourself with the **Control** class, the class that forms the foundation of all controls, including the form. The **Control** class is part of the **WinForms** namespace and is derived from the **Component** class.

The **Control** class is very involved, with class members that include:

- Static properties that set the color scheme, modifier key (Ctrl, Shift, and Alt) status, and mouse position and state.
- Static methods that manage control handles and determine whether a character is a mnemonic character, a character that follows the first instance of "&" in a string.
- Public instance properties that handle accessibility features, drag and drop, manage the collection of controls, and determine the state of the control, such as focus and enabled, name, size, and position of the control.
- Public instance methods that create the control, manage its window order and visibility, and refresh, update, and reset the control.
- Protected properties and methods that manage the internal workings of the control and raise events.
- Public instance events that are raised and can be handled within your code. This class is rich in events due to the many possible ways a user might interact with a control. They include mouse events, including drag-drop events, change of status, and appearance events.

A good many of the controls derive most of their properties, methods, and events from the **Control** class. For this reason, when discussing controls in the rest of this chapter, the information on members of the **Control** class won't be repeated. However, in the section on creating custom controls, these members will be discussed in greater detail.

Control Navigation

Users must have a way to navigate through the controls on a **Form**. Most Windows users now know that hitting the Enter key after entering data in a control will attempt to trigger the click event of the default mouse button (explained in detail in the next section). Most users will move to the next control by clicking on that control with their mouse, giving *focus* to the control. When a control has focus, all user interface events will be triggered by that control.

One set of properties common to all controls is the **TabStop**. When the **UseTabStops** property is enabled for controls, the user is allowed to use the Tab key on the keyboard to move from control to control. You can control the order and to which controls the user can Tab by setting the **TabStop** property (True or False) and the **TabIndex**, an integer specifying the Tab order.

Button

The button first and foremost in any user interface is a powerful, two-position control. It's two-position because the button is either in an up or down state. There are two classes within the **WinForms** namespace, **Button** and **Buttonbase**.

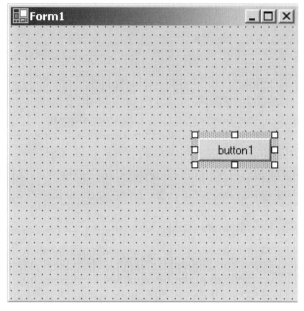

Figure 12.1   Typical Windows **Button** on a **Form**.

An instance of the **Button** class is a typical Windows button (Figure 12.1).

The simplest way to begin using buttons on your **Form** is to select the **Button** from the Visual Studio Toolbox window. Clicking the **Button** on the Toolbox window and then clicking on your **Form** will place the **Button** on the **Form**. At the same time, the code necessary to create a **Button** object is automatically integrated into the **Form** class.

Double-clicking on the **Button** will create the code necessary to create a procedure to handle the click event of the **Button**. There are many **Button** events, but the click event is the default and most often used event of the **Button**. This occurs when someone has clicked and released their mouse over a **Button** object.

You are not restricted to creating **Buttons** using Visual Studio's Form Designer. You can create **Buttons** on the Form by modifying the **Form**'s code in a similar manner to how the Designer adds the code. Refer to Chapter 9 for more in**Form**ation about Form development. You can also create your own custom **Buttons** by inheriting from the **Button** class.

To create an instance of the **Button** class, simply create a new class and inherit from **Button**. Because the Button class's constructor does not accept parameters, you will not have to worry about specifying arguments when creating a new instance of the **Button** class, either when creating a new **Button**, or when dealing with a class derived from **Button**.

```
Class myButton

    Inherits Button

End Class
```

Properties of the Button class not inherited already from the control class include:

- Flatstyle – Sets or Gets the appearance style of the **Button** (Flat or 3D). This member is inherited from the **ButtonBase** class, mentioned earlier in this section.
- Image – The image displayed on the control.
- ImageAlign – The alignment of the image displayed on the control.
- ImageIndex – Sets the image list index value of the image being displayed on the control.
- ImageList – A collection of image objects for display on the control.
- TextAlign – The alignment of text on the control.

All the public instance methods of the **Button** class are derived from the **Object**, **MarshalByRefObject,** and **Control** classes. The public instance events are all inherited from Control except the Disposed method, which is derived from the **Component** class.

- Protected Instance properties (inherited from the ButtonBase class) include:
- CreateParams – Creates parameters.
- DefaultSize – The default size.
- IsDefault – Boolean, True if default.

All of the protected instance methods are derived from either the **Object** or **Control** classes.

Using Buttons   Buttons, for the most part, are used with the click events to run code whenever the event is triggered. They are generally not used as a data-entry type of control, although that purpose is not out of the question. For **Buttons** used as data-entry controls, see the section on **CheckBox** controls. The **Text** property of the **Button** is used to display a text value. This can be anything from "Go" to "Click here to enter the value specified." Of course, the size of the **Button** must be large enough to accept the size of the Text property. You can dynamically change the value of the **Text** property. This is convenient if you want your **Button** to display a different message based on other control properties on the **Form**.

Buttons often make use of the **Enabled** property. Quite often, **Buttons** will remain on the Form with their **Enabled** properties set to False. The **Button** then appears light gray, and will not animate when clicked. In this state, the **Clicked** event of the **Button** will not be triggered if a user clicks their mouse on the **Button**. Dynamically setting the **Enabled** property to True is done when all required fields on the **Form** have been entered. This is a simple way to keep users from updating a Form before required values have been entered.

The **IsDefault** property is set to True when a **Button** is considered to be the "default" **Button** on the **Form**. In other words, when the end-user hits the Enter key, the **clicked** event of the default **Button** will be triggered without using a mouse. It's not required that any **Buttons** on your Form be considered the default **Buttons**. But, when you do have a default **Button**, only one **Button** can be the default. The **IsDefault** property is commonly used when there are **OK** and **Cancel Buttons** on a **Form**. Depending on your preference, either **Button** can be set as the default. But, normally, the **OK Button** is set as the default. When a **Button** is set as the default, the **Button** graphic normally appears with a slightly heavier border to indicate which **Button** is marked as default to the end-user.

TextBox

The most commonly used user interface control is the **TextBox** control. It's a simple box that accepts alphanumeric text and printable characters as input.

There are some properties unique to the **TextBox** control. Here are some of them and the behaviors they control:

AcceptsReturn – This controls whether hitting the Enter key adds a new line into the text in the control, attempts to trigger the **Click** event of the default **Button**, or does nothing if no default **Button** is defined.

AcceptsTab – This controls whether or not Tab characters may be included in the text of the control, or whether hitting the Tab key takes the user to the next control in the Tab order.

MultiLine – This controls whether the **TextBox** control will allow multiple lines of text to be entered.

PasswordChar – When **TextBox** controls are used to accept passwords, the text is not displayed, but instead, the character defined here is displayed.

WordWrap – This controls whether or not text will wrap when the **TextBox** is defined as being multilined.

By default, the maximum length of the value a user can enter into a **TextBox** control is 32,767 characters. You can change this value to limit the length of a value a user can enter by adjusting the value stored in the **MaxLength** property.

Using the TextBox Control   The **TextBox** control is simple to use. When not in **MultiLine** mode, the **Text** property contains the value of the **TextBox** control. Default values can be stored in this property so that they appear when the control first appears. Evaluating the contents of the **Text** property will allow you to use the value entered by the user.

In **MultiLine** mode, the **Lines** property contains a collection of **String** values, one for each line entered into the control. You can also set the default settings in Visual Studio.

Clicking the button next to the **Lines** property launches the String Collection Editor. Enter each line as you want it to appear in the control at runtime. This example shows the code for getting the **Text** property as well as the **Lines** property for displaying both single and **MultiLine TextBox** values.

```
Private Sub button1_Click(ByVal sender As System.Object,
ByVal e As System.EventArgs) Handles button1.Click

    'Valid for Single Line entry only

    console.Write(textBox1().Text)

    'Valid for both MultiLine and Single Line entry

    Dim myline As String

    For Each myline In textBox1().Lines

        console.Write(myline)

    Next

End Sub
```

Most of the members of the **TextBox** control not already inherited from the **Control** class are inherited from the **TextBoxBase** class, which implements the basic functionality required of a **TextBox**. There are only two members unique to the **TextBox** class, the **CharacterCasing** property, which determines whether the case of the **Text** is modified as the user enters it, and the **Scrollbars** property, which determines which scrollbars appear in **MultiLine TextBox** controls.

Label

The **Label** control is important in the Windows user interface. It is a display-only control for displaying text on the **Form**. It's called a **Label** because this is its primary duty. It is used as a label for other controls on the **Form**, or even for the **Form** itself. It can provide titles or directions to the user.

The **Label** control, even though it is primarily used for displaying **Text**, will also display graphics if you set the value of the **Image** property. You can also set a combination of the **ImageList** and **ImageIndex** properties to display more than one graphic in the control.

Setting Label Properties   Because **Label** controls are not used to accept data in a user interface, special attention is paid to proper display of the control. You can set the properties of the **Label** control through the properties window in Visual Studio, or set them programatically like this:

```
Private Sub button1_Click(ByVal sender As System.Object,
ByVal e As System.EventArgs) Handles button1.Click

    Dim newImage As Image

    ' Set the border to a 3D border.

    label1().BorderStyle = System.Windows.Forms.
    BorderStyle.Fixed3D

    ' Set the Image Property to display an image.

    label1().Image = newImage.FromFile("c:\temp\
    ocean.jpg")

    ' Align the image to the Bottom Center.

    label1().ImageAlign = ContentAlignment.BottomCenter

    ' Specify that the text can't display mnemonic
    characters.

    label1().UseMnemonic = False

    ' Set the text of the control.

    label1().Text = "Ocean"

End Sub
```

This example results in the **Label** shown in Figure 12.2. The image does not appear until the **Button** is clicked. Of course, if you are trying to run this sample, you will have to specify an image that is found locally on your hard drive.

Figure 12.2   The **Label** control can be used to display both text and images.

Image of Ocean courtesy of Jason Coombs.

LinkLabel

The Internet has made hyperlinking commonplace, and no longer simply part of a Web page. You can include hyperlinks to documents on the local computer, available over the local area network, or on the Internet. This control, unlike most other controls, does not have a value property that can be inspected during data entry. This is more of an action control rather than a data-entry control. LinkLabels are useful for placing "Help" links, or "More InFormation" links within your application.

   Similar to the **Label** control, the **LinkLabel** control can contain both text and images. One way you may consider using this control is to create a small help icon, such as a small question mark, and use this throughout your application to provide context-sensitive help through a Web browser.

Configuring the LinkLabel Control   Unlike the **Label** control, the color of the text displayed in the **LinkLabel** control is designed to convey information about the link, such as whether the link is active or disabled, and whether the link has been visited. You can keep the defaults assigned to these values or modify the following properties:

ActiveLinkColor – Normally red, this color identifies a link that is in the process of being clicked.

DisabledLinkColor – Normally dark gray, this color identifies a link that is not enabled.

LinkColor – Normally blue, this color identifies a link the user can click.

VisitedLinkColor – Normally purple, this color identifies a link that has already been visited and is still enabled.

These properties accept a **System.Drawing** object where the **Color** property has been set in one of two ways. The first way is to use one of the standard system color names:

```
linkLabel1.DisabledLinkColor = System.Drawing.Color.
Turquoise
```

Or, you can use the RGB color values and the **FromArgb** method:

```
linkLabel1.DisabledLinkColor = System.Drawing.Color.
FromArgb(0,192,192)
```

One thing to keep in mind when selecting the color for these links is whether or not they will all be visible given the background color or image of your Form. You may have to play with these color values a while to find the best colors for your application.

Using the LinkLabel Control   Similar to the Button control, the **LinkLabel** control depends heavily on events to trigger its behavior. The default event for the **LinkLabel** control is the **LinkClicked** event. Behaviors, such as changing the color of the link after it's been clicked and what exactly you want done when someone clicks the link, appear within this event's code. You can launch Web pages or other **Forms** or process any type of code, just as you might in the **Click** event of a **Button** control.

Here is a very simplified example of loading a Web page when the **LinkLabel** is clicked. Notice that the key to loading a Web page is using the **Start** method of the **Diagnostics.Process** class.

```
Private Sub linkLabel1_LinkClicked(ByVal sender As
System.Object, ByVal e As
System.Windows.Forms.LinkLabelLinkClickedEventArgs)
Handles linkLabel1.LinkClicked

    System.Diagnostics.Process.Start("http://www.
    tedcoombs.com")

End Sub
```

Diagnostics.Process Class

*The **Diagnostics.Process** class provides management capability over system processes. It can provide information about running start, exit, and kill processes. One method of the **Diagnostics.Process** class you may find yourself using heavily is the **Start** method. This method is overloaded and can be used to start a process by filename, or even by process start arguments. Windows uses its file type associations to look up the type of application that is launched for various file types. For example, in the case of a Web page, the Web browser associated with Web pages is launched to display the page.*

The **LinkLabel.Link** class defines the text and display state of a **LinkLabel** control. You can define the location of the link using the values in the **Start** property and the length of the text to be displayed by using the **Length** property. In the previous section on configuring the **LinkLabel** control, you learned how the **Enabled** property can be used to enable or disable links. When you only want the link clicked once, you can disable the link in the control's click event after the first click. You can also change other appearance-related properties such as whether or not the link has been visited. Based on the values given to the colors associated with each state of the control, setting the **Visited** property to True should change the color of the link, alerting the user to the fact that the link has already been visited.

It's possible to associate more than a single **Link** object with a single **LinkLabel** control. Instances of the **LinkLabel.Link** class are stored in the **LinkLabel.LinkCollection** for use in the **LinkLabel** control. Use the **Add** and **Remove** methods to add new **Link** objects to the collection. Once you have **Link** objects in your collection, you can use the **Contains** method to find out if **Link** objects exist in the collection and the **IndexOf** method to return the index number of any **Link** object within the collection.

In this example, you see that we need the index of the current link, passed as an argument to the **LinkClicked** event by the **LinkLabelLinkClickedEventArgs**. Using the **IndexOf** method to look up the link in the collection, this code is able to set the **Visited** property of the correct link to True, changing the link's color.

```
linkLabel1().Links(linkLabel1().Links.IndexOf(e.Link)).
Visited=True
```

CheckBox

The **CheckBox** is a commonly used data entry control. It has two states: checked and unchecked. It's a good control when asking the user to enter Yes or No answers. Figure 12.3 represents a typical Windows **CheckBox** in its **checked** state. You can use this control without paying attention to events. The stored state of this control is oftentimes all that is required of it. Of course, the **CheckBox** can make use of any of the events that belong

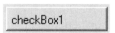

Figure 12.3   Windows CheckBoxes are used for selection of items.

Figure 12.4   A CheckBox can also appear as a **Button**.

to the Control class. By default, Visual Studio will add code to respond to the **Checked-Changed** event.

CheckBoxes can also be shown as **Buttons** by changing the default value of the **Appearance** property from **Normal** to **Button**. Figure 12.4 shows the **CheckBox** with the **Appearance** set to **Button** and in the **unchecked** state. When the **CheckBox Button** is clicked, the **Button** will appear depressed (in the clicked state, not sad).

The most important properties of the **CheckBox** control are the **Checked** and **CheckState** properties. The **Checked** property gets or sets the value of the state of the control, either **checked** or **unchecked**. This is the property you look at when determining a user's input. The other important property is the visual state of the control, stored in the **CheckState** property. By default, both these properties are updated automatically.

You can override the default behavior of updating the **Check** and **CheckState** properties automatically. The AutoCheck property determines whether the **Checked** and **CheckState** values are set automatically when the user checks or unchecks the control. When the AutoCheck property is set to False, it's up to you to set the **Checked** and **CheckState** values in the **Click** event handler.

Some of the other properties you can use for this control include the **CheckAlign** and **ThreeState** properties. The **CheckAlign** property determines the alignment of a check-box on a **CheckBox** control. Of course, this property is not valid when the **Appearance** property is set to **Button**. The **ThreeState** property allows the **CheckBox**, when not in **Button** appearance, to accept three states. There is a checked state, an unchecked state, and an indeterminate state. When the control is in the indeterminate state, the graphic appears as a light gray check instead of black and white. The **Checked** property returns True when in either the checked or indeterminate state. So, to determine which of the three states the control is in, inspect the **CheckState** property. That property will return one of three enumerated values: **Checked**, **Indeterminate**, or **Unchecked**.

The **CheckBox** control has a few events beyond those inherited from the **Control** class; they are:

- AppearanceChanged
- CheckedChanged
- CheckStateChanged

The **AppearanceChanged** property only changes when the Appearance property is changed and does not change when other physical appearances of the control change, such as the **CheckState**. With the **AutoCheck** property set to True, both the **Checked-Changed** and the **CheckStateChanged** events will fire when a user clicks in the control.

Using the CheckBox Control   The following is an example of a simple data-entry window that involves two **CheckBox** controls and a Button control. Notice in this example that the **CheckState** property of each **CheckBox** control is examined in the **Click** event of the **Button**. The Form for this example appears in Figure 12.5.

```
Private Sub Button1_Click(ByVal sender As System.Object,
ByVal e As System.EventArgs) Handles Button1.Click

    If checkBox1().CheckState = CheckState.Checked Then

        console.Write("Value 1 Selected  ")

    End If

    If checkBox2().CheckState = CheckState.Checked Then

        console.Write("Value 2 Selected")

    End If

End Sub
```

ListBox

The **ListBox** control displays a list of indexed string values and allows a user to select one or more items from the list, highlighting the selected item in the list. The user can scroll through the list if the entire list is not visible within the control at one time.

Using the **ListBox** control is a two-step process. The first process is to place a **ListBox** control on the Form. You can select this control from the Visual Studio Toolbox window. The second process is to create the **String** collection that will be displayed as the items in the list. Figure 12.6 shows the String Collection Editor window, accessible by clicking the

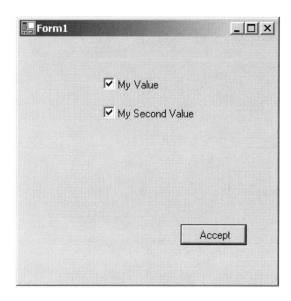

Figure 12.5   The value of two CheckBox controls will be evaluated in the Click event of the **Button**.

Button in the Item property, found in the **ListBox**'s property window. Add **ListBox** items, one per line, into the String Collection Editor window, and click OK when you have finished adding items.

If the items in your list have been entered randomly, as those in Figure 12.6, you may want to use the **Sorted** property. Changing this property to True will cause the items in the list to appear in sorted order.

> **Warning**
> While alpha string values will appear in alphabetical order, numeric values are not sorted in correct numeric order. The number 10 will appear before 9 because the first digit on the left has a lower ASCII value than the number 9.

Figure 12.7 shows a **ListBox** control with the items added in the String Collection Editor shown in Figure 12.6. Notice that a vertical scroll bar has appeared on the right to allow you to scroll through items not visible in the list. Something to know about the scroll bar is that it will "eat" space in the list area. The size of the control does not change when a scroll bar is present. Instead, the area where the list is displayed is resized to incorporate the scroll bar. If the number of items in your list is dynamic, where sometimes a scroll bar appears and sometimes it doesn't, you might consider setting the **Scroll-**

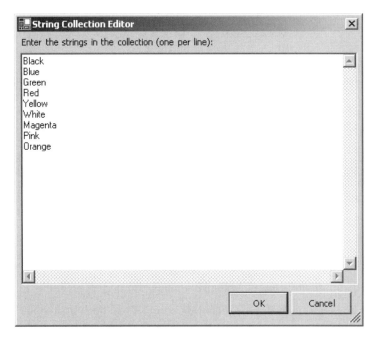

Figure 12.6 The String Collection Editor is the fastest way to create the items in a **ListBox** control.

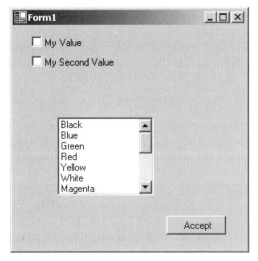

Figure 12.7 The **ListBox** control displays a scroll bar when all the items are not visible at the same time.

Always Visible property to True, turning on the scroll bar all the time. You can then size your control appropriately. When the length of the string to display in the item is too long to fit within the width of the control, a horizontal scroll bar appears along the bottom.

Customizing the ListBox   You can further configure the **ListBox** in several ways. First, you can choose whether or not you want the user to be able to select more than one item from the list. For example, if you are displaying a list of states and asking users to select the state where they live, you don't want multiple select capability. However, if you are asking them to select all the products from your catalog that they would like to order, you would like them to select as many as they want. The property that controls selection is **SelectionMode**. There are four possible values for the **SelectionMode**:

None – No items are selectable.

One – A single item is selectable.

MultiSimple – Any number of items are selectable.

MultiExtended – Any number of items are selectable and the user can use keys such as shift and Ctrl with the arrow keys to select blocks of items and multiple items.

ListBoxes have one failing. They take up a lot of screen "real estate"; in other words, space on the window is valuable, and a control that takes up too much room on the window is expensive in terms of valuable space. One way to solve this problem is to set your **ListBox's MultiColumn** property to True. This will cause the **ListBox** to place the items in columns, given the height of the **ListBox**. A horizontal scroll bar allows you to navigate to the various columns.

Adding and Removing Items   You've seen how easy it is to add items to a **ListBox** collection using the String Collection Editor (Figure 12.6). This is simple and easy if you're creating a static list of items from which to choose. But more often than not, you don't know before runtime what items you will want to appear in your list and you'll need to add them in your code. There are three methods for adding items in code.

Items.Add – Appends an item to the end of the list.

Items.Insert – Inserts an item at a specific point in the list.

Items.InsertRange – Adds an array of items in a single block.

This example adds three items in the **ListBox** when the **Button** on the **Form** is clicked. The return value of the **Add** method is the index of the position in the array where the item was added. The following example adds the items to the **ListBox**, then writes 012 into the console window.

```
Private Sub button1_Click(ByVal sender As System.Object,
ByVal e As System.EventArgs) Handles button1.Click
```

```
      Dim iPosition As Integer

      iPosition = listBox1().Items.Add("Purple")

      console.Write(iPosition.ToString)

      iPosition = listBox1().Items.Add("Green")

      console.Write(iPosition.ToString)

      iPosition = listBox1().Items.Add("Red")

      console.Write(iPosition.ToString)

  End Sub
```

You can use this same code even if you have already added items using the manual method in Visual Studio. The items will simply be appended to the end of the list. The previous example added three items. The preferred method for adding more than a single item into the list is to use the **AddRange** item. Before we get to that method, if for some reason you want to add several items not using the **AddRange** method, you should also use the **BeginUpdate** and **EndUpdate** methods. They will keep the control from repainting each time an item is added to the list. Here is the same code showing the use of the **BeginUpdate** and **EndUpdate** methods.

```
Dim iPosition As Integer

listBox1().BeginUpdate()

iPosition = listBox1().Items.Add("Purple")

console.Write(iPosition.ToString)

iPosition = listBox1().Items.Add("Green")

console.Write(iPosition.ToString)

iPosition = listBox1().Items.Add("Red")

console.Write(iPosition.ToString)

listBox1().EndUpdate()
```

The **AddRange** method is used when adding many items to the collection of items at the same time. If you add items using the String Collection Editor, you will see that this is how Visual Studio adds those items into the **ListBox**. This is copied from the Form code after using the String Collection Editor to add three items:

```
Me.listBox1.Items.AddRange(New Object() {"Blue", "Red",
"Green"})
```

To use the **AddRange**, first create an array of objects and then add them using the **AddRange** method like this:

```
Dim myItems(3) As Object

myItems(0) = "Pink"

myItems(1) = "Purple"

myItems(2) = "Yellow"

listBox1().Items.AddRange(myItems)
```

So far, you've seen how you can append items to the list and add them in bulk. There is one more method for adding items that allows you to insert them into any position in the list you want. The Insert method accepts two arguments; the index number of the position in the list and the object you want to add to the list. Here is an example that adds an item to the second position in the list. Remember that this is a zero-based array.

```
Private Sub button1_Click(ByVal sender As System.Object,
ByVal e As System.EventArgs) Handles button1.Click

    listBox1().Items.Insert(1, "Purple")

End Sub
```

There are also methods for removing items from the list. The **Remove** method accepts an object that it finds in the list, then removes the item from the list. In this example we add the color Purple, launch a **MessageBox**, and as soon as the **MessageBox** is closed, remove the item from the list again.

```
Private Sub button1_Click(ByVal sender As System.Object,
ByVal e As System.EventArgs) Handles button1.Click

    listBox1().Items.Insert(1, "Purple")

    messagebox.Show("I've added the color")
```

```
        listBox1().Items.Remove("Purple")

End Sub
```

The **RemoveAt** method selects an item to remove based on the index number passed in as an argument. Make certain that the index exists or you'll throw an exception.

```
        listBox1().Items.RemoveAt(2)
```

The **Items.Clear** method removes all the items from the collection.

```
listBox1().Items.Clear()
```

Once you clear all your items you will have to add items again before you can use the ListBox. All items, no matter how they were added, will be removed.

Using the ListBox Control   To best understand how to use the **ListBox** control, you should know how information is stored in the control. First, the **ListBox.ObjectCollection** object contains all the items displayed in the listbox. The **ListBox.SelectedObjectCollection** contains all the items the user has selected. When the **MultiSelect** property is set to either **MultiSimple** or **MultiExtended**, the user may select any number of items. Because this collection contains only the values of the selected items, another collection contains the index values of the selected items so you know where they are in the list. This collection is called the **ListBox.SelectedIndicesCollection**.

The **ObjectCollection** contains the index, the object, and the selected state of the item. The **SelectedObjectCollection** contains only the selected items, not their indexes. You can easily find out how many items were selected using the **Count** property of the **SelectedObjectCollection**. This is an important value, especially if you are going to iterate through the collection. Here's an example:

```
Private Sub button1_Click(ByVal sender As System.Object,
ByVal e As System.EventArgs) Handles button1.Click

Dim iSelected, i As Integer

    iSelected = listBox1().SelectedItems.Count()

    For i = 0 To (iSelected - 1) 'iSelected is not zero-
    based

        console.Write(listBox1().SelectedItems.Item(i))

Next

End Sub
```

This example iterates through the **SelectedItems** collection using the **Count** property to know how many times to loop. If you need the corresponding index number of one of the items, you can expect to find it in the identical position within the **ListBox.SelectedIndices** collection.

CheckedListBox

By design, the **CheckedListBox** control allows for multiple selection of items. Rather than simply clicking the item, with the selected items appearing highlighted, the list of items appears with a checkbox next to each item and selected items appear checked. In many ways this control is similar to the **ListBox** control. Add items in the same manner in which you would add items to the **ListBox** control.

> **Note**
> The **SelectionMode** property is overridden in this control and only allows you to select One or None.

One property that is different from the **ListBox** control is the **CheckOnClick** property. With this value set to False, simply clicking an item in the list will not place a check in the box. You must click again to check the box. Changing this value to True will check the box on the first click. Even though the default value for this property is False, single-clicking to select an item and placing a check in the check box is more intuitive.

Figure 12.8 shows how the **CheckedListBox** control appears similar to a **ListBox**, but with checkboxes to the left of the items. Notice also that the most recently selected item

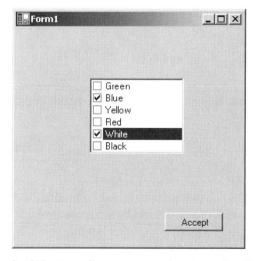

Figure 12.8 A **CheckedListBox** allows you to select items in a list using a checkbox.

is also highlighted, while the previously selected item appears only with a check mark in the box next to the item.

Using the CheckedListBox   Also similar to the **ListBox** control, the values of the items, selected items, and selected indices are stored in collections. The **CheckedItems** collection stores the selected items, while the **CheckedIndices** collection stores the corresponding indices of the items in the **CheckedItems** collection. Here is a sample where the **Click** event of a **Button** iterates through both collections to display the index and value of the selected items.

```
Private Sub button1_Click(ByVal sender As System.Object,
ByVal e As System.EventArgs) Handles button1.Click

    Dim iSelected, i As Integer

    iSelected = checkedListBox1().CheckedItems.Count()

    For i = 0 To (iSelected - 1) 'iSelected is not zero-
    based

        console.Write(checkedListBox1().CheckedIndices.
        Item(i))

        console.Write(checkedListBox1().CheckedItems.
        Item(i))

        console.Write(vbCrLf)

    Next

End Sub
```

This example writes the index and value of the items selected in the **CheckedListBox** into the console window.

ComboBox

The **ComboBox** control is similar to the **ListBox** with the added ability to type text into the control's edit field. Another difference between the **ListBox** and the **ComboBox** is that the **ComboBox** hides the list until specifically requested by the user. When requested, the list drops down to display a specified number of items (Figure 12.9). The **MaxDropDown-Items** property maintains this value. Of course, if you specify five for the number of items, and you only have two in the list, the drop down will only display two items.

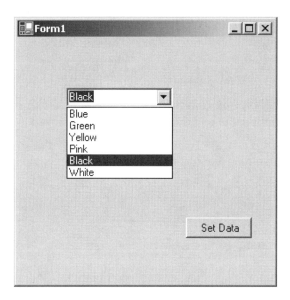

Figure 12.9   Enter or select text from a list in the ComboBox control.

The **ComboBox** is by design a single entry control. You cannot select multiple items from the list in this control. Selecting from the list adds the value into the control's text box.

Configuring the ComboBox   The **ComboBox** control is more configurable than either the **ListBox** or **CheckedListBox**. This is because this control has both edit features and drop-down list capabilities the other two controls do not have.

One of the first things you will want to configure is the **ComboBox** style. The style is set in the **DropDownStyle** property. Here are the three styles:

Simple – Allows users to edit data in the edit box, select from a list, the list is fixed, not a drop down.

DropDown – Allows users to edit data in the edit box or select from a drop down list; this is the default style.

DropDownList – The edit box is disabled, allowing the user to select items from the drop down list only.

Using the ComboBox   When a user selects a value, the selected value is stored in the **SelectedItem** property, and the corresponding index of the item is stored in the **SelectedIndex** property. Here is an example:

selectedItem – Handle to the selected object.

selectedIndex – Integer value of the index of the selected item.

selectedText – Text value of the edit box. When DropDownList is specified as the DropDownStyle, the value of selectedText is an empty string.

This sample uses the **Try** and **Catch** blocks to display values set in the **ComboBox**. The expressions will throw an exception, caught in the **Catch** block when no value exists.

```
Private Sub button2_Click(ByVal sender As System.Object,
ByVal e As System.EventArgs) Handles button2.Click

    Try

        console.Write(comboBox1().SelectedItem.ToString)

    Catch

        console.Write("selectedItem not found")

    End Try

    console.Write(vbCrLf)

    Try

        console.Write(comboBox1().SelectedText)

    Catch

        console.Write("selectedText not found")

    End Try

    console.Write(vbCrLf)

    Try

        console.Write(comboBox1().SelectedIndex.ToString)

    Catch

        console.Write("selectedText not found")
```

```
        End Try

    End Sub
```

DomainUpDown

The **DomainUpDown** control is a string selection control that is just like a **ListBox**. This control consists of an edit box with up and down arrows that allows you to scroll through a collection of string values. Already mentioned in relation to selection-type controls, screen real estate is at a premium. The **DomainUpDown** control is the winner in the category of screen space conservation. The selection list of a **DomainUpDown** control always remains invisible, with only the current selection appearing in the text box.

Add items to the **DomainUpDown** control in the same manner you would add them to a **ListBox**. At design time you can use the String Collection Editor, launching it from the **Items** property in the Properties tab window for the control. At runtime you can add items to the collection using the **Add** method of the Items object like this:

```
domainUpDown1.Items.Add("Red")
```

Maintain the items in the string collection in the same manner as the **ListBox** control.

Using the DomainUpDown Control   Similar to the **ComboBox**, because the **DomainUpDown** control does not have multiple selection capability, the result of the user selection is stored in the **SelectedItem** and **SelectedIndex** properties. Here is an example that examines the result of the user's input:

```
Private Sub button1_Click(ByVal sender As System.Object,
ByVal e As System.EventArgs) Handles button1.Click

    messagebox.Show(domainUpDown1().SelectedItem.ToString)

End Sub
```

An important thing to keep in mind is that the **Text** property appears in the text box when the control first launches. The **SelectedItem** property will contain nothing at this point and the **SelectedIndex** property will equal −1 (negative one). Trying to display the contents of these properties while they contain nothing will throw an exception. Also, once you have scrolled using the arrow keys, the **Text** property will no longer be displayed. In other words, using this control, once you've scrolled you can never return to a state where **SelectedItem** and **SelectedIndex** equal nothing. If "Nothing" is a choice, you should add it to your list of selectable choices.

The **Text** property, on the other hand, always contains a value. Examining this value will return any default **Text** property as well as any item you may have selected from the list. Once an item has been selected, the **Text** and **SelectedItem** properties will be equivalent.

Here is another difference between the **Text** and **SelectedItem** properties. The user can type a value into the text box that is not currently in the list. Examining the **Text** property will show the value typed in by the user. Of course, if nothing was selected from the list, the **SelectedIndex** property will still equal −1. So, in your application, you might first look to see the value of **SelectedIndex**. If it equals a value greater than −1, you can look in the **SelectedItem** property for the result. If it equals −1, then you can look in the **Text** property to see if the value is default or if the user typed in a value.

This control is for string values only. When you want to scroll through numeric values, use the **NumericUpDown** control.

NumericUpDown

The **NumericUpDown** control is a scrollable selection control for selecting numeric values. It is similar to the **DomainUpDown** control in its operation, but quite different in how it is managed programatically.

The **NumericUpDown** control does not have a collection of items from which to choose. Instead, you specify a selection range and a value amount to increment. The properties that set the range and increment are:

Maximum – Maximum value in the range. This value must be within the range of the data type you are allowing your user to select. This value can be either a positive or a negative number.

Minimum – The Minimum value is the minimum value in the selectable range. This value can be either a positive or a negative number.

Increment – The increment property specifies the amount the value shown in the control increments or decrements each time an arrow key in the control is clicked. This value can be a decimal value. It cannot be a negative number.

You can **Form**at the numeric value that appears in the control by adding a comma as a thousands separator. The **ThousandsSeparator** property can be either True or False. You can also specify the number of decimal places your number displays by entering a value in the **DecimalPlaces** property.

The selected value will appear in the **NumericUpDown** control's **Value** property. This example displays a string representation of the selected number in a **MessageBox**.

```
messagebox.Show(numericUpDown1().Value.ToString)
```

You can also use the many other methods of the **Value** property to convert the number to other types or per**Form** numeric evaluation.

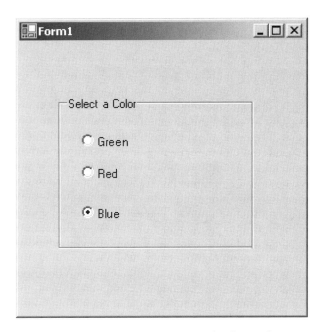

Figure 12.10 RadioButtons allow you to select a single choice from a group of choices.

RadioButton

The **RadioButton** control is another selection control. Similar to the **CheckBox** control, the **RadioButton** offers an on or off user input. The main difference is that a single **RadioButton** is never used alone. It's not impossible to use a **RadioButton** alone, but the power of the **RadioButton** lies in the fact that each **RadioButton** interacts with other **RadioButtons** in a group (see Figure 12.10). As one **RadioButton** is selected, all the other **RadioButtons** in the group are deselected. That is how the control got its name. Old-style car radios had push **Buttons** to select preselected stations. As one **Button** was pushed in, the currently pushed-in **Button** would pop out.

Configuring RadioButton Controls

RadioButtons can be configured as either circular checkboxes, or as **Buttons** that can be toggled (Figure 12.11). With the **Appearance** property set to **Normal**, the **Radio-Buttons** appear as checkboxes. Setting the property to **Button** will change their appear-

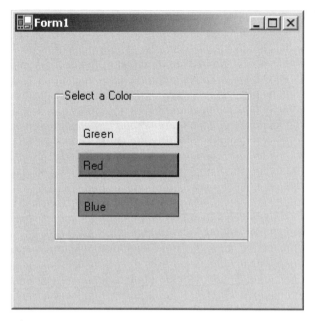

Figure 12.11 RadioButtons can appear as round checkboxes or **Buttons**.

ance to **Buttons**. They have identical behavior in either appearance. As shown in Figure 12.11, changing the **BackColor** property can create a more effective user interface.

In a manner similar to Label controls, **RadioButton** controls can display text, an image, or both. Figure 12.12 shows how adding the small paintbrush image to each control gives the **Form** a more professional appearance and adds to the user-friendliness of your application.

When at least one **RadioButton** within a group of **RadioButtons** has its **Checked** property set to True, at least one **RadioButton** in the group will continue to have a **Checked** value set to True. When **RadioButtons** are first placed on the Form, they carry their default **Checked** value, which is False. That means that when an application first starts, no **RadioButton** appears checked. At design time, you might consider setting at least one of the **RadioButton's Checked** property to True as a default value. If you need one of the options to be that none of the **RadioButtons** appear checked, consider placing a **Reset Button** on the Form that forces all the **Checked** property values to False.

Using RadioButton Controls   All **RadioButtons** within a container object will interoperate as a group. As mentioned in Chapter 9, a **Form** is a container object. The easiest configuration of **RadioButtons** exist when all the **RadioButtons** on a **Form** need

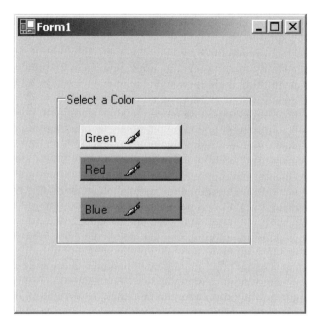

Figure 12.12   Adding images to **RadioButton** Controls can improve usability.

to interact. If you need more than a single group of **RadioButtons** on a single **Form**, you must contain these **Buttons** within another group object that can be placed on the **Form**, creating subgroups. The two controls that create subgroups are the **GroupBox** control and the **Panel** control.

The **GroupBox** control, once it's placed on the Form, can be configured as visible or invisible by setting the **Visible** property to True or False. If you still want the grouping ability of the **GroupBox**, but don't wish to place a frame around your controls, you can set the **GroupBox's** Visible property to False. When the **GroupBox** is visible it can also act as an instructional Label, as shown in Figure 12.10.

The **Checked** property contains the value of the **RadioButton**. This example shows an example of **RadioButtons** used to select a color. Adding an **OK Button** to the **Form** shown in Figure 12.12 to process the results of the other data entry controls results in the following code:

```
Private Sub button1_Click(ByVal sender As System.Object,
    ByVal e As System.EventArgs) Handles button1.Click

        If radioButton1().Checked Then
```

```
                    console.Write("Green")

          End If

          If radioButton2().Checked Then

                    console.Write("Red")

          End If

          If radioButton3().Checked Then

                    console.Write("Blue")

          End If

    End Sub
```

There is nothing inherently bad about this last example but it is crude. When collecting data in an object-oriented environment, it's much simpler to create a class designed to collect values. An instance of this **results** class can do things such as validation as values are assigned to this object. Rather than waiting for a **Button** click, as in this example, you can use one of the control's events. Almost all controls that allow values to be changed have some type of value-changed event. For **RadioButtons** this event is the **Checked-Changed** event. Here is an idea of how you might want to update a data collection object (the code to create this object is not included in this example):

```
Private Sub radioButton1_CheckedChanged(ByVal sender As
System.Object, ByVal e As System.EventArgs) Handles
radioButton1.CheckedChanged

If radioButton1.Checked Then

     ResultObject.Color = "Green"

End if

End Sub

Private Sub radioButton2_CheckedChanged(ByVal sender As
System.Object, ByVal e As System.EventArgs) Handles
radioButton2.CheckedChanged
```

```
If radioButton2.Checked Then

    ResultObject.Color = "Red"

End if

End Sub

Private Sub radioButton3_CheckedChanged(ByVal sender As
System.Object, ByVal e As System.EventArgs) Handles
radioButton3.CheckedChanged

If radioButton1.Checked Then

    ResultObject.Color = "Blue"

End if

End Sub
```

When the **OK Button** on the Form is clicked, all of the Form values have already been validated and collected. The Form has only to pass back a single object containing the values of the **Form's** controls.

GroupBox and Panel Controls

The **GroupBox** and **Panel** controls are container objects. These controls have no data-entry capabilities of their own. Instead, both these controls act as containers for other controls. All of the controls within a container object, Form, **GroupBox**, or **Panel**, are affected by the **Enabled** property of the container object. When the **Enabled** property of a container object is set to False, all of the controls within the container are also disabled.

Some controls, such as **RadioButton** controls, are affected by their container object. In the section on **RadioButton** controls you saw one implementation of the **GroupBox** control and how **RadioButtons** interact with each other within a container object.

The main differences between the **GroupBox** and **Panel** controls are that **GroupBox** controls can display captions and **Panel** controls can contain scroll bars.

Both controls can be made invisible, or configured to have different border types and background colors. When designing user interfaces they provide a convenience of designing a Form in units, where all the controls within a container, once designed, can be moved around as a unit.

The **Panel** control is unique in its ability to have two areas: a visible region and a region larger than the visible area that also contains controls. The user then has the option to scroll to different areas of the *Panel* control using the **Panel's** scroll bars.

Tip

While having the ability to display a large user interface within a small visible window using the **Panel** control is intriguing, it's not the most user-friendly way to conserve screen real estate. Consider using one of the other space-saving controls, such as the **Tab** control.

ListView

The **ListView** control is the most involved control covered so far in this chapter. This control manages the display of a list of items. Each item in the list has a text caption and can also display an image.

The ListView control allows you to view the data in one of four views:

LargeIcon – Displays large icon images next to the text.

SmallIcon – Displays small icon images next to the text.

List – Displays the list in a single column with small icons next to the text.

Report – Displays the list in multiple columns.

Configuring the ListView Control   Adding Items into the **ListView** control is similar to other list-type controls. Editing the **Items** property in the ListView Item Collection Editor is an easy way to add items to the list at design time. Here are the steps you need to follow after adding the **ListView** from the Toolbox:

1. Click the Add **Button** and the list item appears in the left window of the editor.
2. Set the properties of the item in the window on the right.
3. Add subitems by clicking the **SubItems** property in the window on the right for each list item.
4. Set the properties for each subitem.
5. Click the OK **Button** to save the changes.

Similar to a **ListBox**, you can set this control so that users can select multiple items from the list. Set the **MultiSelect** to True if you want to allow multiple item selection. The **ListView** control can be set up with columns, each column with its own title. You can configure the control so that sorting of the items can be done by column.

Using the ListView Control   Items in the **ListView** control are stored in the **ListItems** property. As with the **ListBox** control, the values of the selected items are held in the **SelectedItems** and the **SelectedIndices** collection. The **ListViewItem** object is stored in the **SelectedItems** collection and can be retrieved like this:

```
Private Sub button1_Click(ByVal sender As System.Object,
  ByVal e As System.EventArgs) Handles button1.Click
```

```
        Dim myitem As ListViewItem

        For Each myitem In listView1().SelectedItems()

                console.Write(myitem.ToString)

        Next

    End Sub
```

You can refer to the **ListBox** control for more information about how to retrieve and use the information held in collections.

TreeView

The **TreeView** control is designed to display a tree-structured list of items. Each item is considered a node in the tree, starting with the root node. You can add as many root nodes to the tree and as many child nodes (branches) as you wish. To configure a **TreeView** control, place a **TreeView** control on the **Form**, right-click the control, and launch the properties window. Click the **Button** next to the **Nodes** property. This launches the **TreeNode** Editor window (Figure 12.13).

The **TreeNode** object is used to create nodes within the **TreeView** control. The constructor of the **TreeNode** class accepts both the text caption for each node and the ability to supply a collection of other **TreeNode** objects. Hierarchies are created by embedding more collections of **TreeNode** objects within each node.

This code snippet shows the **AddRange** method of **TreeView**, adding a complete tree hierarchy.

```
    treeView1().Nodes.AddRange(New
    System.Windows.Forms.TreeNode() {New
    System.Windows.Forms.TreeNode("2001", New
    System.Windows.Forms.TreeNode() {New
    System.Windows.Forms.TreeNode("January"), New
    System.Windows.Forms.TreeNode("February"), New
    System.Windows.Forms.TreeNode("March", New
    System.Windows.Forms.TreeNode() {New
    System.Windows.Forms.TreeNode("1"), New
    System.Windows.Forms.TreeNode("2")})})})})
```

Every node in the tree includes a caption and even an optional graphic. The user can use the small plus and minus signs in the tree to expand and collapse the lists beneath each node. The user can then select a node by clicking on it with a mouse.

Here is how to handle the user selection in your code. The **TreeNode** object is returned from any user selection. The **TreeNode** class has an incredible number of properties, allowing you to view not only the current selection using the **Text** property, but the

Figure 12.13 The TreeNode Editor is used to construct the hierarchical tree.

previous and next nodes, the first and last nodes, and the full path (**FullPath** property) starting at the root, as we show in this next example. Each node is separated by a forward slash (/) in the path.

```
Private Sub button1_Click(ByVal sender As System.Object,
ByVal e As System.EventArgs) Handles button1.Click

    Dim selectedvalue As New TreeNode()

    selectedvalue = treeView1().SelectedNode()

    messagebox.Show(selectedvalue.FullPath)

End Sub
```

An entire book could be written about this control alone. There are methods for programatically expanding and collapsing the tree, navigating through the tree, and numerous events for reacting to user input. This section is merely an introduction to this powerful control. Refer to the CLR documentation for full details.

Clipboard

> **Note**
> The Clipboard object appeared in beta versions and may not be included in release versions.

Not all user interface elements are composed of visible controls. Interacting with an application user can take on many **Forms**, based on the requirements of the desired action. One of those requirements is moving data between different parts of the same application, or different applications. There is a semi-manual way to move this data, using the Windows Clipboard as the intermediate storage area. Most people are familiar with Copy and Cut commands in most Windows applications. These commands place selected data into the Clipboard for temporary storage. The Paste command places the data, stored in the Clipboard, into another application capable of accepting the data.

Visual Basic .Net has a **Clipboard** class that provides methods to save data to the Clipboard as well as to fetch data from the Clipboard.

> **Note**
> Unlike visual controls, the **Clipboard** class cannot be inherited.

The **Clipboard** is a unique and powerful object due to its ability to save many different data formats. The predefined **Clipboard** formats are defined by the DataFormats class and listed in Table 12.1.

Most people are familiar with the manual methods of copying data to the **Clipboard**. You can also add data programatically using the **SetDataObject** method of the **Clipboard** object. Here's an example:

```
Private Sub button1_Click(ByVal sender As System.Object,
ByVal e As System.EventArgs) Handles button1.Click

    Clipboard.SetDataObject("My test")

End Sub
```

In this example, the string data is written to the **Clipboard** object. Even after the application closes, you can paste the values in the **Clipboard** to other applications. Just as you can save data to the **Clipboard** within your application, you can also retrieve data from the **Clipboard**. All data returned from the **Clipboard**, regardless of the data format, is

Table 12.1 Clipboard Data Formats

Format	Description
Bitmap	Bitmap (BMP) format
CommaSeparatedValue	Comma-separated value (CSV) format
Dib	Device Independent Bitmap (DIB) format
Dif	Data Interchange Format (DIF)
EnhancedMetafile	Enhanced metafile format
FileDrop	File drop format
Html	Text containing HTML tags
Locale	Culture format
MetafilePict	Metafile format
OemText	Original Equipment Manufacturer (OEM) text format
Palette	Palette format
PenData	Pen data format
Riff	Resource Interchange File Format (RIFF)
Rtf	Rich Text Format (RTF) text
Serializable	Text from a serialized object
StringFormat	String objects
SymbolicLink	Symbolic link format
Text	ANSI text format
Tiff	Tagged Image File Format (TIFF)
UnicodeText	Unicode text format
WaveAudio	Wave (WAV) audio file format

returned as an object that implements the **IDataObject** interface using the **GetDataObject** method.

You may or may not know the data format of the information you are retrieving from the Clipboard. In the latter case you can use the **GetFormats** method of the **IDataObject** interface to retrieve a list of each format in which the data might be saved. Some applications store the same data in multiple formats so that many types of applications may view the data. In the next example, Button1 sets the value of the **Clipboard** while **Button2** retrieves the value as an **IDataObject**, and then determines the formats the value is saved in and prints them to the console window.

```
Private Sub button1_Click(ByVal sender As System.Object,
ByVal e As System.EventArgs) Handles button1.Click

    Clipboard.SetDataObject("My test")
```

```
End Sub


Private Sub button2_Click(ByVal sender As System.Object,
ByVal e As System.EventArgs) Handles button2.Click

    Dim ClipData As IDataObject

    Dim sDataFormat() As String 'array of strings

    Dim sFormattype As String

    ClipData = Clipboard.GetDataObject()

    sDataFormat = ClipData.GetFormats(True)

    For Each sFormattype In sDataFormat

        console.Write(sFormattype)

    Next

End Sub
```

Notice in this example that the data formats are returned as an array of strings. This particular example returns data in the **System.String**, **UnicodeText**, **Text**, and **Rich Text** Formats.

Once you have the data stored in the object that supports the **iDataObject** interface, use the **GetData** method, passing in the data type, to get the data in a particular format. This next example is an expansion of the previous example. Rather than write out the various data types, the data is saved as text data into the text property of a **TextBox** control on the **Form**. (**TextBox** controls are covered later in this chapter.)

```
Private Sub button2_Click(ByVal sender As System.Object,
ByVal e As System.EventArgs) Handles button2.Click

    Dim ClipData As IDataObject

    Dim sDataFormat() As String 'array of strings

    Dim sFormattype As String
```

```
    ClipData = Clipboard.GetDataObject()

    textBox1().Text = ClipData.GetData(DataFormats.Text,
    True).ToString

End Sub
```

Note

Since all Windows applications share the **Clipboard**, the contents of the Clipboard are subject to being overwritten by other applications.

ToolBar

Building a Windows graphic user interface has slowly changed over the years. This was once a menu-oriented environment, but today users rely on toolbars to simplify their application use. Visual Basic .Net includes a control for creating a toolbar in your application.

When you place the **ToolBar** control on your Form it automatically snaps to the top of the Form, where toolbars are normally situated. You can further configure the **ToolBar** control by setting some of its properties, such as:

BorderStyle – Sets the border of the **ToolBar** to none, FixedSingle, or Fixed3D.

ButtonSize – Sets the size of the **ToolBar Buttons** by setting the height and width in pixels.

Divider – Sets whether or not the **ToolBar** will display a 3D line along the top of the control.

DropDownArrows – Sets whether or not arrows will appear next to drop-down **Buttons**.

Setting up the **ToolBar** involves adding **Buttons** to the ToolBar. **Buttons** are not added using **Button** controls, but rather **ToolBarButtons** are added using the properties editor for the **ToolBar** control. Clicking the **Button** next to the **Buttons** property launches the ToolBarButton Collection Editor. This utility will help you populate the **ToolBarButtonCollection** object manually at design time.

Click the Add **Button** beneath the **Members** column to add a new **Button** to the collection. The properties for that **Button** will appear in the column on the right, as shown in Figure 12.14. When configuring the **ToolBarButton** object, you can select how the **Button** appears. Here are the choices:

- PushButton
- ToggleButton
- Separator
- DropDownButton

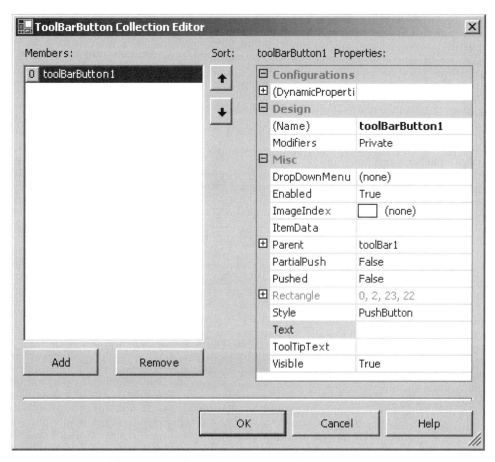

Figure 12.14 Add items into the ToolBarButtonCollection object using this editor.

Notice that one of the selections in the previous list is **Separator**. You can define a **ToolBarButton** to be a separator between other **Buttons**. The **Button** will not appear as a **Button**, and will not be enabled in any way.

The **ImageIndex** collection will contain the image that can appear on your **ToolBar-Button**. This can be one of the most important property features, as a good icon can make or break your toolbar. Many people have studied how humans view icons, and how they are interpreted. Make your icon simple and clear as to its functionality.

You can also add **Buttons** to the **ToolBar** programatically. Use either the **Add** or **Insert** methods of the **ToolBarButtons**.

```
    Private Sub button1_Click(ByVal sender As System.Object,
ByVal e As System.EventArgs) Handles Button1.Click

  'Create new ToolBarButton instances

  Dim MyButton1 As New ToolBarButton()

  MyButton1.Text = "Display"

  Dim MyButton2 As New ToolBarButton()

  MyButton2.Text = "Save"

  Dim MyButton3 As New ToolBarButton()

  MyButton3.Text = "Print"

  Dim MyButton4 As New ToolBarButton()

  MyButton4.Text = "Clear"

  'Add ToolBarButtons to the ToolBar Control

  toolBar1.Buttons.Add(MyButton1)

  toolBar1.Buttons.Add(MyButton2)

  toolBar1.Buttons.Add(MyButton3)

  toolBar1.Buttons.Add(MyButton4)

End Sub
```

Once the **Buttons** have been added you will need to add the code that will process the **ButtonClick** event for the control.

Using the ToolBar Control   ToolBarButton objects are very similar in functionality. Double-clicking on a **ToolBarButton** object will automatically add code to handle the object's **ButtonClick** event. One critical difference is that the same event is triggered no matter which **Button** is clicked. You must first determine which **Button** was clicked to know how to handle the code.

The following code snippet shows the code to launch a **MessageBox** when the **Display ToolBarButton** is clicked.

```
Private Sub toolBar1_ButtonClick(ByVal sender As
System.Object, ByVal e As
System.Windows.Forms.ToolBarButtonClickEventArgs) Handles
toolBar1.ButtonClick

Dim iButton As Integer

        iButton = toolBar1().Buttons.IndexOf(e.Button)

        If iButton = 0 Then

            'Display code

            Dim selectedvalue As New TreeNode()

            selectedvalue = treeView1().SelectedNode()

            messagebox.Show(selectedvalue.Text & " " &
            selectedvalue.Index.ToString & " parent: " &
            selectedvalue.FullPath)

        End If

        If iButton = 1 Then

            'Save code here

        End If

        If iButton = 2 Then

            'Print code here

        End If

        If iButton = 3 Then

            'Clear code here

    End If

End Sub
```

The **ToolBar** controls normally provide shortcuts to functionality already in a menu, and generally do not introduce new functionality. This is a guideline, and not a hard-and-fast rule.

Table 12.2   Enumerated ColorDepth values

Enumeration	Description
Depth16Bit	16-bit image
Depth24Bit	24-bit image
Depth32Bit	32-bit image
Depth4Bit	4-bit image
Depth8Bit	8-bit image

ImageList

Some of the controls covered in this chapter accept lists of images, normally stored within an **ImageList** object. For instance, the **ListView**, **TreeView**, and **Toolbar** controls all accept **ImageList** objects.

Each image, either a bitmap or icon, added to the ImageList is stored in the **ImageCollection** object. This collection object is created automatically when you set values into the **Images** property of the **ImageList** object. You can also set the sizes of the images within an **ImageCollection** by setting the **ImageSize** property.

You can further affect changes to the images within the **ImageCollection** by setting the **ColorDepth** and **TransparentColor** properties. The **ColorDepth** property allows you to set the number of colors available to the images. The default is an enumerated value: Depth4Bit. The ColorDepth Enumerations are listed in Table 12.2 (above).

In addition to the **ColorDepth**, you can also set the **TransparentColor** property. This property allows you to identify which color in a range of colors will appear transparent, allowing you to view the graphic image beneath it. This property accepts a system.drawing.color object as an argument.

The ImageList object can draw stored images to the screen using the Draw method.

ContextMenu

Most Windows users are familiar with the context menu. This is the menu that appears when you right-click on a Windows object. Whenever a context menu has been set for an object, the pop-up menu will list frequently used commands for that object.

To create a **ContextMenu** object, select **ContextMenu** from the Toolbox and click on the Form. You will notice that a **ContextMenu** object appears at the top of the Form as well as a reference to the object in a window beneath the Form. Because this is a nonvisual object, you can click on the reference to the object beneath the Form to set its properties.

Once you've added the **ContextMenu** control to the Form, click on it to begin adding menu items, as shown in Figure 12.15.

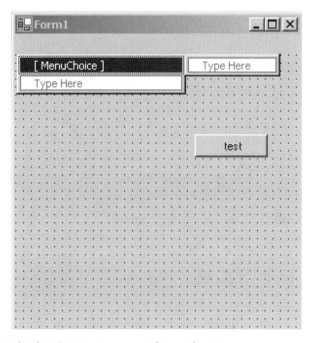

Figure 12.15 Edit the **Context** menu right on the Form.

You can add ContextMenu items programmatically. Creating the menu object is simple.

```
Dim myContextMenu as New ContextMenu()
```

If only menus were that easy to create. Before the **ContextMenu** object can be useful you have to add **MenuItems** to it. First, create the **MenuItem** objects:

```
Dim menuItemNew as New MenuItem

Dim menuItemOpen as New MenuItem

Dim menuItemSave as New MenuItem
```

Set the **Text** properties of each **MenuItem** object like this:

```
menuItemNew.Text = "&New"

menuItemOpen.Text = "&Open"

menuItemSave.Text = "&Save"
```

Note
The Ampersand (&) denotes the shortcut key.

Add the new **MenuItem** objects to the **ContextMenu** using the Add method:

```
myContextMenu.MenuItems.Add(menuItemNew)

myContextMenu.MenuItems.Add(menuItemOpen)

myContextMenu.MenuItems.Add(menuItemSave)
```

To add submenus to existing **MenuItem** objects, you can use the **Add** method of the **MenuItem** objects to add additional **MenuItems** like this:

```
Dim menuItemFile as New MenuItem

menuItemFile.Text = "&File"

menuItemNew.Add(menuItemFile)
```

ContextMenus wouldn't do much good if they didn't do anything. To associate an action with a menu selection you can use the **Click** event of the menu choice. Here is an example:

```
Private Sub contextMenu1_Click(ByVal sender As
System.Object, ByVal e As System.EventArgs) Handles
menuItemFile.Click

        messagebox.Show("test")

End Sub
```

This example handles the **Click** event for the **menuItemFile MenuItem** object. To add many menu items quickly, simply copy and paste the click event code and change the name of the **Sub** and the name of the object that appears after the **Handles** keyword. In the editor, the various events will appear for you to select. Menu items are normally limited to the **Click** event.

The **ContextMenu** must now be associated with one or more controls. Set the **ContextMenu** property of any control you wish to have a context menu for. When using the Visual Editor, clicking in the **ContextMenu** property will list any **ContextMenu** objects you've already created, allowing you to select them from the drop-down list. Or, as always, you can set the property in your code like this:

```
ListBox1.ContextMenu = myContextMenu
```

MainMenu

Creating the main menu for your application is simple using the **MainMenu** control. Its use is very similar to the **ContextMenu** control in the previous section. However, the **MainMenu** has almost no properties and is therefore easier to configure.

Once you add a **MainMenu** control onto the Form, you can configure menu items exactly as with the **ContextMenu** control. You also handle click events of the MenuItems to trigger functionality.

The important thing to know about constructing a main menu is not necessarily how to use and configure the **MainMenu** control. You should follow the Windows standard for creating a main menu. One of the advantages of the Windows operating system is that it created a standard for all applications to follow. Before Windows, every application operated differently, and just navigating the menus took time to learn. Today, Windows applications are enough alike that even a novice can understand how to navigate through basic menus.

The **File** menu selection always comes first. Normally, the first three selections in this menu are **New**, **Open**, and **Close** followed by a separator. You can add a separator into a MainMenu control by right-clicking the visual editor where it says "Type Here" and selecting **Insert Separator**. The File menu also includes **Save** and **SaveAs**, **Print**, **Most Recently Used** files, and **Exit**.

The next main menu selection is always **Edit**. The normal selections in this menu choice are **Undo**, (Separator), **Cut**, **Copy**, **Paste**, (Separator), **Select All**, (Separator), **Find**, and **Replace**.

The main menu normally has a Window menu choice for selecting and configuring windows on the desktop or in the application. The selections are **New Window**, **Arrange All**, **Cascade**, and a list of open windows with the current window checked.

The last menu selection is always the **Help** menu. This can have various menu selections, depending on the Help system you are using. Normally, the last menu selection is the **About** application selection, which offers information about the application such as the name, version number, and contact information.

DateTimePicker

The **DateTimePicker** control is a visible control that allows the user to select a date and time. The control initially appears like a **ComboBox** control until the user clicks in the control. Depending on how you have the properties of the **DateTimePicker** control, it can be used to easily set the date, the time, or both. When configured to select a new date, a calendar, like the one shown in Figure 12.16, appears beneath the control and allows the user to click a new date.

To configure the **DateTimePicker** control to allow different **Form**ats, set the **Format** property. It includes the following choices:

Figure 12.16 A calendar pops up when the user clicks in the DateTimePicker control.

Long – Displays the day of the week and the date.

Short – Displays the date in mm/dd/yyyy format.

Time – Displays the time in hours, minutes, and seconds.

Custom – Allows you to create your own custom format based on standard date/time formatting.

When either the **Long** or **Short** formats are specified, the control displays a calendar when the user clicks the control. When the **Time** format is set, the user can modify the time. No special pop-up appears. When the **Custom** format is selected, the control looks to the **CustomFormat** property for formatting instructions. An example of a custom format might be:

MMMM dd, yyyy hh:mm

This example displays the date as August 22, 2001 12:01. When the user clicks the control that allows selection of both date and time, the date and time are editable by hand, and the date is also selectable by clicking the drop-down arrow, causing the calendar to appear beneath the control.

To use the **DateTimePicker** control in your application to accept user input, you can evaluate the Value property. This example prints the **Value** property, a **DateTime** type value, as a string by using the **ToString** method.

```
Private Sub button1_Click(ByVal sender As System.Object,
ByVal e As System.EventArgs) Handles button1.Click

    messagebox.Show(dateTimePicker1().Value.ToString)

End Sub
```

MonthCalendar

The **MonthCalendar** control allows you to display a calendar like the one displayed in Figure 12.16 on your Form. This control is used to display and select dates. Unlike the **DateTimePicker** control, this calendar control is not designed to disappear.

The **MonthCalendar** control can display date ranges up to a week by default, and also allows users to select a date range also up to a week or the maximum value set in the **MaxSelectionCount** property. The calendar is very configurable. You can change which day of the week appears in the far-left column. You can turn on the **Today** property, which identifies today's date on the calendar, and even allows you to place a red circle in the date.

When using the **MonthCalendar** control to accept user input, you can examine the **SelectionRange**, **SelectionStart**, and **SelectionEnd** properties to view the date or date range entered by the user.

```
Private Sub button1_Click(ByVal sender As System.Object,
ByVal e As System.EventArgs) Handles button1.Click

        messagebox.Show(monthCalendar1().SelectionRange.
        ToString)

End Sub
```

Earlier in this section, I mentioned that the **MonthCalendar** control did not disappear like the **DateTimePicker** control. Here is a little explanation of how you can make the **MonthCalendar** control mimic the **DateTimePicker** control.

1. Add a **TextBox** control, **TextBox1**, to the **Form**.
2. Add a **MonthCalendar**, **monthCalendar1**, to the **Form**.
3. Set the **Visible** property of the monthCalendar control to False.
4. Add some code to handle the **Enter** event of the **TextBox** control like this:

```
Private Sub textBox1_TextEnter(ByVal sender As
System.Object, ByVal e As System.EventArgs) Handles
textBox1.Enter

    monthCalendar1().Visible = True

End Sub
```

This sample code makes the **monthCalendar** visible when anyone clicks in the **TextBox** control.
5. Write some code to handle the **DateChanged** event of the **MonthCalendar** control like this:

```
Private Sub monthCalendar1_DateChanged(ByVal sender As
System.Object, ByVal e As
System.Windows.Forms.DateRangeEventArgs) Handles
monthCalendar1.DateChanged

    textBox1().Text =
    monthCalendar1().SelectionStart.ToString

    monthCalendar1().Visible = False

End Sub
```

This sample code adds the value selected from the calendar into the **TextBox** and then makes the **MonthCalendar** control invisible again.

PictureBox

The **PictureBox** control is not normally used as a data-entry control but is an important control for displaying images on a container object such as the Form. Setting the Image property of the **PictureBox** control sets the image that will appear in the control.

The **PictureBox.Image** property accepts a bitmap object. Create a bitmap object and load it into the **Image** property like this:

```
Dim mypic As New System.Drawing.Bitmap("c:\temp\me.jpg")

pictureBox1().Image = mypic
```

Replace the path and filename in the **Bitmap** constructor with the actual path and file-name of the image you would like displayed in the **PictureBox**.

The **PictureBox** control can display static images, or by dynamically changing the value of the **Image** property, you can change the picture that appears. This is very handy for displaying images stored in a database. For example, an employee management application may display information about an employee alongside of the employee's photo.

The **PictureBox** is not normally used as a user input control, although it can be enabled by setting the **Enabled** property to True, and then code can be entered as event handlers. For example, the **PictureBox** can respond to events such as the **Click** event, **Enter**, **Drag** and **Drop** events, and many other change-of-configuration events.

RichTextBox

The RichTextBox control allows the user to enter formatted text. Unlike other text controls, which allow text to be entered in a set font, this control allows formatting such as tabs, embedded URLs, word wrapping, and much more.

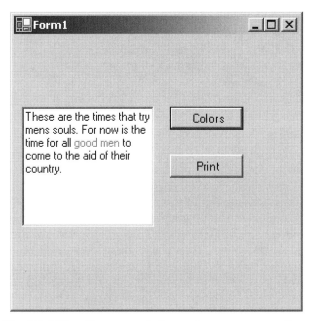

Figure 12.17   The **RichTextBox** control allows the user to enter Formatted text; *good men* appears gray.

When a user enters text into the control, it will appear with the default font. To further **Form**at the text, the user must select (highlight) the text (see Figure 12.17). Once text has been selected it may be formatted using the following properties:

- SelectionBullet
- SelectionColor
- SelectionFont
- SelectionHangingIndent
- SelectionIndent
- SelectionRightIndent

Here is an example of changing the color of selected text by setting the value returned from the **ColorDialog** (covered later in this chapter).

```
Private Sub ColorSelect_Click(ByVal sender As
System.Object, ByVal e As System.EventArgs) Handles
ColorSelect.Click
```

```
              Dim myResult As New DialogResult()

              colorDialog1().ShowDialog()

              richTextBox1().SelectionColor =
              colorDialog1().Color


   End Sub
```

Users can load a file into the **RichTextBox**, edit its contents, and save it back in Rich-Text format. Enable this feature using the **LoadFile** method and **SaveFile** methods.

You can enable other word processor–like features such as the ability to find words or characters within the text using the **Find** method. Similar to Microsoft Word, the Rich-TextBox also has the abilities to automatically detect URLs and display them as hypertext links. Also like a word processor, you can call **Undo** and **Redo** methods to allow corrections. The **CanRedo** property must be set to **True** to allow these other two methods to operate.

Protect sections of the text within the control using the **SelectionProtected** property. This is a great feature if you are creating user entry **Form**s to be saved in Rich Text **Format**. Protect labels and other text you do not want the user to edit. Then allow editing of other portions of the text.

Similar to the **TextBox** control, the **Text** property of the **RichTextBox** control sets the text to be displayed in the control. The **Lines** property accepts a collection of **String** objects, one for each line.

ErrorProvider

The **ErrorProvider** indicates to the user that a control on the Form has an error. When an error occurs, an icon appears next to the offending control and when the user places the mouse over the control, a tooltip appears displaying the error description (Figure 12.18).

Add the **ErrorProvider** to the **Form**. Once it has been added, you can modify the properties of each control on the **Form** to use the **ErrorProvider** in the Error property. They should each say "Error on ErrorProvider1," or whatever your **ErrorProvider** object is named.

HelpProvider

The **HelpProvider** control provides pop-up or online Help for controls. This is a nonvisual control. Adding the **HelpProvider** control to the Form places a reference to the object beneath the Form.

The **HelpProvider** keeps a collection of references to each control for which it provides Help.

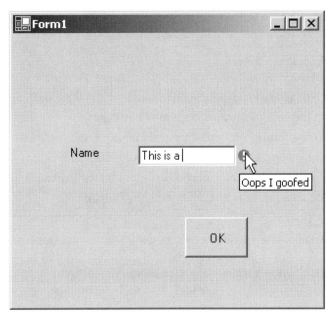

Figure 12.18   The ErrorProvider places an error icon and displays a tooltip next to the control.

Help Files provide Help information and must be associated with the **HelpProvider** by setting the **HelpNameSpace** property. The value set in the **HelpNameSpace** property is the full path to the Help file. Two types of Help files can be designated here:

- Compiled Help File (.chm) – also known as a chum file.
- HTML File – also known as a Web page.

Set the type of Help provided by calling **SetHelpNavigator** and setting the **Help-Navigator** property. You can also set a keyword for context-sensitive help by setting the **SetHelpKeyword** property.

Dialogs

Dialog windows are an important part of creating a Windows user interface. They are not controls you place on a **Form**, but instead **Forms** themselves. These dialogs are usually single purpose and transitory. They provide immediate and sometimes instantaneous functionality, and then go away.

Common to all dialog windows is the return value. Dialogs return a DialogResult object. This object contains one of the enumerated values shown below:

Abort – The dialog was aborted, normally by an Abort **Button**.

Cancel – The dialog was canceled, normally by a Cancel **Button**.

Ignore – The dialog value is to be ignored, normally by an Ignore **Button**.

No – The dialog value is No, normally set by a No **Button**.

None – There is no return value, which usually means the dialog is still open.

OK – The dialog value is OK, normally set by an OK **Button**.

Retry – The dialog value is Retry, normally set by a Retry **Button**.

Yes – The dialog value is Yes, normally set by a Yes **Button**.

The values listed above are enough to know what the user did to exit the dialog but offer no clue as to what may have been chosen while the dialog was open. The following sections discuss some of the more common system dialogs, and the properties you will need to inspect to discern what the user selected from the dialog.

Dialogs also share some common events. Two events of particular interest are:

OnApply – Raises the Apply event.

OnHelpRequest – Raises the **HelpRequest** event.

Not every dialog has an **Apply Button**. Should you choose to allow this **Button**, you can also handle the **OnApply** event. The same is true for Help. If you choose to have a Help **Button**, you can also handle the **OnHelpRequest** event.

OpenFileDialog

The **OpenFileDialog** is one of the more commonly used dialog windows. It allows users to select one or more files by browsing through the folders on their disk drives or network drive, or allows the user to type in a path and file name. Figure 12.19 shows the **Open-FileDialog** window.

Customize the way the **OpenFileDialog** searches and displays files by setting the object's properties. There are many properties, but here are a few of the important ones for configuring the display and its behavior:

AddExtension – Sets whether or not the file extension is automatically added.

DefaultExt – This sets a default file extension. When a user excludes an extension from a filename, the default extension is appended.

Filter – Adds filters for the user to select for limiting the file types to display.

InitialDirectory – This sets the starting folder for the dialog.

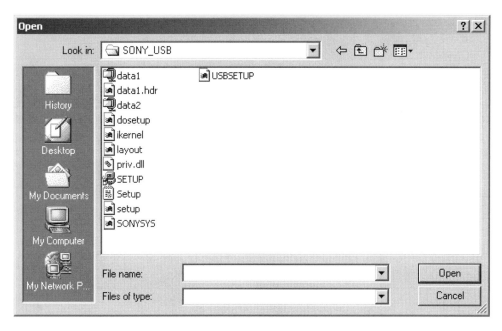

Figure 12.19 The OpenFileDialog is one of the most familiar of all dialog windows.

MultiSelect – Determines if the user can select more than one file.

Title – The Dialog window's title bar.

To use the information entered by the user, your application must look at either the **FileName** property, or if you have **MultiSelect** enabled, look at the **FileNames** property. The **FileNames** property is a collection of file names represented as **Strings**. Here is an example that simply prints out the full path and file name of each file selected by the user:

```
Private Sub button1_Click(ByVal sender As System.Object,
ByVal e As System.EventArgs) Handles button1.Click

    openFileDialog1().ShowDialog()

    Dim myfile As String

    For Each myfile In openFileDialog1().FileNames

        console.Write(myfile)
```

```
        Next

    End Sub
```

Rather than printing the output, as this sample has, you would use the file names to open the files. Also, this sample has the dialog opened by clicking a **Button**. This code would be more appropriate in the click event of a **MainMenu MenuItem** object labeled "Open." This control is used together with classes found in the **System.IO** namespace to open files. Here is an example of opening or creating each file specified:

```
For Each myfile In openFileDialog1().FileNames

        System.IO.File.Open(myfile, IO.FileMode.
        OpenOrCreate)

    Next
```

This will open the file, but this sample is limited. Normally you would assign the output of the **Open** method to a **FileStream** object.

> **Note**
> The **OpenFileDialog** class cannot be inherited.

SaveFileDialog

The **SaveFileDialog** is quite similar to the **OpenFileDialog** with one distinction; rather than selecting files to open, it allows the user to identify the path and file name of a currently open file to be saved to disk. The **SaveFileDialog** allows you to specify which file you are currently trying to save, as you can only save one file at a time. You can also choose a new location for the file to be saved by browsing the folders on the hard drive. Or you can save to a network drive by selecting **My Network Places** from the **Save In** dropdown list (see Figure 12.20).

This is not really a data-entry control, so you are limited to examining the return value of the Dialog to see if the user actually clicked the **Save Button** rather than the **Cancel Button**. This control is used together with classes found in the **System.IO** namespace to save files.

PrintDialog

Many applications require the ability to send a file to the printer. The **PrintDialog** lets users select a printer and choose what pages of the document to print.

Add the **PrintDialog** to your application by selecting it from the Visual Studio Toolbox window and clicking on your Form. A reference to this nonvisual control will appear in the space beneath your Form.

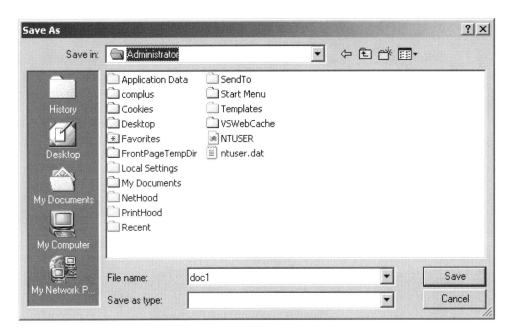

Figure 12.20 The SaveFileDialog is similar in appearance to the OpenfileDialog.

Configure the behavior and appearance of your PrintDialog by setting the following properties:

AllowPrintToFile – Enables and disables the ability to print a document to file, enabling and disabling the checkbox on the dialog.

AllowSelection – Enables and disables the selection radio **Button**.

AllowSomePages – Enables or disables the ability to print a range of pages.

ShowHelp – Displays the Help **Button**.

ShowNetwork – Displays the Network **Button**.

Printing in Visual Basic .Net is a little complex.

In this example, the **Print Button**'s click event starts the process by creating a new **PrintDialog** object and a **PrintDocument** object, both necessary for the print process. (Also see Figure 12.21.) Set the **Name** property of the **PrintDocument** object and then store the **PrintDocument** object into the **PrintDialog** object's Document property. You're now ready to launch the **PrintDialog** using the **ShowDialog** method.

Next, we need to create an event handler for the document's **PrintPage** event. Using **AddHandler**, we assign the **PrintPageHandler** procedure as the event handler. An event

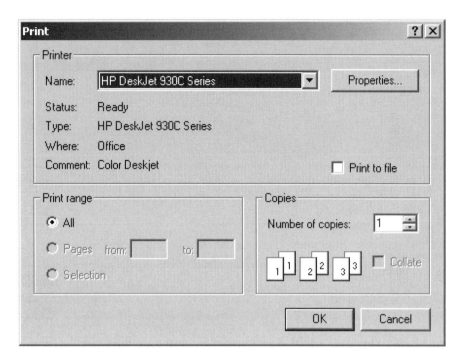

Figure 12.21   The PrintDialog allows you to send documents to the printer.

is raised each time a new page is ready to print. In the event code PrintPageHandler, you draw into the page to be printed using the **Graphics.DrawString** method.

```
Public Class Form1

    Inherits System.Windows.Forms.Form

#Region " Windows Form Designer generated code "

    Public Sub New()

        MyBase.New()

        InitializeComponent()

    End Sub
```

```
Public Overrides Sub Dispose()

    MyBase.Dispose()

    If Not (components Is Nothing) Then

        components.Dispose()

    End If

End Sub

Private Printfont As Font

Private StreamToPrint As IO.StreamReader

Private WithEvents Print1 As
System.Windows.Forms.Button

Private components As System.ComponentModel.Container

Private Sub <System.Diagnostics.DebuggerStepThrough()>
InitializeComponent()

    Me.Print1 = New System.Windows.Forms.Button()

    Me.Print1.Location = New System.Drawing.Point(160,
    120)

    Me.Print1.TabIndex = 0

    Me.Print1.Text = "Print"

    Me.AutoScaleBaseSize = New System.Drawing.Size(5,
    13)

    Me.ClientSize = New System.Drawing.Size(292, 273)

    Me.Controls.AddRange(New
    System.Windows.Forms.Control() {Me.Print1})
```

```
        Me.Text = "Form1"

    End Sub



    Private Sub Print1_Click(ByVal sender As
System.Object, ByVal e As System.EventArgs) Handles
Print1.Click

        Dim prdialog As New PrintDialog()

        Dim prdoc As New
        System.Drawing.Printing.PrintDocument()

        prdoc.DocumentName = "test document"

        prdialog.Document = prdoc

        prdialog.ShowDialog()

        AddHandler prdoc.PrintPage, AddressOf
        Me.PrintPageHandler

        prdoc.Print()

        prdoc.Dispose()

        prdialog.Dispose()

    End Sub

    Private Sub PrintPageHandler(ByVal sender As Object,
ByVal ev As Drawing.Printing.PrintPageEventArgs)

        Dim linesPerPage As Single = 0

        Dim yPos As Single = 0

        Dim count As Integer = 0
```

```
        Dim leftMargin As Single = ev.MarginBounds.Left

        Dim topMargin As Single = ev.MarginBounds.Top

        Dim line As String = Nothing

        linesPerPage = ev.MarginBounds.Height /
        Printfont.GetHeight(ev.Graphics)

        While count < linesPerPage

            line = StreamToPrint.ReadLine()

            If line Is Nothing Then

                Exit While

            End If

            yPos = topMargin + count *
            Printfont.GetHeight(ev.Graphics)

            ev.Graphics.DrawString(line, Printfont,
            Brushes.Black, leftMargin, yPos, New
            StringFormat())

            count += 1

        End While

        If Not (line Is Nothing) Then

            ev.HasMorePages = True

        Else

            ev.HasMorePages = False

        End If

    End Sub
```

```
#End Region

End Class
```

PageSetupDialog

The **PageSetupDialog** is a dialog box that enables users to configure page settings for documents destined for printing. Users can manipulate margin settings, printer settings, and paper orientation. This dialog is normally launched from the application's **MainMenu**, and found as a menu item of the **File** menu, located above the **Print** menu selection.

As the application developer, you can decide how much control to give the users in configuring their page setup. Configure the **PageSetupDialog** using the following properties:

AllowMargins – Enables or disables margin-setting ability.

AllowOrientation – Enables or disables the ability to change between portrait and landscape mode.

AllowPaper – Enables or disables the ability to set paper size and source.

AllowPrinter – Enables or disables the ability to print directly from this dialog.

MinMargins – Configures the minimum margin that can be set in this control.

ShowHelp – Shows or hides the Help **Button**.

ShowNetwork – Shows or hides the Network **Button**.

The Document contains the **PrintDocument** object while the **PageSettings** property either gets or sets the modified page settings. The **PrinterSettings** property contains the printer settings sent to the printer when the user clicks the **Print Button** (when enabled).

FontDialog

The **FontDialog** allows users to select choices related to the appearance of text. This dialog returns two objects: **Font** and optionally **Color**. Figure 12.22 shows the **FontDialog** set to accept both font and color information.

The properties of the **FontDialog** allow you to control the types and styles of fonts, as well as which font features can be set in the dialog window. They include the following:

AllowSimulations – Allows GDI font simulations.

AllowVectorFonts – Allows the selection of vector-based fonts.

AllowVerticalFonts – Allows the selection of vertical fonts.

FixedPitchOnly – Allows the selection of fixed-pitch fonts only.

MaxSize – Sets the maximum point size.

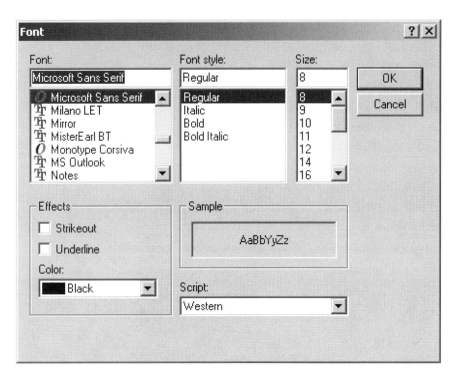

Figure 12.22 The FontDialog lets users select fonts already installed on the system.

MinSize – Sets the minimum point size.

ShowApply – Shows an Apply **Button** on the dialog.

ShowColor – Shows a color selection control on the dialog.

ShowEffects – Shows the effects area of the dialog.

ShowHelp – Shows a Help **Button** on the dialog.

The **FontDialog** returns a **Font** object that can be used to set the font properties of other objects, accepting **Font** objects. Almost all of the controls included in the Visual Studio Toolbox accept **Font** objects to configure the text display. Remember that container objects, such as the **Form**, affect the display of other controls contained in them. So, changing the **Font** properties of the **Form** will also, for example, change the **Font** of the text of a **Button**.

Font   The properties of the **Font** object returned from the **FontDialog** will give you the information selected by the user. Here are the properties:

Bold – Is the font bold or not?

FontFamily – The text name of the font, such as Helvetica or Arial.

GdiCharSet – The value of the graphics display character set.

GdiVerticalFont – Is this font a GDI Vertical Font or not?

Height – The height of the font in pixels.

Italic – Is the font set in italics?

Name – The face name of the font.

Size – The size of the font.

SizeInPoints – The size of the font in points.

StrikeOut – Will the font appear with strikeout characters?

Style – The style of the font.

Underline – Will the font appear with underline characters?

Unit – The unit of measure for this font.

This code sample shows how you can create a **DialogResult** object that accepts the return value of the **FontDialog**. This return value is important because you will want to ignore any changes in Font when the user exits the dialog with anything other than either an **Apply** or **OK** result. If it's all right to change the font based on user selection, look in the Font property of the FontDialog for the result.

```
Private Sub button1_Click(ByVal sender As System.Object,
ByVal e As System.EventArgs) Handles button1.Click

    Dim myresult As New DialogResult()

    myresult = fontDialog1().ShowDialog()

    If myresult = DialogResult().OK Then

    messagebox.Show(fontDialog1().Font.FontFamily.Name)

        console.Write(fontDialog1().Font.Name.ToString)

    End If

End Sub
```

This sample displays the FontFamily name in a **MessageBox** and prints the Font name in the console window. Just add a **Text Box** from the toolbox. You wouldn't normally print the results like this. Instead, you would plug them into the **Font** property of another object like this:

```
Private Sub button1_Click(ByVal sender As System.Object,
ByVal e As System.EventArgs) Handles button1.Click

    Dim myresult As New DialogResult()

    myresult = fontDialog1().ShowDialog()

    If myresult = DialogResult().OK Then

        textBox1().Font = fontDialog1().Font

    End If

End Sub
```

Color When you set the **ShowColor** property of the **FontDialog** to True, a color selection control appears in the Effects section of the dialog. This allows the user to select a font color from a list of 16 basic system colors.

The result of user color selection is returned within a **DialogResult** object. This next code sample displays the **Color** object within a message box. Four values are displayed that make up the RGBA color composition: Red, Green, Blue, and Alpha. Each color channel is represented by an integer from 0 to 255. The red, green, and blue channels make up the color, while Alpha represents the transparent pixel color. There is no way to set the transparent color in this dialog, so by default the Alpha always equals 255 for each of the 16 color selections.

```
Private Sub button1_Click(ByVal sender As System.Object,
ByVal e As System.EventArgs) Handles button1.Click

    Dim myresult As New DialogResult()

    myresult = fontDialog1().ShowDialog()

    If myresult = DialogResult().OK Then

        messagebox.Show(fontDialog1().Color.ToString)

        console.Write(fontDialog1().Font.Name.
        ToString)
```

```
            End If

    End Sub
```

Just as with the **Font** property, you would not normally print out the color, but instead use it to set the font color property within a control. Here is an example that sets both the **Font** and the **ForeColor** properties of the **ActiveForm**:

```
Private Sub button1_Click(ByVal sender As System.Object,
ByVal e As System.EventArgs) Handles button1.Click

    Dim myresult As New DialogResult()

    myresult = fontDialog1().ShowDialog()

    If myresult = DialogResult().OK Then

        Form1.ActiveForm.Font = fontDialog1().Font

        Form1.ActiveForm.ForeColor = fontDialog1().Color

    End If

End Sub
```

ColorDialog

The **ColorDialog** enables users to select a color that can be used to customize other controls. The **ColorDialog** has two display modes, one that allows custom colors, and one that only allows users to select from preselected solid colors. Custom colors may appear solid, but they are in fact combinations of colored pixels *dithered* together to appear as a new color. Dithered colors are achieved by creating varying combinations of Red, Blue, and Green, and a scale of 0 (meaning no pixels of this color) to 255, which is the maximum intensity (a third of all the pixels) of this color.

Configure the ColorDialog by setting the following properties:

AllowFullOpen – Enables or disables the Define Custom Colors **Button**.

AnyColor – Enables or disables the selection of any color.

FullOpen – Configures the control to initially show or not show the custom color selection.

ShowHelp – Shows or hides the Help **Button**.

SolidColorOnly – Enables or disables the selection of only solid colors.

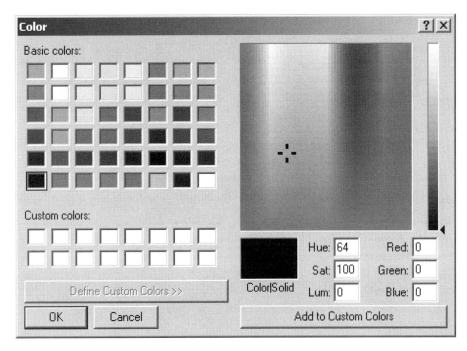

Figure 12.23 Applications that allow color changes make use of the ColorDialog.

The **Color** property of the **ColorDialog** contains the color selected by the user. Use the **Color** object returned in this property to set colors of other objects accepting **Color** objects.

Add another **Button** to the **Form** and change the name to **ColorSelect**. In this example, the **Color** object returned from the dialog is used to change the background color of the **Button** used to launch the **ColorDialog** (see also Figure 12.23):

```
Private Sub ColorSelect_Click(ByVal sender As
System.Object, ByVal e As System.EventArgs) Handles
ColorSelect.Click

    colorDialog1().ShowDialog()

    ColorSelect().BackColor = colorDialog1().Color

End Sub
```

MessageBox

The **MessageBox** is an important user-interface item. Although most developers do not think of the lowly **MessageBox** as a dialog window, it fits all the requirement of being one. It's a transitory window that is designed to display text messages, and allows the user to click a response to the message. In this way, it operates in a similar manner to other dialog windows we've already covered. Admittedly much simpler than the other dialogs, the **MessageBox** is an equally important part of the user interface.

MessageBox windows are launched using the **Show** method. This method has 12 overloaded constructors that allow you to configure the display of the **MessageBox** by passing differing numbers and types of arguments.

> **Text** – The message text to display.
>
> **Caption** – The caption that appears in the Window header of the MessageBox.
>
> **Owner** – A property of an object that determines the owner (container) of the object.
>
> **MessageBoxButtons** – A combination of **Buttons**, such as Abort, Retry, and Ignore (Figure 12.24)
>
> **Icon** – A preconfigured Windows MessageBox icon. Figure 12.24 shows the error icon.
>
> **DefaultButton** – Identifies which **Button** is the default when the user hits the Enter key.
>
> **MessageBoxOptions** – Configures where and how the MessageBox is displayed.

MessageBox objects always display text. They can be further configured to display **Buttons**, options, and an icon. Additionally, you can also identify a specific object over which the **MessageBox** should appear.

The **MessageBox**, like other dialogs, returns a **DialogResult** object. Here is an example you might find in the **Catch** block of a Try-Catch exception handling block:

```
Dim myResult As New DialogResult()

myResult = messagebox.Show("My test", "caption text",
MessageBoxButtons.AbortRetryIgnore, MessageBoxIcon.Error,
MessageBoxDefaultButton.Button1,
MessageBoxOptions.DefaultDesktopOnly)

If myResult = DialogResult().Retry Then

    'add code to retry whatever failed.

End If
```

When displaying text only, the **MessageBox** appears with an **OK Button**. Because the **MessageBox** is a modal dialog, no other user action can be taken until the user clicks the **OK Button** on the **MessageBox**.

Figure 12.24   The **MessageBox** can be configured to allow several types of user response.

Custom Controls

You can create custom controls by inheriting from any of the controls already discussed in this chapter and customizing them for your own needs. You can also start from a lower level and create controls that are based on lower-level, foundational classes, which provide functionality. Unfortunately Visual Basic .Net does not support multiple inheritance, giving your new controls the ability to inherit from multiple classes. It does, however, support the ability to implement several interfaces. The WinForms Interfaces are listed in Table 12.3. When implementing an interface you must implement each of the members defined in the interface.

Table 12.3   WinForms Interfaces

Interface	Description
IButtonControl	Allows a control to act like a button on a form.
IContainerControl	Provides the functionality for a control to act as a parent for other controls.
IDataGridColumnEditingNotificationService	Provides Data Grid Editing feedback notification.
IDataObject	Provides a format-independent mechanism for transferring data.
IFeatureSupport	An interface for retrieving feature information from the current system.
IMessage	FilterAn interface that defines a message filter.
IWin32Window	Provides an interface to expose Win32 HWND handles.

In addition to implementing interfaces, the Common Language Runtime classes include a great number of base classes for building custom controls. These include:

UserControl – An empty control. This is the base class for all controls. It is derived from the Form, and thus has all the same abilities.

ContainerControl – The base class for all controls that contain other controls.

Control – The parent control for controls with a visual representation.

UpDownBase – This class implements basic functionality for any control that has an up-and-down scroll ability.

VScrollBar – A Windows vertical scroll bar.

HScrollBar – A Windows horizontal scroll bar.

ControlPaint – This class has members used to paint user interface elements.

CommonDialog – The base class for dialog window controls.

FormatControl – This class has functions for **Form**atting text displayed in a control.

ListManager – Takes care of the position and bindings of list members.

Implementing interfaces and creating custom controls is time-consuming and involved but rewarding. Chapter 18 will go into greater detail concerning component and custom control creation.

Summary

Not every control found in the Toolbox was covered in this chapter, but the controls that are important for constructing a working user interface were explained. Because all controls are all derived from the same base classes, you'll find that the properties and behaviors of any control should closely match the ones covered in this book.

Visual Basic .Net gives you the ability to create custom controls by using inheritance. You can inherit many of the standard controls, extending their behaviors or customizing their appearance. You can also start from some of the underlying base classes from which other controls are derived to create your own unique classes.

The next chapter covers databases and data handling. Some of the controls in this chapter are capable of being *bound* to a database. This means that their values are pulled from data storage. Chapter 13 will revisit some of the controls covered here to explore their data-binding capabilities.

Databases 13

A database is an external program designed for the storage and retrieval of information. Communicating with databases is done through classes in the **System.Data** namespace, which make up what is known in Visual Basic .NET as ADO.NET. ADO stands for Active Data Objects.

Many applications have a need to store and retrieve data in a database. Most business applications are known to be "data-centric" because they are designed primarily to retrieve, display, and store information.

To achieve maximum efficiency of design, applications of today are configured in layers or tiers: the display tier, the processing tier, and the database tier. As we explore the classes in the **System.Data** namespace in this chapter, we will try to give examples of three-tier application design.

Data Access

Data access to ODBC data sources is accomplished through a managed provider. There are currently two providers available: Microsoft SQL Server 7.0 and Provider for OLE DB providers.

The DataTable

The **DataTable** object represents a data source or table in a database. This is one of the key objects in data manipulation in Visual Basic .NET. It's a key object because it is used in the **DataSet** and **DataView** objects.

DataTable objects are designed to contain data from a data source, usually a database management system. Just as database tables contain columns, **DataTable** objects contain a collection of **DataColumn** objects in a **ColumnsCollection** property. Columns and their definitions form the storage-handling capability of a database table. Defining **Data-Columns** is also known as defining the *table schema* of the **DataTable**. The complete table and column design is known as the *database schema*. Each **DataColumn** object defines the

313

type of data that is stored in the column. Like variables, columns are designed to hold a single data type.

The **DataTable**, completely oblivious to where data originates, still has the ability to use the data stored in memory. It has the ability to move through the data, change the data, create views, apply filters, and sort the data. Later in this chapter you'll see how you can tie a **DataTable** object to the **DataSource** of a **Control** object, populating the values in a data-bound control.

DataTable objects are created either by having the values filled in by **DataSet** commands or constructed manually. The next section explains how to populate the **Data-Table** using the **DataSet** object. When building the **DataTable** programmatically, begin by defining the **DataColumn** objects, adding them to the **DataColumnCollection**.

The **DataColumn.DataType** property defines the data type. You can further customize the **DataColumn** object by setting properties such as:

AllowNull – Enables or disables the ability to leave the column blank when adding a new row into the database.

ReadOnly – Protects the data stored in the column from being edited or changed.

Expression – Constructs the value of this column dynamically based on an expression.

Adding rows programmatically is done using the **NewRow** method of the **DataTable**. The **NewRow** method returns a new **DataRow** object, which has columns defined that match the schema defined when adding **DataColumns**. When adding rows, you can also define constraints on the data that is entered into a row. Add **Constraint** objects to the **DataTable's Constraint** collection to ensure the integrity of the data added into the database.

> **Note**
> The maximum number of rows a **DataTable** can store is 16,777,216.

DataTable Events   When users add, change, or delete rows, events are triggered, allowing you greater flexibility in responding to the user during data entry. Changes to the **DataTable** object trigger the following events:

- RowChanged Event
- RowChanging Event
- RowDeleted Event
- RowDeleting Event

The DataSet

When you think of a database, you think of a container defined with columns and containing rows of data. This is exactly how you can imagine the **DataSet**, except that it is held entirely in memory instead of written to disk. The **DataSet** is simply a container object that contains one or more **DataTable** objects and the objects used to create relationships between **DataTables**.

As shown in more detail in the next section, the **DataAdapter** object acts like a bridge, mapping physical columns of data in a data source to the user-defined columns in a **DataTable** object.

The **DataSet** contains another object used to define the relationship between tables. Each table in the relationship must share a common field. This means that the column that is defined must have the same data type and size defined, as well as contain data in that column that will match in both tables. A relationship creates a parent–child relationship between tables.

Understanding Relations   Most modern database management systems are considered *relational*. A relational database is one where information in one table is tied together (related) to information in another table based on primary and secondary keys. These are columns in the related tables that match, forming the ability to relate two or more tables. For example, a database may have a table that contains a list of all employees, their names, and their employee id numbers. Another table may contain information about the employees' salary history. The second table need not store the employee name, only the employee id number. The two tables are then related based on the key, id number.

The **DataTable** object contains a collection of **DataRelation** objects in its **RelationsCollection** property. These define the relations each table maintains with other tables. Whenever a **DataRelation** object is added to the collection, two additional objects are automatically created: the **UniqueConstraint** and **ForeignKeyconstraint**.

When data values in a column are intended as keys, they must be unique. This uniqueness is managed by the **UniqueConstraint** object. The **ForeignKeyConstraint** object manages the interaction with related tables. For example, when data in one table is deleted, will the delete cascade throughout all related tables? An example of this would be deleting an employee. Information related to the deleted employee should also be deleted or something known as orphaned records will be created. These are rows for which no identifying or related information appears in the parent table.

The **DataRelation** object does the work of the SQL **Join** command. The relationship between the two tables is dynamic and can be changed. It's also possible to have many levels of parent–child relationships between multiple tables.

The DataView

SQL (Structured Query Language), used by most modern relational databases, has the ability to create a view. A *view* is a type of saved query that acts like a database table. The data continues to reside in the original tables; only the way of viewing the data changes.

The same ability exists in the .NET data framework using the **DataView** object. This object has the same ability to offer a customized view of a **DataTable**. The **DataView** object can be used in many cases in the same manner as a **DataTable**. For example, many data-bound controls that bind to **DataTable** objects can also bind to the **DataView** object.

Using a Database

Data-centric applications allow users to view, add, change, and delete data. This data can be textual or binary data, such as multimedia graphics and sounds. The data used in these applications can be created by the application, retrieved from the Internet, entered by the user, or retrieved from archival storage in a database. Of course, the data's source can be any combination of these, and some we haven't thought of.

The most common way of storing data is using a database management program, like Microsoft's SQL Server, or products by Oracle, Sybase, Informix, or many others not listed here. There are several kinds of database management systems: nonrelational, relational, and object-oriented, to name a few. This chapter discusses the most commonly used type, the relational database.

The database can store user information as well as information about itself. For example, later in this chapter we discuss data-bound controls, which retrieve their values ultimately from a database. It's also possible to store serialized objects in a database, a concept known as object persistence, and reinstantiate them in your program when needed.

How you construct your Visual Basic .NET programs that make use of a database depends on the database you select, such as Microsoft's SQL Server or anything else. This example demonstrates the use of Microsoft's SQL Server.

> **Note**
> To use with Microsoft's SQL server, Visual Basic .NET must be version 7.0 or later.

Making a Connection

When making a connection to a database, the first thing you will need is a connection string. This contains the initial catalog, data source, or data source name, and optionally the type of security to use.

```
Dim connectString As String = "Initial
Catalog=Northwind;Data Source=localhost;Integrated
Security=SSPI;"
```

Next you will need to create a connection to the database. This is done using one of the **Connection** classes (in this example we use SQLConnection), passing in the connection string created in the first step.

```
Dim dbNorthwind As SqlConnection = New
SqlConnection(connectString)
```

Note
The Northwind database is the sample database that comes installed with Microsoft SQL Server. Because many people have this database already installed (Figure 13.1), the samples in this chapter use that database. You can adapt these samples to your own custom database.

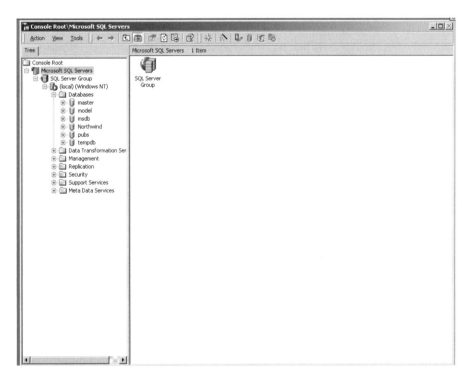

Figure 13.1   The Northwind database comes installed as a sample in SQL Server.

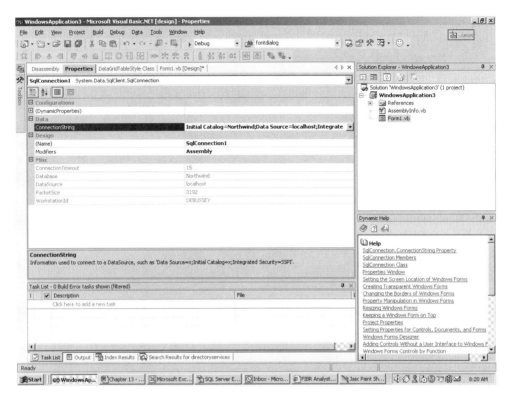

Figure 13.2 Read-only properties of the connection object populate when you enter a **ConnectionString**.

If you choose, you can add a connection object by selecting the connection object type (**OleDbConnection** or **SQLConnection**) from the Toolbox window and clicking on the **Form**. The one property that is not read-only is the **ConnectionString** property. Add a connection string in the Properties window exactly as you would programmatically. You will notice that all the read-only properties populate from the values defined in the **ConnectionString**. This is a great way to know if your **ConnectionString** is formatted properly. When it's malformed, these properties will not populate correctly. Correctly populated values are shown in Figure 13.2.

Using the DataAdapter

The **DataAdapter** forms the bridge between the **DataSet** and the data source (in many cases a database) for the purpose of retrieving and saving data. One of the most powerful methods of the **DataAdapter** is Fill, which sets the contents of the **DataSet** to match data in the data source. The Update method of the **DataAdapter** calls the appropriate INSERT, UPDATE, or DELETE commands to make changes to the data source. Each row in the **DataSet** is evaluated to see if a new row should be added, an existing row modified, or a row deleted.

The Northwind database is installed with 13 tables (not counting the system tables). In this next step we add a **DataAdapter** object for the Employees table. Once again, because we are communicating with an SQL Server database, we use **SQLDataAdapter**.

```
Dim daEmployees As SqlDataAdapter = New SqlDataAdapter()
```

The **SQLDataAdapter** object acts as a bridge between the **DataSet** and a Microsoft SQL Server database. It's used together with the SQLConnection object, created in the previous step, and the SQLCommand object. When working with databases other than Microsoft SQL Server, refer to Table 13.1 to see which objects to use.

The **DataAdapter** object has methods that facilitate data storage and editing as well as mapping results to the **DataSet**:

DeleteCommand – This property contains the SQL **Delete** command, used during delete.

InsertCommand – This property contains the SQL **Insert** command, used while adding new data.

SelectCommand – This property contains the SQL **Select** command, used for retreiving rows.

TableMappings –This provides the mapping between the **DataSet** object and the columns returned from the database.

UpdateCommand – This property contains the SQL **Update** command for changing data.

This example uses **TableMappings** to add a new mapping to the Adapter object:

```
daEmployees.TableMappings.Add("Table", "Employees")
```

Open the connection to the database using the **Open** method of the **SQLConnection** object.

```
dbNorthwind.Open()
```

Table 13.1 Adapter, Connection, and Command Objects by Database Type

Database Type	Connection Object	Adapter Object	Command Object
SQL Server	SQLConnection	SQLAdapter	SQLCommand
Other Database	OleDbConnection	OleDbAdapter	OleDbCommand

Create a new **SQLCommand** object by passing in the SQL command as a string. In this example we are selecting all the columns from the Employees table in the Northwind data connection.

```
Dim cmdEmployees As SqlCommand = New SqlCommand("SELECT *
FROM Employees", dbNorthwind)
```

The command object must be told how to interpret the commands given to it as either text or a stored procedure in the database. Set this value to **CommandType.Text** when not using stored procedures. Otherwise, this property should contain the name of the stored procedure containing the appropriate SQL command.

```
cmdEmployees.CommandType = CommandType.Text
```

Set the **SelectCommand** property of the **DataAdapter** object to the **SQLCommand** object you just created.

```
daEmployees.SelectCommand = cmdEmployees
```

Adding a DataAdapter Visually

In addition to adding a **DataAdapter** programmatically, you can select the appropriate **DataAdapter** (either **OleDbDataAdapter** or **SQLDataAdapter**) from the Toolbox window and click on the Form. This launches the **DataAdapter** Configuration Wizard. You can choose to configure the **DataAdapter** object using the Wizard, or by setting the properties of the **DataAdapter** in the Properties window (see Figure 13-3). You can launch the Configuration Wizard at any time by clicking the link in the bottom of the Properties window.

When setting **DataAdapter** properties manually, the first thing you should fill in is the **ConnectionString**. It will be the same **ConnectionString** created earlier in this chapter. That will self-fill some of the read-only properties of the **DataAdapter**.

When filling out the **CommandText** property, a Visual Studio Query Builder tool will pop up. Select the table from the list. You will see an additional window pop-up allowing you to select one, several, or all the columns. You can see the Query Builder construct the SQL statement in the window. The next step is to configure the **DataSet** (see "Adding a **DataSet** Visually").

Configuring the DataSet   Now that we have the key components configured, it's time to create the **DataSet** object. This is the key object used for storing and manipulating data from the database. We'll call it *ds* for short.

```
Dim ds As New DataSet("Employees")
```

The **Fill** method adds or refreshes rows in the **DataSet** object. In this example, there are no rows currently in the object, so rows are added.

```
daEmployees.Fill(ds)
```

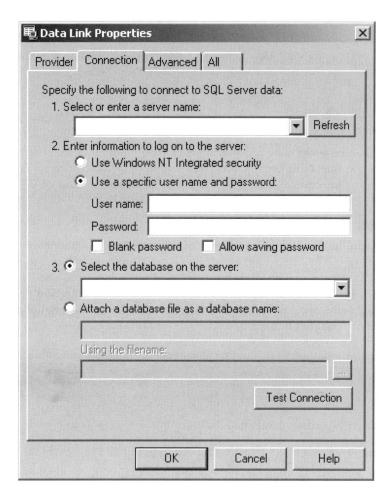

Figure 13.3 Set the **DataLink** properties to set the **Connection** property of the **DataAdapter**.

The **DataSet** now contains a set of rows that match those in the database table, stored in memory. This example also has a second table that we will eventually relate to the first table. The next step, then, is to create a second set of **SQLDataAdapter** and **SQLCommand** objects:

```
Dim daTerritories As SqlDataAdapter = New SqlDataAdapter()

daTerritories.TableMappings.Add("Table",
```

```
"EmployeeTerritories")

Dim cmdTerritories As SqlCommand = New SqlCommand("SELECT
* FROM EmployeeTerritories", dbNorthwind)

daTerritories.SelectCommand = cmdTerritories

daTerritories.Fill(ds)
```

Notice that the results were added into the existing **DataSet** object. There was no need to create a new one. Now, because everything we need is in memory, we no longer need the database connection. So, we close it using the **Close** method of the Connection object.

```
dbNorthwind.Close()
```

The data in the **EmployeeTerritories** table is incomplete without its relation to the **Employees** table. The key field in both tables is the **EmployeeID** field. To relate the two tables you must create a **DataRelation** object, Dimension two **DataColumn** objects, one for each key field (column), and then create the new **DataRelation** object, giving it a meaningful name, and passing in the two key **DataColumn** objects. Use the Relations property of the **DataSet** to store the relation. Your **DataSet** can store as many relations as needed.

```
Dim mydatarelation As DataRelation

Dim datacolPrime As DataColumn

Dim datacolSec As DataColumn

' Get the parent and child columns of the two tables.

datacolPrime =
ds.Tables("Employees").Columns("EmployeeID")

datacolSec =
ds.Tables("EmployeeTerritories").Columns("EmployeeID")

mydatarelation = New
System.Data.DataRelation("employees2territories",
datacolPrime, datacolSec)

ds.Relations.Add(mydatarelation)
```

The data is now in memory, sitting in a **DataSet**, with the relationship set between the two tables. It's now time to use the data.

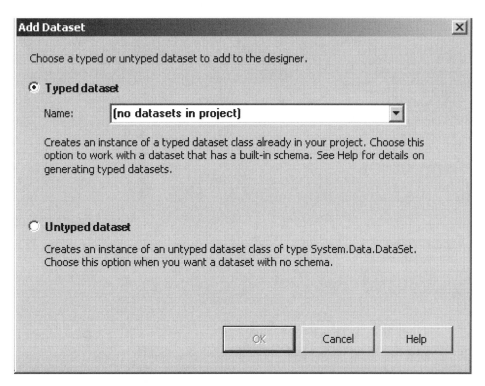

Figure 13.4   Configure **DataSet** objects visually using the Wizard.

Adding a DataSet Visually

So far, we've talked about how to create a **DataSet** programmatically. In this book we've tended to discuss creating things visually using the visual development environment and then how to create them programmatically. In this case, it was more important to understand the foundations of how each of the data types are created and how they interact. Now, it's on to the visual development environment.

When viewing a Form in Visual Studio, you can select the Data tab in the Toolbox window. Select a **DataSet** and click on the **Form**. This launches a Wizard that will help you create the **DataSet**. Figure 13.4 shows you the first window of the Wizard, allowing you to choose between a **DataSet** that already has a schema, defined programmatically, and an empty **DataSet**, one that will have its schema defined later.

If you've visually created the **DataAdapter**, as described previously in this chapter, you will find a link at the bottom of the **DataAdapter** properties window that allows you to

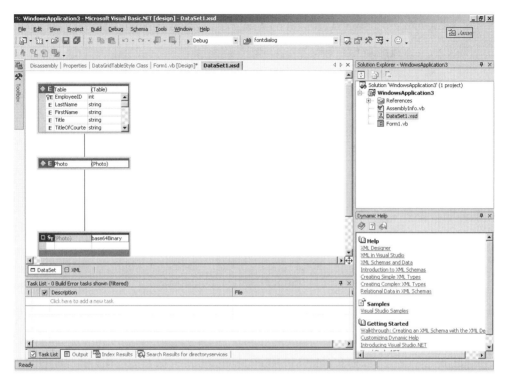

Figure 13.5 The **DataSet** schema is stored as an XML schema file.

create the **DataSet**. Once the **DataSet** is configured, you can click the link in the properties window that appears that allows you to view the schema. Notice that the schema is stored as an XML schema (.XSD) file in the project window. The schema will appear visually, as shown in Figure 13.5.

Data-bound Controls

Most of the controls in the **System.Windows.Forms** namespace are *data aware*. This means that they have the built-in ability to accept data from a **DataSet** object to display in the control. To start off, we'll use the **CheckedListBox** control to display the last names of the employees in the **Employee** data table. The first example is going to show the entire **Form** example, and subsequent examples will assume that the **DataSet** has already been created.

```
Imports System.Data

Imports System.Data.SqlClient

Imports System.Windows.Forms

Public Class Form1

    Inherits System.Windows.Forms.Form

    Dim ds As New DataSet("Employees")

    Dim mytable As New DataTable()

#Region " Windows Form Designer generated code "

    Public Sub New()

        MyBase.New()

' The call to the private getdata() procedure is done here
in

' the constructor so that the data connection is set
first.

        getdata()

        InitializeComponent()

    End Sub

    Protected Overloads Overrides Sub Dispose(ByVal
    disposing As Boolean)

        If disposing Then

            If Not (components Is Nothing) Then

                components.Dispose()
```

```
            End If

        End If

        MyBase.Dispose(disposing)

    End Sub

    Friend WithEvents Button1 As
    System.Windows.Forms.Button

    Dim connectString As String = "Initial
    Catalog=Northwind;Data Source=localhost;Integrated
    Security=SSPI;"

    Dim dbNorthwind As SqlConnection = New
    SqlConnection(connectString)

    Friend WithEvents CheckedListBox1 As
    System.Windows.Forms.CheckedListBox

    ' Create an SqlDataAdapter for the Employees table.

    Dim daEmployees As SqlDataAdapter = New
    SqlDataAdapter()

    Private Sub getdata()

        daEmployees.TableMappings.Add("Table",
        "Employees")

        dbNorthwind.Open()

        Dim cmdEmployees As SqlCommand = New
        SqlCommand("SELECT * FROM Employees", dbNorthwind)

        cmdEmployees.CommandType = CommandType.Text

        daEmployees.SelectCommand = cmdEmployees

        Console.WriteLine("The connection is open.")
```

```
    daEmployees.Fill(ds)

    Dim daTerritories As SqlDataAdapter = New
    SqlDataAdapter()

    daTerritories.TableMappings.Add("Table",
    "EmployeeTerritories")

    Dim cmdTerritories As SqlCommand = New
    SqlCommand("SELECT * FROM EmployeeTerritories",
    dbNorthwind)

    daTerritories.SelectCommand = cmdTerritories

    daTerritories.Fill(ds)

    dbNorthwind.Close()

    Console.WriteLine("The connection is closed.")

    Dim dr As DataRelation

    Dim datacol1 As DataColumn

    Dim datacol2 As DataColumn

    datacol1 =
    ds.Tables("Employees").Columns("EmployeeID")

    datacol2 = ds.Tables("EmployeeTerritories").
    Columns("EmployeeID")

    dr = New System.Data.DataRelation
    ("employees2territories", datacol1, datacol2)

    ds.Relations.Add(dr)

End Sub

Private components As System.ComponentModel.Container

<System.Diagnostics.DebuggerStepThrough()> Private Sub
```

```
    InitializeComponent()

        Me.CheckedListBox1 = New
        System.Windows.Forms.CheckedListBox()

        Me.SuspendLayout()

        Me.CheckedListBox1.Location = New
        System.Drawing.Point(136, 8)

        Me.CheckedListBox1.Name = "CheckedListBox1"

        Me.CheckedListBox1.Size = New
        System.Drawing.Size(120, 94)

        Me.CheckedListBox1.TabIndex = 1

        'Instantiate the DataTable object

        mytable = ds.Tables("Employees")

        Me.CheckedListBox1.DataSource = mytable

        Me.CheckedListBox1.DisplayMember = "LastName"

        Me.AutoScaleBaseSize = New System.Drawing.Size(5,
        13)

        Me.ClientSize = New System.Drawing.Size(292, 273)

        Me.Controls.AddRange(New System.Windows.Forms.
        Control() {Me.CheckedListBox1, Me.Button1})

        Me.Name = "Form1"

        Me.Text = "Form1"

        Me.ResumeLayout(False)

    End Sub

#End Region

End Class
```

This example creates a **DataSet** object using the steps outlined in the previous section. Some of the objects are defined in different places, depending on the scope that is needed by the object. For instance, the **DataSet** and **DataTable** objects are defined in the parent **Form**.

To set the data that will fill the **CheckedListBox** control, we set the control's **Data-Source** and **DisplayMember** properties. First, we instantiate the **DataTable** object with the **Employees** table. We then set the **DataSource** to that **DataTable** object. Lastly, we choose the column that will be used to populate the control and store it in the **DisplayMember** property like this:

```
mytable = ds.Tables("Employees")

Me.CheckedListBox1.DataSource = mytable

Me.CheckedListBox1.DisplayMember = "LastName"
```

Visually Configuring Data-bound Controls

Once you've visually added all the various data objects that create the **Connection**, **DataAdapter,** and **DataSet**, binding controls to the data is a snap. Add the controls as you normally would. For instance, in this example case, we add a **ComboBox** to the **Form**. Opening the properties window for the **ComboBox** (or other control) you will see the **DataSource** and **DisplayMember**. Clicking the **DataSource** will display all the data sources you have already configured. Selecting a **DataSource** now allows you to select the **DisplayMember**. For this example, we've selected **City** as the **DisplayMember**.

> **Note**
> You cannot modify the **Items** collection once you've set the **DisplayMember** property. The field you've selected in the **DisplayMember** will appear in place of the **Items** collection.

The DataGrid

The **DataGrid** control (Figure 13.6) allows you to view, change, and delete data from a **DataSet** object in row and column format. You can drop a **DataGrid** control onto a **Form** by selecting it from the Toolbox window and clicking the place on the Form where you'd like to place the control. Resize and customize the control using the **DataGrid** properties.

There are numerous ways to customize this control. For example, some of the properties you can use to customize the control include:

AllowSorting – Allows or disallows the ability for the user to click a column title to sort the data by column.

AlternatingBackColor – Sets or unsets alternating background colors in rows. Alternating background colors can aid in viewing long lists of data, especially if it becomes necessary for the user to scroll to the right to view data.

BackColor – Gets or sets the background color of the grid.

BackgroundColor – Gets or sets the background color of the control not including the grid area. (See BackColor to set the grid background color.)

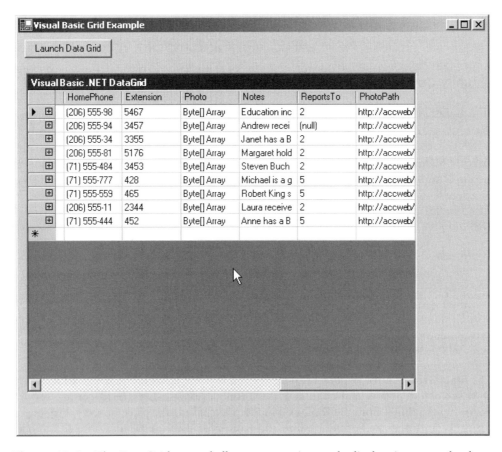

Figure 13.6   The DataGrid control allows you to view and edit data in row and column form.

Like most controls, you can create a **DataGrid** object programmatically. The following example adjusts the size of the **Form** dynamically to allow enough room for the **DataGrid**. You can set the **Form** size to this size initially, or change it on the fly as this example does. Refer to Chapter 12 for more information on adding controls to a **Form** programmatically. The most important line of code in this example is the one that binds the control to the **DataSet** named Employees. The **DataSet** was created in the example earlier in this chapter.

```
Me.ClientSize = New Size(600, 500)

Dim myGrid As New DataGrid()

myGrid.Location = New Point(10, 50)

myGrid.Size = New Size(500, 400)

myGrid.CaptionText = "Employee Information"

Me.Controls.Add(myGrid)

myGrid.SetDataBinding(ds, "Employees")
```

This is also the place in the code where you would customize the appearance of the grid, setting background colors and the appearance of data in the grid.

Once the **DataGrid** is populated, the user can navigate and edit data in the control. To validate data, you can create event handlers that handle both the **ColumnChanging** and **RowChanging** events. Here, you can test the values being entered by the user to determine if they meet business rules or data constraints. For example, your database might allow the entry of employees from a particular district. When attempting to add an employee with an address in the wrong district, you can disallow this action, alerting the user.

When determining which row–column location (cell) currently has focus, you can view the **CurrentCell** property of the **DataGrid**. You can also use the **HitTest** method to determine where in the **DataGrid** a user has clicked. Call this method in the **MouseDown** event. The **HitTest** method returns the row and column index of the cell in which the user has clicked in a **HitTestInfo** object.

When you make changes using the **DataGrid**, you are making changes to the **DataSet**, not the data stored in the database. Remember that the **DataSet** is an in-memory copy of the data stored in the database. You can use the **GetChanges** method of the **DataSet** to return a copy of the **DataSet,** including all changes made since the last time the **DataSet** was loaded or the **AcceptChanges** method was called, a method that commits changes to the **DataSet**. Use the **DataAdapter's Update** method to save changes back to the data source.

System.Data Classes

The **System.Data** namespace classes listed in Table 13.2 contain the abilities needed to build and maintain a database-centric application. In the previous section we've already introduced some of the more important classes in this namespace. You may want to review the other classes and the enumerations available in Table 13.3.

Use these classes together with classes found in the **System.Data.Common** namespace. The classes in this namespace include the **DataAdapter**, **DataTableMapping**, **DataColumnMapping**, and the **RowUpdatingEventArgs** and **RowUpdatedEventArgs**.

Refer to the description next to each class to discover its functionality.

Table 13.2   Classes

Class	Description
Constraint	An object that enforces data integrity within one or more DataColumn objects.
ConstraintsCollection	A collection of Constraint objects for a DataTable.
DataColumn	Represents a single data column.
DataColumnChangeEventArgs	Represents the arguments passed to the ColumnChange event handler.
DataColumnCollection	A collection of DataColumns grouped for a DataTable.
DataException	Errors thrown by data objects in this namespace.
DataRelation	Represents a parent–child relationship between two tables.
DataRelationCollection	A collection of DataRelation objects.
DataRow	Represents a row of data in a DataTable.
DataRowChangeEventArgs	Represents the arguments passed to the RowChange event handler.
DataRowCollection	A collection of DataRow objects.
DataRowView	Represents a customized view of a DataRow.
DataSet	Represents an in-memory cache of data.
DataSetDescriptionAttribute	Property, event, or extender for a description for Visual Design tools.
DataTable	A single table of in-memory data.
DataTableCollection	A collection of DataTable objects stored in the DataSet object.
DataView	A custom view of a DataTable or related DataTables used the same way you would use a DataTable. DataViews can be bound to data-bound controls.
DataViewManager	Manages the default settings in the DataViewSettingCollection.
DataViewSettingCollection	Read-only collection of DataViewSetting objects.

Table 13.2 Classes

Class	Description
DbConcurrencyException	The error thrown when the number of rows affected by an SQL Update operation is zero.
DeletedRowInaccessibleException	Error thrown when attempting action on a deleted row.
DuplicateNameException	Error thrown when attempting to add a duplicate name in a database.
EvaluateException	Error thrown when the expression of a DataColumn is invalid.
FillErrorEventArgs	Provides data to the FillError event handler of a DataAdapter object.
ForeignKeyConstraint	Represents an action restriction enforced on a set of columns in a primary key/foreign key relationship when a value or row is either deleted or updated.
InRowChangingEventException	Error thrown when EndEdit is called in the RowChanging event.
InternalDataCollectionBase	The base functionality for creating collections.
InvalidConstraintException	Error thrown for an invalid constraint.
InvalidExpressionException	Error thrown for an invalid expression in a DataColumn.
MergeFailedEventArgs	Properties passed to the event handler for a failed merge attempt. This happens normally when the target and source have the same primary key.
MissingPrimaryKeyException	Error thrown when a process requires a DataTable PrimaryKey that is not set.
NoNullAllowedException	Error thrown when an attempt is made to add a row containing a Null value when it is not allowed by the DataColumn.
PropertyCollection	A collection of properties that can be added to the DataColumn.
ReadOnlyException	Error thrown when a user attempts to change a read-only value.
RowNotInTableException	Error thrown when attempting an operation on a nonexistent DataRow.
StateChangeEventArgs	Provides data to the StateChange event handler.
StrongTypingException	Error thrown when a Null value is accessed in a strongly typed DataSet.
SyntaxErrorException	Error thrown when the expression property of a DataColumn contains a syntax error.
TypedDataSetGenerator	Creates a strongly typed DataSet.

Table 13.2 Classes

Class	Description
TypedDataSetGeneratorException	Error thrown when a name conflict occurs when creating a strongly typed DataSet.
UniqueConstraint	A special constraint on a DataColumn where all rows must contain a unique value.
VersionNotFoundException	Error thrown when attempting to return a DataRow that has been deleted.

Enumerations

The enumerations used in the **System.Data** classes have made configuring the behavior of the classes listed in Table 13.2 much simpler. The enumerations and a description are included in Table 13.3.

Table 13.3 Enumerations

Enumeration	Description
AcceptRejectRule	Actions that occur when the AcceptChanges or RejectChanges method is invoked on a DataTable with a ForeignKeyConstraint.
CommandBehavior	Descriptions of the results and effect on the database of the query command.
CommandType	How a command string is interpreted.
ConnectionState	Current state of the connection to a data source.
DataRowAction	Action taken on a DataRow.
DataRowState	The state of a DataRow object.
DataRowVersion	Version (deleted or not) of a DataRow.
DataViewRowState	Version of data in a DataRow.
DbType	The data type of a field, a property, or a Parameter object of a .NET data provider.
IsolationLevel	Transaction locking behavior for the connection.
MappingType	Specifies how a DataColumn is mapped.
MissingMappingAction	The action that occurs when a mapping is missing from a source table or a source column.
MissingSchemaAction	The action to take when adding data to the DataSet and the required DataTable or DataColumn is missing.
ParameterDirection	The type of a parameter within a query relative to the DataSet.

Table 13.3   Enumerations

Enumeration	Description
PropertyAttributes	The attributes of a property.
Rule	The action that occurs when a ForeignKeyConstraint is enforced.
SchemaType	Specifies how to handle existing schema mappings when performing a FillSchema operation.
SqlDbType	SQL Server data types.
StatementType	Type of SQL query to be used by the OleDbRowUpdatedEventArgs, OleDbRowUpdatingEventArgs, SqlRowUpdatedEventArgs, or SqlRowUpdatingEventArgs class.
UpdateRowSource	Specifies how query command results are applied to the row being updated.
UpdateStatus	Specifies the action to take with regard to the current and remaining rows during an Update.
XmlReadMode	How to read XML data and a relational schema into a DataSet.
XmlWriteMode	How to write XML data and a relational schema from a DataSet.

Summary

Working with data in Visual Basic .NET involves more objects than ever before. Your head may be swimming with all the various objects necessary to work with data right now. Eventually, it will all become clear. One reason for this large number of objects is the .NET concept of separating the objects that manage data from the data source. In this manner, objects, such as the **DataSet**, can manipulate data without caring where it came from, as you would in previous versions of Visual Basic working with **RecordSets**. With this new separation between data and data source, you can write custom code to extract data from an LDAP server, other directory service, relational database, object database, XML file, or other type of data storage.

Whether you create the objects discussed in this chapter programmatically or use the Visual Designers, the resulting **DataSet** and **DataView** objects can be bound to visual controls for building powerful, data-bound user interfaces. Using the **DataGrid** control, you can create a customizable data editing user interface with very little trouble at all.

The objects in the .NET data namespaces are tied to XML, with data schemas and data stored internally in XML format or written out in that form using specialized methods for that purpose. The next chapter delves into XML, where we will revisit some of the objects in this chapter as they relate to XML.

XML Application Basics 14

XML, short for **Ex**tensible **M**arkup **L**anguage, is a means of identifying data in a text document for the purpose of data interchange. It has become the de facto standard for data interchange over the Internet and is quickly moving into place as the standard for data interchange between all types of applications.

This chapter first introduces some of the basic concepts of XML followed by an explanation of how XML forms the foundation of much of the data handling in Visual Basic .NET. Additionally, the Common Language Runtime provides a set of classes that allow you to create, navigate, and edit XML documents and XML schemas.

Introduction to XML

Markup languages use tags, identifiers that appear like this: <tag>. Some markup languages, such as HTML, the basis for Web pages, use tags to format text. XML, on the other hand, uses tags to identify data by name. For example, <First Name> Bob </First Name> is a tag that identifies a first name, contains the data "Bob," and then contains a close tag, identifying the end of the First Name information.

XML is defined by three basic standards:

- The Extensible Markup Language (XML 1.0) – http://www.w3.org/TR/REC-xml
- XML Pointer Language and also XML Linking Language – http://www.w3.org/TR/1998/WD-xptr-19980303 and http://www.w3.org/TR/1998/WD-xlink-19980303 .
- Extensible Stylesheet Language – http://www.w3.org/TR/xsl/

Before you launch into reading the specifications found at the Web sites listed above, consider reading this brief explanation of how modern XML specifications are written using Extended Backus–Naur Form (EBNF).

Extended Backus–Naur Form (EBNF)

A way of describing the XML syntax called EBNF (Extended Backus-Naur Form) was recently developed. This form is a set of rules, known as productions. *Each production is preceded by a number in brackets, so that each rule (production) can be referred to by number. You may be reading a technical document that refers to production 12 or production 4. These are shortcuts to specific rules about XML syntax.*

Each EBNF production describes a particular part of the of the XML syntax. Here is the EBNF production for the XML Name:

```
[4] NameChar ::= Letter | Digit | '.' | '-' | '_' | ':' |
CombiningChar | Extender
[5] Name ::= (Letter | '_' | ':') (NameChar)*
```

Production 4 defines the term **NameChar**. *Once defined in a specification, you can refer back to Production 4 to find the definition of the term so there is no ambiguity. Next, the double-colon-equals character (::=) reads* is defined as. *The vertical bar (|) represents a logical OR (| is also called a pipe character).*

Translating the EBNF Production 4 to something more like English might read:

```
NameChar is defined as a letter or a digit or a period or
a dash or an underscore or a color or a combining
character or an extender.
```

Each one of these options is also defined within the WC3 standards document. For example, **Extender** *is defined in Production 89. Note in Production 5, shown above, parentheses can be used to create subexpressions. Production 5 can be read as:*

```
Name is defined as a letter or an underscore or a colon,
followed by a NameChar. The asterisk tells you that there
can be any number of NameChars (including zero).
```

EBNF is very exact and unambiguous. Programmers are used to reading complex expressions built using symbols. It may be a bit more difficult for someone first looking at these rules to completely understand them. But because the expressions are exact, this method can be used to define the syntax of languages and are then useful in building computer applications that will parse the syntax of that language.

The XML Schema

XML Schemas are an XML language for describing and constraining the content of XML documents. Here's an example of an XML document that defines information about a Visual Basic programming book:

```
<?xml version="1.0" encoding="utf-8">

<book isbn="1-8841-3393-2">

    <title>1001 Visual Basic Programmers Tips</title>

    <author>Ted Coombs</author>

    <description>Great Visual Basic 6.0
book.</description>

    <subject>

        <tip>An Introduction to Programming</tip>

        <description>Basic programming
        principles.</description>

    </subject>

    <subject>

        <tip>How Visual Basic Stores Source Files</tip>

        <description>Explanation of file
        storage.</description>

    </subject>

</book>
```

To get started creating a schema we begin by creating a new document that opens an xsd schema element. This defines the type of schema being created.

```
<?xml version="1.0" encoding="utf-8">

<xsd:schema xmlns:xsd="http://www.w3.org/2000/10/
XMLSchema">

<xsd:element name="book">

 <xsd:complexType>

 <xsd:sequence>
```

This last element, **sequence**, is a *compositor*, which defines a sequence of subelements. Because book is composed of other elements, instead of simply having a value, it is considered a *complex type*. Schema items that do not contain other definitions, but simply a value, such as the **name** item, are *simple types*. Notice that each element type is preceded by the schema type.

Continuing on, we continue the creation of the schema by defining more simple types:

```
<xsd:element name="title" type="xsd:string"/>

<xsd:element name="author" type="xsd:string"/>
```

Notice that the schema is defining the structure, and not the data that will end up in this structure. Once you're finished defining the schema, make certain each of your tags are closed:

```
</xsd:complexType>

</xsd:element>

</xsd:schema>
```

Now that you've seen a small sample schema, it's time to look at the real thing. Here is the XML schema for the **DataSet** created in the chapter on databases:

```
<xsd:schema id="DataSet1"
targetNamespace="http://www.tempuri.org/DataSet1.xsd"
xmlns="http://www.tempuri.org/DataSet1.xsd"
xmlns:xsd="http://www.w3.org/2001/XMLSchema"
xmlns:msdata="urn:schemas-microsoft-com:xml-msdata"
attributeFormDefault="qualified"
elementFormDefault="qualified">

 <xsd:element name="DataSet1" msdata:IsDataSet="true">

  <xsd:complexType>

   <xsd:choice maxOccurs="unbounded">

    <xsd:element name="Table">

     <xsd:complexType>

      <xsd:sequence>
```

```xml
<xsd:element name="EmployeeID" msdata:ReadOnly=
"true" msdata:AutoIncrement="true" type="xsd:int"
/>

<xsd:element name="LastName" type="xsd:string" />

<xsd:element name="FirstName" type="xsd:string" />

<xsd:element name="Title" type="xsd:string"
minOccurs="0" />

<xsd:element name="TitleOfCourtesy"
type="xsd:string" minOccurs="0" />

<xsd:element name="BirthDate" type="xsd:dateTime"
minOccurs="0" />

<xsd:element name="HireDate" type="xsd:dateTime"
minOccurs="0" />

<xsd:element name="Address" type="xsd:string"
minOccurs="0" />

<xsd:element name="City" type="xsd:string"
minOccurs="0" />

<xsd:element name="Region" type="xsd:string"
minOccurs="0" />

<xsd:element name="PostalCode" type="xsd:string"
minOccurs="0" />

<xsd:element name="Country" type="xsd:string"
minOccurs="0" />

<xsd:element name="HomePhone" type="xsd:string"
minOccurs="0" />

<xsd:element name="Extension" type="xsd:string"
minOccurs="0" />
```

```
                <xsd:element name="Photo" minOccurs="0">

                  <xsd:simpleType>

                    <xsd:restriction base="xsd:base64Binary" />

                  </xsd:simpleType>

                </xsd:element>

                <xsd:element name="Notes" type="xsd:string"
                minOccurs="0" />

                <xsd:element name="ReportsTo" type="xsd:int"
                minOccurs="0" />

                <xsd:element name="PhotoPath" type="xsd:string"
                minOccurs="0" />

              </xsd:sequence>

            </xsd:complexType>

          </xsd:element>

        </xsd:choice>

      </xsd:complexType>

  <xsd:unique name="Constraint1" msdata:PrimaryKey="true">

      <xsd:selector xpath=".//Table" />

      <xsd:field xpath="EmployeeID" />

    </xsd:unique>

  </xsd:element>

</xsd:schema>
```

In case it wasn't obvious, the xmlns elements define namespaces that contain element and attribute type definitions.

The XML Document

The XML schema described in the last chapter allows you to describe data that is stored in an XML document. You can match the values described in the XML document that follows with the XML schema, which describes this document to get a full picture of the data here. This XML document was created by using the **WriteXML** method of the **DataSet** object created in Chapter 13. The document was lengthy so this sample shows only a single record.

```xml
<?xml version="1.0" standalone="yes"?>

<Employees>

  <Employees>

    <EmployeeID>2</EmployeeID>

    <LastName>Fuller</LastName>

    <FirstName>Andrew</FirstName>

    <Title>Vice President, Sales</Title>

    <TitleOfCourtesy>Dr.</TitleOfCourtesy>

    <BirthDate>1952-02-19T00:00:00.0000000-
08:00</BirthDate>

    <HireDate>1992-08-14T00:00:00.0000000-07:00</HireDate>

    <Address>908 W. Capital Way</Address>

    <City>Tacoma</City>

    <Region>WA</Region>

    <PostalCode>98401</PostalCode>

    <Country>USA</Country>

    <HomePhone>(206) 555-9482</HomePhone>
```

```
    <Extension>3457</Extension>

    <Photo>Binary data omitted for brevity</Photo>

    <Notes>Andrew received his BTS commercial in 1974 and
    a Ph.D. in international marketing from the University
    of Dallas in 1981.  He is fluent in French and Italian
    and reads German.  He joined the company as a sales
    representative, was promoted to sales manager in
    January 1992, and to vice president of sales in March
    1993.  Andrew is a member of the Sales Management
    Roundtable, the Seattle Chamber of Commerce, and the
    Pacific Rim Importers Association.</Notes>

<PhotoPath>http://accweb/emmployees/fuller.bmp</PhotoPath>

  </Employees>

  <EmployeeTerritories>

    <EmployeeID>2</EmployeeID>

    <TerritoryID>01581</TerritoryID>

  </EmployeeTerritories>

</Employees>
```

This data is from the sample data in the Northwind database, included with SQL Server 2000. You can see that the representation of the data is very straightforward, and more importantly, because the XML standard is experiencing such wide adoption, this data can be read by many systems on many platforms.

Using the DataSet

Before launching into the classes that make up the **System.XML** namespace, we'll take another look at the **System.Data.DataSet** object. In previous versions of Visual Basic, XML was treated differently, as hardly more than an input and output format. XML is now completely integrated into the CLR data-handling classes, and in fact, forms the foundation of how data is handled in memory. A **DataSet** object, storing its data in XML form, has the ability to read and write XML schemas and data documents. These XML documents are then transportable through HTTP, and can be understood by any XML 1.0–compatible software.

Data that resides in a **DataSet** (see Chapter 13 for information about **DataSet** objects) can be viewed and manipulated, accessing rows (records) in random order, or sequentially, row by row. Remember, the **DataSet** doesn't care about the data source. That's the job of the **DataAdapter** (with one exception, XML schemas and data). The DataSet object can handle XML directly.

The **DataSet** has several methods for handling the data, in XML format, and XML schema. Here is a list of the XML handling methods in the **DataSet** class:

GetXML – Returns the data, stored in the DataSet, in XML format.

GetXMLSchema – Returns the path to the XML schema that describes the data in the DataSet.

InferXMLSchema – Infers the XML schema from a file or TextReader into the DataSet.

ReadXML – Reads the XML schema and XML-formatted data into the DataSet.

ReadXMLSchema – Reads an XML schema into the DataSet.

WriteXML – Writes the data in a DataSet in XML format (example in previous section).

WriteXMLSchema – Writes the structure of the DataSet as an XML schema.

The next example reads an XML schema from file. Once the **DataSet** object has read the schema from file (or stream), the schema of the **DataSet** object is set. In fact, this example proves, by using the same **WriteXML** method used to write the schema provided by the **DataAdapter** object in the last chapter, the two schema files are identical.

```
Private Sub Button1_Click(ByVal sender As System.Object,
ByVal e As System.EventArgs) Handles Button1.Click

    Dim ds As New DataSet()

    'read XML schema from file

    ds.ReadXmlSchema("c:\temp\dataset1.xsd")

    'write the XML schema back to file

    ds.WriteXmlSchema("c:\temp\xmlschema2.xsd")

    MessageBox.Show("file written")

End Sub
```

To run this example you will have to have an XML schema file called dataset1.xsd stored in the \temp folder of your C: drive. This code snippet then writes a new file back to the C:\temp folder. Use Notepad to examine the contents of both files.

Once your **DataSet** object has a schema, you can begin adding data into the schema. Another way for your **DataSet** object to acquire a schema is to automatically create one on the fly by reading an XML data file. This is a one-step process for loading data into the **DataSet** and creating the schema at the same time.

```
Private Sub Button1_Click(ByVal sender As System.Object,
ByVal e As System.EventArgs) Handles Button1.Click

    Dim ds As New DataSet()

    'read XML Data from file

    ds.ReadXml("c:\temp\xmlschema2.xsd", XmlReadMode.Auto)

    ds.WriteXmlSchema("c:\temp\xmlschema3.xsd")

    MessageBox.Show("data read and schema written")

End Sub
```

Now, examining xmlschema3.xsd again reveals the same schema as the one initially loaded using the **XmlSchemaRead** method. The difference here is that not only does the **DataSet** have the schema, it's completely loaded with data, too. The point of all this is that the **DataSet** object can use XML data in your application as simply, or even more simply, than data from a database.

Note
If you are familiar with the XML Document Type Declaration (DTD), and wondered why we have not discussed it here, it's because the XML schema is replacing the DTD and provides a richer and more powerful way of describing data.

Programming XML

The classes in Visual Basic .NET provide the mechanism for manipulating, organizing, sharing, and transferring your data. Table 14.1 contains a list of the classes in the **System.Xml** namespace. One of the embedded CLR namespaces not listed in Table 14.1 is the **System.Xml.Schema** namespace. Before taking a look at the classes in Table 14.1, we need to begin with the **Xml.Schema.XmlSchema** class.

Table 14.1 XML Namespace Classes

Class	Description
NameTable	Implements a single-threaded XmlNameTable, which is a table of atomized string objects. It provides a way for the XML parser to use the same string object for all repeated element and attribute names, making object pointer comparisons rather than processor-expensive string comparisons.
XmlAttribute	An attribute. Valid and default values for the attribute are defined in a DTD or schema.
XmlAttributeCollection	A collection of attributes that can be accessed by name or index.
XmlCDataSection	Used to quote or escape blocks of text to keep that text from being interpreted as markup language.
XmlCharacterData	Provides text-manipulation methods that are used by several classes.
XmlComment	The content of an XML comment.
XmlConvert	Encodes and decodes XML names and provides methods for converting between CLR types and XSD types.
XmlDataDocument	Allows structured data to be stored, retrieved, and manipulated through a relational DataSet.
XmlDeclaration	The XML declaration node.
XmlDocument	An XML document.
XmlDocumentFragment	A lightweight object that is useful for tree insert operations.
XmlDocumentType	The document type declaration.
XmlElement	An XML element.
XmlEntity	An XML entity declaration.
XmlEntityReference	An entity reference node.
XmlException	Information about the last exception.
XmlImplementation	Defines the context for a set of XmlDocument objects.
XmlLinkedNode	The node immediately preceding or following this node.
XmlNamedNodeMap	A collection of nodes that can be accessed by name or index.
XmlNamespaceManager	Resolves, adds, and removes namespaces to a collection and provides scope management for these namespaces. This class is used by the XsltContext and XmlReader classes.
XmlNameTable	Table of atomized string objects. This provides an efficient means for the XML parser to use the same string object for all repeated element and attribute names in an XML document.
XmlNode	A single node in a document.

Table 14.1 XML Namespace Classes

Class	Description
XmlNodeList	An ordered collection of nodes.
XmlNodeReader	A reader that provides fast, noncached, forward-only access to XML data in an XmlNode.
XmlNotation	A notation declaration.
XmlParserContext	Provides all the context information required by XmlTextReader or XmlValidatingReader to parse an XML fragment.
XmlProcessingInstruction	A processing instruction, which XML defines to keep processor-specific information in the text of the document.
XmlQualifiedName	An XML qualified name. (See the XML Namespace sidebar.)
XmlReader	A reader that provides fast, noncached, forward-only access to XML data. Implemented as XmlTextReader, XmlValidatingReader, and XmlNodeReader.
XmlResolver	External XML resources named by a Uniform Resource Identifier (URI).
XmlSignificantWhitespace	Whitespace between markup in a mixed content mode. This is also referred to as significant whitespace. These nodes will be created automatically at Load time only if the PreserveWhitespace flag is true.
XmlText	The text content of an element or attribute.
XmlTextReader	A reader that provides fast, noncached, forward-only access to XML data. Derived from the XmlReader class.
XmlTextWriter	A writer that provides a fast, noncached, forward-only way of generating streams or files containing XML data that conforms to the W3C Extensible Markup Language (XML) 1.0 specification and the namespaces in XML specification.
XmlUrlResolver	Resolves external XML resources named by a Uniform Resource Identifier (URI).
XmlValidatingReader	A reader that provides DTD, XDR, and XSD schema validation.
XmlWhitespace	Whitespace in element content. These nodes will be created automatically at Load time only if the PreserveWhitespace flag is true.
XmlWriter	A writer that provides a fast, noncached, forward-only way of generating streams or files containing XML data that conforms to the W3C Extensible Markup Language (XML) 1.0 specification and the namespaces in XML specification.

Programming the XML Schema

So far in this chapter we've taken a look at how to load an XML schema into a **DataSet** object, but we still need to see how to construct a **DataSet** programmatically.

> **Note**
> XML schemas are saved in text format. Therefore, it's possible with enough diligence to create and type the entire schema by hand into a text editor like Notepad.

Begin creating a schema by first creating an **XmlSchema** object. Remember to add **Imports System.Xml.Schema** to the head of your file. Then begin creating the elements that make up the schema by defining **XmlSchemaElement** objects, as shown below:

```
Dim schema As New XmlSchema()

Dim eMother As New XmlSchemaElement()

schema.Items.Add(eMother)

eMother.Name = "mother"

eMother.SchemaTypeName = New XmlQualifiedName("string",
"http://www.w3.org/2001/XMLSchema")
```

The **XmlSchemaElement**, eMother in this example, is added to the **Schema** using the **Add** method of the **Items** property. Further configure the element by setting the **Name** and **SchemaTypeName** properties of the **XmlSchemaElement** object.
The **XmlQualifiedName** contains the *qualified name* of the element.

The XML Namespace

The purpose of the XML namespace is to distinguish between duplicate element types and attribute names. The namespace itself is a collection of element types and attribute names. This allows any element type or attribute name to be uniquely identified by a two-part name. The first part of the name is the XML namespace name, followed by a colon and a local name, the name of the actual element or attribute. This allows you to have duplicate attribute or element names in the same XML document which have different actual definitions. The XML namespace does not provide that different definition. That is the purpose of the schema.

An XML document has one namespace for element type, and a namespace for each element type that contains the attributes that define and apply to that element type. That is the entire purpose of the XML namespace. It serves no other purpose other than to create a two-part naming system.

*Each XML namespace is uniquely identified by a URI, which serves as its name. Unlike Web URIs the URIs used to uniquely identify namespaces will not resolve to a document, or anything else for that matter. It's just a human-readable way to create a globally unique name. The alternative would be a GUID, which is a long, barely readable number, not very handy as a name. Namespaces are declared in XML documents using the **xmlns** attribute. The first form of the attribute (xmlns:prefix) declares a prefix associated with the XML namespace. The second form (xmlns) declares the default XML namespace.*

Namespace declarations have a scope. The scope is that they apply to the elements in which they are declared, and all subelements and attributes. To make certain the namespace is in scope throughout an XML document, make certain to declare the namespace in the root element of the document.

Anyone can create an XML namespace. The one requirement is that you assign a unique URI as the name. When using the URI of your company, make certain no one else in your company uses the same URI to create a different namespace.

To use an XML namespace in your XML document, no matter who created it, declare it as mentioned above, then use the prefix with element and attribute names in the form: prefix:name. Element names without a prefix will assume the default XML namespace is being used. Attribute names cannot be defined in a default namespace.

Here is an example that creates an entire schema programmatically in the click event of a **Button** control:

```
Imports System.Xml 'Add to the head of the file

Imports System.Xml.Schema 'Add to the head of the file

Private Sub Button1_Click(ByVal sender As System.Object,
ByVal e As System.EventArgs) Handles Button1.Click

    Dim ds As New DataSet()

    Dim schema As New XmlSchema()

    Dim eMother As New XmlSchemaElement()

    schema.Items.Add(eMother)
```

```
    eMother.Name = "mom"

    eMother.SchemaTypeName = New XmlQualifiedName
    ("string", "http://www.w3.org/2001/XMLSchema")

' <xsd:element name="dad" type="string"/>

    Dim eFather As New XmlSchemaElement()

    schema.Items.Add(eFather)

    eFather.Name = "dad"

    eFather.SchemaTypeName = New XmlQualifiedName
    ("string", "http://www.w3.org/2001/XMLSchema")

' <xsd:element name="grandpa" type="string"
  substitutionGroup="dad" />

    Dim egrandpa As New XmlSchemaElement()

    schema.Items.Add(egrandpa)

    egrandpa.Name = "grandpa"

    egrandpa.SubstitutionGroup = New XmlQualifiedName
    ("dad")

    egrandpa.SchemaTypeName = New XmlQualifiedName
    ("string", "http://www.w3.org/2001/XMLSchema")

' <xsd:element name="grandpa" type="string"
  substitutionGroup="dad" />

    Dim estepdad As New XmlSchemaElement()

    schema.Items.Add(estepdad)

    estepdad.Name = "stepdad"

    estepdad.SubstitutionGroup = New XmlQualifiedName
    ("dad")
```

```
        estepdad.SchemaTypeName = New XmlQualifiedName
        ("string", "http://www.w3.org/2001/XMLSchema")

    ' <xsd:element name="family">

        Dim eFamily As New XmlSchemaElement()

        schema.Items.Add(eFamily)

        eFamily.Name = "family"

        ' <xsd:complexType>

        Dim complexType As New XmlSchemaComplexType()

        eFamily.SchemaType = complexType

    ' <xsd:choice minOccurs="0" maxOccurs="unbounded">

        Dim choice As New XmlSchemaChoice()

        complexType.Particle = choice

        choice.MinOccurs = 0

        choice.MaxOccursString = "unbounded"

    ' <xsd:element ref="mom"/>

        Dim momRef As New XmlSchemaElement()

        choice.Items.Add(momRef)

        momRef.RefName = New XmlQualifiedName("mom")

    ' <xsd:element ref="dad"/>

        Dim dadRef As New XmlSchemaElement()

        choice.Items.Add(dadRef)
```

```
        dadRef.RefName = New XmlQualifiedName("dad")

        schema.Compile(AddressOf ValidationCallbackOne)

        schema.Write(Console.Out)

End Sub

Public Shared Sub ValidationCallbackOne(ByVal sender As
Object, ByVal args As ValidationEventArgs)

        Console.WriteLine(args.Message)

End Sub
```

This example creates the following schema:

```
<?xml version="1.0" encoding="Windows-1252"?>

<schema targetNamespace="" xmlns="http://www.w3.
org/2001/XMLSchema">

  <element name="mom" type="string" />

  <element name="dad" type="string" />

  <element name="grandpa" substitutionGroup="dad"
type="string" />

  <element name="stepdad" substitutionGroup="dad"
type="string" />

  <element name="family">

    <complexType>

      <choice minOccurs="0" maxOccurs="unbounded">

        <element ref="mom" />

        <element ref="dad" />
```

```
            </choice>

        </complexType>

      </element>

  </schema>
```

Most of the concepts in this schema have been discussed earlier in the chapter. Notice that one of the attributes used in the grandpa and stepdad elements is *substitutiongroup*. Using a substitutiongroup is similar to the concept of object-oriented inheritance. A parent element (*head element*), in this case "dad," can have elements that are derived. Head elements can be used by themselves, or declared as abstract, similar to an abstract class. In this case, an abstract head element cannot be used in a document, only members of its substitutiongroup. Lastly, elements can be defined as *final*, rather than abstract. Elements declared as final will not allow new elements to be derived from them.

Programming the XML Document

The **Xml.XmlDocument** class implements the W3C Document Object Model (DOM), and represents an in-memory tree representation of an XML document. In other words, an XML document is a text document, complete with XML member tags, attributes, and data. The **XmlDocument** class also contains methods that allow navigation and editing of the data in an XML document.

The XML Document Object Model (DOM) is a programming interface for XML documents. The DOM defines the methods an XML document can be accessed. Using the DOM, you can create new XML documents, navigate through the document, and add, change, and delete elements.

In addition to methods in the **XmlDocument** class, there are **XmlReader** and **Writer** classes that parse data from the nodes within an XML document and write well-formed XML to a stream or file. A well-formed XML document is simply a document that conforms to the XML standard. The XML document is shaped like a tree with a root node, and child nodes that represent the branches of the tree. You can use the **ChildNodes** property of the **XmlDocument** object to obtain a list of all the child nodes within the document tree.

You can continue navigating through the nodes within the document by using properties such as **FirstChild** and **LastChild**, which returns the first and last child of a node, **HasChildNodes**, to see if the node has children and **ParentNode**, to find the parent of a child node. You can also move among *siblings*, which are child nodes of the same parent. The **PreviousSibling** and **NextSibling** properties return the previous and next child nodes of the same parent node.

To create a new XML node, use the **CreateNode** method of the **XmlDocument**. You can also use the **CreateTextNode** method to create nodes used as either elements or attributes. The next example uses the **CreateTextNode** to create the text node used as the price value.

```
Imports System.Xml 'Add to the head of the file

Imports System.Xml.Schema 'Add to the head of the file

Private Sub Button1_Click(ByVal sender As System.Object,
ByVal e As System.EventArgs) Handles Button1.Click

    Dim xdocument As New XmlDocument()

    xdocument.LoadXml(("<book genre='programming' ISBN='1-
    88413393-2'>" & "<title>1001 Visual Basic Programming
    Tips</title>" & "</book>"))

    Dim elem As XmlElement = xdocument.CreateElement
    ("price")

    Dim text As XmlText = xdocument.CreateTextNode
    ("57.95")

    xdocument.DocumentElement.AppendChild(elem)

    xdocument.DocumentElement.LastChild.AppendChild(text)

    xdocument.Save(Console.Out)

End Sub
```

This sample outputs the following XML:

```
<book genre="programming" ISBN="1-88413393-2">

<title>1001 Visual Basic Programming Tips</title>

<price>57.95</price>

</book>
```

For the purpose of storing structured data, the **XmlDataDocument** class has been derived from **XmlDocument**. It's the **XmlDataDocument** class that allows you to use the **DataSet** object to provide a row-column view of your data.

The XmlTextWriter Class   In discussing XML documents it's important to know how to programmatically create a well-formed XML document. The **XmlTextWriter** class outputs streams or files containing well-formed XML. The **XmlTextWriter** implements the **XmlWriter** class and has methods, such as **WriteStartElement**, **WriteAttributeString,** and **WriteElementString**, that make writing an XML document simple. Here is an example of a procedure that accepts values and writes them in XML format. The **XmlTextWriter** outputs the XML as a stream to the Console window.

```
Imports System.Xml 'Add to the head of the file

Imports System.Xml.Schema 'Add to the head of the file

Shared Sub WriteXML(ByVal writer As XmlWriter, ByVal isbn
As String, ByVal title As String, ByVal author As String,
ByVal pages As Integer)

    writer.WriteStartElement("Book")

    writer.WriteAttributeString("ISBN", isbn)

    writer.WriteElementString("Title", title)

    writer.WriteElementString("Author", author)

    writer.WriteElementString("Pages", XmlConvert.ToString
    (pages))

    writer.WriteEndElement()

End Sub

Private Sub Button1_Click(ByVal sender As System.Object,
ByVal e As System.EventArgs) Handles Button1.Click

    Dim xwriter As New XmlTextWriter(Console.Out)

    xwriter.Formatting = Formatting.Indented
```

```
        WriteXML(xwriter, "1-88413393-2", "1001 Visual Basic
        Programmers Tips", "Ted Coombs", 927)

        xwriter.Close()

    End Sub
```

This example produces the following output:

```
<Book ISBN="1-88413393-2">

  <Title>1001 Visual Basic Programmers Tips</Title>

  <Author>Ted Coombs</Author>

  <Pages>927</Pages>

</Book>
```

Using the XmlReader Class   You can hardly talk about the **XmlWriter** class without talking about the **XmlReader** class next. **XmlReader** objects allow your application to read through XML documents in a forward only manner. You cannot navigate in a random access manner. The **XmlReader** object's methods provide access to the data as you navigate through the document.

The **XmlReader** keeps track of its location as it steps through the document by defining a *current node,* or position of the cursor. The current node gives you access to the LocalName of the element and any namespace URI. Of course, you have access to any value stored within an element by accessing the **Value** property. When the current node is an element, you also have access to information about attributes using the **HasAttributes** and **AttributesCount** properties.

Use the **XmlReader.Read** method to move the cursor through the XML document. The **XmlReader** class is labeled as **MustInherit** and therefore must be implemented in a derived class. The **XmlReader** class is implemented in the following classes:

XmlTextReader – A quick and dirty **XmlReader** type.

XmlValidatingReader – Validates data using the XML schema, expands entities, and supports default attributes.

XmlNodeReader – Reads XML data from an **XmlNode**.

The first call to the **Read** method moves the cursor to the first node in the XML document. Prior to that, no current node is set. Read continues moving through the document until it reaches the end, at which time, **Read** simply returns **False**.

Introduction to SOAP

SOAP (Simple Object Access Protocol) is an open, standards-based interoperability protocol that uses XML to provide a common messaging format to link together applications and services across the Internet. The SOAP standard can be found at the following Web address:

http://www.W2.org/TR/SOAP

Primarily, the SOAP protocol defines the syntax of XML messages used by computers communicating with one another. Because of this standardized way of formatting XML messages, SOAP allows a new class of application known as a *Web Service*. New applications can be built by using the services of Web Service applications located throughout the Internet. Each portion of the application communicates using the standardized SOAP messaging protocol.

The four areas covered by the SOAP specification are:

The SOAP envelope format.

Encoding rules for how language types are mapped to XML in a SOAP message.

Remote Procedure Call format that defines how function calls are expressed in a SOAP message.

An HTTP binding standard.

Here is the Microsoft sample SOAP message:

```
<?xml version="1.0" encoding="UTF-8" standalone="no"?>

<SOAP-ENV:Envelope

SOAP-ENV:encodingStyle="http://schemas.xmlsoap.org/
soap/encoding/"

  xmlns:SOAP-ENV="http://schemas.xmlsoap.org/soap/
  envelope/">

  <SOAP-ENV:Body>

    <SOAPSDK1:Add xmlns:SOAPSDK1="http://tempuri.org/
    message/">
```

```
    <a>333</a>

    <b>888</b>

    </SOAPSDK1:Add>

  </SOAP-ENV:Body>

</SOAP-ENV:Envelope>
```

The first line sets the character set used in the message. The second line contains the envelope element, always the root of a SOAP message. The namespace (see The "XML Namespace") will always be named http://schemas.xmlsoap.org/soap/envelope/. The **body** element contains the actual SOAP message.

The classes to implement SOAP in Visual Basic .NET can be found in the **System.Xml.Serialization** namespace. They are listed in Table 14.2, and as this is simply a brief introduction to the SOAP standard, more detail will not be provided about the classes and their uses.

In general, classes in the **Xml.Serialization** namespace are used to serialize (write out in text form) objects into XML format. This process involves taking an object's public properties and fields and writing them out in XML format. It's a way of saving the state of an object in XML format, whether written to a stream or ultimately to a file. SOAP provides a mechanism for sharing this serialized data in a standardized format.

Table 14.2 SOAP Classes in the System.XmlSerialization Namespace

Class
SoapAttributeAttribute
SoapAttributeOverrides
SoapAttributes
SoapCodeExporter
SoapElementAttribute
SoapEnumAttribute
SoapIgnoreAttribute
SoapIncludeAttribute
SoapReflectionImporter
SoapSchemaExporter
SoapSchemaImporter
SoapSchemaMember
SoapTypeAttribute

Summary

XML is as important to data sharing as HTML is to the World Wide Web. Applications no longer need to concern themselves with incompatible data types. XML provides a way to store data, as well as for other applications to discover the structure of the data using an XML schema. Not only is XML a method for managing data between applications, it can also form the foundation for managing data within an application, as it does in Visual Basic .NET.

The next chapter moves away from data handling and back into some basic application-building capabilities. Threads are the processes in which programs run, and modern Windows applications can have more than one thread running at the same time. Creating threads is easy—getting them to play nicely is the challenge we pick up in the next chapter.

Threads 15

In the past, Visual Basic programs ran synchronously. This means that if the program needed to wait for something to happen, such as user input or the result of an Internet call, the entire program sat and waited until the input was given or processing was completed before continuing.

Visual Basic .NET joins the league of serious programming languages by allowing the program to branch into subprograms called *threads*. The operating system, such as Microsoft Windows, manages the processing time of your computer's brain, the microprocessor. When a software application runs, it runs in what is called an AppDomain. Each AppDomain has at least one thread, but can contain many threads.

Threads are considered the basic unit to which the operating system can allocate processor time. In an operating system that supports multitasking, the processor's time is divided among all the threads, giving them the appearance of running simultaneously. In a computer that has more than one microprocessor, threads can run simultaneously, one per microprocessor.

Each thread runs independently, and contains its own exception handlers, scheduling priority, and a set of structures used by the operating system to save the thread until it is scheduled to run. Each time the operating system switches between threads, the currently running thread is saved in these structures until its turn to run again, when it is restored. This way, one thread can sit waiting for an event to be triggered, or involve itself in time-consuming calculations while the other threads continue with their own processing. Visual Basic .NET employs a *free thread model*.

The primary class used for creating and controlling threads is the **System.Threading.Thread** class. This chapter helps you better understand threads, and helps you utilize them in your application.

When to Use Threads

Each thread uses system resources. Therefore, using too many threads can seriously slow a computer's performance. With this warning out of the way, use threads whenever you have a process within your program that may take some time to complete, and you need the program to continue to run. For example, reading and writing to a database, loading Web pages, or streaming media to or from your program. Any time your program needs to wait, whether for user input from the keyboard or mouse, or for processing that takes significant time, launch a new thread to handle that process.

Tip
Remember that just because your development computer may have two microprocessors and a gigabyte of RAM doesn't mean that every computer that runs your program will be equally equipped. Develop your program with the lowest acceptable performance in mind. This may mean that your program has limits to who can run your program. Just be aware of those limits.

Creating Threads

To create a new thread, simply create a new **System.Threading.Thread** object and pass a **ThreadStart** delegate to the constructor. Remember that a delegate is the code that is assigned to handle an event, in this case the starting of a thread.

```
Public Delegate Sub Threadstart()
```

This example demonstrates starting a thread when a button on a form is clicked. The first thing that happens is that a new **ThreadStart** delegate is created. The **ThreadStart** delegate points to the method used when the thread begins its execution and is required when creating and starting a new thread.

```
Dim Count As Integer

Private Sub button1_Click(ByVal sender As System.Object,
ByVal eval As_ System.EventArgs) Handles button1.Click

        'Create the ThreadStart delegate

        Dim thrdStart As Threading.ThreadStart = New_
        Threading.ThreadStart(AddressOf DigitCounter)

        'Create the thread

        Dim mythread As Threading.Thread = New_
        Threading.Thread(thrdStart)

        mythread.Start() 'starts the thread
```

```
            While (count < 10)

                'repeat until the number 9

            End While

            mythread.Abort() 'Stops the thread

            mythread.Join() 'Wait until the thread finishes

    End Sub

    Sub DigitCounter()

            Do

                Threading.Interlocked.Increment(count)

                Console.WriteLine("Count is ", count)

                Threading.Thread.Sleep(100)

            Loop

    End Sub
```

Notice that the thread delegate function accepts no parameters. You may often want to pass in parameters when starting a thread. You can do this by setting properties on the object that exposes the **Threadstart( )** function before starting the thread.

To start the thread, once it's been created, call the **Start** method of the thread object. The method is asynchronous, meaning that it handles the business of starting the thread without blocking the continued execution of the program. It will return immediately after being called, possibly even before the thread has actually started. In the Thread States section, beginning on page 365, you will find two methods you can use to determine the actual state of the thread, since you can't depend on the return of the Start method to tell you that the thread has started. Use the **Thread.IsAlive** and **Thread.ThreadState** methods to keep you abreast of the thread's actual condition.

One of the properties of the **Thread** object is the **ApartmentState**. This property tells the CLR whether this thread can run in a multithreaded apartment model, or a single-threaded apartment model. You can set this property only once. This property is important for communicating with COM objects, because they are required to know what apartment model the thread is designed to run within.

Thread Communication

Threads need the ability to communicate with one another. Without this ability, the program thread that spawned a new thread would never know when its child thread has completed its task. In these cases you can use the synchronization classes, **ManualResetEvent** and **AutoResetEvent**. With thread syncronization there are two event states: **signaled** and **nonsignaled**. Events have handles just like **Mutexes,** where you can also use the **WaitHandle** method. (See "Synchronizing with Mutexes," next page.)

A thread that is waiting for an event is *blocking*. In other words, the thread cannot continue until the blocking event allows it to continue. It will continue to block the processing of code until it is signaled by another thread with either the **ManualResetEvent.Set** or the **AutoResetEvent.Set** methods.

> **Note**
> When using **ManualResetEvent** you are required to use the **Reset** method to reset the state back to **nonsignaled**. **AutoResetEvent**, as its name suggests, will return to the **nonsignaled** state immediately following notification that an event has been signaled.

Synchronizing Threads

Managing more than one thread can be a bit tricky. Imagine the complexity of having more than one thread trying to open the same file, set a global variable, or write to the same serial port. This can create conflicts known as deadlocks and race conditions.

Multiple threads running simultaneously may want to communicate with other threads. This communication might be in the form of a shared value that each thread updates, or by alerting other threads about the state of each thread, such as when it has completed its task and is exiting.

Visual Basic .NET has special objects for avoiding multiple thread conflicts known as *synchronization objects*. The most basic example of synchronization is to safeguard access to a shared counter variable from deadlock and race conditions. Use the **Threading.Interlocked** class for this purpose.

Interlocking

When you want to use shared variables, you can use the **System.Threading.Interlocked** class to help make updating the shared variables simpler. The class has four methods:

CompareExchange – Evaluates two variables, and when they are equal, updates the shared variable.

Decrement – Decreases the value of a shared, numeric variable.

Increment – Increases the value of a shared, numeric variable.

Exchange – Sets the value of a numeric or object value as an atomic operation.

When incrementing the counter use:

```
Interlocked.Increment(counter)
```

Or to decrement the counter:

```
Interlocked.Decrement(counter)
```

> **Note**
> An action is **atomic** if it cannot be interrupted, partially executed, or terminated. This avoids interruption by threads while an operation is taking place. One thread must wait until an atomic operation is over before attempting the same operation.

Monitor

You can also lock access to an object's resources by using the **Monitor** class. The **Monitor** class synchronizes threads using locks and wait signals. The **Monitor** class has the ability to accept and release the sync block using one of its six members:

Enter – Obtains a lock on the monitor.

Exit – Releases the monitor lock.

Pulse – Notifies a waiting thread that the object's state has changed.

PulseAll – Notifies all waiting threads that the object's state has changed.

TryEnter – Nonblocking Enter. This is similar to Enter, but will either not block or block for a limited amount of time.

Wait – Waits for notification from the Pulse or PulseAll methods.

Use the **Monitor.Enter(*object*)** method. When processing of the object has been completed, use the **Monitor.Exit(*object*)** method. The object is then released and other threads, which may have been paused while waiting their turn to process the common object, will start their processing in a first in first out (FIFO) method.

Synchronizing with Mutexes

A more advanced way to create synchronization in threads involves the **Mutex** class. Mutex stands for "mutual exclusion." A **Mutex** is a primitive that ensures exclusive access to a shared resource. A **Mutex** also allows you to synchronize threads between various running applications (interprocess synchronization). Here's another way to think of mutexes. During road construction, when the road crew has reduced traffic to a single lane, that lane is a single shared resource, and if it weren't for the mutex (the guys on either side of the construction who alternate stop/slow signs), cars coming from both directions might attempt to use the shared resource at the same time.

The drivers of the cars are programmed to pay attention to the mutex, and they all have to cooperate and follow their programming or there can still be an accident. Nothing will stop a poorly behaved driver, or section of code, from violating the rules and using the shared resource at the wrong time, so it's up to the programmer to make sure that this transgression doesn't happen.

Any place in the code that attempts to use a shared resource, especially if it is going to make changes to it, must call one of the wait functions and wait for a signal prior to performing those changes on that shared resource.

There are times when it is okay by design, depending on the application, for code to read the shared resource while other code is in the process of changing it. But if code that makes changes to the shared resource does not use a mutex, it will cause unpredictability and changes will, at various times, get lost by being overwritten immediately by other changes. If this is acceptable to your program, then you don't need to use a mutex.

The **Mutex** object can be obtained from a thread running in any process. Once you've gotten the Mutex object, use the **GetHandle** method. The handle returned is necessary for use in the blocking methods, **WaitHandle.WaitAny** and **WaitHandle**.

To request ownership of the **Mutex,** you can use the **Wait** method. The **Wait** method is overloaded and accepts different sets of parameters.

Wait(object) – Accepts the object on which to wait.

Wait(object, integer) – Accepts the object as well as an integer that specifies a number of milliseconds to wait until giving up and returning from the method.

Wait(object, integer, boolean) – The last argument is the exitContext. When True, the synchronization domain is exited before the wait, and reacquired.

Once a **Mutex** lock is acquired by a running thread, any thread wishing to acquire the **Mutex** lock will be suspended, pending the release of the **Mutex**. A synchronized thread object holds the following references:

- A reference to the thread that currently holds the lock.
- A reference to the ReadyQueue – Threads waiting to obtain a lock.
- A reference to the WaitingQueue – Threads waiting for notification from Pulse or PulseAll.

Thread States

A Thread state is not a northern state where wool is spun into thread. Rather, **Thread-State** is a property of the **Thread** class. The ThreadState property provides more addi-

Table 15.1   Thread States

Thread State	Description
Aborted	The thread has been aborted. This thread is entered when the thread responds to the Abort request.
AbortRequested	A request has been made for the thread to abort. This state is entered when another thread calls Abort.
Background	The thread is running in the background.
Running	The thread is executing (running). This state is entered when the thread starts. This state is maintained when another thread calls Interrupt or Resume.
Stopped	The thread has stopped.
StopRequested	A request has been made for the thread to stop.
Suspended	Execution of the thread has been suspended. This state is entered when the thread responds to the Suspend request.
SuspendRequested	A request has been made for the thread to suspend execution. This state is entered when another thread calls Suspend.
Unstarted	The thread has not been started.
WaitSleepJoin	The thread is blocking on a call to Wait, Sleep, or Join.

tional information about the state of the thread than do the **IsAlive** and **IsBackground** properties.

Although a **Thread** can be in many states at the same time, it must be in at least one state. The **Thread** object's **Thread.ThreadState** property contains the current state or states of the **Thread**. Possible **Thread** states are listed in Table 15.1.

Threads can be in certain states at the same time, but not just any combination of states. A possible scenario would be a **Thread** in the **WaitSleepJoin** state, blocking on a call to either **Wait**, **Sleep**, or **Join**, receiving a call to **Abort** from another **Thread**. In this case, the **Thread** would be in both the **WaitSleepJoin** state, as well as the **AbortRequested** state. In order to store multiple states, the state information is stored in a bit mask saved in the **ThreadState** property. Here are the decimal values used in creating the bit mask:

Running – 0

SuspendRequested – 2

Background – 4

Unstarted – 8

WaitSleepJoin – 32

Suspended – 64

AbortRequested – 128

Aborted – 256

Newly created **Threads** begin in the **unstarted** state.

Thread.IsAlive

It's useful to know if a thread is still alive. A thread is considered alive if it has been started and has not been aborted or stopped. The **IsAlive** property returns True when the thread is alive and False when it's dead. Here is an example that launches a new **Thread** that displays a **MessageBox** while the first thread is looping, waiting for the value of an **Integer** variable to change from 1 to 0. The return value from the **MessageBox** causes the **Threading.Interlocked.Decrement** method to be called. This causes the parent thread to abort the child thread and display a new **MessageBox** anouncing the death of the child thread.

```
Dim MyAlert as Integer = 1

Private Sub button1_Click(ByVal sender As System.Object,
ByVal e As System.EventArgs) Handles Button1.Click

    'Create the ThreadStart delegate

    Dim thrdStart As Threading.ThreadStart = New
    Threading.ThreadStart(AddressOf threadstuff)

    'Create the thread

    Dim mythread As Threading.Thread = New
    Threading.Thread(thrdStart)

    mythread.Start() 'starts the thread

    Do While myAlert = 1

        'do something until my alert is True

    Loop

    mythread.Abort() 'Stops the thread

    mythread.Join() 'Wait until the thread finishes
```

```
        MessageBox.Show("It is " &mythread.IsAlive.ToString &
        "that the child thread lives.")

    End Sub

    Private Sub threadstuff()

        MessageBox.Show("in the threadstuff method")

        If DialogResult().OK Then

            Threading.Interlocked.Decrement(myAlert)

        End If

    End Sub
```

The **IsAlive** property provides a general idea of the state of the thread. For more detailed information, you will need to inspect the **ThreadState** property. This was described in the section of this chapter with that heading (page 365).

Thread.Sleep

Thread.Sleep causes a thread to go to sleep for a specified number of milliseconds. Passing a 0 as a parameter causes the **Thread** to yield its processor time to all the other **Threads**. This next example is similar to the previous example, with some distinct differences. First of all the thread we are going to cause to go to sleep is the main (parent) **Thread**. So, the first thing we need is a reference to the parent thread. In this example, we get a reference to the currently running **Thread** by using the static **CurrentThread** method of the **Thread** class. The return value is stored as a **Thread** object called **thisthread**. We then create and launch the second thread, that now has nothing to do with changing the value of any shared variables; it simply launches the **MessageBox**.

As soon as the second **Thread** is launched, the parent **Thread** is put to sleep for 10 seconds using this command:

```
    thisthread.Sleep(10000)
```

The **Sleep** method then gives up all the CPU cycles allotted to it to other running threads, in this case **mythread. Add Imports System.Threading**:

```
    Private Sub button1_Click(ByVal sender As System.Object,
    ByVal e As System.EventArgs) Handles Button1.Click
```

```
        Dim thisthread As Thread

        thisthread = Threading.Thread.CurrentThread

        Dim thrdStart As Threading.ThreadStart = New
        Threading.ThreadStart(AddressOf threadstuff)

        Dim mythread As Threading.Thread = New
        Threading.Thread(thrdStart)

        mythread.Start() 'starts the thread

        thisthread.Sleep(10000)

        mythread.Abort() 'Stops the thread

        mythread.Join() 'Wait until the thread finishes

        MessageBox.Show(mythread.IsAlive.ToString)

    End Sub

Private Sub threadstuff()

        MessageBox.Show("in the threadstuff method")

End Sub
```

There are two possible things that can happen in this example. The first is that the user clicks the **OK** button in the **MessageBox** immediately, then waits until 10 seconds have transpired, and then sees the **MessageBox** alerting them to the fact that the child thread has been successfully aborted, checking the value of the **IsAlive** property. The second thing is that the user does not immediately click the **OK** button, and instead goes to get coffee and then returns. By then, the parent thread has woken from its nap, and has sent an **Abort** request to the child thread. You will need to have read the section on **Thread States** to know that the second thread then enters two thread states at the same time. It is running, waiting for the user to click the **OK** button, and has also entered the **AbortRequested** state. As soon as the user clicks the **OK** button in the **MessageBox**, the second thread aborts.

Thread.Suspend

Thread.Suspend is similar to **Thread.Sleep**. Unlike **Thread.Sleep**, calling **Thread-.Suspend** does not cause the processing to stop immediately. Processing will suspend when the **Thread** enters a state where it is safe to enter a suspended state. It will then remain in a suspended state until **Thread.Resume** is called by a running **Thread**.

```
' A running thread calls suspend.

mythread.Suspend()

' A running thread calls resume.

mythread.Resume()
```

Unlike **Sleep**, the **Thread** cannot wake itself up because it has no timer. It depends on another **Thread** to cause it to resume processing.

Thread.Interrupt

Thread.Interrupt interrupts a thread that is in the **WaitSleepJoin** state. The interrupt is immediate. If the child **Thread** is not currently in the **WaitSleepJoin** state, the interrupt is held in queue until the **Thread** enters that state, at which time it will be immediately interrupted. The following example demonstrates how a **Thread.Interrupt** can be held in suspense. The primary **Thread** sends an **Interrupt** the moment it starts the **Thread**. The **Thread** is not currently in the **WaitJoinSleep** state because it is waiting for the user to respond to the **MessageBox** before **Thread.Sleep** is called. When the user finally clicks the **OK** button on the **MessageBox**, the **Thread** enters the **WaitJoinSleep** state, only to be immediately interrupted by the waiting **Interrupt**.

```
Imports Sytem.Threading

Dim icounter As Integer

Private Sub button1_Click(ByVal sender As System.Object,
ByVal e As System.EventArgs) Handles Button1.Click

    Dim thisthread As Thread

    thisthread = Threading.Thread.CurrentThread

    Dim thrdStart As Threading.ThreadStart = New
    Threading.ThreadStart(AddressOf threadstuff)
```

```
    Dim mythread As Threading.Thread = New
    Threading.Thread(thrdStart)

    mythread.Start() 'starts the thread

    mythread.Interrupt() 'immediatly call the Interrupt
    method.

    Do While icounter = 1

    Loop

    mythread.Abort() 'Stops the thread

    mythread.Join() 'Wait until the thread finishes

    MessageBox.Show("done")

End Sub


Private Sub threadstuff()

    MessageBox.Show("in the threadstuff method")

    Dim childthread As Thread

    childthread = Threading.Thread.CurrentThread()

    Try

        childthread.Sleep(10000) 'sleep for 10 seconds

    Catch

        Console.Write(Now)

        MessageBox.Show("Thread Interrupt Exception
        Thrown")
```

```
      End Try

      Threading.Interlocked.Decrement(icounter)

End Sub
```

Here is another example of using Thread.Interrupt:

```
Imports System.Threading 'Add

Private Sub button1_Click(ByVal sender As System.Object,
ByVal e As System.EventArgs) Handles Button1.Click

      Dim thisthread As Thread

      thisthread = Threading.Thread.CurrentThread

      Dim thrdStart As Threading.ThreadStart = New
Threading.ThreadStart(AddressOf threadstuff)

      Dim mythread As Threading.Thread = New
Threading.Thread(thrdStart)

      mythread.Start() 'starts the thread

      Console.Write(Now)

      thisthread.Sleep(20000) 'sleep for twenty seconds

      mythread.Interrupt()

      mythread.Abort() 'Stops the thread

      mythread.Join() 'Wait until the thread finishes

      MessageBox.Show(IIf(mythread.IsAlive, "I'm
alive.", "I'm dead now."))

      End Sub

      Private Sub threadstuff()
```

```
            MessageBox.Show("in the threadstuff method")

            Dim childthread As Thread

            childthread = Threading.Thread.CurrentThread()

            Try

                childthread.Sleep(45000) 'sleep for 45 seconds

            Catch

                Console.Write(Now)

                MessageBox.Show("Thread Interrupt Exception
                Thrown")

            End Try

        End Sub
```

Thread.Join

Thread.Join waits for either another **Thread** to die or for an amount of time to elapse. It returns True when the **Thread** dies or False if the time elapses before the **Thread** dies. It's a strange name, because **Join** doesn't seem like you're just waiting for something to die, but that's actually what you're waiting for.

```
    Thread.Join([integer or timespan])
```

When no argument is passed to **Join**, the method waits indefinitely.

> **Note**
> **Thread.Interrupt** can interrupt a waiting **Thread** with a **Thread.Join**.

Whenever a **Thread** takes a while to die, because of lengthy processing code in the **Finally** block, you'll want to make your program wait until the **Thread** is actually dead. The **Thread.Join** method is used to let you know when the thread is actually dead.

Thread.Abort

Thread.Abort kills any running thread, including those that are sleeping, waiting, or suspended. Unlike other actions that pause **Thread** processing, this action kills the **Thread**

permanently. You can not restart a **Thread** that has been aborted. The **ThreadAbortexception** is thrown, and not handled by **Catch**. Any statements in a **Finally** section of a Try – End Try block are executed.

Like other actions that cause suspension of processing, **Thread.Abort** waits for a safe point to finally kill the **Thread**. See **Thread.Join** for more information about waiting for the thread's actual death. Similar to **Thread.Join**, you can pass an argument that specifies a time period to wait for successful completion of the abort process. The method returns True if the abort is successful in the allotted time, and False if it fails to complete in time.

Once a thread has been aborted, it cannot be restarted.

Thread.Suspend

Because a stopped thread cannot be restarted, the **Thread.Suspend** method allows you to stop a thread temporarily, starting it again with the **Thread.Resume** method.

Thread.Resume

Thread.Resume starts the processing of a thread that has been suspended. You can't use this method to restart a thread that has been stopped or aborted.

Thread Scheduling

All **Threads** have a *priority*. Processor time is scheduled based on a **Thread**'s priority. Higher priority **Threads** are executed first. When all high-priority **Thread** processing has been completed, lower priority **Threads** are executed. A higher priority **Thread** will always preempt lower priority **Threads**. **Thread** priorities can be changed dynamically. For example, an application running in the foreground may be changed to run in the background. This is true when a Windows application is minimized, or no longer the application with focus (moved between foreground and background).

> **Note**
> Threads created in the runtime are normally given the priority of *Normal*.

Thread Pooling

The ability to queue work to be performed by one or a pool of threads is important in multithreaded applications. The **System.Threading.Threadpool** class provides a method for managing queues, **QueueUserWorkItem**. This method accepts a **WaitCallBack** delegate that represents the function to call when a **Thread** is released from the queue to perform its task. You can use an overloaded version of this method to pass state information to the delegate function.

The thread pool handles creating new threads in the pool automatically.

Note
Threads in a pool are managed by the pool. Therefore, the **WaitCallBack** functions should not terminate the current thread.

Foreground and Background Threads

Background and foreground **Threads** are identical, with one exception. A foreground **Thread** has the ability to keep the runtime alive, while the background **Thread** does not. In other words, upon the death of the last foreground thread, all background **Threads** will also die.

The **IsBackground** property merely sets the importance of a **Thread**, and does nothing to change the way processing occurs unless a background **Thread** is left running when an application terminates. The runtime simply shuts down the application and all the background threads.

Threads are foreground by default. To change a **Thread** to be a background **Thread**, change the **IsBackground** property of the **Thread** object to **True**.

Summary

Every application has at least one thread. Whether you use more than one thread in your application or not, it's important to understand how threads operate, and how the operating system might interact with your application, changing the priority of your application's thread.

There are types of applications that lend themselves to multithreading. For example, network communications applications would be very difficult to write without threads. You can have each communication session run in a different thread, enabling the application to carry on more than one session at a time.

Threads are simple to create, but more challenging when it comes to synchronizing thread interaction. The common language runtime brings a powerful ability to Visual Basic .NET. The next chapter teaches you how to create Windows Services applications.

Creating Windows Services 16

Many computer applications do not provide functionality directly to the end user. Instead, those applications manage resources that other applications use and share. These applications also provide functionality that must always be available regardless of who uses the computer. A *Windows Service*, sometimes simply known as a *service*, can be thought of as an extension of your operating system. It begins running when your system boots and continues running until it is either manually stopped or the operating system shuts down. Another important characteristic of these applications is that they rarely have a user interface. The tasks services perform rarely relies on an end user. Instead, services run in the background.

Services resemble UNIX daemon processes and often implement the server side of a client-server application. (See Chapter 18 for a more complete explanation of server applications.) One example of a service, commonly found on computers running Windows 2000 Server, Windows XP and computers running Windows NT, is a Web server application. Web servers run as services, quietly in the background, serving Web pages to client applications that request them.

The Web server begins running when the operating system starts, without the aid of an administrator or other human intervention. And, because a typical Web server does not require a user interface other than the occassionally used configuration interface, it runs invisibly. In fact, Internet Information Server, the Web server that runs on most Windows servers, does not have a user interface at all, but rather relies on plug-in applications to a server administrator to set its configuration.

The Windows Service Components

Before launching into building a service, it's important to understand the components involved in Windows services. Three components are required to run a service:

- A service application
- A Service Control Program (SCP)
- A Service Control Manager (SCM, pronounced *scum*)

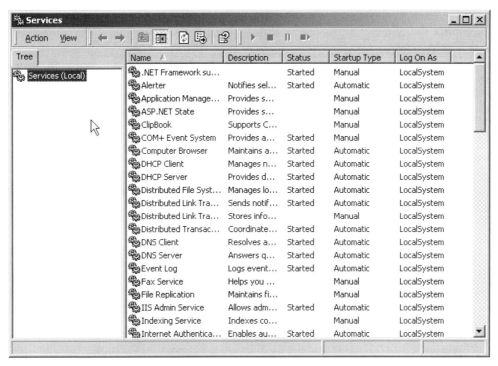

Figure 16.1 The Windows Services Applet lets you visually manage Windows Services.

Of the three component types, the service application is the one you build. They are functionality-driven, with no concern about building a user interface. When building a service application, memory constraints are a concern. Because these applications run silently in the background, they are often overlooked as consumers of Windows resources, such as memory and CPU time. Try to keep your applications memory- and processor-friendly.

The Service Control Program (SCP) is an application that provides a user interface to handle the management of Windows services. You have probably seen the visual manager in your Windows Control Panel applet or in Windows 2000 and Windows XP by selecting Services from the list of Administrative Tools in the Startup Menu. The Windows Services Applet is shown in Figure 16.1.

This application communicates with the Service Control Manager (SCM) to give you manual control over how services start up, and the ability to start, stop, pause, and resume services. It's also the case that applications include their own SCP, which allows an administrator to modify settings used by the service the SCP manages. Windows Server operating systems supply built-in SCPs that provide general stop, pause, and continue functionality.

The Service Control Manager maintains a database of services and device drivers and is responsible for starting and stopping them automatically. The SCM is itself a Windows Service. The Windows operating system supplies the SCM that starts services according to their start parameters. In this chapter you will learn how to create a service application and a Service Control Program (SCP).

Programming a Service

Before Visual Basic .NET, to write Windows Service applications you had to use a low-level language such as Visual C++ or utilities such as srvany.exe or other third-party utilities. It's now quite simple to build this type of application.

Begin by creating a new Visual Basic .NET application. When the project's type window appears select Windows Service. This will create a new, nonvisual application using the services template. Your application development environment will launch without a **Form** (Figure 16.2).

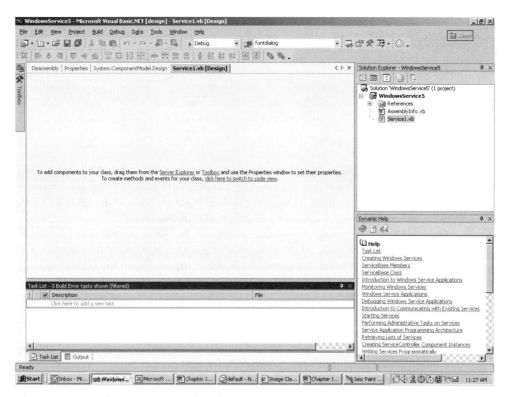

Figure 16.2   The services template launches a nonvisual development environment.

The template creates the following code:

```
Imports System.ServiceProcess

Public Class Service1

    Inherits System.ServiceProcess.ServiceBase

#Region " Component Designer generated code "

Public Sub New()

    MyBase.New()

    ' This call is required by the Component Designer.

    InitializeComponent()

    ' Add any initialization after the
InitializeComponent() call

End Sub

' The main entry point for the process

Shared Sub Main()

    Dim ServicesToRun() As System.ServiceProcess.
    ServiceBase

    ServicesToRun = New System.ServiceProcess.ServiceBase
    () {New Service1}

    System.ServiceProcess.ServiceBase.Run(ServicesToRun)

End Sub

Private components As System.ComponentModel.Container

<System.Diagnostics.DebuggerStepThrough()> Private Sub
InitializeComponent()
```

```
      components = New System.ComponentModel.Container()

      Me.ServiceName = "Service1"

  End Sub

  #End Region

  Protected Overrides Sub OnStart(ByVal args() As String)

      ' Add code here to start your service.

  End Sub

  Protected Overrides Sub OnStop()

      ' Add code here to stop your service.

  End Sub

  End Class
```

The application, rather than inheriting from **Form**, inherits from **System.Service-Process.ServiceBase** and imports **System.ServiceProcess**.

```
  Imports System.net.sockets

  Imports System.ServiceProcess

  Public Class Service1

      Inherits System.ServiceProcess.ServiceBase

  #Region " Component Designer generated code "

      Public Sub New()

          MyBase.New()

          ' This call is required by the Component Designer.

          InitializeComponent()
```

```vb
        ' Add any initialization after the
        InitializeComponent() call

    End Sub

    ' The main entry point for the process

    Shared Sub Main()

        Dim ServicesToRun() As System.ServiceProcess.
        ServiceBase

        ServicesToRun = New System.ServiceProcess.
        ServiceBase () {New Service1}


        System.ServiceProcess.ServiceBase.
        Run(ServicesToRun)

    End Sub



    Private components As System.ComponentModel.Container

    <System.Diagnostics.DebuggerStepThrough()> Private Sub
    InitializeComponent()

        components = New System.ComponentModel.Container()

        Me.ServiceName = "Service1"

    End Sub

#End Region

    Protected Overrides Sub OnStart(ByVal args() As
    String)

        startlistening()
```

```
        End Sub


        Protected Overrides Sub OnStop()

            ' Add code here to perform any tear-down necessary
            to stop your service.

        End Sub

        Private Sub startlistening()

            Dim myListener As New TcpListener(8080)

            myListener.Start()

            Console.Write("waiting")

            Dim mySocket As Socket = myListener.AcceptSocket()

            Dim myMessage As String = "Hi There"

            Dim byteMessage As Byte() =
            System.Text.Encoding.ASCII.GetBytes(myMessage.
            ToCharArray())

            mySocket.Send(byteMessage, byteMessage.Length,
            Net.Sockets.SocketFlags.DontRoute)

            myListener.Stop()

            mySocket.Close()

        End Sub

  End Class
```

Notice that the first line in **Sub Main( )** declares **ServicesToRun** as type **System.ServiceProcess.ServiceBase**. Then, **ServicesToRun** instantiates a new **ServiceBase** object, and passes the services as part of the constructor. Each service must be instantiated using the **New** operator, like this:

```
ServicesToRun = New System.ServiceProcess.ServiceBase()
{New Service1, New Service2, New Service3}
```

This sample is a typical network server application. This happens to be one of the samples from the Building Network Applications chapter. Instead of running the application with a user interface, as in Chapter 18, it is being run as a service.

Note
You cannot start your Windows Service application from the Visual Studio Debugger. Your Windows Service application must first be installed (see "Installing a Service").

Installing a Service

Before you can install your new Window Service application, you must add a **ServicesInstaller** object to your application. Add the installer by right-clicking in the Design window. Select Add Installer from the pop-up menu. This will add a ProjectInstaller.vb file to your Solution Explorer. It will also add a tab to your visual design window. In this window you will see a **ServiceInstaller** object and a **ServiceProcessInstaller**.

Right-click on these two objects to set their properties. In the **ServiceInstaller** object you can set the startup type of the application. The **StartupType** property choices are: **Manual**, **Automatic**, or **Disabled**.

Set the **DisplayName** property with the text you would like to appear in Service Control Programs that manage services. The **ServiceName** property is filled in automatically with the name of the service. In our example, it is **Service1**.

The **ServicesDependedOn** property is a collection of service application names on which this service depends. This list should include any service that needs to be started for this service to start. In reverse, when the service upon which this service depends is stopped, a notification is sent to all dependent services. Editing this service displays the String Collection Editor.

Edit the **ServiceProcessInstaller** properties. The first property is the **Account** property specifying under what account this application will run (see the next section, "Service Accounts"). When the **Account** is set to **User**, you can enter the **Username** and **Password** of the account under which this service will run.

One of the tools that ships with the .NET Framework is the installer tool known by its filename: **installutil.exe**. Running **installutil.exe** is the final step required before running your service. This program does the installation and sets all the required settings in the System Registry.

Installutil.exe is a command line application, and needs to be run from the Command Prompt. When run, **installutil.exe** executes the installers (the objects you just added). The application begins a transaction that can be rolled back in case the installation fails. That way, you don't fill your Registry up with garbage information. **Installutil.exe** accepts the following command line parameters:

/u – Uninstall

/Logfile=logfilename – This writes installation log information, if any, to a logfile.

/LogtoConsole – Writes the log to the output console.

/ShowCallStack – When an exception occurs, the stack is printed to the log.

The **installutil.exe** program will let you know whether or not your service was successfully installed. It's output is a bit verbose, but if you read through it generally you can get an idea what went wrong, if the install is unsuccessful.

Once the service has been installed, you can use any SCP or the Windows Server-Explorer to start the service. It is normally unnecessary to reboot your computer after installation. Start the Services Management Console, then find your service and start it (Figure 16.3).

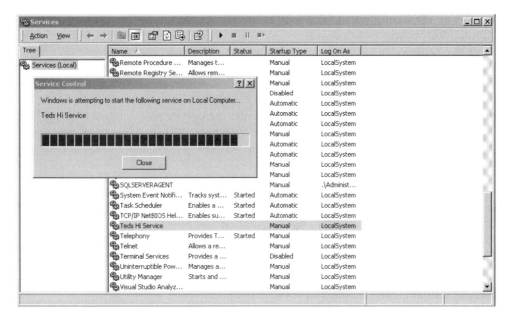

Figure 16.3 Starting your service from the Services Management Console.

Service Accounts

When setting the properties of the **ServiceProcessInstaller**, you are asked to choose the account under which the Windows Service application will run. There are four enumerated Security Account types:

LocalService

LocalSystem

NetworkService

User

By default, Windows Services applications are set to run under the User account. What account the service runs under has significant security issues. The Local System account is extremely powerful. For example, all of the Windows 2000 user-mode operating system components runs under this security account. This includes the Windows 2000 Session Manager, the Win32 Subsystem process, the local security authority subsystems, and, most importantly, the WinLogon process.

The Local System account owns almost every defined privilege, such as the ability to take ownership of files, create security tokens, reboot the machine, and allow access to the system account. The Local System account is more powerful than any local or domain account in terms of the security ramifications on a local system.

Creating a Service Controller

The **ServiceController** class allows you to build an application that connects to the Windows SCM and allows you to control other services, whether running or not. Writing your own SCP gives you a great deal more control over how services operate. The built-in Microsoft Management Console snap-in does not support custom commands or give you much more than rudimentary control over services.

A service controller can be embedded within any application. For example, perhaps your application needs to modify some of the parameters used by a Web server. Your application can handle shutting down the Web service, changing the parameters, and restarting the Web server. Or, perhaps a security monitoring program senses an incursion or denial of service attack. The services can be shut down to protect system resources and alert a remote operator, even to the point of paging an administrator or sending an email message. Even though this book does not cover creating Web applications, you can embed a service controller in a Web application using ASP.NET.

To get started, add a **ServiceController** object to an application. Remember, the SCP can be a service itself, but is more often a standalone application or embedded in other applications. The **ServiceController** object can be in applications with a user interface to allow user interaction with a service, or placed within an application, user interface or not, to perform automated tasks on a service or services.

When adding a **ServiceController** object, you must first use the Imports **System.serviceProcess** directive. If Visual Studio complains that **System.serviceProcess** is not a part of framework, you may have to add a Reference. To add a Reference:

1. Right-click on the References folder in the Solution Explorer.
2. Choose to Add Reference.
3. When a dialog pops up that allows you to choose a new reference, scroll down to the reference labeled System.ServiceProcess.dll.
4. Select it by clicking on the dll.
5. Click the Select button.
6. Finally, click the **OK** button.

Your application will now have access to the classes provided in the **ServiceProcess** library.

Here is a code snippet that shows a **ListBox** on a **Form**, populated with the names of all the services running on a machine:

```
Private Sub Button1_Click(ByVal sender As System.Object,
ByVal e As System.EventArgs) Handles Button1.Click

    Dim mySCParray As ServiceController()

    Dim mySCP As ServiceController

    mySCParray = ServiceController.GetServices()

    For Each mySCP In mySCParray

        ListBox1.Items.Add(mySCP.ServiceName)

        Console.Write(mySCP.ServiceName & vbCrLf)

    Next

End Sub
```

The **GetServices** method of the **ServiceController** class is a shared method that returns a collection of **ServiceController** objects. Each one of these **ServiceController** objects returned by the **GetServices** method is capable of managing each of the services that the **ServiceController** object is bound to.

Here is a simple, working SCP written in Visual Basic .NET. It involves two **Forms**. **Form1** is the primary user interface and **Form2** is the pop-up that allows you to stop, start, and pause a service:

```vbnet
Imports System.serviceProcess

Public Class Form1

    Inherits System.Windows.Forms.Form

    Dim soarray As Object()

#Region " Windows Form Designer generated code "

    Public Sub New()

        MyBase.New()

        'This call is required by the Windows Form
        Designer.

        InitializeComponent()

        'Add any initialization after the
        InitializeComponent() call

    End Sub

    'Form overrides dispose to clean up the component
    list.

    Protected Overloads Overrides Sub Dispose(ByVal
    disposing As Boolean)

        If disposing Then

            If Not (components Is Nothing) Then

                components.Dispose()

            End If
```

```
        End If

    MyBase.Dispose(disposing)

End Sub

Friend WithEvents ListBox1 As System.Windows.Forms.
ListBox

Friend WithEvents Button1 As System.Windows.Forms.
Button

Friend WithEvents Button2 As System.Windows.Forms.
Button

'Required by the Windows Form Designer

Private components As System.ComponentModel.Container

'NOTE: The following procedure is required by the
Windows Form Designer

'It can be modified using the Windows Form Designer.

'Do not modify it using the code editor.

<System.Diagnostics.DebuggerStepThrough()> Private Sub
InitializeComponent()

    Me.Button1 = New System.Windows.Forms.Button()

    Me.ListBox1 = New System.Windows.Forms.ListBox()

    Me.Button2 = New System.Windows.Forms.Button()

    Me.SuspendLayout()

    'Button1

    Me.Button1.Location = New System.Drawing.
    Point(192, 16)
```

```
Me.Button1.Name = "Button1"

Me.Button1.TabIndex = 1

Me.Button1.Text = "Load"

'ListBox1

Me.ListBox1.Location = New System.Drawing.
Point(16, 48)

Me.ListBox1.Name = "ListBox1"

Me.ListBox1.Size = New System.Drawing.Size(240,
160)

Me.ListBox1.TabIndex = 0

'Button2

Me.Button2.Location = New System.Drawing.
Point(184, 240)

Me.Button2.Name = "Button2"

Me.Button2.TabIndex = 2

Me.Button2.Text = "Configure"

Me.Button2.Enabled = False

'Form1

Me.AutoScaleBaseSize = New System.Drawing.Size(5,
13)

Me.ClientSize = New System.Drawing.Size(292, 273)

Me.Controls.AddRange(New System.Windows.Forms.
Control() {Me.Button2, Me.Button1, Me.ListBox1})
```

```
        Me.Name = "Form1"

        Me.Text = "Form1"

        Me.ResumeLayout(False)

    End Sub

#End Region

    Private Sub Button1_Click(ByVal sender As
    System.Object, ByVal e As System.EventArgs) Handles
    Button1.Click

        ' Declare a new ServiceController object

        Dim mySCParray As ServiceController()

        ' The GetServices method returns a
          ServiceController.

        mySCParray = ServiceController.GetServices()

        'Make a clone of the mySCParray collection

        soarray = mySCParray.Clone

        Dim mySCP As ServiceController

        'load the listbox

        For Each mySCP In mySCParray

            ListBox1.Items.Add(mySCP.ServiceName)

        Next

        Button2.Enabled = True

    End Sub
```

```
Private Sub Button2_Click(ByVal sender As
System.Object, ByVal e As System.EventArgs) Handles
Button2.Click

    Dim mySCP As ServiceController

    Dim status As ServiceControllerStatus 'enumerated

    ' Declare a new Form of type Form2. Assumes Form2
    has already been created

    Dim configForm As New Form2()

    mySCP = soarray(ListBox1().SelectedIndex)

    configForm.Label1().Text = mySCP.DisplayName

    configForm.configSCP = mySCP

    status = mySCP.Status

    'Set the enabled state of the buttons based on
    status

    Select Case status

        Case ServiceControllerStatus.Paused

            configForm.Button1.Enabled = False 'start

            configForm.Button2.Enabled = True 'stop

            configForm.Button3.Enabled = False 'pause

            configForm.Button4.Enabled = True
            'continue

            configForm.Label2.Text = "Paused"
```

```
            Case ServiceControllerStatus.Running

                configForm.Button1.Enabled = False

                configForm.Button2.Enabled = True

                configForm.Button3.Enabled = True

                configForm.Button4.Enabled = False

                configForm.Label2.Text = "Running"

            Case ServiceControllerStatus.Stopped

                configForm.Button1.Enabled = True

                configForm.Button2.Enabled = False

                configForm.Button3.Enabled = True

                configForm.Button4.Enabled = False

                configForm.Label2.Text = "Stopped"

        End Select

        configForm.Show()

    End Sub

End Class
```

Add a new **Form** using the Solution Explorer, as explained in Chapter 9. Add two **Labels** and five **Buttons**. Four of the **Buttons** are used to start, stop, pause, and continue the service; the **Labels** are for displaying the name of the service and its current status. The fifth **Button** closes the window. Figure 16.4 shows you the way that **Form2** was designed with callouts for easier reference.

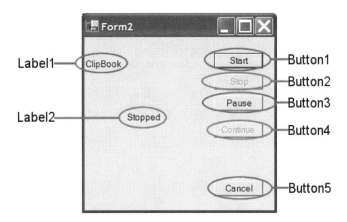

Figure 16.4 **Form2** while the program is running.

This is the code for **Form2**:

```
Imports System.serviceProcess

Public Class Form2

    Inherits System.Windows.Forms.Form

    Public configSCP As New ServiceProcess.
    ServiceController()

'+ Windows Form Designer Generated Code

    Private Sub Button1_Click(ByVal sender As
    System.Object, ByVal e As System.EventArgs) Handles
    Button1.Click

        configSCP.Start()

        configSCP.Refresh() 'refreshes the property values

        Me.Close()

    End Sub
```

```vb
Private Sub Button2_Click(ByVal sender As
System.Object, ByVal e As System.EventArgs) Handles
Button2.Click

    configSCP.Stop()

    configSCP.Refresh() 'refreshes the property values

    Me.Close()

End Sub

  Private Sub Button3_Click(ByVal sender As
  System.Object, ByVal e As System.EventArgs) Handles
  Button3.Click

    If configSCP.CanPauseAndContinue Then

        configSCP.Pause()

        configSCP.WaitForStatus
        (ServiceControllerStatus.Paused)

        configSCP.Refresh()

        Me.Close()

    Else

        MessageBox.Show("Can not pause this service.")

    End If

End Sub

Private Sub Button4_Click(ByVal sender As
System.Object, ByVal e As System.EventArgs) Handles
Button3.Click

    configSCP.Continue()
```

```
            configSCP.WaitForStatus
            (ServiceControllerStatus.Running)

            configSCP.Refresh() 'refreshes the property
            values

           Me.Close()

       End Sub

      Private Sub Button5_Click(ByVal sender As
      System.Object, ByVal e As System.EventArgs) Handles
      Button5.Click

           Me.Close()

      End Sub

End Class
```

Warning!
This is a working Service Control Program and can stop, start, pause, and continue running services. Do not stop services in your operating system you are unfamiliar with. This can cause your system to crash, requiring a reboot of your operating system.

The application returns to the main window after changing the service's status. Before returning, the **Refresh** method is called, resetting the property values in the control. You could also change the status, and wait for the actual status of the service to change using the **WaitForStatus** method. This often takes a few seconds to occur. Then, you can redisplay the new actual status and update the enabled states of the buttons accordingly.

Further Service Configuration

There is much more control over a service other than simply starting, stopping, and pausing it. First of all, one of the things shown, but not discussed, in the previous sample is the fact that the Service Control Program was able to check the **ServiceController** object to see if it's possible to pause, continue, and stop an application. The **ServiceController's CanPauseAndContinue** property will tell you if a service will allow the SCP program to pause and continue the service. The **CanStop** property alerts the SCP to the service's ability to be stopped by the SCP. There may be critical services that will not allow you to stop them in your application, not matter what security privileges your application has.

Your application can also check the value of **CanShutdown** to see if the service will be notified when the system is shutting down. Services that do housekeeping at shutdown should be notified when the system is shutting down so they can close files, save data, or do whatever housekeeping is required before allowing the system to completely shut down.

In addition to all the stopping and starting, you can issue a custom command to the service by calling the **ExecuteCommand** method. This method accepts an integer value that acts as a flag to the service, telling it which command to execute. The result of the ExecuteCommand method has no effect on the state of the service, that is, running, stopped, or paused.

Summary

Windows Services applications are the invisible workhorses that provide a great deal of the many client-server applications that make today's networking possible. It's appropriate that they are symbolized by the icon. Internet servers, such as DNS, DHCP, SMTP, and POP3, are essential to modern networks.

Applications other than traditional Internet servers may run as a service. There are services that listen for incoming connection requests and manage communications, such as NetMeeting and PCAnywhere. Other services operate as a part of the operating system and simply provide local machine and local area network support, such as the Print Spooler.

The next chapter shows you how you can build components using Visual Basic .NET. Application developers realize they no longer have to reinvent the wheel each time they write a program. They make use of components they can plug right into their applications. There is an excellent market for components, and now that Visual Basic .NET allows you to create components using managed code, the market is even greater.

Components are encapsulated mini-programs that provide some specific bit of functionality to full applications. By themselves, components do nothing. They do, however, provide important functionality to programs that make use of them. Components provide the ability to "plug" reusable code into your Visual Basic .NET application. You saw how this was done by plugging in components in the form of controls, such as the **Button** control or **ListBox** control. But all components are not visual. Some provide functionality without a user interface. For example, a developer might design a component that provides special mathematical processing capability.

As you now know, Visual Studio .NET provides many visual components that can be used in your Visual Basic .NET applications. This chapter will help you understand how those components are included in your application, while also giving you an idea of how to create your own components.

The **System.ComponentModel** namespace provides classes that are used to build the runtime and design-time behavior of controls and components. The namespace also includes classes that allow the component developer to provide licensing functionality with their components. The classes in this namespace are divided into the following categories:

Component classes

Licensing

Attributes

Descriptors

Converters

The Component

You are already familiar with some of the basics of the **Component** class. This is the class from which the **Form** controls, discussed in Chapter 12, are derived. When creating components, it's important to have a specific goal in mind. Remember that components are not applications, but rather reusable code snippets that perform a very specific task. Therefore, keep the design goal of your component focused. For example, a visual component should allow the user to interact in a single manner, that is, type text here or click there. Nonvisual components should also provide a limited amount of functionality, such as connect to this server or perform this math function. You'll find that by limiting the function of your component it will become more generic, and you will be more likely to use it in other applications. You might also consider marketing your component commercially if it provides some unique service important to other developers.

Building Components

You'll find that working with components is all about understanding the interfaces that are implemented in the various classes involved. For instance, the **Component** class implements the **IComponent** interface, which allows the sharing of objects between applications.

Three classes are involved in giving a Component the ability to provide services to various applications:

Component – This class is the provider of services.

Container – This class encapsulates **Components.**

Site – This class provides information about what **Containers** encapsulate which **Components**.

Components can be hosted in **Container** objects that implement the **IContainer** interface. **Components** have the ability to interact with their containers by getting services and querying the container's services. When a **Container** hosts a component, it creates a *site*, which is a class that implements the **ISite** interface. The site is used as an intermediary between the **Container** and **Component**. Each uses the site when communicating with the other. Classes that implement the **ISite** interface merely have to implement the following members:

Component – The actual component associated with the site.

Container – The actual container associated with the site.

DesignMode – Whether or not the component is in design mode.

Name – The name of the component.

Before this gets confusing, this example shows how simple this is:

```
Public Class mycomponent

    Inherits System.ComponentModel.Component

End Class
```

```
Public Class mycontainer

    Inherits System.ComponentModel.Container

End Class
```

Once you have both the **Component** and **Container** classes, use the **Add** method of the **Container** to add the **Component** to the **Container's** collection (**Component-Collection** class) of **Components,** like this:

```
Dim newcomponent As New mycomponent()

Dim newcontainer As New mycontainer()

newcontainer.Add(newcomponent)
```

To later remove a **Component** from the **Container**, use the **Container's Remove** method. The Container also has a CreateSite method that it uses to create the site. Remember, the site keeps track of **Component – Container** relationships.

To add a component into your application using Visual Studio .NET select **Add Component...** from the **Project** menu. Select the name of the component you wish to add from the **Add New Item** window. This adds a new design tab to your Visual Studio designer window. You will also see the component added to your Solution Explorer window.

The Component Designer allows you to build nonvisual components. Don't add visual controls such as buttons. They will appear on the design surface but you won't be able to use them. You can, however, drop nonvisual components such as the MessageQueue component onto the design surface. The Component Designer also creates the following code:

```
Public Class Component1

    Inherits System.ComponentModel.Component

#Region " Component Designer generated code "

    Public Sub New(Container As System.ComponentModel.
    IContainer)

        MyClass.New()

        'Required for Windows.Forms Class Composition
        Designer support
```

```
            Container.Add(me)

    End Sub

    Public Sub New()

        MyBase.New()

        'This call is required by the Component Designer.

        InitializeComponent()

        'Add any initialization after the
        InitializeComponent() call

    End Sub

    'Required by the Component Designer

    Private components As System.ComponentModel.Container

    'NOTE: The following procedure is required by the
     Component Designer

    'It can be modified using the Component Designer.

    'Do not modify it using the code editor.

    <System.Diagnostics.DebuggerStepThrough()> Private Sub
    InitializeComponent()

        components = New System.ComponentModel.Container()

    End Sub

#End Region

End Class
```

Once you've dropped other nonvisual components onto the design surface, you can manipulate them by right-clicking them and modifying their properties, or double-clicking them and allowing the designer to generate code for you.

Client and Server Components

Client components are similar to the controls we've already used to create user interfaces. They have properties and abilities and are implemented in each copy of the application we deliver. This is the type of component you will want to implement on a computer not connected to a server through a network. The .NET Framework gives you the ability to create a different type of component known as a server-side component.

Server-side components have all the same capabilities as client components, but instead of residing on the client machine, the component lives on the server. This makes it possible for clients to make use of components simply by referring to them on the server. This makes distributing an application much simpler, as the underlying code to support the component does not need to be distributed with the application. The downside to this, of course, is that the server must always be accessible for the application to run.

Designers

Visual Basic .NET, based on the .NET Framework, is completely extensible. The .NET Framework has been designed so that there is a tight integration between the runtime and design time portions of the application's code base. Visual Basic .NET objects responsible for managing the design time behavior of a component are known as *designers*. This is not to be confused with the designer tools built into Visual Studio .NET. Designers are objects specifically designed to manage the behavior and appearance of components by implementing the **System.ComponentModel.Design.IDesigner** interface.

The classes used to build designers are in the **System.ComponentModel.Design** namespace. The **ComponentDesigner** class serves as the base class for derived designers and provides the base functionality of a designer by implementing the **IDesigner** Interface.

Normally, it is not necessary to code a designer from scratch. Objects that implement the IComponent interface are already set up to have the ComponentDesigner as their designer.

Root designers allow a component to be the root object in the Visual Studio .NET design environment. For example, **Form** and **UserControl** objects have root designers that allow them to appear in both design mode and code view within Visual Studio .NET. Each type can have several designers associated with it, with a limit of a single designer of each type.

Designers have the following three primary functions:

They create and modify the design time user interface for the component being designed.

They modify the object's properties, attributes, and events.

They also add verbs, which are actions that can be performed on a component at design time.

At design time, each component gets a name and connection that allows it to access underlying designer services. That way, the designer interacts with the user and Visual Studio to perform actions such as automatic code generation.

Designers are associated with components using the **System.ComponentModel. DesignerAttribute**. The constructor of this attribute accepts an Assembly-qualified string type name, or an actual type reference. Attributes are explained in greater detail later in this chapter.

Component Relationships   There is a way to associate components. Take, for example, grouping components with a group box, or the button controls you add to a menu or ToolBar object. You want to keep these components associated with one another. The **AssociatedComponents** property of **ComponentDesigner** keeps track of component associations. When an action takes place on a component that has associations, Visual Studio .NET determines which components should be part of the operation, such as move, cut, copy, and paste.

Using Designers   Designers are commonly used to adjust the appearance of components within the Visual Studio design surface. You can also modify and add properties using a designer. This happens automatically in many cases. Consider, when adding a control to your project, the name and location are filled in for you. This is the action of the designer, as it has nothing to do with the component itself.

One of the things a designer does is keep track of the property selections you make, passing them to the component at the appropriate time. This keeps your control from disappearing when you select the **Visible** property to **False**.

The **ComponentDesigner** class has methods that allow you to change the properties of a component at design time:

PreFilterProperties

PostFilterProperties

PreFilterAttributes

PostFilterAttributes

PreFilterEvents

PostFilterEvents

It's normal practice to add and remove items using the **PreFilter** methods and modify existing items in the **PostFilter** methods. The ComponentDesigner has a dictionary for maintaining the values added or modified at design time.

Verbs   When your component has common actions that are performed on it, you can expose the actions as a *verb* of the component. We've seen how verbs work when adding controls, which also add hyperlinks that have "wizard-like" actions. These are actually verbs of the component. These same verbs are usually accessible by right-clicking on the component and selecting the actions from the pop-up menu.

DesignerVerbs are menu commands linked to an event handler. They are added to a component's context menu and the Properties window at runtime. **DesignerVerb** objects contain the verb's string name, the delegate to invoke when the verb is invoked, and an optional command ID, usually assigned by Visual Studio .NET. **TemplateEditing Verbs** are inherited from **DesignerVerb** and can only be invoked by the template editor.

Changes in a component's state are broadcast through the **IComponentChangeService**. Other services monitor this service to update the states of other components that may be affected by another component's change. For example, the change of font on the **Form** will affect the font on components placed on the **Form**.

The **IComponentChangeService** has two event notifications: **OnComponentChanging** and **OncomponentChanged**. The first event always fires, but the second event only fires if the change actually occurs. In other words, if you abort the change, the **OnComponentChanged** event will not fire.

Component Licensing

Once you've worked hard building a component, you may consider that it has value to others in the development community. In other words, you think that you can sell licenses to your component. .NET Framework has included classes that make adding licensing functionality to your component fairly simple.

The **System.ComponentModel** namespace includes the **License, LicenseProvider,** and **License Manager** classes for providing licenses to assemblies. The **License** class is the abstract base class for all licenses and has a single property, the **LicenseKey**. Licenses are granted to specific instances of a component by specifying a **LicenseProvider**.

The **LicenseManager** class adds a license to a component and manages the **LicenseProvider**. An implementation of the **LicenseProvider**, the **LicFileLicenseProvider**, is included in the CLR to provide licensing similar to COM components and uses text license files. The **LicFileLicenseProvider** class provides the **GetLicense** and **IsKeyValid** methods.

To add a **LicenseManager** to your component, add the **LicenseProviderAttribute** to the control like this:

```
<LicenseProvider(GetType(LicFileLicenseProvider))> Public
Class MyComponent
```

The next section discusses attributes and how to use them in detail. Within your component instantiate a new **License** object:

```
Private license As License = Nothing
```

In the constructor of the component, set the license object using the **Validate** method of the **LicenseManager** class, passing in the name of your component.

```
Public Sub New()

    license = LicenseManager.Validate(GetType(MyComponent),
    Me)

End Sub
```

Attributes

Attributes are a means of adding custom attributes to any element of the MetaData, such as the MetaData for a class or property. In this manner, custom or application-specific information can be stored at compile time, and retrieved at runtime, by tools that read the MetaData.

Creating Attributes

The **Attribute** class is used as the base class for all derived custom attributes. To create a custom attribute, create a new class derived from the **Attribute** class like this:

```
Public Class MyAttribute

    inherits Attribute

    ' Attribute code here

End Class
```

When constructing your own custom attribute, you can control how your attribute is used by specifying the **AttributeUsage Attribute** in your new derived class. To set the value of the **AttributeUsage Attribute,** it is necessary to define the following parameters:

ValidOn – Dictates which elements the attribute is valid on, defined by the Attribute-TargetEnumeration, whose values are listed in Table 17.1.

AllowMultiple – Can be specified multiple times for a given element.

Inherited – Indicates whether the attribute can be inherited by a derived class or overridden members.

Table 17.1 AttributeTargets Enumeration

Member Name	Description
All	Apply to any element.
Assembly	Apply to an assembly.
Class	Apply to a class.
Constructor	Apply to a constructor.
Delegate	Apply to a delegate.
Enum	Apply to an enumeration.
Event	Apply to an event.
Field	Apply to a field.
Interface	Apply to an interface.
Method	Apply to a method.
Module	Apply to a module.
Parameter	Apply to a parameter.
Property	Apply to a property.
ReturnValue	Apply to a Return value.
Struct	Apply to a value type.

Here is an example of defining an attribute using the **AttributeUsage Attribute**:

```
<AttributeUsage(AttributeTargets.Method Or
AttributeTargets.Field Or AttributeTargets.Property)>
Public Class MyAttribute
```

Notice that the values are combined in this example using a bitwise **Or** to indicate when the attribute usage is valid.

Using Attributes

Visual Basic .NET includes a number of attributes that control runtime behavior. Add attributes to an element by preceding the element's name and keywords with the attribute surrounded by <>. This example shows an attribute added to a class by preceding the name of the class with the attribute and its value like this:

```
<TypeConverter(GetType(MyClassConverter))> Public Class
MyClass
```

This example adds a **TypeConverterAttribute**, a predefined attribute (covered later in this chapter), to the **MyClass** definition. To add an attribute to a property, precede the property name with the attribute like this:

```
<Browsable(True)> Public Property MyProperty as String
```

The **Browsable** attribute is explained later in this section.

Attributes are stored in a collection called the **AttributeCollection**. Unlike other collections, the **AttributeCollection** is read-only. You cannot use methods of this collection to add or remove **Attributes**. You can, however, query the collection using the **Contains** and **Matches** methods.

Being able to query the **AttributeCollection** is an important feature. However, it might be easier to get all the attributes in the collection and iterate through them. This is because it's not guaranteed that all attributes will be known at runtime. It's possible for a developer to create and add a custom attribute, beyond those attributes provided by the .NET Framework for controlling components.

Use the shared methods **GetCustomAttribute** and **GetCustomAttributes** to retrieve the entire collection of attributes for a given element.

You can allow attributes to appear in a properties window by declaring the attribute to be of type **BrowsableAttribute**. When the **Browsable** property is set to **True**, the default, the attribute can be edited at design time in the properties window for the object being modified. When **Browsable** is set to **False**, the attribute does not appear and cannot be modified at design time.

```
<Browsable(True)> Public Property MyProperty as String
```

Deploying Components

Assemblies are the unit of deployment for components. Unlike COM objects, .NET components no longer require the use of a GUID (Globally Unique Identifier), and therefore require the use of a strong name.

Each component will run within a specific security context, depending on the security context of where the component is deployed. Here are some of the security contexts:

Local Machine - The component has full access to all machine capabilities. The components can execute unmanaged code, and can be installed using simple file copy.

Local Computer Zone – Full trust, unrestricted access to machine resources.

Intranet Zone – Restricted to accessing the user interface, isolated storage, the ability to read some environment variables.

Internet Zone – Safe access to the user interface and isolated storage.

Restricted Zone – The component is not authorized to run.

MS Strong Name – Fully trusted, unrestricted.

Strong Names

Strong names are unique names for your assembly, created using public–private key cryptography. When deploying your component such that several applications on a single machine might use it, a strong name is required.

To create a strong name, use the Strong Name tool (sn.exe) included with the .NET Framework. The following command line generates a public–private key pair. The result is stored in a file that you name. The example name is somekey.snk:

```
sn -k somekey.snk
```

Note
The key pair can be stored in a file on your computer or stored using your computer's Cryptographic Service Provider (CSP).

Depending on how you've chosen to store your key pair (see note) will determine the next step. You must create a custom attribute in your code so that the compiler will output the source with a strong name. For key pairs stored in a file, use the **System.Reflection.AssemblyKeyFileAttribute**. For keys managed by the CSP, use **System. Reflection.AssemblyKeyNameAttribute**.

Begin by setting the assembly level file attributes at the beginning of your code. This example sets the value of the AssemblyKeyFileAttribute to the name of the key pair file created by the Strong Name tool:

```
Imports System.Reflection

<assembly: AssemblyKeyFileAttribute("somekey.snk")>
```

Delay Signing

It's common in some organizations to restrict access to the private key used in signing code. This limits a "developer gone mad" from ruining the corporate reputation by releasing some nasty bit of code, signed with the company's digital signature. It's this digital signature that determines if users of the assembly will trust it or not.

Because of this security measure used by some companies, the developer may not have access to the private key when building an assembly. For this reason, there is an ability to delay the signature of the assembly by saving a space for the digital signature.

At build time, you supply the public key, which is stored in the Public Key field of the assembly's manifest. A space is then reserved for the digital signature. You later include the signature to the file.

Tip
Generate a digital signature using the Strong Name tool by specifying the **-R** command line switch.

To alert the compiler that you want to use delay signing, include the AssemblyDelaySignAttribute, setting it to True. You will still need to include the **AssemblyKeyFile attribute**. Here is an example:

```
Imports System.Reflection

<assembly: AssemblyKeyFileAttribute("somekey.snk")>

<assembly: AssemblyDelaySign(True)>
```

To test your compiled component prior to signing it and releasing it for distribution, you can tell the system to overlook the fact that a signature was not included. This is also done using the Strong Name tool:

```
sn -Vr DelaySign.dll
```

When you're ready to ship the code, the person responsible for managing the company's private key will use the Strong Name tool to sign the assembly, like this:

```
sn -R DelaySign.dll somekey.snk
```

When using the CSP to manage your key pair, use the **-c** command-line switch to the Strong Name tool to set the name of the CSP. Sign an assembly using the CSP using **-Rc** rather than just the **-R** as in the previous example, passing in the assembly and container as command-line arguments. For further help on using the Strong Name tool, simply run the tool without switches or arguments from the command line like this:

```
sn
```

Help will be displayed in the Command window.

Descriptors

Descriptors are structures that define attributes or functionality of objects or processes. An example of a Descriptor is the **MemberDescriptor** class. This class represents an array of attributes for a member and defines the properties and methods that provide access to attributes in the array. **MemberDescriptor** serves as the base class for the following classes:

EventDescriptor – Provides a description of an event.

PropertyDescriptor – Provides a description of a property.

Even though **MemberDescriptor** serves as a base class for **EventDescriptor** and **PropertyDescriptor**, it does not normally serve as the base class for other descriptors. New classes are normally derived from the other two descriptor classes, whose members are listed below.

EventDescriptor provides the following abstract, MustOverride, properties and methods:

ComponentType – Contains type of the component this event is bound to.

EventType – Contains the type of delegate for the event.

IsMulticast – Contains a value indicating whether the event delegate is a multicast delegate.

AddEventHandler – Binds the event to a component.

RemoveEventHandler – Unbinds the delegate from the component so that the delegate no longer receives events from the component.

PropertyDescriptor provides the following properties and methods:

Converter – Contains the type converter for this property.

IsLocalizable – Indicates whether this property should be localized.

GetEditor – Returns an editor of the specified type.

PropertyDescriptor also provides the following abstract, MustOverride, properties and methods:

ComponentType – Contains the type of component this property is bound to.

IsReadOnly – Indicates whether this property is read-only.

PropertyType – Gets the type of the property.

CanResetValue – Indicates whether resetting the component changes the value of the component.

GetValue – Returns the current value of the property on a component.

ResetValue – Resets the value for this property of the component.

SetValue – Sets the value of the component to a different value.

ShouldSerializeValue – Indicates whether the value of this property needs to be persisted.

Type Converters

The **System.ComponentModel** namespace also includes classes for converting one object type into another. Throughout this book you've seen examples of the most common type of converter, the **ToString** conversion, where objects are converted to type **String**.

TypeConverter objects perform type conversion. They are bound to a class with a **TypeConverterAttribute** like this:

```
<TypeConverter(GetType(MyClassConverter))> Public Class
MyClass

    ' Class code inserted here.

End Class
```

Here is an example of using a **TypeConverter** to convert a value to a **String**:

```
Dim Int As Integer = 5

Console.WriteLine(TypeDescriptor.GetConverter(Int).Convert
ToString(Int))
```

This next example from the Framework documentation is the best example of using the **TypeConverter** to convert a string value into an different object type and to list the standard values an object supports.

```
Dim c As Color =
CType(TypeDescriptor.GetConverter(GetType(Color)).Convert-
FromString("Red"), Color)
```

This example lists the standard values supported by the object:

```
Dim c As Color

For Each c In
TypeDescriptor.GetConverter(GetType(Color)).GetStandardVal
ues()
Console.WriteLine(TypeDescriptor.GetConverter(c).ConvertTo
String(c))Next c
```

Summary

Components are the foundation of modern application development. In the perfect developer world, it's only necessary to create a framework in which components can run and interact with each other. Whether your components live on standalone machines or run from a server, the .NET Framework has made it much simpler to create and distribute components. Strong Names have replaced the concept and hassle of GUIDs. Digitally signed components can be trusted by developers that recognize you, the developer, or the company you work for.

This chapter gets you started by extending the Visual Studio .NET design user interface. Designers help component developers maintain greater control over how their components are used while offering users of the component simpler control over the component.

Now that you have a better idea of how components are constructed in the .NET environment, you'll be able to have some great ideas of how to build network communications components, discussed in the next chapter.

Applications that communicate over a network have been around for decades. A class of networks, known generically as public data networks, of which the Internet is one, required that applications that communicate over them adhere to strict communication lexicons, also known as a *protocol*. Many people find the word *protocol* scary. It only means that both sides of a conversation decide on what words to use, and what they mean before communicating with each other. Some protocols have less than 10 such words. For example, the HTTP protocol has less than 10 words in its vocabulary, and the entire World Wide Web is based on this protocol.

The application protocols, used over public data networks, became so popular that they were employed on private local area networks. When Internet-type applications run on local area networks, the network is called an Intranet. The only difference between the Internet and an Intranet is the limited scope of public access to the Intranet.

There have been many network application protocols over the years, but most have fallen by the wayside. Those that remain do so partially because they pose a minimal security risk, and are allowed to pass through security firewalls, or they are just so heavily used, they must be allowed to exist and operate. A few of these include:

Email – POP3, SMTP

File transfer – FTP

World Wide Web – HTTP

Ping

Telnet

The actual number of protocols in use is quite hefty, and range from complex data exchange protocols and security protocols to the simple Network Time Protocol (NTP).

Writing network applications involves two things: creating socket coummunication connections between at least two computers (sometimes more in a broadcast application) and following the proper protocol in your application. There are two ways to accomplish these tasks. The first and easiest is to use a set of classes with built-in socket communications abilities, and built-in knowledge of the protocol you want to use. A good example of this type of class is the **WebClient** class covered in the next section. The other way to accomplish the task is to build your own socket communications layer, also using classes in the **system.Net** namespace, and then learn the protocol of the application type you are writing. The Internet makes this easy, because most public protocols are defined in a public standard document called an RFC (Request For Comment). Standards groups define the protocol, and then publish these protocols. For instance, the Network Time Protocol is published in RFC 1119. There are many places on the Internet where you can view an RFC. Perhaps the easiest to remember is http://rfc.net. One of the things of interest you can view there is a list of all RFCs. For example, you can read the RFC written in 1969 by Vinton Cerf, RFC 0020 *ASCII Format for Network Interchange*.

This chapter will cover the classes in the **system.Net** namespace.

Domain Name Service

The Domain Name Service (DNS) is a system by which human-readable names are assigned to IP addresses. Most people on the planet are now familiar with domain names and just about every company now has a Web page (www.somecompany.com). It is essential that you understand how the DNS system works to be able to develop more complex network applications.

First, a high-level introduction to DNS reveals that it's simple, but not as simple as many people believe. Figure 18.1 gives you a simple graphic view of the system. Here is a step-by-step walk-through of what happens when a computer requests that a domain name be translated into an IP address. Low-level socket communications cannot work with domain names; they must first have an IP address. The high-level classes, such as WebClient, look up the IP address behind the scenes.

User requests Internet resource using a domain name.

Application looks in local computer setup for the IP address of a name server.

The user's computer sends a request to the name server, asking it to translate a domain name into an IP address.

If the name server can perform that request, it returns an IP address to the user's computer.

If the name server does not know the IP address, the name server contacts the InterNIC and asks what name server is *authoritative* for that particular domain.

The InterNIC responds to the name server with the IP address of the authoritative name server for that domain.

The user's name server contacts the authoritative name server and asks it to resolve the domain name to an IP address.

The authoritative name server delivers the IP address to the name server.

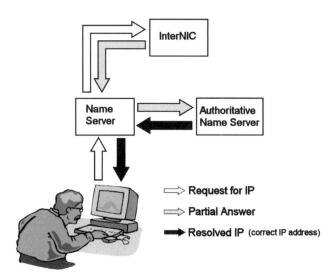

Figure 18.1 The DNS system has three layers.

The user's name server returns the IP address to the user's application, which uses it to contact another application running at the designated IP address.

When you register a domain name with the InterNIC, or some other domain name registrar, you are not assigned an IP address. Rather, you designate a computer, running a DNS server, to be your authoritative name server for your domain. Your domain name must then be entered into the database of the authoritative name server, along with IP address information.

IP address information is stored as a Long type. But for human readability it is displayed in String format as a *dotted quad.*

The IP Address

An IP address is a 32-bit number, divided into 4 parts, each an octet in the range of 0 to 255. Each octet is separated by a dot, and the resulting format is called dotted decimal notation, *or simply a* dotted quad. *The IP address is a unique number that identifies a single network resource.*

Each octet of the IP address identifies the resource in continually finer detail. The first octet describes the class of network. There are three classes: A, B, and C. Class A networks describe networks with a large number of computers attached. The first quad has a range of 0 to 127, with 0 and 127 reserved. The 126 usable addresses can then each support networks with 16,777,126 computers attached.

> *Class B networks use the first two octets to identify them, and the first octet is numbered in the range between 128 and 191. There are 16,320 possible Class B networks each of which can support 65,536 computers.*
>
> *Class C addresses use the first three octets and are used to identify networks with a smaller number of attached hosts. This class is identified by the first octet in the range of 192 to 233. There are 2,080,800 possible Class C networks, each supporting up to 244 computers.*
>
> *There is a special range of IP addresses reserved for private networks. These IP addresses will not be resolved across the Internet, but used for local networks only. For Class A networks, use the IP address range of 10.0.0.0 to 10.255.255.255, Class B is 172.16.0.0 to 172.31.255.255, and Class C is 192.168.0.0 to 192.168.255.255.*

Net.DNS Classes

Before getting into the nitty-gritty of the DNS classes, it's important to understand the difference between an *asynchronous* network connection and a *blocking* network connection. An asynchronous connection allows the program to continue while waiting for a response from the network. Once a response is received, an event is fired, calling the Call-Back (Delegate) supplied to the asynchronous method. If a connection is not asynchronous, it's blocking, and all program processing (at least in the current thread) is held up until a response is received, or the connection times out.

The **Net.Dns** namespace contains classes that manage information involving domain names, host names, and IP addresses. Domain names are two-part names specifying a network domain and a top-level domain, separated by a dot. Every domain name on the Internet is unique. Network domains do not have to be unique, but the combination of a network domain and a top-level domain must be. A host name is the network name of a single computer. A fully qualified domain name is one that begins with a host name, followed by a dot and then the domain name (mycomputer.mynetwork.com).

> **Note**
>
> When the World Wide Web was in its infancy, network administrators named the computer that hosted the Web servers "WWW." For absolutely no reason at all, this became a standard. The "WWW" host name, or even supplying a host name, is optional.

Each host on the Internet has a set of information that describes it, and the **Net.DNS.IPHostEntry** class is used to get and set that host information. The **IPHostEntry** class is a helper to the **DNS** class and has three properties:

AddressList – A list of all IP addresses associated with a host.

Aliases – A list of aliases associated with the host.

HostName – The DNS name of the host.

The following example uses the **Net.Dns.GetHostByName** method to create a populated instance of the **IPHostEntry** class. The **Net.Dns.GetHostByName** class is one of the methods of the DNS class listed after this sample.

```
Private Sub button1_Click(ByVal sender As System.Object,
ByVal e As System.EventArgs) Handles button1.Click

    Dim hostinfo As New Net.IPHostEntry()

    Dim hostIP As Net.IPAddress

    hostinfo = Net.Dns.GetHostByName("www.science.org")

    For Each hostIP In hostinfo.AddressList

        console.Write(hostIP.ToString)

    Next

End Sub
```

This example writes an IP address in dotted quad notation to the console window. When there is more than one IP address associated with a host, this example should print each of them. The following is a list of the methods provided by the DNS class:

BeginGetHostByName – Asynchronous call to retrieve IPHostEntry information.

EndGetHostByName – End the Asynchronous call to retrieve IPHostEntry information.

BeginResolve - Asynchronous call to DNS to retrieve an IP address by host name.

End Resolve – End the Asynchronous call using BeginResolve.

Resolve – Resolves a host name of IP address in dotted quad to IPHostEntry information.

GetHostByAddress – Get host information by IP address.

GetHostByName – Get host information by supplying the fully qualified domain name.

GetHostName – Gets the host name of the local machine.

IPToString – Converts an IP address in Long format to a dotted quad String form.

Sockets

Even though the .NET Framework provides a set of high-level classes for managing Web communication and file transfers, the really exciting thing that has happened to Visual

Basic is the inclusion of socket programming capability. This was not possible in Visual Basic prior to this version. I am going to go into detail about sockets, even though you may rarely use them directly, because knowing how sockets work will help you use the high-level classes that manage application protocols like HTTP much more efficiently. Also, you will not be restricted to these protocols. Using the **Socket** class, you will be able to build communications capabilities into your application that supports any type of network application protocol.

Intro to Sockets

Many of the terms in network communications are taken from a physical thing applied to networking concepts. The term *port* was already discussed. The socket is one of the basic concepts of network communications. A *socket* is an object that connects an application with a network protocol. Earlier in the chapter we discussed application protocols. Network protocols are the syntax understood by look networks, allowing them to transport data from one network resource to another.

Sockets encapsulate low-level networking functionality. As a programmer, you don't have to worry about all the details of constructing, sending, receiving, and reading packets. You simply have to create a socket object, and tell it what you want it to do. This functionality is built into the **Net.Sockets.Socket** class.

Sockets are known by their transport types. Table 18.1 lists the transport types that can be set by enumeration in the **SocketType** property of the **Socket** class. There are two basic transport types: those that make a connection, such as TCP, and those that are connectionless, such as UDP.

TCP (Transmission Control Protocol), or ConnectionOriented socket connections, are used when your application cares about the data its sent has been received on the other end. As the name suggests, the network transport protocol is all about control. This level of control ensures data integrity. The downside to this is that server software must maintain tens, hundreds, thousands, or even millions of simultaneous socket connections. The connection is also constantly sending information about the status of the packets sent and received. It's an efficient yet data intensive connection type. Despite that, many network applications rely on ConnectionOriented socket connections.

Table 18.1   Socket Transport Types

Transport Type	Description
All	All transport types.
Connectionless	The transport type is connectionless, such as UDP.
ConnectionOriented	The transport type is connection oriented, such as TCP.
Tcp	TCP transport.
Udp	UDP transport.

UDP (User Datagram Protocol), or connectionless sockets, simply broadcast data to an intended endpoint, and that's that. If data is lost along the way, it's up to the receiving application to request new data. The socket itself will not maintain a connection and will not know whether the data arrived or not. Therefore, this network transport protocol is perfect for broadcasting messages across a network.

Client–Server at the Socket Level

Another way in which sockets are identified is by their initial behavior. One type of socket listens for incoming socket connections and the other type connects to a listening socket. Once a connection is established, sockets do not differ in function. Sockets, once connected, send and receive data until one side closes the connection.

The significance of this initial behavior is that applications that operate as a server create a listening socket, waiting for connections from clients, that create sockets that connect to listening sockets.

Creating a Socket

Creating a socket involves knowing several things about the type of socket you want to create ahead of time. The socket constructor accepts three arguments:

AddressFamily – The type of addressing scheme for the network on which the socket will be communicating.

SocketType – The socket type.

Protocol Type – The underlying protocol used by the socket to communicate.

Here is an example of creating a new socket object:

```
Dim myListeningSocket As New Net.Sockets.Socket(
Net.Sockets.AddressFamily.NetBios,
Net.Sockets.SocketType.Stream,
Net.Sockets.ProtocolType.Tcp )
```

Visual Studio will help you create the new socket by popping up an enumeration of each argument. Simply select an enumerated value from the list, depending on the network type you are writing the application to operate on. These values can be set dynamically. You can specify the type of network the application is going to be running on in a configuration file. You can then set the arguments of the socket constructor based on the network type.

The TcpClient

Visual Basic .NET includes a **TcpClient** class built on top of the **Socket** class to make some of this a little easier. Simply pass in the fully qualified domain name, and the port on which you want to communicate. You won't need to add a protocol specifier, such as HTTP://, because the port will identify what application with which you want to communicate.

```
Private Sub Button1_Click(ByVal sender As System.Object,
ByVal e As System.EventArgs) Handles Button1.Click

    Dim myclient As New Net.sockets.TcpClient("mail.
    mailserver.com", 25)

    Dim myStream As IO.Stream = myclient.GetStream()

    Dim reader As New IO.StreamReader(myStream, System.
    Text.Encoding.ASCII)

    MessageBox.Show(reader.ReadLine())

End Sub
```

This example communicates with the Simple Mail Transport Protocol (SMTP) application on port 25 at mail.mailserver.com, a fictitious domain. Change the mail.mailserver .com entry with a valid mailserver domain and this application will return the first response. In an actual application you would know details about the protocol and the data you should be receiving. This will help you adjust what StreamReader methods you should use for reading data from the stream. Normally, the next step is to respond to the initial server response. Here is a longer example showing a brief interaction with the SMTP server.

```
Private Sub Button1_Click(ByVal sender As System.Object,
ByVal e As System.EventArgs) Handles Button1.Click

    Dim myclient As New Net.sockets.TcpClient
    ("mail.mailserver.com",25)

    Dim myStream As IO.Stream = myclient.GetStream()

    Dim reader As New IO.StreamReader(myStream, System.
    Text.Encoding.ASCII)

    Dim writer As New IO.StreamWriter(myStream, System.
    Text.Encoding.ASCII)

    Dim respstring
```

```
       writer.AutoFlush = True

       Do While reader.ReadLine() > ""

            MessageBox.Show(reader.ReadLine())

            writer.WriteLine("HELP")

            Do While True

                 respstring = reader.ReadLine()

                 MessageBox.Show(respstring)

                 If respstring = "" Then

                      Exit Do

                 End If

            Loop

            Exit Do

       Loop

       myclient.Close()

    End Sub
```

This example, once it receives the initial response from the SMTP server, sends the HELP command. Most major application protocols support that command. The SMTP server responds by sending a list of the supported commands. From this point on, it's up to you to send the correct command and any required parameters, such as the password and user name.

You can read the RFC documents to understand the complexities of creating network client applications for the different protocols, or in most cases, you can simply send a HELP message to find out what commands are supported and try to carry on the conversation with the server in your application. The one exception to this is FTP. The FTP protocol carries on a conversation on two different ports. This is because FTP has a command channel and a data transfer channel. You may want to refer to the RFCs to create an FTP client.

The TCPListener

To create an application that listens (acts as a server) you must create a listening socket. You can do this by creating a new socket, as explained earlier in the chapter, calling the **Bind** method and then the **Listen** method. Once again, the .NET Framework has a class in the **Net.Sockets** namespace that makes this simpler, called the **TCPListener** class. Here is an example of its use:

```
On the first line of the code add:

Imports.System.Net.Configuration

Imports.System.Net.Sockets

'Then add the following code near the end of the Form
class.

Private Sub Button1_Click(ByVal sender As System.Object,
ByVal e As System.EventArgs) Handles Button1.Click

    Dim myListener As New TcpListener(8080)

    myListener.Start()

    Console.Write("waiting")

    Dim mySocket As Socket = myListener.AcceptSocket()

    Dim myMessage As String = "Hi There"

    Dim byteMessage As Byte() = System.Text.Encoding.
    ASCII.GetBytes(myMessage.ToCharArray())

    mySocket.Send(byteMessage, byteMessage.Length,
    Net.Sockets.SocketFlags.DontRoute)

    myListener.Stop()

    mySocket.Close()

End Sub
```

Note

To test your application without writing your own custom client, you can use Telnet to carry on a communication session with your application. For this example, open a Web browser and enter the following: Telnet://*IP address of your computer*:8080. The port number, 8080 in this example, is completely arbitrary.

This is a network server application in less than 10 lines! Granted, this server doesn't do much. When you connect, it simply sends the message "Hi there" and then disconnects. I call this my network Hi There server.

Looking at this application in detail, when the button is clicked, the first thing that happens is that the **TcpListner** is created and told to listen on port 8080. You can choose another port, but be careful not to choose a port already in use by your computer, as an exception will be thrown if you do. Start the new **TcpListener** object listening by calling the **Start** method.

Here is the important part. Notice that the **AcceptSocket** method returns a socket. This is a type of hand-off mechanism. If the listening socket had to carry on the conversation with the client, everyone would have to wait in line until the conversation was done before the listening socket could pay attention to the next client trying to connect. That would be a disaster for a server trying to handle many connections at the same time.

The new socket handles the new communication session. This is just a simple example. A better plan is to create an object that creates a new socket, and have the **AcceptSocket** method pass the socket to the new object. In this way, your application can handle many socket connections at the same time.

Humans communicate in text, but computers need to pass their data around in byte form. So, after creating your message, it needs to be converted to a **Byte** array before being sent to the client. Remember that the Client will expect to receive a **Byte** array as a **Stream**.

Use the **Send** method of the socket to send the **Byte** array. You must also include the size of the message you are sending followed by any socket flags you want to send. The socket flags are an enumeration.

You now have an idea of the low-level way in which client and server applications communicate with each other. Using low-level sockets to create the connection involves a certain amount of housekeeping, although you have a greater amount of freedom when it comes to choosing your network and protocol type. But, for the most part, most people will be communicating over the Internet in local area network that uses the TCP protocol. The **TcpClient** and **TcpListener** classes have merely simplified the housekeeping of creating a TCP socket connection. There are even higher-level application protocol-level classes that use the **TcpClient** and **TcpListener** classes. For example, here's a code snippet that uses the WebRequest and WebResponse classes:

```
Dim myRequest As WebRequest =
    WebRequest.Create("http://www.tedcoombs.com")
```

```
Dim myResponse As WebResponse = myRequest.GetResponse()

' Code to handle the response goes here...

myResponse.Close()
```

These classes are also the parents to derived classes such as the FileWebRequest and FileWebResponse classes. This next section goes into greater detail in the most popular Internet application, the Web, and using the WebClient class.

```
TcpListener myListener = new TcpListener(13);

myListener.Start();

// Program blocks on Accept() until a client connects.
Socket mySocket = myListener.AcceptSocket();

// Get current date and time.
DateTime now = DateTime.Now;
String strDateLine = now.ToShortDateString() + " " +
now.ToLongTimeString();

// Convert to byte array and send.
Byte[] byteDateLine = System.Text.Encoding.ASCII.GetBytes
(strDateLine.ToCharArray()); mySocket.Send
(byteDateLine,byteDateLine.Length,0);
```

Building Web Applications

The World Wide Web, once only a network application, has become the environment in which many applications either run or share data. Your Visual Basic .NET application can take advantage of classes in the **System.Net** namespace classes to manage communications between the Web browser and server.

Before launching into using the Web classes, a little foundation in how the Web operates might help you. The World Wide Web is a client–server application. This means that an application has the ability to listen for communications over a software *port*. An application with listening ability is known as a *server*. Another or sometimes even the same application has the ability to send requests to a server and receive information sent back from a server. These are known as *clients*. The port that client and server applications communicate through is not a physical port, but rather a means of routing information to applications running on a TCP/IP network.

Applications that communicate over a network need to know two important things: one is the IP address of the computer they are communicating with and the other is the port on which the application is communicating. Information that flows over the network is enclosed in packets, each addressed with this destination information. Because information does not flow over a network in a steady stream but in presized chunks enclosed in electronic packets, the packets must also be numbered, so they can be put back together again on the receiving end. Because of the dynamic packet routing ability of a TCP/IP network such as the Internet, it's possible that not all packets will arrive in the same order. The numbering of packets, or even enclosing your data in packets, is nothing you have to concern yourself with at the application level. This all happens down at the network layer.

You will have to be aware of the IP address and the port number over which you would like to communicate. Once again, the port is not a physical port, but sometimes it's easiest to talk about it as though it were a physical port. Each port has a number, and applications choose one or more ports over which they will communicate. It's a little like deciding on which radio channel you communicate over a walkie talkie or CB radio. We'll discuss ports in more detail later in this chapter. For now, it will suffice to know that the World Wide Web uses port 80 as its communication port.

The WebClient

So far in this chapter you've learned how Internet applications work at the socket level and a little about how the Web works. The **Net.WebClient** class, obviously a class designed to be used as a client portion of an application, provides members designed for communicating with a Web server.

Begin by creating a new **WebClient** object:

```
Dim myWebClient As New System.Net.WebClient()
```

The **WebClient** object, to be useful, will first have to have its **BaseAddress** property set with the URL of the server it will be contacting:

```
myweb.BaseAddress = "http://www.tedcoombs.com"
```

Note
The WebClient object will accept the protocol designators HTTP, HTTPS, and FILE.

This is the base address. It may not be the full path to the exact resource you are requesting or referring. This **BaseAddress** property is used in conjunction with other properties to fully identify a network resource. For example, in the next example, the **OpenRead** method accepts the URL of the document to download. When the

BaseAddress property contains a value, the argument passed to the **OpenRead** method must be a path relative to the **BaseAddress**. When the **BaseAddress** value is empty, the method will accept a full URL. Similar to previous examples, this example has a method that returns **Stream**. So, you will need to create a **StreamReader** object to read the **Stream**. This example reads the results, one line at a time, in a **Message-Box**. You will think of better things to do with the result than read it one line at a time.

```
Private Sub Button1_Click(ByVal sender As System.Object,
ByVal e As System.EventArgs) Handles Button1.Click

    Dim myweb As New System.Net.WebClient()

    Dim myStream As IO.Stream

    Dim myresult As Windows.Forms.DialogResult

    myweb.BaseAddress = "http://www.tedcoombs.com"

    myStream = myweb.OpenRead("default.asp")

    Dim reader As New IO.StreamReader(myStream, System.
    Text.Encoding.ASCII)

    Do While True

        myresult = MessageBox.Show(reader.ReadLine(),
        "hi", MessageBoxButtons.OKCancel)

        If myresult = DialogResult.Cancel Then

            Exit Do

        End If

    Loop

End Sub
```

The WebClient can also accept data as a Byte Array using the **DownLoadData** method:

```
Dim myweb As New System.Net.WebClient()

Dim myByteResult() As Byte

myweb.BaseAddress = "http://www.tedcoombs.com"

myByteResult = myweb.DownloadData("default.asp")
```

In this next example, the **OpenRead** method of the **WebClient** object returns a **Stream** then looks at the **ResponseHeaders** property of the **WebClient**. Web clients and servers share information behind the scenes in the form of response and request headers. The server learns about the client, such as what type of Browser is being used, and the client learns about the server. Here is a code snippet that lets you look at what a server returns:

```
Private Sub Button1_Click(ByVal sender As System.Object,
ByVal e As System.EventArgs) Handles Button1.Click

    Dim myweb As New System.Net.WebClient()

    Dim resultStream As System.IO.Stream

    Dim results As String()

    Dim myheader As String

    Dim headerCollection As System.Net.WebHeaderCollection

    myweb.BaseAddress = "http://www.tedcoombs.com"

    resultStream = myweb.OpenRead("default.asp")

    resultStream.Close() 'this is required to release
    resources.

    headerCollection = myweb.ResponseHeaders

    results = headerCollection.AllKeys()

    For Each myheader In results
```

```
        Console.Write(myheader & " = " &
    headerCollection.Get(myheader) & vbCrLf)

      Next

    End Sub
```

This code snippet writes the following values into the console window:

```
Server = Microsoft-IIS/5.0

Date = Thu, 09 Aug 2001 14:27:05 GMT

Content-Length = 2451

Content-Type = text/html

Set-Cookie = ASPSESSIONIDGQGGGNAC=
KKDLDPEAEPNELJOKEJAKJGCI; path=/

Cache-control = private
```

Looking Forward

The Web is an exciting place to create powerful applications. You can also write powerful server-side applications using Active Server Pages (ASP.NET). Look for *ASP.NET Programming* by this author.

The QueryString

When a client application sends a request to a Web server, it can include a set of parameters called a *query string*. The query string is a set of name–value pairs that follow the name of the requested resource. The query string begins with a question mark and is followed by any number of name value pairs, separated with an ampersand (&). Here's an example of a URL that includes a query string:

```
http://www.mycompany.com/default.asp?employeeid=12345
```

Most of the high-level protocol handling classes that accept **Url** objects in the **Net** namespace have a **QueryString** property. This is a collection of name–value pairs. Both the name and value in the collection are stored as a string. For values you need to use in date or numeric format in your application you will have to convert them after retrieving values from the **QueryString**. You can use the **QueryString** property to set the values in the **QueryString** collection destined for the server as part of the request. Use the Add method of the **QueryString** like this:

```
myweb.QueryString.Add("book", "Visual Basic .NET")
```

You can also refer to the **QueryString** property when evaluating the query string sent to an application acting as a server. Use the Get method to evaluate individual *keys*. A key is the name portion of a name–value pair. This is how a server application would get the value sent in the last example:

```
Dim StringResult as String

StringResult = MyWeb.QueryString.Get("book")
```

The **QueryString** is automatically populated by HTML forms that use the **Get** method instead of the **Post** method. Query strings are one way state is managed in a Web application; cookies are another.

Cookies

Cookies are name–value pairs that can be sent by a Web server and stored on the client's machine. The cookie is associated with the URL of the server, so that only the Web site that "dropped" the cookie can retrieve it from the user's (client) hard drive once it has been stored there.

Cookies are a way for Web servers to store information about the user who visited their site and save state information. The **Net.Cookie** class accepts name–value pairs in its constructor like this:

```
Dim mycookie As New Net.Cookie("Book", "Visual Basic
.NET")
```

The constructor can be empty. You can set name and value pairs of a **Cookie** by setting the **Name** and **Value** properties.

Each **Cookie** object can store a great deal of information. For example, you can store a comment with the cookie as an explanation by setting the **Comment** property:

```
mycookie.comment = "This is your book selection."
```

Set the URI of the site the cookie is associated with by setting the **CommentURI** property. Notice that to convert a string to a **Uri** object, the following example passes the string into the constructor of a new **Uri** object.

```
Dim myURI As New Uri("http://www.tedcoombs.com")

mycookie.CommentUri = myURI
```

You can also set the domain of the cookie rather than use the domain that may be sent by the Server.

```
mycookie.Domain = "tedcoombs.com"
```

One of the most important properties of the Cookie object is the Expires property. This will affect the long-term behavior of the cookie.

```
mycookie.Expires = "01/01/80"
```

Setting the **Expires** property to a date in the past will cause the Cookie, dropped by your server application, to expire the moment the Browser (client) is no longer communicating with your application. This is a good way to temporarily store cookies on someone's site to keep track of state information between Web pages.

State Information and the Web

The World Wide Web is a stateless environment. In other words, when values are set on one page, they are not automatically carried to the next page of your application. When values are set, such as those entered into a form, the values must be passed to the next page. This can get pretty inconvenient if some of the information must be common to all of the pages.

State information (the values of any variables set on a page) are often set in cookies stored on the client's machine. Then, on each subsequent page, values can be retrieved using name – value pairs from the cookie. The downside to this, is that many people have cookies turned off as a security measure in their Web browser software. When this happens, if your application relies on cookies to maintain state information, you will have to have a fallback position, such as passing values in the QueryString.

When the Expires property of a **Cookie** object is set to some date in the future, the cookie is saved on the client's computer until the expiration date. This is the way cookies are made persistent.

File WebRequest

The Hypertext Transport Protocol is only one of the ways to retrieve a file from the Web. It uses the HTTP protocol to download files. You can also use the FILE:// scheme to retrieve a local file by using the **FileWebRequest** class in the **System.Net** namespace.

```
Dim myStream As IO.Stream

    Dim myFile As FileWebRequest =
WebRequest.Create("FILE:///c:/temp/dsc00001.jpg")
```

```
      Dim myresponse As FileWebResponse =
   myFile.GetResponse()

      myStream = myresponse.GetResponseStream()
```

The **GetResponse** method starts a blocking request for the file transfer, as shown above. Notice that the WebRequest class was used and that a FileWebRequest was returned after determining that the protocol type was FILE://. To make an asynchronous (nonblocking) connection, you can use the **BeginGetResponse** and **EndGetResponse** methods.

Instead of the **GetResponse** method, you can also use the **GetRequestStream** method. This outputs the file data as a stream to make it easier to write the result out to a file. Just as with the **GetResponse** and **BeginGetResponse** methods, the **GetRequest-Stream** blocks while the **BeginGetResponse** and **EndGetResponse** are asynchronous.

Summary

Almost all major computer applications are now designed to be network-aware. This can mean that the application has several levels of network communications ability built into it. Some applications are network-aware because online help is provided using Web pages, rather than compiled help files. Other applications receive real-time data from the Internet, either through the World Wide Web, or a proprietary application, and still others are used to send data out over the Internet.

Network applications can use either a proprietary protocol or one defined by a public standard, such as an RFC. When local area networks use these Internet applications, they are known as Intranets. Intranet applications can also communicate with applications running on the global Internet. Most of these applications use the HTTP protocol to push and pull data over port 80, the software port used by the Web. In this way, applications can be assured to get through most network firewalls.

Visual Basic .NET makes use of the new ability to develop socket-level applications rather than simply using preprogrammed COM objects, such as the Internet Transfer Control (ITC). The ITC was never really ready for the production environment. Now, you can develop your own network applications with their own protocol or write applications that communicate with any of the standard public protocols. The Common Language Runtime has the ability to communicate using Web communication classes, such as the Web client, as well as handle file downloads. File handling was another feature that required third-party components in previous versions.

The System.Net namespace also contains classes that manage the authentication modules an application uses. The namespace also has the GlobalProxySelection class, which contains a default proxy instance for HTTP requests. Everything you need to create a network application is now available in Visual Basic .NET. The next chapter covers graphics and drawing. You may find that using classes from the System.Drawing namespace allows you to create graphics on the fly and deliver them over the network.

Computers have become much more than simple word processors and number crunchers. They are now used for communications and mulitmedia entertainment. Almost every aspect of our lives can be supplemented with some computer functionality. Fewer people are running to the drug store to drop off film to be developed, and now rely on their computers to view their digital photography. Graphics and computer drawing functionality has become an increasingly important computer function.

The **System.Drawing** Namespace defines an extremely powerful set of classes to provide many levels of graphics functionality. Table 19.1 lists the classes in the **System.Drawing** Namespace and gives a short description of each class. The **System.Drawing.Drawing2D** namespace provides a set of classes for advanced two-dimensional drawing and vector graphics, while the System.Drawing.Imaging namespace provides advanced GDI+ imaging functionality, which includes the ability to display any graphic format. Finally, the System.Drawing.Text namespace provides font and text support to the graphics abilities of Visual Basic .NET.

This chapter will introduce you to some the classes, structures, and enumerators included in the **System.Drawing** namespace.

System.Drawing namespace

The **System.Drawing** namespace includes several other subnamespaces. They include:

System.Drawing.Design - Classes that extend design-time user interface (UI) logic and drawing.

System.Drawing.Drawing2D - Classes that provide advanced two-dimensional and vector graphics functionality.

System.Drawing.Imaging - Classes that provide advanced GDI+ imaging functionality.

System.Drawing.Printing - Classes that allow you to customize printing.

System.Drawing.Text - Classes that allow users to create and use collections of fonts.

It is beyond the scope of this book to completely cover every class or aspect of the **System.Drawing** classes. To adequately cover each of these namespaces, you would end up with a book that would no longer fit under your arm. The skills you've learned in this book so far will allow you to use the .NET Framework documentation to become familiar with the many classes in these namespaces. The **System.Drawing** classes are a bit more complex. For this reason, I've chosen to focus a little more on this topic. Of course, it would take an entire book to adequately cover even this topic. So, let this serve as a simple introduction.

To get started with the **System.Drawing** classes, let's take a look at two classes you will most frequently use: **System.Drawing.Image** and **System.Drawing.Bitmap**.

The Image Class

The **Image** class decodes a number of different image formats and forms the base of the Bitmap, Icon, and Metafile derived classes.

There are two static methods of the **Image** class that are particularly important: **Image.FromFile** and **Image.FromStream**. These methods load the bitmap, icon, or metafile into the **Image** object so that it can be manipulated. Because many images are stored in file form, the **FromFile** method makes loading an image directly from a file saved on the local computer easy, by simply passing in the path and filename as a String argument.

```
Dim myphoto As Image

myphoto.FromFile("c:\temp\photo.jpg")
```

FromFile is great when loading images stored on the local computer. In the world of the graphic Internet, it is simpler to load an image from a Stream, as many Internet-related objects such as the HttpPostedFile return images as streams. This code passes the decoded bits from the HttpPostedFile object to the Image decoding class:

```
System.Drawing.Image img =
System.Drawing.Image.FromStream(upload.PostedFile.InputStr
eam)
```

Of course, a common piece of functionality is the ability to save the **Image** to a file or stream. Use the **Save** method of the **Image** passing in either the name of the file or the **Stream** in which you want the **Image** saved.

The Bitmap Class

Certain image types are composed of *pixels*. Pixels, short for "picture elements," are the individual dots of light that appear on your computer monitor. The higher the resolution of your monitor and graphics card setting, the more pixels your monitor will display. Bitmap images are stored as pixel representations. When displayed, the bitmap file tells every single pixel what color to display on the monitor.

Here is a sample that creates a new bitmap object using the **New** operator to create the object. The bitmap constructor accepts a string that corresponds to the path and filename of the image you want to load.

```
Dim MyImage As New Bitmap("c:\temp\myphoto.jpg")
```

The **Bitmap** class has two static methods:

FromHIcon – Creates a Bitmap by converting a Windows handle to an icon.

FromResource – Creates a Bitmap from a Windows resource.

The **Bitmap.Flags** property is inherited from **Image.Flags** and stores attribute flags as integers.

Bitmap images can have multiple frames that hold the image in different resolutions. This allows the image to be shown in different resolutions, depending on the resolution of the local display system. Each frame stored in the image has a frame dimension, represented as a GUID in the **FrameDimensionList** property. This property can be used with the **GetFrameCount** method, which returns the number of frames in the image. This example, after loading a bitmap image, prints the GUID list to the console window:

```
Dim myphoto As New Bitmap("c:\temp\myphoto.jpg")

Dim Guids As Guid()

Dim aguid As Guid

Guids = myphoto.FrameDimensionsList

For Each aguid In Guids

    Console.Write(aguid.ToString & vbCrLf)

Next
```

The **Height**, **Width**, **HorizontalResolution,** and **VerticalResolution** properties provide detailed information about the size and resolution of the image, so you can adjust sizes of controls to accommodate your image by adjusting the properties of the control dynamically. Here is a code snippet that prints these values for an image to the Console window:

```
Private Sub Button1_Click(ByVal sender As System.Object,
    ByVal e As System.EventArgs) Handles Button1.Click
```

```
    Dim myphoto As New Bitmap("c:\temp\myphoto.jpg")

    Console.Write("Height:" & myphoto.Height.ToString &
    vbCrLf)

    Console.Write("Width:" & myphoto.Width.ToString &
    vbCrLf)

    Console.Write("H Resolution:" & myphoto.
    HorizontalResolution.ToString & vbCrLf)

    Console.Write("V Resolution:" & myphoto.
    VerticalResolution.ToString & vbCrLf)

End Sub
```

This example prints the following values in the Console window (this works differently, depending on what picture you specify):

```
Height:194

Width:203

H Resolution:20

V Resolution:20
```

A **SizeF** structure, which contains the height and width of the image, can also be obtained from the **PhysicalDimension** property. A **Size** structure, also the height and width, is returned from the **Size** property.

The **PixelFormat** property returns an enumerated value that represents the format of the pixels. For example, loading the JPG image in the last example returns the **Format24bppRgb** format. This enumerated value translates to a 24 bit-per-pixel format with 16,777,216 colors; 8 bits each for red, green, and blue. The **RawFormat** is represented as a GUID.

Displaying Images

One of the simplest ways to display an **Image** on a **Form** is to use the **PictureBox** control. The Image property of the **Picturebox** control accepts an **Image** type. Select the **PictureBox** control from the Toolbox and drag it onto the **Form**.

In this example we then set the **Picturebox** control's size to **AutoSize** by setting the **PictureBoxSizeMode.AutoSize** property (see also Figure 19.1).

Note
You should set the **Image** property of the **PictureBox** control before attempting
to use **PictureBoxSizeMode.AutoSize**.

```
Private Sub button1_Click(ByVal sender As System.Object,
ByVal e As_ System.EventArgs) Handles button1.Click

    Dim picturewindow As New Form()

    Dim mypicturebox As New PictureBox()

    mypicturebox.Image = New Bitmap("c:\temp\
    myphoto.jpg")

    mypicturebox.SizeMode = PictureBoxSizeMode.
    AutoSize

    mypicturebox.Location = New Point(1, 1)

    picturewindow.Controls.Add(mypicturebox)

    picturewindow.Show()

End Sub
```

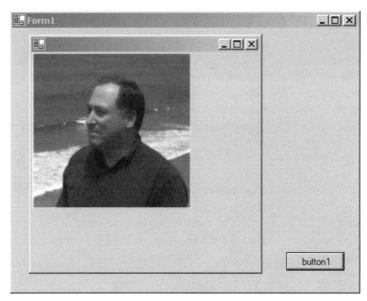

Figure 19.1 The PictureBox control contains a JPG image on this new form.

Table 19.1   Basic Drawing Classes

Drawing Class	Description
Bitmap	Extends Image class, encapsulates pixel data for the image and its attributes (see Note below).
Brush	An abstract base class that defines brush objects that are used to fill graphic shapes.
Brushes	Class that defines brushes. There is a property in this class for each standard color.
ColorConverter	Class that converts colors from one data type to another.
ColorTranslator	Class that translates graphics to and from GDI+ (see Note below).
Cursor	Class used to define the mouse pointer object.
CursorConverter	Class used to convert cursors from one data type to another.
Cursors	Class that defines cursors.
Font	Class defines fonts and their characteristics, such as font face, style, weight, and size.
FontConverter	Class used to convert fonts from one data type to another.
FontFamily	An abstract class that defines certain basic font styles that share characteristics but vary in style, such as sans serif.
Graphics	Class that encapsulates a GDI+ drawing surface.
Icon	Class used to represent Windows icons.
IconConverter	Class used to convert the icon data type to another.
Image	Abstract class that defines the functionality of bitmaps, icons, cursors, and metafiles.
ImageAnimator	Class that provides the functionality for animating images.
ImageConverter	Class that converts images from one data type to another.
ImageFormat	ConverterClass used to convert images from one format to another.
PenPen	Class used to define pens that draw lines and curves.
Pens	Class used to define pens of all standard colors.
PointConverter	Class used to convert a point structure from one data type to another.
RectangleConverter	Class used to convert a rectangle structure from one data type to another.
Region	Class used to describe, with paths and rectangles, the interior of a graphic shape.
SizeConverter	Class used to convert a size structure from one data type to another.
SolidBrush	Class that defines a monochrome brush used in filling graphics.
StringFormat	Class that encapsulates text layout information.
SystemBrushes	Class that defines brushes for Windows system–wide colors.
SystemColors	Class that defines Windows system–wide colors.

Table 19.1   Basic Drawing Classes

Drawing Class	Description
SystemIcons	Class that defines Windows system–wide icons.
SystemPens	Class that defines Windows system–wide pens.
TextureBrush	Class that defines a brush that fills graphic shapes with bitmap images.
ToolboxBitmapAttribute	Class that defines images used with components.

The Graphics Class

The **Graphics** class provides methods for drawing to the display device. Classes such as **Rectangle** and **Point** encapsulate GDI+ primitives. The **Pen** class is used to draw lines and curves, while classes derived from the abstract class **Brush** are used to fill the interiors of shapes. Table 19.2 lists the various enumerations for the **Graphics** classes. Notice that the **BrushStyle** is one of those enumerations. You cannot use the **Brush** class directly; you must use an inherited brush such as:

SolidBrush – A single-colored brush used to fill graphic shapes and patterns.

TextureBrush – A brush that uses an image to fill the interior of a shape.

LinearGradientBrush – A brush that paints with a linear gradient (a rainbow-like pattern of colors).

> **Note**
> The GDI+ Graphics Device Interface is also known as GDI2k. This is Microsoft's new desktop graphics interface, which improves integration of 2-D and 3-D graphics. It includes capabilities such as alpha blending, antialiasing, texturing, and advanced typography and imaging.

Many of the classes in the **System.Drawing** namespaces accept structures as parameters. These structures define multivalued elements, such as the red, blue, and green parts of a color or the x and y coordinates of a point. Structures, once defined, make managing some of the classes much easier. Table 19.3 lists the various structures used in graphics programming.

Table 19.2   Enumerations

Enumeration	Description
BrushStyle	Defines a variety of brush styles that can be applied to brushes.
ContentAlignment	Specifies alignment of content on the drawing surface.
FontStyle	Specifies style information applied to text.
GraphicsUnit	Specifies the unit of measure for the given data.
KnownColor	Specifies the known system colors.
PenStyle	Defines different styles that a pen can be created with.
PolyFillMode	Specifies the different ways a region's overlapping polygons may be filled.
StringAlignment	Specifies the alignment of a text string relative to its layout rectangle.
StringDigitSubstitute	Specifies style information applied to String Digit Substitute.
StringFormatFlags	Specifies the display and layout information for text strings.
StringTrimming	Specifies how to trim characters from a string that does not completely fit into a layout shape.
StringUnit	Specifies the units of measure for a text string.

Another way to make using the graphics classes easier are the enumerations listed in Table 19.2. These groups of attributes allow you to easily select the correct parameter from a list when using Visual Studio .NET.

Table 19.3   Structures

Structure	Description
Color	Represents an RGB color.
Point	Represents an ordered pair of x and y coordinates that define a point in a two-dimensional plane.
PointF	Represents an ordered pair of x and y coordinates that define a point in a two-dimensional plane.
Rectangle	Stores the location and size of a rectangular region. For more advanced region functions use a Region object.
RectangleF	Stores the location and size of a rectangular region. For more advanced region functions use a Region object.
Size	Represents the size of a rectangular region with an ordered pair of width and height.
SizeF	Represents the size of a rectangular region with an ordered pair of width and height.

Fun with the GUI

Controlling the graphic effects on controls allows you to create an interesting graphic user interface. Modify the way controls appear by fading, animating, and modifying their appearance. You can also use some of the other graphic classes to add geometric figures to a special graphic region and then map the shape of controls to the region.

Opacity

Here's an example of using the **Opacity** property of the **Form** to make the application semitransparent. An **Opacity** of 1 is fully visible (completely opaque), while a decimal value equals a percentage of transparency (partially opaque).

```
Private Sub Button1_Click(ByVal sender As System.Object,
    ByVal e As System.EventArgs) Handles Button1.Click

    If Me.Opacity = 1 Then

        Me.Opacity = 0.5

    Else

        Me.Opacity = 1

    End If

End Sub
```

This sample toggles between completely opaque and 50% opaque by clicking the button. The result is shown in Figure 19.2. Notice that you can see the Visual Studio application right through the **Form**. One of the uses of this property is to create fading transitions. You can open a new **Form** that slowly appears by changing the **Opacity** value in a loop.

The GraphicsPath

This next example program shows you how to use the **GraphicsPath** of the **Drawing2D** namespace. Paths are used to draw outlines of shapes. As this example shows, a **GraphicsPath** can be composed of one or more geometric shapes. This example adds an ellipse and a pie shape to the **GraphicsPath**.

Each geometric shape we've added is a *figure*. Figures can be *open* or *closed*. An open figure is one where the points, lines, and curves do not stop and start at the same point. A

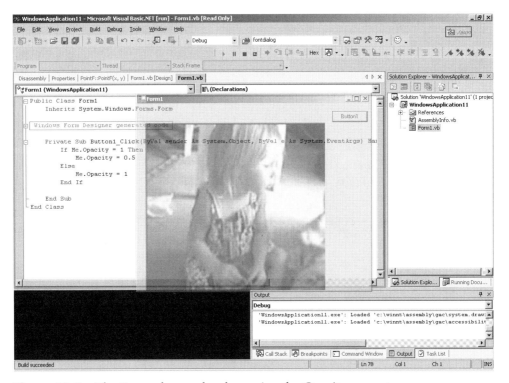

Figure 19.2 The Form plays peek-a-boo using the Opacity property.

closed figure is one where the geometic shape starts and stops at a coincident point (there is no way into the interior of the object from outside the object). Refer to Figure 19.3.

You can quickly close an open figure by using the **CloseFigure** method of the **GraphicsPath**. The figure is then closed by drawing a line from the begin point to the end point.

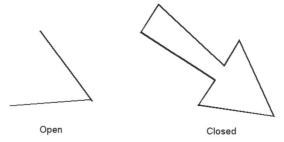

Open   Closed

Figure 19.3 Open figures do not start and stop at the same point, as closed figures do.

Figure 19.4   The form conforms to the defined Region.

Each time a figure is closed, a new figure is started in the **GraphicsPath**. You can also start a new figure by calling the **StartFigure** method.

In this example, a **Rectangle** and **Pie** are added to the **GraphicsPath**. A **Region** describes a graphic area that consists of paths and rectangles. A new **Region** is created, passing in the **GraphicsPath** we've created and used to modify the **Form's Region** property. The result (Figure 19.4) appears when the button is clicked.

```
Private Sub Button1_Click(ByVal sender As System.Object,
    ByVal e As System.EventArgs) Handles Button1.Click

    Dim GraphPath As New Drawing2D.GraphicsPath()
```

```
Dim OD As Integer = Me.ClientSize.Height 'Outside
Diameter of ellipse

Dim rect As New Rectangle(1, 1, 125, 125) 'Boundary of
pie

GraphPath.AddEllipse(0, 0, OD, OD)

GraphPath.AddPie(rect, 30, 45)

Me.Region = New Region(GraphPath)

    End Sub
```

Summary

Volumes have been written about graphics programming. Visual Basic .NET now has a powerful set of classes that allow you to manipulate and use graphic images in your applications. You can use the graphics classes to create new graphics, display and modify existing graphics, or modify the user interface in new, wonderful, and strange ways.

The next chapter completes the book by taking a look at Directory Services. From Windows 2000 forward, Active Directories are an essential part of the operating system. Learn how to access the low-level directory storage of Active Directories as well as create your own data storage in an LDAP directory.

Directory Services 20

An Active Directory is a way of storing information that provides a single, unified view of all objects on a network. Active Directory is based on LDAP, the Lightweight Directory Access Protocol, which is itself a paired-down version of the x.500 protocol. Data is stored within the Active Directory in a tree-structured form and is available to both users and applications.

The Active Directory Service Interfaces (ADSI) is a set of objects used to access Active Directories. ADSI programming, although not difficult, takes a little getting used to. First, the data stored in an active directory is actually stored in a standard SQL database, such as MS SQL Server. You can think of LDAP as an object-oriented front end to the data stored in the database. Although active directories are not true object databases, the end result is very similar. This object-oriented method of storing data lends itself to a unique way of referencing individual data items.

The path to a network item is constructed based on a series of information, beginning with the directory where the information is stored. There are several types of directories found on servers such as Windows NT, Windows 2000, and Windows XP. One such directory is IIS, which stores information about every aspect of every resource within Internet Information Server. Another type of directory is an LDAP directory. Originally conceived to store information about people within an organization, LDAP has grown far beyond its white pages origin.

An LDAP Primer

To understand accessing information in an active directory, or LDAP repository, it's important to know a few basics. An LDAP server contains *entries*. Each entry in an LDAP server is defined by an object class (similar to a data type). An object class is defined by a schema that determines the attributes that make up the object class. Notice that we only mention attributes and not methods. Because this is a data storage mechanism, all we need are attributes. The schema, also stored using the same directory structure, defines the data types of the attributes, very much like determining the field (column) types in a database.

443

Attributes in an LDAP server can be marked as required, and as multivalued. At least one attribute of an LDAP object must be required, and that is the naming attribute. Each instance of an LDAP object (entry) has a name, and it's up to you or the designer of the LDAP schema to determine which attribute will be the naming attribute. Most often, the naming attribute is the common name attribute, or *cn* for short.

Every entry in the LDAP server is uniquely identified by a *distinguished name* (DN). A DN is very much like the path to a file on your hard drive, it's hierarchical and continues to the root. The root of a DN varies by the amount of information required to locate a specific directory. For example, the root of the DN could be a country, signified in LDAP by the "c" attribute. The next level of information may be the one that identifies the organization, or "o." Identifying the organization is often sufficient to identify a root for the distinguished name. You can further identify an entry in an LDAP server by an organizational unit, or "ou." Finally, you can identify the individual entry by the naming attribute, normally "cn" (common name).

An example of a DN is one that locates Joanna Jones in the Marxley Corporation directory:

o=Marxley Corporation, ou=Accounting Personnel, cn=J12394

The organization is Marxley Corporation, the organizational unit is Accounting Personnel, and the common name is Joanna's employee id number. The cn must be unique, and therefore using Joanna's name does not guarantee uniqueness. There is another way to write this DN that includes the type of directory server, the domain on which the directory server is running, the port on which the directory server is listening, and finally the DN. Instead of a comma delimiting the DN, it is delimited with forward slashes like this:

LDAP://myhost.marxleycorp.com:1234/cn=J12394/ou=Accounting
Personnel/o=Marxley Corporation

Beyond LDAP

It was mentioned earlier that LDAP servers are not the only directory services in the Windows operating system. For example, the MetaBase that manages all of the Internet Information Services (IIS) is also stored in a directory, similar to LDAP.

The syntax for accessing the IIS Metabase for information about a particular Web server instance is:

IIS://localhost/W3SVC/*Webserver*/root

Modifying values in the IIS Metabase from within your application allows you to maintain complete control over even the tiniest parameter of Internet Information Server. Many time-consuming tasks, such as building a complex Web site directory structure, complete with virtual directories and physical path mappings, can be completely automated.

IIS is only one example of how administration can be automated using an active directory. It also provides a single point of access for system management of user accounts, clients, servers, and applications.

The System.DirectoryServices Namespace

Before you can begin using classes from the **System.DirectoryServices** namespace, you must add a reference to System.DirectoryServices.dll. Add a reference by clicking on the References icon in the Solution explorer and selecting the appropriate file from the pop-up window. If you prefer, you can select **Add Reference** from the **Project** menu.

Once you've added a reference to the System.DirectoryServices.dll, you will notice that your design environment will change slightly to accept these new classes. For example, in the Component tab of the Visual Studio Toolbox, you will notice two additional components, **DirectoryEntry** and **DirectorySearcher**. In the editor, you will have access to the classes in the **DirectoryServices** namespace listed in Table 20.1.

Table 20.1   Classes in the DirectoryServices Namespace

Class	Description
DirectoryEntries	Contains child entries of an entry in the active directory.
DirectoryEntry	Encapsulates an entry in the active directory hierarchy. An entry is a node on the tree.
DirectorySearcher	Performs queries against the active directory.
DirectoryServicesPermission	Directory services permission.
DirectoryServicesPermissionAttribute	This is the Metabase attribute for directory services permissions. Attributes were covered in Chapter 17.
DirectoryServicesPermissionEntry	A directory services permission Entry.
DirectoryServicesPermissionEntryCollection	A collection of directory services permission entries.
PropertyCollection	Contains the properties of a DirectoryEntry.
PropertyValueCollection	Contains the values of a DirectoryEntry property.
ResultPropertyCollection	Contains the properties of a SearchResult instance.
ResultPropertyValueCollection	Contains the values of a SearchResult property.
SchemaNameCollection	Contains a list of the schema names that the SchemaFilter property of a DirectoryEntries object can use.

Table 20.1   Classes in the DirectoryServices Namespace

Class	Description
SearchResult	Encapsulates a node in the active directory hierarchy that is returned during a search through DirectorySearcher.
SearchResultCollection	Contains the SearchResult instances that the active directory hierarchy returned during a DirectorySearcher query.
SortOption	Specifies how to sort the results of a search.

The DirectoryEntry

DirectoryEntry objects represent nodes within one of the following types of directory services:

Internet Information Services (IIS://)

Lightweight Directory Access Protocol (LDAP://)

Novell NetWare Directory Service (NDS://)

Novell NetWare 3.*x* (NWCOMPAT://)

Windows NT v.5, Windows 2000, and Windows XP (WinNT://)

The node, or **DirectoryEntry,** has properties (also known as attributes) that are defined in the Active Directory schema. The **DirectoryEntry** can also have values. Here's something you'll want to know about values that differs from traditional database tables. When you define a table, you create a row and column format for storing data within a database. That means that if a particular column is not filled in for a particular row, an empty space is stored where that data would have gone. This is not the case with LDAP. Only attributes that actually have values are stored in the **DirectoryEntry**. This is significant because when referencing properties, they may just not exist for one **DirectoryEntry**, while existing for others.

DirectoryEntries can optionally be defined as parents, capable of containing other objects. The objects one object type can contain are defined in the LDAP schema.

Begin creating a **DirectoryEntry** object by dragging the object from the Toolbox window onto your application design surface. Figure 20.1 shows the **DirectoryEntry** object in the nonvisual design area.

Once you've added the **DirectoryEntry** object to your application, you can right-click on the object and edit its properties. The **AuthenticationType** property contains an enumerated value that determines what authentication type the **DirectoryEntry** object will use when contacting and authenticating with the directory server. When the **Authen-**

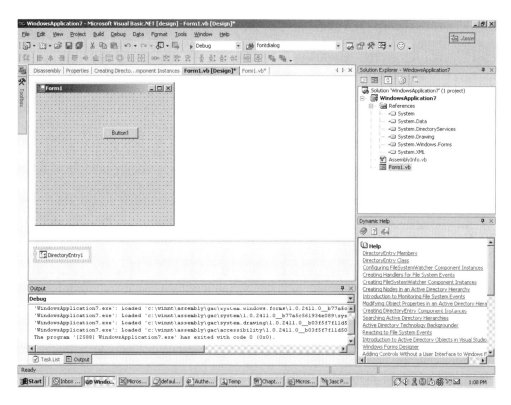

Figure 20.1 The **DirectoryEntry** object appears in the nonvisual object area of the Visual Studio design surface.

ticationType is other than **None** or **Anonymous**, the **Password** and **Username** properties must contain values that match a user with sufficient security privileges to retrieve or set information in the directory. The **ADSIPropertyCache** property determines whether or not the ADSI property cache is used. The default value for this property is **True**.

The **Path** property contains the full path to the entry in the active directory. Use the syntax described earlier in this chapter to create the path. It is entered as a String value.

The **DirectoryEntry** does not require a method to be called to "fill in" its values. Rather, when the **DirectoryEntry** object is created, the connection to the directory server is established, a reference to the object within the directory service is given to the **DirectoryEntry** object. So, for practical purposes, it is the object and all of its children. This example shows how a **DirectoryEntry** object is first set up with the **Path**, **User-**

name, and **Password**. In a Button's click event there is code that iterates through the children of the node. In this case, examining the path, you see that the node is the **Members** container object. The **Members** node does not contain attributes other than its ability to act as a parent to **User** objects. (User objects are an object type defined in this directory's schema. Directory schemas vary in design.)

> **Note**
> The examples in this chapter cannot be run without access to an LDAP server. If you have access to an LDAP server, you can replace the host.mycompany. com:1001 with the actual fully qualified domain name and port number of the LDAP server, and replace the organization (o) with the proper organization and organizational unit (ou) with the appropriate value.

```
DirectoryEntry1.Path = "LDAP://host.mycompany.com:1001/
o=My Company/ou=Members"

DirectoryEntry1.Username = "cn=administrator,ou=Members,
o=My Company"

DirectoryEntry1.Password = "password"
```

Once the object has been created, the **Children** property contains references to each of the node's children. This code loops through each of the children, each a **DirectoryEntry** object, and writes out the Name property, which in this case is the **cn** attribute value of the object (child node).

```
Private Sub Button1_Click(ByVal sender As System.Object,
ByVal e As System.EventArgs) Handles Button1.Click

    Dim children As DirectoryServices.DirectoryEntries

    Dim child As DirectoryServices.DirectoryEntry

    children = DirectoryEntry2.Children()

    For Each child In children

        Console.Write(child.Name & vbCrLf)

    Next

End Sub
```

Important Note
To minimize confusion between properties of an object, such as the DirectoryEntry object, and the values stored in the directory, we will refer to the values in the directory by their commonly used name, attributes. This is confusing because the object names and methods refer to attributes as properties. Both are correct, but in this discussion can be confusing. Therefore, the term *properties* refers to the properties of classes in the .NET Framework, and the term *attribute* refers to the attributes/properties of a directory services entry.

You will want to have access to more than just the **Name** property of the **DirectoryEntry**. Each **DirectoryEntry** also has a **Properties** property. Use the **Item** method of the **Properties** property to return the value stored in the attribute as a **PropertyValueCollection**. You see in this next example that two variables are created of type **PropertyValueCollection**, **cn** and **pw**. Passing the actual name of the attribute as specified in the schema, you will instantiate the values of the cn and pw values.

Note
Oftentimes, the directory schema has a display name and an actual name for an attribute. This is to make displaying attributes of an entry more human-readable. To access the values of an attribute, you must use the actual name of the attribute, and not the user-friendly name.

```
Private Sub Button1_Click(ByVal sender As System.Object,
ByVal e As System.EventArgs) Handles Button1.Click

    Dim children As DirectoryServices.DirectoryEntries

    Dim child As DirectoryServices.DirectoryEntry

    Dim cn As DirectoryServices.PropertyValueCollection

    Dim pw As DirectoryServices.PropertyValueCollection


    children = DirectoryEntry2.Children()

    For Each child In children

        cn = child.Properties.Item("cn")
```

```
            pw = child.Properties.Item("userpassword")

        Try

                Console.Write(cn.Item(0).ToString & " = ")

                Console.Write(pw.Item(0).ToString & vbCrLf)

        Catch

        End Try

    Next

End Sub
```

This example uses the **Item** method of the **PropertyValueCollection**, passing in a zero-based index value. This prints the **cn** and **user-password** attribute values for each child within the organizational unit **Member**. In this example, I cheated a little and passed a zero as the index number. I knew in advance that these attributes had only a single value. Attributes in a directory are multivalued-capable, and you should assume that an attribute has more than a single value when testing for values.

The **DirectoryEntry** object can be used for much more than simply viewing attributes and values stored in a directory. It's also capable of modifying values. Using the Add method, as shown below, we add a String value to the **Country-Name** attribute (the actual name of the attribute as defined by the schema is the letter c). Entries into the directory are transactional, and changes will not be saved into the entry until you commit the changes using the **CommitChanges** method of the **DirectoryEntry** object.

```
Private Sub Button1_Click(ByVal sender As System.Object,
ByVal e As System.EventArgs) Handles Button1.Click

    DirectoryEntry2.Path = "LDAP://host.mycompany.
    com:1001/o=My Company/ou=Members/cn=Ted"

    DirectoryEntry2.Properties.Item("c").Add("USA")

    DirectoryEntry2.CommitChanges()

    MessageBox.Show("Value changed.")

End Sub
```

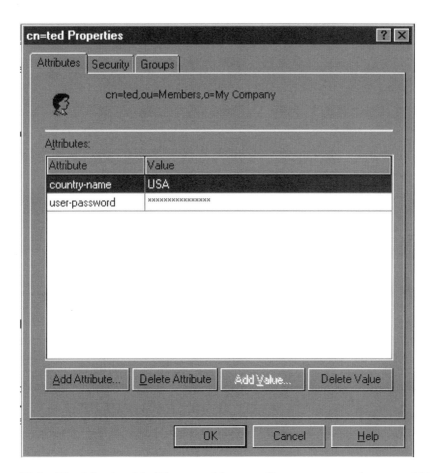

Figure 20.2 The Membership Directory Manager allows us to see values set within a directory node.

Figure 20.2 shows that the value, USA, is actually set for the **Country-Name** attribute using the Microsoft Membership Directory Manager application to view the results.

The previous example demonstrated adding a new attribute value. You can also use the **AddRange** method to add an array of values to the entry. You may want to change values rather than add them. This next example shows you how to change the value of the attribute we added in the previous example:

```
Private Sub Button1_Click(ByVal sender As System.Object,
   ByVal e As System.EventArgs) Handles Button1.Click
```

```
        DirectoryEntry2.Path = "LDAP://host.mycompany.
        com:1001/o=My Company/ou=Members/cn=Ted"

    DirectoryEntry2.Properties.Item("c").Item(0) = "US"

    DirectoryEntry2.CommitChanges()

        MessageBox.Show("Value changed.")

End Sub
```

For items that are multivalued, you will have to already know the index value of the item you want to change.

The LDAP Schema

You will be viewing and modifying the contents of most active directories, such as IIS or the WinNT active directories. Other, more generic directory services, such as NDS or LDAP, can be used to store any type of data. Each directory type normally comes with some sort of predefined schema. For example, the Microsoft LDAP servers have a container defined called Members that contain Member objects. Member objects have many possible attributes defined in the schema, almost anything you can think of to describe a person, that is, first and last name, address, phone, fax, and even URLs to link this member to online resources, such as the Member's homepage.

The Microsoft Member schema is very complete if you want to create a "white pages" type of personnel directory. If your requirements extend beyond the items found in the schema, you will want to expand or modify the existing schema. With the ability to change the directory's schema, you can store any type of data, and form relationships between objects.

The schema is stored in a container in the same way that the Member entries in the Members container are stored in the previous examples. So, to view and modify the schema, it is only important that you know two things: the path to the schema and the attributes that make up a schema item. LDAP is very object oriented, and therefore, schema items are directory entry objects, just as any other type of entry.

Here is sample code that lets you display all the schema items defined in the schema:

```
Private Sub Button1_Click(ByVal sender As System.Object,
ByVal e As System.EventArgs) Handles Button1.Click

    Dim DirectoryEntry1 As New System.DirectoryServices.
    DirectoryEntry()
```

```
    DirectoryEntry1.Path = "LDAP://host.mycompany.com:
    1001/o=My Company/ou=Admin/cn=schema"

    DirectoryEntry1.Username = "cn=administrator,
    ou=Members,o=My Company"

    DirectoryEntry1.Password = "password"

    Dim SchemaItem As DirectoryServices.DirectoryEntry

    Dim SchemaItems As DirectoryServices.DirectoryEntries

    SchemaItems = DirectoryEntry1.Children

    For Each SchemaItem In SchemaItems

        Console.Write(SchemaItem.Name & vbCrLf)

    Next

End Sub
```

This example prints the name of each schema item to the Console Window. Be aware that the path to the schema in directories may vary. You should consult the documentation of the directory you are trying to access and modify to learn the exact path.

Within a schema there are two types of objects defined, **classSchema** and **attribute-Class**. Schema Items identified as a **classSchema** are the items that eventually become **DirectoryEntry** objects, and **attributeClass** items are the attributes that define a **DirectoryEntry**. Schema Items in a Microsoft LDAP server have the attributes listed in Table 20.2.

Using the methods covered already for adding new items into the directory, you can add new schema items, filling in the appropriate items from Table 20.2. The complete information on required attributes of schema items can be found in the documentation for the directory you are modifying. Here is an example that defines the Member object's schema:

cn = member

objectClass = classSchema

displayName = member

u2GovernsID = 1.2.840.113556.1.4.611.1103010708051500150108150101130009121504000120004151202100000708

description = a member account

schemaIDGUID = {6D12FCF9-B836-11D0-9601-00C04FC30E1A}

rdnAttID = cn

possSuperiors = organization

mustContain = objectClass

mayContain = description

isContainer = 0

containerType = 0

isSecurityPrincipal = 1

Table 20.2 Schema Item Attributes

Schema Attribute	Description
cn	Common name of the schema item.
objectClass	This is always **classSchema** for schema items that define attributes and **attributeClass** for schema items that define objects.
displayName	This is a friendly name for the schema item (don't use this except to look at).
u2GovernsID	A very long id number.
description	Description of the schema item.
schemaIDGUID	A GUID (Globally Unique Identifier) that identifies an object in the schema.
possSuperiors	Defines the possible parents of this schema type, e.g., organizationalUnit.
mustContain	Defines a list of required attributes this object requires (for object definitions only).
mayContain	Defines a list of optional attributes for this object (for object definitions only).
isContainer	Boolean value determining of this object can contain other objects, set as 1 or 0.
containerType	Type of container, normally equals 0.
attributeSyntax	Defines the value type of an attribute, e.g., UnicodeString, Integer, Date.
isSecurityPrincipal	Boolean value that determines if this is a security principle object, 1 or 0. A security principle is an object involved in security issues, such as the ability to login or access a secured Web site.

Using the DirectorySearcher

Active Directories are optimized for searching. It is possible to instantiate a **Directory-Entry** object for each node, and search through attribute values until you find the object you are looking for. Luckily, it's not necessary to do that in Visual Basic .NET. You can use the **DirectorySearcher** object to return a subset of **DirectoryEntries**.

Create a **DirectorySearcher** by dragging a **DirectorySearcher** component from the Toolbox onto the application design surface, or create one programmatically, as shown in the next example. When creating these objects programmatically, it's important to know that a **DirectorySearcher** is tied to a **DirectoryEntry** object by serving as the **SearchRoot** of the **DirectorySearcher**. The **DirectorySearcher.SearchRoot** property specifies the starting point of the search within the tree-structured directory.

The **DirectorySearcher** has a **Filter** property that allows you to limit which entries in the directory appear in the set of results stored in the **SearchResultCollection** object. Here are the three rules to follow when creating the Filter expression as a String value:

Enclose Filter expressions within parentheses.

Use the $<, <=, =, >=, >$ relational operators to form expressions.

Build compound expressions using the prefix operators & (AND) and | (OR).

The **DirectorySearcher.Filter** property will filter the results of the search to objects of a particular class by specifying (objectClass=*objectclassname*). The default (objectClass=*) allows all object types. In this next example, the filter expression is short and sweet. We just filter such that the only result returned is the one where the cn = Mary.

```
Private Sub Button1_Click(ByVal sender As System.Object,
ByVal e As System.EventArgs) Handles Button1.Click

    Dim DirectorySearcher1 As New DirectoryServices.
    DirectorySearcher()

    Dim DirectoryEntry1 As New DirectoryServices.
    DirectoryEntry()

    DirectoryEntry1.Password = "password"

    DirectoryEntry1.Path = "LDAP://host.mycompany.com:
    1001/o=My Company/ou=Members"

    DirectoryEntry1.Username = "cn=administrator,
    ou=Members,o=My Company"
```

```
        DirectorySearcher1.PropertiesToLoad.AddRange(New
        String() {"ADsPath", "Name", "ADsPath", "Name",
        "ADsPath", "Name"})

        DirectorySearcher1.SearchRoot = DirectoryEntry1

        DirectorySearcher1.Filter = "(cn=Mary)"

        Dim result As DirectoryServices.SearchResult

        For Each result In DirectorySearcher1.FindAll()

            Console.WriteLine(result.GetDirectoryEntry.Path &
            vbCrLf)

            Next

    End Sub
```

This example writes the complete LDAP path to the one item returned to the Console Window. Your result will vary depending on the LDAP path to the item you select in your query. Customize your search results by specifying sort criteria in the **Directory-Searcher.Sort** property. In order to set this property, you will need to create a **SortOption** object, setting the **SortOption.Direction** and **SortOption.PropertyName** values.

SortOption.Direction accepts an enumerated value of either **Ascending** or **Descending**. The **SortOption.PropertyName** value is set to the name of the attribute on which you'd like your results sorted.

Active Directory Services

Active directories form the foundation of system administration in Windows 2000 and Windows XP. You can use the same **DirectoryService** classes to access and modify items in the active directories. The types of information managed in an active directory include computers, users, printers, shared resources, security, and more. Here is a list of the standard container objects in an active directory:

Name spaces

Country

Locality

Organization

Organizational unit

Domain

Computer

Continuing down the tree, here is a list of the standard "leaf" objects:

User

Group

Alias

Service

Print queue

Print device

Print job

File service

File share

Session

Resource

This simple code snippet will access your computer's Active Directory and print a top-level list of objects. Using the **DirectoryEntry** object, you can navigate to any portion of the Active Directory and view settings or make modifications.

```
Private Sub Button1_Click(ByVal sender As System.Object,
ByVal e As System.EventArgs) Handles Button1.Click

    Dim DirectoryEntry1 As New System.DirectoryServices.
    DirectoryEntry()

    DirectoryEntry1.Path = "WinNT://mydomain"

    Dim SchemaItem As DirectoryServices.DirectoryEntry

    Dim SchemaItems As DirectoryServices.DirectoryEntries

    SchemaItems = DirectoryEntry1.Children

    For Each SchemaItem In SchemaItems

        Console.WriteLine(SchemaItem.Name)

    Next

End Sub
```

Replace "mydomain" in the Path with the actual domain name of your computer. Depending on whether your computer is connected to the Internet, this may or may not be an Internet domain name.

This example gives you an idea of connecting to the active directory. You should refer to Active Directory Management documentation before modifying items within active directories.

Summary

Active Directories form the heart of Microsoft operating systems, and directory services such as NDS and LDAP form the foundation of many other types of data management systems. The object-oriented nature of directory-based storage mechanisms has given rise to a powerful way to manage data. This is one reason active directories are used to manage features within your operating system and tools such as Internet Information Services.

Encapsulating ADSI within the .NET Framework allows developers to begin using directory services both as a means of data storage and for the automation of system administration. It seems fit to close this last chapter with a discussion of an object-oriented way to manage data using a very object-oriented .NET Framework of classes.

Appendix

WinForms Enumerations

Enumeration	Description
AccessibleEvents	Events that are reported by accessible applications.
AccessibleNavigation	Values for navigating between accessible objects.
AccessibleRole	Values representing possible roles for an accessible object.
AccessibleSelection	Choose how an accessible object will be selected or receive focus.
AccessibleStates	Choose values representing possible states for an accessible object.
AnchorStyles	Select how a control anchors to the edges of its container.
Appearance	The appearance of a control.
ArrangeDirection	Direction in which the system arranges minimized windows.
ArrangeStartingPosition	Starting position that the system uses to arrange minimized windows.
BootMode	Mode the computer was started in.
Border3DSide	Sides of a rectangle on which to apply a three-dimensional border.
Border3DStyle	Style of a three-dimensional border.
BorderStyle	Border style for a control.
BoundsSpecified	Bounds of the control to use when defining a control's size and position.
ButtonBorderStyle	Border style for a Button control.
ButtonState	Appearance of a Button.
CaptionButton	Type of caption Button to display.
CharacterCasing	Choose case of text within a TextBox control.
CheckState	State of a control, such as a checkbox, that can be checked, unchecked, or set to an indeterminate state.

WinForms Enumerations

Enumeration	Description
ColorDepth	Number of colors used to display an image in an ImageList control.
ColumnHeaderStyle	Styles of the column headers in a ListView control.
ComboBoxStyle	ComboBox style.
ControlStyles	Determines the style and behavior of the control.
DataGrid.HitTestType	Specifies the part of the DataGrid control on which the user has clicked.
DataGridLineStyle	The style of gridlines in a DataGrid.
DataGridParentRowsLabelStyle	Determines how the parent row labels of a DataGrid control are displayed.
DateTimePickerFormat	Date and time format the DateTimePicker control displays.
Day	The day of the week.
DialogResult	The return value of a dialog box.
DockStyle	The position and way in which a control is docked.
DragAction	How a drag-and-drop operation should continue.
DragDropEffects	Determines the effects of a drag-and-drop operation.
DrawItemState	State of an item that being drawn.
DrawMode	How the elements of a control are drawn.
ErrorBlinkStyle	Constants specifying when the error icon supplied by an ErrorProvider should blink to alert the user that an error has occurred.
ErrorIconAlignment	Constants specifying the locations that an error icon can appear in relation to the control with an error.
FlatStyle	Determines when the appearance of a control is flat rather than 3-D.
FormBorderStyle	Border styles for a Form.
FormStartPosition	Starting position of a Form.
FormWindowState	Form display state.
FrameStyle	The frame style of the selected control.
GridItemType	The valid grid item types for a PropertyGrid.
HelpNavigator	Constants indicating which elements of the Help file to display.
HorizontalAlignment	Determine the horizontal alignment of text relative to an element of the control.
ImeMode	A value that determines the Input Method Editor status of an object when the object is selected.

WinForms Enumerations

Enumeration	Description
ItemActivation	The user action that is required to activate items in a list view control and the feedback that is given as the user moves the mouse pointer over an item.
ItemBoundsPortion	A portion of the list view item from which to retrieve the bounding rectangle.
Keys	Key codes and modifiers.
LeftRightAlignment	Select whether an object or text is aligned to the left or right of a reference point.
LinkBehavior	Choose the behaviors of a link in a LinkLabel control.
ListViewAlignment	Alignment settings in the ListView control.
MdiLayout	The layout of multiple document interface (MDI) child windows in an MDI parent window.
MenuGlyph	The image to draw when drawing a menu with the ControlPaint.DrawMenuGlyph method.
MenuMerge	The behavior of a MenuItem when it is merged with items in another menu.
MessageBoxButtons	Constants defining which buttons to display on a MessageBox.
MessageBoxDefaultButton	Constants defining the default button on a MessageBox.
MessageBoxIcon	Constants defining which information to display.
MessageBoxOptions	Options on a MessageBox.
MonthCalendar.HitArea	Defines constants that represent areas in a MonthCalendar control.
MouseButtons	Constants that define which mouse button was pressed.
Orientation	The orientation of controls or elements of controls.
PictureBoxSizeMode	Positioning of an image within a PictureBox.
PropertySort	Choose how properties are sorted in the PropertyGrid.
RichTextBoxFinds	How a text search is carried out in a RichTextBox control.
RichTextBoxScrollBars	The type of scroll bars to display in a RichTextBox control.
RichTextBoxSelectionTypes	The type of selection in a RichTextBox control.
RichTextBoxStreamType	The types of input and output streams used to load and save data in the RichTextBox control.
RightToLeft	A value indicating whether the text appears from right to left, such as when using Hebrew or Arabic fonts.
ScrollBars	Which scroll bars will be visible on a control.
ScrollButton	The type of scroll arrow to draw on a scroll bar.
ScrollEventType	The type of action used to raise the Scroll event.

WinForms Enumerations

Enumeration	Description
SelectionMode	The selection behavior of a list box.
Shortcut	Shortcut keys that can be used by menu items.
SizeGripStyle	The style of the sizing grip on a Form.
SortOrder	How items in a list are sorted.
StatusBarPanelAutoSize	How a panel on a status bar changes when the status bar resizes.
StatusBarPanelBorderStyle	The border style of a panel on the StatusBar.
StatusBarPanelStyle	Selection determining whether a panel on a status bar is owner-drawn or system-drawn.
TabAlignment	The locations of the tabs in a tab control.
TabAppearance	The appearance of the tabs in a tab control.
TabDrawMode	Selection determining whether the tabs in a tab control are drawn by the parent window, or drawn by the operating system.
TabSizeMode	Selection determining the sizing of tabs in a tab control.
TickStyle	The location of tick marks in a TrackBar control.
ToolBarAppearance	The type of toolbar to display.
ToolBarButtonStyle	The button style within a toolbar.
ToolBarTextAlign	The alignment of text on the toolbar button control.
TreeViewAction	The action that raised a TreeViewEventArgs event.
UICues	The state of the user interface.
View	Selection determining how list items are displayed in a ListView control.

Index